Milestones

of

Motherhood

CLARE COOPER

To Som,

with warm wishes + much
light for your path.
Clare Cooper.

Milestones

of

Motherhood

A celebration of women's
transformation through mothering

CLARE COOPER

Mother's Milk Books

First published in Great Britain in 2020 by Mother's Milk Books

ISBN 978-1-9162437-1-2

Although the author and publisher have made every effort
to make sure that information regarding health issues was correct when going to press,
this book is not intended as a replacement for the expertise and medical advice of physicians.
The reader should consult with a doctor before making any decisions regarding their health.

Typeset in Georgia and Wenceslas
by Teika Bellamy.
Wenceslas font designed by Manfred Klein.
Printed and bound in Great Britain by Imprint Digital, Devon
using responsibly sourced paper.
https://digital.imprint.co.uk

First published in 2020 by Mother's Milk Books
www.mothersmilkbooks.com

For mothers everywhere ~
recognise that never are your efforts wasted,
but always love invested.

For Surya, Shanti and Sol,
my children, my teachers.

Contents

'My Girls', by Katrina Rourke   8

'Letting Go', by Angela Topping   9

Foreword, by Teika Bellamy   11

Introduction: The Mothering Journey   13

Chapter One   Beginning the journey – Conception and Pregnancy   25

Chapter Two   Journeys of Labour and Birth   55

Chapter Three   First Times   83

Chapter Four   Breastfeeding Journeys   115

Chapter Five   The Mothering Path   155

Chapter Six   A Mother Again   187

Chapter Seven   Challenging Times   213

Chapter Eight   Changing the Legacy   263

Chapter Nine   Journeys of Identity   289

Chapter Ten   Journeys of Independence and Letting Go   315

Chapter Eleven   The Qualities of the Mother   339

Resources   347

Reflections on Your Own Journey   351

Acknowledgements   355

About the Author   357

My Girls

My dearest girls what can I say
to show my love and gratitude on this October day.
My soul was lost, damaged and bruised,
slowly suffocating, being consumed.
But then you came along, shining your light,
filling me with love, happiness and insight.
You lifted the blindfold and forced me to see the darkness
living within me.
My dearest girls, I may have helped you learn and grow
but you, my dears, have taught me more than you will ever know.
You've taught me patience, tolerance and love
you've given me the power and strength to change for the good.
You are my favourite song, the sweetest taste, my serenity and joy,
my happy place.
An endless flow of illuminating glee, bursting, rushing, radiating
within me.
The colours of your rainbow hearts flooded into my soul,
transforming, fixing, making me whole.
My dearest girls you make my world so sweet.
I will love you always. You make me complete.
Love mam xx

KATRINA ROURKE

Letting Go

First you hold them like a secret
you only suspect is true.
Then soft knockings from within
tap out messages for you.
Slowly the body allows escape,
you hold them in your arms,
dazed and milky, full of love,
pledged to defend from harm.
Then you hold them to your heart
and put them to the breast.
But they learn to walk away
like any other guest.

ANGELA TOPPING

First published in *Musings on Mothering,* edited by Teika Bellamy
(Mother's Milk Books, 2012) and then in *Letting Go,* by Angela
Topping (Mother's Milk Books, 2013)

Foreword
by Teika Bellamy

Back in 2013, Clare submitted an essay entitled 'Milestones' to the Mother's Milk Books Writing Prize, which ended up being commended by the prose category judge, Susan Last, and then published in the anthology, *Parenting*, which came out in 2014.

About Clare's essay, Susan wrote: "I liked the idea at the centre of this piece, of examining the milestones of parenthood alongside those of the growing child – it expands on the idea that when a child is born, so is a mother – which is a concept that I personally have found important in my own parenting journey. I enjoyed being invited to reflect on how motherhood has changed me, and reading the author's own experience."

I, too, found the essay to be enlightening as well as thought-provoking. I knew that becoming a mother had affected me deeply, but I'd never before had the chance to vocalise all the shifts that had occurred within me because of this life change. I couldn't help thinking that, surely, more women would appreciate the chance to explore their own milestones of motherhood. So... being the kind of person who "thinks in books" I contacted Clare and asked her if she'd be interested in greatly expanding on her essay, i.e. writing a book! Clare agreed, contracts were signed, and then came a few years of Clare writing and rewriting the book amidst raising, and home schooling, her family (not to mention her yoga teaching and being a forest school leader!). Meanwhile, busy with a publishing schedule that had to be pieced around freelance work and family life, I carved out time to edit and produce this book.

Milestones of Motherhood has been many years in the making. Much love – from Clare, the wonderful mother-contributors, and myself – has been poured into it. Yet it is only fitting that this book has been created with much love, because only then can it begin to reflect back the enormous love that mothers are capable of.

Thank you, Clare, for shedding light on the many milestones of the incredible journey that is motherhood. Thank you mothers, everywhere, for all that you do, every day, with so much love.

Introduction
The Mothering Journey

As mothers we have the precious privilege of seeing our babies and children grow and change day by day and year by year. We share their smiles and triumphs, tears and tumbles, learning and challenges, and hold them physically and emotionally through their paths of childhood.

As I begin this book, my youngest son has just turned two. Although he only says a couple of words, every day he amazes me as he shows just how much he understands. As we are getting ready for a day out he brings over my shoes and drags my bag across the floor so he can put his little tractor inside. The first day we bought bunk beds for his elder sisters he learned to climb the ladder even though he was only eight months old and could not yet walk. Every day he learns, and every day I recognise a little more of who he is, and who he is becoming. Bedtimes see my eldest daughter now easily reading stories to her younger siblings for fun, books she struggled to read only months earlier.

As mothers we witness many of these tiny milestones, the small fragments of learning, the many ordinary, yet magical, moments which together become the vibrant mosaic of childhood. We have the privilege of sharing and nurturing our children's journeys of exploration and investigation as they discover the world and their place in it.

Our children's growth and milestones are clearly visible, eagerly-awaited and celebrated by many, and this is exactly the way it should be. They are precious, bewitching beings; dependent, awesome and deserving of our full love and attention. Their growth is biologically and socially expected and their learning is chronological and inextricably linked to their development. Yet as mothers, we too are learning and growing at a rate paralleled to theirs, yet our own path, our experiences of deepening into love, trust, wisdom and understanding, whilst nonetheless transformative, passes by largely unnoticed.

Milestones of Motherhood explores these transformative, inner journeys of mothering; the growth, deepening, challenge and learning we encounter as we strive to love and nurture our children. With contributions from over fifty women, *Milestones of Motherhood* explores our awakening and transformation through our initiation into mothering – conception, pregnancy, birth and breastfeeding –

then explores our continuing learning and transformation as we guide and nurture our children through childhood, adolescence and into independence. Far from losing ourselves to motherhood as we sometimes fear, let us perceive mothering in a new light; as a transformative process with the potential to ignite passion, strength, growth and learning. Learning to love our children invites us to discover new aspects of ourselves, to surrender, learn and discover; to find, know and love ourselves in a fundamentally different way.

"Being a mum changed me in many ways, most of which I'd never have guessed at and all of which I'm very thankful for. It was almost as though there was another me inside just waiting to come out and blossom, and it was only through giving birth and raising a child that the other me could be born."

Fran, Mother to Emma, 35, Jack, 32 and Edward, 29

We do not become new people, but rather we become *more* of the women we are. We awaken to new parts of ourselves, slough off old ways of thinking and being, uncovering new elements of ourselves. And it is for this reason that transformation through motherhood has the potential to be so potent; for perhaps the first time, we are not learning to fulfil a job description or study a curriculum, but rather we are growing more deeply into *ourselves* and our own authenticity.

The landscapes of mothering

Our mothering work occurs simultaneously across our inner, emotional and outer, practical landscapes. Let us envisage these different spheres as the landscapes within and around us. Our outer landscapes describe the terrain of our homes, our bodies and the physical work we do. It is upon our outer, physical landscapes that we take care of our baby's needs; we hold and cuddle, feed, rock and carry, it is the sphere of our home and the multitude of activities which constitute our physical nurturing. Such outer landscapes do not exist independently, but are informed and guided by our inner world.

Our inner landscapes describe our mental, emotional and spiritual life; our feelings, emotions, thoughts, philosophies, ideals, plans, reflections and sensations. Our inner world, whilst largely hidden from view, is the driving force which animates our actions and relationships. Our inner world houses our instinct and intuition, our hopes, fears, dreams, anxieties, and the landscapes upon which we

14

experience joy, anxiety, learning, courage, strength, love, trust and understanding.

There is constant interaction, communication and feedback occurring between our landscapes, informing our perceptions, behaviour, reflections and learning. Neither sphere exists in isolation; what happens in one affects the other; as above, so below. Upwelling love within prompts action across our outer landscapes; we pick up our baby, breathe in her soft scent and hold her close. In turn such practical actions create ripples of feedback within, replenishing our inner reserves of love, trust, connection and understanding which prompt further nurturing action now and in the future; change in one sphere ignites change across another.

Our landscapes do not exist in isolation, but swirl and interact with our children, partner, friends, community and culture in a constant state of feedback. Interactions and feedback with our baby is constant, detailed and intense; clunky at first, yet becoming finely tuned as we give ourselves the time and space to connect, listen and respond. For in the beginning, we are fledglings, as embryonic in our maternal development as our babies are in life outside our womb. Our bodies and hormones provide the biology and our instincts awaken love and wisdom, yet we must learn to channel and sculpt these raw materials into the art, work and flow of mothering. We develop as mother and child, a dyad, step by step, side by side, through constant interaction across our shared landscapes, each teaching, guiding and learning from the other.

Dolphins locate food through echolocation, sending sound waves through the ocean which scan the vicinity and bounce back as they recognise squid and jellyfish, guiding the dolphins to pitch their course accordingly. As mothers we embody a similar process, constantly sending and receiving signals to and from our baby, building complex, detailed knowledge of, and relationship with, our baby's landscapes. Much of this happens without our conscious effort; we observe our baby, we respond, our baby observes us and in turn responds, voicing emotions and needs for food, comfort, sleep, and company.

We observe, reflect and feel our way forward, stumbling many times. Our learning curve is steep, intense and constant, at times leaving us overwhelmed, wrung out, desperate and confused. Yet this is our initiation into the furnace of transformation; motherhood tears away our previous ways of being, the heat of the intensity renders us molten, we fear for our very survival, unable to see our way out of the furnace. Yet we continue, soon to resurface; reforming, tentatively transforming, remodelling ourselves for the task in hand.

Feedback between our landscapes reinforces our intuition, creating confidence. In the beginning we are uncertain, yet with time, as we realise we *can* understand what our baby is communicating and *are* able to respond. We develop greater trust; trust in ourselves to know, and in our baby to communicate and let us know. Such milestones accrue over the years, deepening our confidence and understanding, developing our inner reserves of courage, wisdom and determination. These become the sturdy foundations of our mothering endeavours. Through persevering in getting to know and love our babies through the challenges, we develop milestones of empathy, compassion and communication. These awaken us to the power, strength and sensitivity of our inner resources, igniting wisdom which informs our onward path.

Balance brings harmony and authenticity

We feel harmonious, happy and at peace when our inner, emotional and outer, physical landscapes resonate; *what we do feels right*. And when our actions and feelings do not align, disharmony and anxiety reign. I first experienced such disharmonies shortly after the birth of my first daughter. Kind hospital midwives urged me to let them take her whilst I slept, yet all I wanted to do was keep her close, sleeping across my chest. As I followed their instructions and let her go, my insides began to churn and adrenaline surged to the extent that I pressed the buzzer and asked for her to be returned. As I received her across my chest and she snuggled close, the inner raging of adrenaline and stress dissolved; my baby was back and all was well. What followed were intense months of discovering what our culture expects regarding baby care and what my inner landscapes were prompting. I learned a great deal through this challenging period, and now understand how this time of uncertainty was *transformation*; a transformation which became my foundation and initiation into mothering and understanding our mothering landscapes and milestones of change.

As women living in a culture which urges us to strive for success and recognition in the outer world, to trust experts and accrue status, wealth and recognition, the transition to mothering can be unsettling to say the least. The shock of birth, the constancy of our baby's needs and the intensity of awakening instincts and emotions is hugely disorientating. We fear we are losing ourselves, our stability and all that we have worked for and become. And in a way we are, for the mothering change is irreversible. Yet we can re-envision this intense time of confusion as *transformation*; for if we let it, motherhood has the potential to peel away layers of insecurity and cultural conditioning, awakening us to new depths of truth, wisdom, love and integrity we hold within. Opening ourselves up to loving our children fiercely re-forms us completely. We develop eyes of empathy, compassion and understanding, and an unshakeable knowing of the power, strength and wisdom embodied within our Femininity.

Landscapes of love

Mothering is a journey of learning to love upon our inner landscapes, and putting this love into action across our outer terrain. We must learn to know, love and trust our babies, children and teens again and again through the many cycles of their development. With experience we grow to recognise the features of our mothering morphology as various manifestations of *love, trust and understanding*. Each change in the geography brings new opportunity for learning; the terrain will change, but the elemental basis is one. Just as the element of water can be a cloud, iceberg, river, pond, waterfall, drought, or vast ocean, our milestones of love, trust, understanding and surrender remain constant yet shift their shapes constantly.

Our experiences of transformation through love are vast and varied. Maternal love flows, manifests and creates with abundant variation, different for each of us and changing over time. Sometimes it is simply love itself which *is* the milestone; feeling the overwhelming depth of emotion and awakening responsibility, or a fleeting flutter of warmth and tenderness and a gentle, shared smile in a time of darkness and isolation. Love, too, is a forebearer of transformation and healing as we learn to open ourselves up to loving unconditionally.

Yet such feelings are not solely emotional experiences, for much of our inner maternal experiences are orchestrated hormonally, influenced by, and influencing, our experiences of pregnancy, birth, breastfeeding, bonding, pleasure and nurturing. Therefore milestones upon our inner landscapes are also milestones of intellect and understanding as we come to realise the impact, influence and interplay our hormones hold and how we can create changes to nurture, and be nurtured by, our hormonal wisdom.

The love we feel for our children urges us to become better mothers and better people. We are in awe of our new baby and feel inspired to be the best parent we can be for this treasured being. If our own childhood has not been as filled with love and nurturing as it could have been, we may worry and doubt our abilities to care for the innocent being we hold in our arms. Yet this is where mother love can become a powerful catalyst of transformation; we love our baby *so* much we want to be as good as we possibly can for her, so we may choose to explore our own childhood, and as one mother explained, re-parent ourselves so we can be as good as we can be for our own child and not replicate past, less than nurturing, patterns.

We grow up and grow into ourselves, learning more of our capabilities and competencies, our strength, courage and determination. We come to understand more fully milestones of power, learning what it means to be empowered, confident and comfortable in our Femininity. Our milestones are reciprocal; strength grows from love, and increasing strength enables us to continue loving them so fully.

Alongside strength, the transformative power of love yields forgiveness, compassion and understanding. Through this foundation of maternal love we develop empathy for our children's feelings; we hope to see the world through their eyes and strive to understand the immature thoughts and feelings behind their constant needs and often trying actions. Such love and empathy helps us deal with frustrations, exhaustion and overwhelm which come with nurturing little ones, and we develop milestones of deepening understanding, compassion, endurance and patience.

Our milestones are reciprocal and interconnected, therefore milestones of love, empathy and compassion developed for our children work on ourselves also. They create ripples throughout our being, offering opportunities to heal, deepen in self-awareness and bring love, forgiveness and understanding to parts of ourselves which may be hurt and vulnerable. Perhaps the most transformative milestone of all is allowing the unconditional love we feel for our babies to embrace ourselves also, creating waves of healing, release and renewal across our landscapes.

For as much as in the beginning the challenge is learning to give so constantly to our babies and children, a little further along, we must learn the milestone of receiving, of giving to ourselves. Here mothering has the potential to be life changing, life enhancing and healing. We can invite the unconditional love we have cultivated for our children to work its healing magic upon ourselves; healing our tired, worn out and overlooked bodies, hearts and minds, replenishing and renewing ourselves, allowing us to know and love ourselves more deeply and to love and nurture our children as we would like.

We can grow to be gentle on ourselves, to love, forgive and accept ourselves for our mistakes and perceived shortcomings. We can grow in empathy, understanding and acceptance, recognising we are doing our best, holding ourselves with understanding and unconditional love rather than judgement and criticism. We can cultivate a more positive, nurturing relationship with ourselves as well as our children, knowing the benefits of this expand outwards to all of those we love and beyond.

Milestones of trust

Alongside love, mothering is a journey of trust; trusting ourselves and our babies. Yet unlike love, trust is more difficult to recognise and quantify; trust comes with experience and interaction between our inner and outer landscapes, and with our baby. Generally the people we trust are those we know well. Our trust grows out of knowing them, knowing how they are likely to respond and knowing they will be there for us as they have been previously.

And this is the way trust grows between mother and baby, it develops over time as we both come to understand and predict one another's communication and behaviour. Our milestones of trust are twofold; trust with our babies and trust of ourselves. For as we come to understand our babies, so too do we come to know and understand ourselves. Whilst at first we may be doubtful of our abilities, with time we develop the ability to understand, to act with confidence and to listen to and act upon our instinct and intuition. We become more confident in listening to the advice of others and being able to discern what is right for our baby. We learn to pass the opinions of others through our inner compass, trusting ourselves to know what resonates with us, and what we will let pass by.

Such milestones repeat and deepen throughout our journey, each becoming a thread woven into the foundational fabric of our relationships. And such trust is not an end in itself, but an energy or cloak which enfolds and informs our onward journey. For there is much of mothering and life which we cannot control, instead we must let go and surrender into what may unfold, from the process of conception, pregnancy and birth, through childhood, adolescence and independence. And it is into trust which we surrender, although often it feels scary, as though we are letting go into nothingness. Yet with reflection and experience we can see that we are letting go into trust; trust of our children, ourselves, the goodness of others and the unfolding process and development of life.

Qualities of the mother

As mothers we frequently judge ourselves and others on snapshots of the practical actions we take and our children's behaviour. Such judgement fails to recognise the practical and emotional constancy and enormity of the mothering role, creates division and feelings of failure as well as overlooking the complexities of our children's needs. Such harshness and judgement grossly overlooks the constant work we undertake upon our inner landscapes, for a mother's inner world is just, if not more, as busy and important as her visible actions. It is within the realms of heart, feeling, thought and mind that we constantly risk assess, plan, consider and evaluate how our children are doing and formulate the many actions we need to take to keep them safe and well.

Yet there is little recognition, and even mocking of this inner path. So much of the literature and discussion during pregnancy focusses on the practical side; nutrition, exercise, health, birth, feeding, sleep and weaning. There is surprisingly little mention of our inner emotional growth, expansion, deepening and development, and when our emotions are discussed it is usually only in the context of anxiety and depression; when our inner landscapes are deemed pathological. Naomi Stadlen in *What Mothers Do* and *How Mothers Love*, and Lucy Pearce in *Moods of Motherhood*, offer detailed and intimate insights into our inner maternal worlds, paying tribute and recognition to our constant inner work.

We *constantly* undergo vast emotional growth, deepening and transformation through our thoughts, feelings and realisations, of which depression and anxiety are just one part. At any one time many of us are as active and busy across multiple layers of our inner worlds as we are outwardly caring for our children. We hold space for overwhelming surges of love, emotion, thought, doubt, fear and the frightening, and at times heavy, sense of responsibility. Through sitting with such feelings, with time we find our way and deepen further into milestones of identity and authenticity.

We grapple with issues of trust, confidence and decision making, processing competing, and at times, contradictory feelings. Likewise, we may experience a resurfacing of issues, emotion and memories from our own past or childhood, awoken through the intensity and emotion of mothering. Such work within our inner landscapes is the alchemy of transformation; we deepen in self-awareness and mothering can ignite the process of letting go, healing, learning and renewal. We are inspired to recast and remodel ourselves to be as capable as possible of loving and caring for our children. Our inner landscapes are the crucible of transformation; changes occurring deep within igniting emotional growth and practical change.

And rather than perceiving such sensitivity and emotionality being the weakness of the Feminine as is so often portrayed, rather it is one of our foremost strengths. For it is through our feelings and inner reflections we grow in emotional capacity, develop intuition and increase our capability for empathy. Deepening into our inner landscapes increases our emotional awareness and fluency, enabling us to move beyond judgement of both ourselves and others, enabling us to see, with eyes of understanding and compassion. Far from weakness, such fluency is the life breath of mothering, enabling us to nurture and understand our children's vital emotional development, as well as developing qualities sorely needed by the wider world.

Yet there remains little recognition and value of such inner, emotional work and the capacity for compassion mothering ignites. Visitors focus on the loveliness of our baby whilst magazines, employers and the wider culture focus on us getting 'back to normal' as soon as possible, which usually means losing weight, getting quickly back to work and being busy, social and productive. We generally lack the quiet, sensitive spaces to rest, discover, process, reflect upon and share our inner journeys. Such personal lack of space to nurture and recognise these inner elements of Femininity is indicative of the values of our wider culture, yet as women feeling these stirrings within, we are beginning to create and seek out such spaces for ourselves.

Times *are* changing and motherhood ignites fierce transformation. We live in times where talk of the Divine Feminine, Womb Yoga and Conscious Menstruality is happening. And Lucy Pearce in her books *Burning Woman* and *Medicine Woman* and Uma Dinsmore-Tuli through *Yoni Shakti* reignite lost archetypes of Feminine strength, power and wisdom. We are beginning to see the personal and ecological devastation of a society built upon outer accumulation only. A new balance is being sought and inner awakening through motherhood is a potent contributor to this transformation.

As mothers we understand personally the immense value, power and strength inherent in nurture, compassion and empathy. We hold hope and vision for the future; we are invested in it for the wellbeing of our children. From such personal, intense, inner experiences, we understand better than most how these *Qualities of the Mother* could bring much needed transformation throughout our communities and wider economic, political and educational systems. It is clear to see how decision making with compassion and nurture at the fore would revolutionise our current exploitative relationships with nature and humanity.

Motherhood is a potent energy for change, yet before we can begin to realise such changes in the outer world, first we must let them birth into being within the quiet, fertile, inner landscapes of our hearts and womb spaces. We must learn; learn to love, nurture and connect with our children and our inner wisdom, and as we develop through the life work of mothering, we cultivate these *Qualities of the Mother*, qualities which our wider world is thirsting for.

Whilst *Milestones of Motherhood* focusses upon women's transformation, men walk a parallel journey of potential growth and awakening through fatherhood. Exploring men's experiences of knowing, loving and parenting their children and the inner growth, transformation and expression of Masculinity this inspires is a valuable and much needed area for greater exploration. Men's awakening to qualities of love, nurture, connection and protection through learning to love and care for their babies and children is a journey rich in potential for personal and much needed wider social, structural and environmental change. Steve Bidduph, William Sears and Patrick Houser make valuable contributions to this field, their work honouring the role and value of fathering and providing much inspiration, insight and guidance.

Sharing the journey

Milestones of Motherhood does not set out to give advice or stipulate parenting approaches, but rather creates a space to recognise, value and validate the work and worth of the mothering journey and its transformative potential. *Milestones of Motherhood* seeks to challenge the judgement and dogmatism existing between various parenting approaches, instead shining light upon the inner journeys of mothering; recognising we are all simply women doing the best we can to love and nurture our children with the resources and inner capacities we possess at the time.

Let the voices within this book hold the space for you as you begin your own journey, or as you pause and look back upon just how far you have come. When you are struggling, facing challenges, fear, exhaustion and overwhelm, know that others have, and do, feel this way at times also. Let the milestones of tending to yourself speak to you, and take respite and comfort in the voices of others walking a similar path. Let their words ignite smiling recognition of your own journey with all its pain and hope, joy and challenge.

Perhaps what we need most as mothers wherever we are on our journey is space; not space as in emptiness or loneliness, but a space in which to be truly held and heard, just as we hold and listen to our children. A space to be honoured and nurtured, held by others who have walked this path too and understand. A space, not to be told what to do, pushed in one direction or another, but space to breathe, explore and be. A space wherein we can rediscover our bodies and Femininity, to let go of ideas of losing baby weight or wrinkles and instead envision our physical bodies as life-giving, life-sustaining powerhouses, to explore our feelings, fears and vulnerabilities and find ways to move and grow forwards. Space and time to ponder, to grieve what went before, to find our feet, grow in confidence in whom we are becoming alongside our growing children. And it is this space which *Milestones of Motherhood* hopes to serve.

It is my hope that the stories and milestones will hold you, resonate with you and your path and reflect back acknowledgement, validation and recognition. I bring together these voices to call for recognition of the valuable life work we do through loving and nurturing our children each day, the transformation this inspires and immense value this makes to the wider world. Let us slough off outdated notions which undervalue time spent nurturing children and instead celebrate the inherent worth held within our actions, recognising that work on the mothering path is never time wasted, but always love invested.

Chapter One
Beginning the Journey – Conception and Pregnancy

We each have different journeys to conception and pregnancy. Many of us have known since childhood we would like children someday, whereas others of us go through a conscious process of transformation before finally feeling ready, and for others of us, this turnaround happens seemingly overnight. Some of us seek to avoid becoming pregnant at all and give little consideration to motherhood, yet find ourselves unexpectedly expecting, and for others of us our journey to conception itself becomes a momentous journey as we navigate our way through assisted fertility or adoption. Whatever our path, conception, pregnancy and birth are times of growth and reorganisation across our landscapes. As our baby is conceived, so is our embryonic *Mother Self* and she grows within, unfolding into being alongside our growing baby.

For those of us who have known since girlhood that we want to become mothers, the decision to conceive is not so much a transformation but more a case of beginning what we have long hoped for at a time we feel ready;

"I always wanted children. From being very young, I'd line up my dolls in cots and tuck them in carefully at night. While other people my age were talking about what career they wanted I was thinking about what job I'd enjoy while waiting to start a family. I found working as a teaching assistant fulfilled this."

Charlotte, Mother to Raffy, 9 months

Others spoke of taking time to explore life as a couple before slowly exploring becoming parents. As Louise illustrates, there are many issues to consider, and this is not always straightforward;

"My husband and I had no experience of children before having our own, other than a bit of babysitting as a teenager. We also expected little or no parental support in the journey ahead. So it was a daunting prospect to venture into parenthood.

However, we decided that we didn't want to grow old having not had the experience and pleasure of having our own children and thought it would be something we'd regret later. Being an only child myself, I wasn't aware of what I'd missed as a child but am growing increasingly so as I get older and would very much have liked a sibling. So, I was keen to have more than one child if nature would allow."

Louise, Mother to Flynn, 3.5 and Rowan, 10 months

Like Louise, many couples do plan consciously the time in their relationship when they would like to begin a family, yet this is not the case for everyone; indeed many women explained that for many years of their adult lives they did not want children of their own. Women spoke of strong feelings opposing motherhood, never imagining themselves to be the type of woman who would become a mother, could be "maternal" or even enjoy having children; simply their passions lay elsewhere.

Interestingly, when women shared these feelings, it was as though they were looking back and smiling at their younger selves. Women spoke of a sudden and overwhelming change as their past convictions vanished, their perspective shifted and they found themselves yearning for a baby, sometimes instantly;

"I never thought I wanted children – I wasn't remotely interested in them or other people's babies. I tried to get myself sterilised when I was 22, assuring the doctor I knew my own mind and was certain I would never want children of my own.

Luckily, my doctor was having none of it and refused, telling me I may feel differently one day. 'Never,' I said, with all the wisdom of my 22 years.

At the age of 28, so suddenly it was almost overnight, I wanted a baby. I have no idea where this came from, it took me by complete surprise and the feeling was so strong it was overwhelming.

I had been married for six years and been a bit hit and miss with contraception at times but had never become pregnant. Now we started actively trying and nothing happened. I'd thought it would happen instantly and when it didn't I noticed myself becoming acutely aware of pregnant women and mothers with prams and toddlers, and my longing for a baby of my own grew stronger and stronger.

Finally, two years later and after one early miscarriage, I became pregnant again, and at the ripe old age of 30 became a mother."

Fran, Mother to Emma, 35, Jack, 32 and Edward, 29

What is this unconscious, unplanned, transformation whereby a woman who had never given babies a minute's thought previously, suddenly finds herself pining, broody, and becoming desperate for a child? How can we as women make sense of this abrupt turnaround which occurs seemingly independent of our conscious selves? Is this drive to mother latent within, lying dormant for years before erupting acutely across our landscapes; a baby of our own becoming the focus of our thoughts and yearning of our heart?

"I was never one of those girls who longed to be a mum, and I was never much interested in playing with baby dolls. I was more of a Sindy and Barbie type, role-playing with toy women who could pick and choose their clothes, careers and men.

Around a year before I became pregnant, I found myself in the gift section of Hillier's Garden Centre, admiring a baby's room sign. *Ssh, baby's dreaming* read the sentiment. This ornament, in all its cuteness and childish simplicity sparked within me an intense desire to have my own child and a nursery door on which to hang such a sign."

Corrine, Mother to Henry, 3

Corrine's experiences are profound; the simplicity of a sign for a baby's nursery which caught her gaze whilst shopping spoke to some part of her deep within, a part she had never connected with previously, and in this moment, awakened an element of her which yearned to be a mother.

Whist we are so often focussed upon establishing our independence, identity, career and other pursuits as younger women, as we mature, many of us do become more consciously aware of our Feminine biology and its time sensitivity. As our perspectives shift, the decision as to whether or not to become a mother can take on a more central, considered role;

"I chose to become a mother when I did because I was in a job which I felt was neither using my talents nor offering me opportunities for advancement. I stuck at it until I bagged my professional qualification then considered the two principal options for change: a new job or a baby. As a married woman approaching the age of thirty, the latter seemed prudent; if I got wrapped up in a fabulous new job I might run the risk of my biological clock 'timing out.'"

Marty, Mother to Jessie, 21 and Lizzie, 16

Becoming pregnant

Once the decision to begin a family has been made, we embark upon journeys of conception, and once again, these journeys are unique and varied. For many couples, journeys to conception are smooth and conscious. We hope and plan to become parents and when we reach the point in our relationship where this feels right, we conceive easily, as was the case for Sharon;

"I had the perfect journey to conception with my first child. My husband and I were about to get married, we had moved and settled into a new country, Canada, and it felt like the right time to start a family. We decided we'd try for a baby and that first try we got pregnant."

Sharon, Mother to Christian, 3 and Jessica, 3 months

"We decided to try for a baby after much discussion, and one thing that was important to us was that it shouldn't become all-consuming. We decided we'd just relax and see what happened, and if after a year or two nothing happened, we'd just carry on with our lives as a couple and be grateful for having more money, free time and sleep! Having said that, as soon as we started trying, I found I was impatient to become pregnant!"

Hazel, Mother to Barnaby, 15 months

Once we have committed to the process of conception, although welcome, this can bring up fears as we begin to spend more time thinking about what it will actually mean to become a mother and all that pregnancy, birth and life with children will bring;

"Although I 'd always wanted children, when it came to starting to try to conceive I actually felt very frightened as well as excited. I've always had a fear of birth and knew once a baby was in there it would have to come out one way or another; that was quite scary. Alongside this it always worried me that because I was so desperate for children, it may not happen for some reason."

Charlotte, Mother to Raffy, 9 months

Charlotte puts into words the mix of different, and at times contradictory, emotions emerging within our inner landscapes. Whilst we may wholeheartedly wish to have a baby, as we begin the actual journey of making this a reality, we become aware of a whole new realm of issues, decisions and anxieties, many of which we cannot control. We are introduced to a milestone of motherhood which recurs throughout our journey – that of surrender. For as much as we would like to plan and have control over the events of our conceptions, pregnancies, births and mothering, what we grow to realise is that, truly, we do not.

Rather we must learn to plan and prepare, to do our best, and then to let go. We begin to accept that we have little control, and instead what we are required to do is to trust, let go and nurture the process as best we can.

Conscious conception and spiritual awakening

Conception can start us thinking about the deeper workings of life. We may think about the beginning of life, the soul or energy of our baby, and if and where this existed before conception. Such musings widen and perhaps challenge our perceptions and understandings; we can ponder the interplay between soul and body, reflecting deeply on the essence and meaning of life.

Some women create a conscious conception whereby the couple connect with the soul or energy of their incoming baby, and consciously dedicate their love making to the conception of this child;

"Before I even met my husband, my daughter was communicating with me through words, pictures and feelings. She even told me her name. I had no idea how motherhood would happen, as there was no man in my life. But within weeks, the love of my life appeared. My daughter's conception was conscious. We chose beautiful music, and had meditated. She was invited into our family."

Veronika, Mother to Bethany, 19 and Eliza 17

For others of us, this can happen slightly differently, whereby the experience of conceiving and the connection with our baby's soul energy brings greater spiritual awareness as we awaken to their presence through our subtle perception;

"I'm certain I know when my son was conceived. I was 39, married only a few months (after a whirlwind transatlantic courtship), and although I'd never been broody, now I was finally in a loving, stable relationship I started feeling a strong desire to be pregnant. On this particular night, I had a dream in which I saw a flower open up, and a baby emerge from it and come to me. The

29

imagery is, of course, straight out of Hans Christian Andersen's Thumbelina – I'm a children's book editor and author, so it's no coincidence I was dreaming in fairy tale images.

I woke up feeling happy, a feeling that stayed with me all day, and feeling particularly warm, close and affectionate towards my husband. When I got home from work, it was a beautiful spring evening, still light, I went for a walk down a country path near our home, and felt very strongly that something wonderful was happening within me. I didn't yet identify it as a pregnancy beginning – but looking back now, I feel sure that's what was happening."

Ronne, Mother to Daniel, 28

Ronne puts into words her perception of the subtle energetic shifts which surround conception whereby the energy of the baby meets our own. Sometimes we can sense this shift through dreams, images and subtle feelings in our merging energies.

My experience with my first daughter is similar; not yet aware I had conceived, I saw subtle, coloured light fill the room and remain for some time. I felt my whole body energy change very slightly and for a few days felt a vibration of absolute love through every cell of my body. It was such a pure and beautiful experience and I knew something very special was happening. Looking back, I feel this was me sensing our daughter's soul energy merging with mine at the beginning of pregnancy.

Such subtle experiences of connection with our babies on an energetic level happen to many of us, yet we may simply not recognise them for what they are, given that our culture has little space or language to describe such things. Many women speak of seeing their baby in a dream, or feeling floaty and different around the time of conception. Motherhood does have the potential to ignite a wave of unexpected spiritual awakening as we begin to reflect, wonder and perceive life in a different way.

"I have five children and can honestly say I was instinctively aware of each one during pregnancy. Each pregnancy connected me with the etheric world in a tangible way. I was aware of something bigger than myself – to me motherhood has always been a spiritual practice, even though there were parts along the way where I wasn't exactly aware of this quality."

Violet, Mother to Sasha, 10, April, 9, Sam and Josh, 7 and Isaac, 2

The experience of the merging of the physical and the spiritual through conception can awaken us to new ways of thinking; heightening and expanding our usual range of perception. Continuing through motherhood, the opening of our bodies and hearts through birthing and loving our babies offers continued opportunities for milestones of awakening, awareness, connection and deepening spiritual understanding.

Journeys to conception can be challenging

Conception itself happens in a single moment. For some of us, this moment occurs early on in our journey, and for others it takes years and a great deal of time, energy and emotion, as Emma and Karen illustrate through their IVF stories.

Whilst some women find themselves conceiving easily, for others, who might have felt ready to become mothers long ago, the journey becomes long, tense and fraught. The decision to try for a baby, which generally begins as an exciting stage in our relationship, can, with time, become increasingly stressful and upsetting if each month continues to bring our period rather than news of a longed-for pregnancy. Stress, anxiety and disappointment cloud our landscapes as we begin to wonder why it is that we are not conceiving and sense that the journey ahead may be more difficult than originally imagined;

"Once married my husband and I looked to start a family. Two years down the line – nothing. I was beginning to feel desperation set in. What was wrong with me? Was there something wrong with my husband? I began talking to my husband about taking tests (this was met with a blank expression), and began to see mothers and children everywhere.

I began to try and reconcile myself to the fact that I might never have children, although deep in my heart I knew, knew I would be a mother – in all honesty that is what I've always wanted most from life.

It wasn't until three years later that I became pregnant and realised what the problem was. I worked for a large global brand and had the boss from hell, my stress levels were through the roof. To cut a long story short, the company went through major reorganisation and my boss decided to leave. When he walked out the door, my stress levels dropped to an all-time low and I conceived pretty much instantly."

Melanie, Mother to James, 1

Melanie's story is remarkable, yet sadly all too common, and brings to light the impact prolonged stress has upon our female health, hormonal balance and fertility. Dr Libby Weaver writes extensively about the dangerous effects of fast-paced, stressful lifestyles on all areas of women's health. Whilst there are many reasons couples experience fertility challenges, as Melanie's story illustrates, learning to see the impact of prolonged stress upon our health, and taking steps to reduce this is a momentous, life-affirming, milestone.

Some women find that some months of adjustments in lifestyle, diet and a reduction in stress create hormonal shifts necessary for conception to occur, yet for many others, journeys to conception require additional support. Such journeys become less joyful, evolving into a process of many steps and stages, with great fluxes of hope, bitterness, emotion and anxiety. A difficult journey to conception gives pregnancy a different tone; we are tentative and hesitant to embrace it, we may protect ourselves emotionally, not letting ourselves get too close to the baby, knowing that nothing is guaranteed until we hold the baby in our arms. Such journeys offer milestones of acceptance, courage, perseverance and surrender;

"We spent the first years of married life enjoying ourselves, going on holidays and working hard! Life was good, we were young, happy and free to do all the things we wanted. I learnt a lot about myself, it was a very valuable time. As time went by though, we started to think more about having a family. My career started to seem less important and other plans started to creep in.

We started to be less careful about contraception and hoped one day we may grow into a family. Time passed and the idea of being a Mum became a much stronger focus, we actively started trying for a baby, but this didn't happen for us. My maternal clock was ticking and I was becoming desperate to be pregnant. Each month that passed with a period became more and more difficult to accept.

Eventually after years of trying we ventured to the doctors, one investigation led to another and I very quickly ended up in hospital having a laparoscopy to investigate what problems there might be. This revealed I had some problems that meant pregnancy might not be as easy to achieve as we'd hoped. I'd had my appendix out as a young child and due to the urgency of the operation quite a bit of damage was done to my Fallopian tubes.

This was very difficult news to hear. I was devastated. By this time

I was so desperate for a baby, it became a near obsession. I couldn't imagine not being a Mum, yet the odds appeared to be stacked against me!

After a few weeks of recovery I decided to hand in my notice at work and take some time out to de-stress. I hoped to find a happier place to be than in a job I no longer cared about! So... we decided to go on a weekend away to celebrate my newfound freedom! To cut a long story short, a lovely hotel, a hot tub, a bottle of wine... I was pregnant!

I never had a period after my operation; the doctor's conclusion was that the dye had flushed out my tube, allowing me to become pregnant, a side effect not expected by anyone! I will never forget the sight of that blue line and the phone call that followed to my husband."

Marie, Mother to Jean, 11 and Lewis, 9

Marie illustrates the journeys of change, longing and letting go many of us find ourselves upon as we strive to become pregnant. The shock and horror of being told by a doctor we may never conceive is beyond devastating. The emotions that follow are some of the hardest we may face as we begin to grieve for the family we may never have and search for reasons why. Yet as Alicja's story shows, pregnancy sometimes can, and does occur, despite receiving such news;

"It took me many years to make the decision, 'I am ready to become a mother.' And once I'd made that decision, I heard from an excellent doctor that I will never have a baby. It was a shock and I cannot describe how I felt. My husband was there for me and convinced me that everything would be OK and not to panic. He was right. After some time, when my GP gave me the right dose of hormones I was feeling better than ever. Soon after, at the age of 27, I became pregnant with my first child. I was so happy! I felt so ready to finally become a mum."

Alicja, Mother to Rozalia 3, and Konrad, 1

Difficult and assisted journeys to conception are hard and trying times. The constant rollercoaster cycle of anticipation and disappointment unfolding alongside our menstrual cycle is stressful, exhausting and emotionally draining. Yet over time, such a journey, with all its milestones and disappointments, can bring with it opportunities for us to cultivate the qualities which serve us well in our onward journey of motherhood. Developing attitudes of acceptance and surrender, and realisations about letting go of the things we cannot control and nurturing what we can, teaches us of flowing with the process. Women spoke of 'letting go, and seeing what happens,' 'no longer being so focussed on trying' and 'enjoying other aspects of life'. Sometimes this letting go is later followed by the news of a pregnancy, and sometimes it is not.

Pregnancy is not the only way we become mothers; fostering and adoption provide alternative routes for many couples. Whilst such journeys certainly have their differences, bringing their own joys and challenges, women speak of a similar process of preparation and letting go in the lead up to receiving their children;

"My boys are adopted – although I do feel I had something of an equivalent journey to pregnancy in preparing emotionally for their arrival. I experienced the beginning of a kind of 'melting away' of small or trivial worries, something which has continued since the boys' arrival three years ago."

Tess, Mother to Adam and Aidan, 8 and Sean, 6

Unexpected pregnancy

Sometimes motherhood arrives in our lives unplanned. Unexpected pregnancy brings intense, mixed thoughts and emotions; we may find ourselves in a state of shock, upon an abrupt path of transformation. Initially we are faced with the decision of whether or not to continue with our pregnancy, which is rarely an easy or straightforward decision.

An unexpected pregnancy may be a surprise, but a happy surprise, albeit one with accompanying fears. We may be shocked, scared, and unsure how things will turn out, but decide to trust in what has happened as being the right thing and, tentatively, we go with the process;

"Discovering I was pregnant was a complete surprise. We had just returned from a fortnight in France, drinking wine, eating brie, smoking. My period was late and the thought occurred to me that I'd been unusually tired and emotional for the second week of the trip, but I pushed it to the back of my mind for at least another week before I took a test. My first thought was 'Oh no! I've pickled my baby in France!' It was a strange mixture of shock, worry and happiness."

Zara, Mother to Izzy, 4

The discovery of an unplanned, yet tentatively welcome, pregnancy can propel us to make almost instant changes. Such immediate changes thrust us onto our path as mothers; we learn to put someone else's needs before our own and instantly make space in our lives and bodies for our baby;

"Needless to say, I quit smoking within a week. We were living with my parents at the time, in order to save up a deposit to buy our first house. It was never under question we would have the baby – fully prepared to move out from my parents' home and abandon our dreams of buying a place of our own, we informed them I was pregnant. They insisted we stay, continue to save up and have the baby, and stay as long as we like."

Zara, Mother to Izzy, 4

For many of us, before we conceive we may not have planned on motherhood and never experienced our own maternal feelings and assume we have no maternal instincts. Yet once we conceive and take our first steps into the terrain of motherhood, planned or otherwise, many of us do find such feelings begin to stir.

Perhaps it is the physiological experience of pregnancy hormones which awaken experiences of maternal instinct. This was certainly the case for Francesca who discovered she was pregnant as a young woman living with alcohol addiction. Acting on a hunch, she took a pregnancy test which confirmed her suspicions. She immediately felt an overwhelming mix of panic, fear, joy, despair, sadness and happiness. Despite her addiction, for which she had not yet sought help, Francesca spoke of feeling an immediate and overwhelming sense of responsibility and protection towards her baby.

It was this intense urge to protect her helpless baby from the harm she knew her drinking could cause that gave her the strength to stay away from alcohol both in that moment, and during her pregnancy, and to later seek help and take control of her addiction. Francesca's story is exceptionally moving and illustrates the depth of transformation mothering can inspire. Her full story is found in Chapter 7, Challenging Times.

Other women made the conscious choice *not* to conceive, choosing to pursue different directions, yet found that sometimes babies have a way of coming into our lives anyway. And whilst we have the choice of whether or not to continue with our pregnancy, this is rarely a simple choice;

"My partner and I had agreed we weren't having children. We both had careers, and were so aware of the state of the world that we decided we didn't want to bring children into this, knowing things were getting worse socially and ecologically.

I'd recently had a lump removed from my breast and had come off the Pill. It was around this time I found I'd become pregnant. It was really hard. We weren't getting on well. I'd had an abortion some years before, and becoming pregnant again all the feelings around that time came flooding back. It was a really hard time, but I didn't want to have another abortion, so I went ahead with the pregnancy."

Amy, Mother to Simon, 25 and Edward, 19

Amy's interview was powerful, moving and deeply heartfelt; as her children are young adults now, there was a lot to talk about. She began talking about her challenging beginnings upon the path of motherhood, her difficult feelings and doubts, yet went on to share how a new element of her awoke and blossomed through mothering, becoming passionate about the meaning and value inherent in nurturing our children.

So whilst we may find ourselves pregnant, worried, uncertain, perhaps alone and with many doubts concerning our abilities, reading the stories of other women who have been there, trusted and grown in knowledge and experience, brings great strength, comfort and inspiration. We learn to be mothers simply by being mothers, learning on the job how to love, care and nurture our children.

Awakening emotional landscapes

Discovering pregnancy brings with it many feelings, often intense, contradictory and simultaneous. We are happy, excited, busy and exhausted, joyful yet anxious, hopeful yet uncertain, overflowing sometimes with love and sometimes with fear. Yet how does our culture hold, guide and nurture our inner emotional experiences?

So often our emotions are waved away as "pregnancy hormones". Whilst hormones certainly contribute to the increased sensitivity and intensity of our emotional experiences, becoming a mother, especially for the first time, is a huge and significant life change. Our experiences are not to be dismissed, diminished or brushed off lightly, but rather nurtured, held and tended. We are awakening, unfolding; our *Mother Self* is emerging. She is fragile, incomplete and as vulnerable and embryonic as our developing babies.

Far from being simply "hormonal", the emotional surges and

shifts we encounter are an integral part of our learning journey. Our whole being reconfigures across all levels to accommodate our baby. We awaken to our inner landscapes of mothering, landscapes of alchemic love, enormity of responsibility and complex emotion, connection and communication. We realise we are changing, letting go of what was before; feelings can be complex, contradictory and intense. We are shedding parts of our previous selves, perhaps unconsciously, yet we are letting go into the unknown, for our *Mother Self* is not yet fully formed. We encounter milestones of surrender, trust and letting ourselves go into an unfolding process of change.

Sadly, we have little cultural guidance as how to navigate and nurture this transformation. Our society, built on the recognition of the outer world, science and material accumulation, has no eyes with which to perceive our inner landscapes. It is all too easy for pregnancy to become a medically managed journey of anxiety and material preparations. How different could this journey be if, collectively, we valued our experiences of the Feminine and the potential for trust and transformation new motherhood ignites?

Yet recognition is occurring, for when we women welcome, explore and embrace our inner experiences we come to recognise the value of these seismic shifts within ourselves and others. Recognition of the sacred, transformative inner landscapes of the Feminine is awakening. We see evidence for this through the emerging presence of Red Tent, Pregnancy Yoga, Womb Yoga, Hypnobirthing, home birth and more widespread support for active, empowered birth in labour wards across the country.

Landscapes of transformation
Difficult childhood and past experiences, or having had less-than-nurturing relationships with our own parents, can cause us to feel reticent about becoming mothers ourselves. We may lack confidence, hold deep fears of replicating negative relationships with our own children, and may doubt our capability to be good, loving mothers. Such fears may intensify through pregnancy, yet motherhood offers immense opportunity for healing the past and doing things differently and in our own way. Women share such journeys in Chapter 8, Changing the Legacy.

"Growing up without strong family values there was a time I didn't want children. We all go through that feeling, I guess, especially when we are given no direction into what motherhood can really be...

Shortly after we started dating, I was expecting a beautiful baby, and the second I found out, I smiled and was flooded by an amazing feeling of happiness and peace.

I could feel this was a girl, through her I'd have to grow and deal with my insecurities, but I didn't know I'd have to face many other challenges, all of which would transform me, take me deep into the depths of pain and then lift me up as the mother I needed to become."

Vanessa, Mother to Lilo, 10, Boo, 8 and Sammy, 1

"I wanted my baby to be a boy, because I'd had a pretty appalling relationship with my mother and feared replicating it with a daughter. But my relationship with my mother improved a lot during pregnancy, and when I eventually produced a girl, I was not at all perturbed."

Marty, Mother to Jessie, 19 and Lizzie, 15

Pregnancy has such potential for healing as we so want to overcome our limitations so we are able to become the best mother we can be for our babies. We return to this milestone again and again along our mothering path; the strength of love we feel for our child causes us to want to make changes in ourselves so we are better able to give the love we so want them to receive;

"Throughout pregnancy I was unsure. I was worried, and felt emotions of my previous abortion returning. I hadn't wanted kids, and now I was pregnant; did I want to be? I was worried about whether I'd be a good mother. I worried that I couldn't do it, and also if I even wanted to. But my health was good. I did lots of walking and took care of myself, that side of things was good."

Amy, Mother to Simon, 25 and Edward, 19

Amy's story continues through the following chapters where we discover how she found herself becoming a loving and insightful mother, discovering overwhelming love and fiercely protective feelings towards her babies. Yet as newly pregnant women, we know only what we feel, and fear, at the time. We are as embryonic as our babies; we do not, as yet, have the benefit of hindsight or experience. We lack the knowledge of how we will grow tremendously and develop the strength, capability, trust and depth of love that will enable us to embrace our babies and cope with the path ahead.

When a baby isn't to be

The emotions of the early weeks are often accompanied by fears of early miscarriage and it is for this reason that many of us choose to keep our pregnancy news to ourselves during the early months. Miscarriage is a fear which lingers around the edges of our inner landscapes and, sadly, the experience of miscarriage is incredibly common too, with one in four pregnancies miscarried.

So few of us speak openly about our losses, meaning miscarriage is an aspect of our Femininity which continues to remain hidden and taboo, and so we tend to suffer, grieve and struggle in fear and isolation. It is only when one woman is brave enough to share her experiences, that others may too share their own.

When women do speak about such losses, it can be difficult and uncomfortable; we rarely have the words or the space to articulate our feelings and those we speak with may be unsure how to respond;

"I had miscarriages which were devastating. The first, prior to having a child was more about the loss of a pregnancy – I didn't understand parenting then. The ones in between children were worse as now I knew what I'd lost."

Ross, Mother to Charley and Chelsea, in their 20's

As Ross illustrates, our experiences of losing our babies are coloured by our experiences of life; before we have children, a miscarriage is a loss of pregnancy, our precious baby, our firstborn, our hopes of motherhood. After such experiences, many of us go on to conceive and become mothers, yet our experiences of these early miscarriages remain with us, silently occupying a tender area of our heartscape.

Our experiences of having children influence our experiences of future miscarriages. As Ross recalls, not only do we grieve for the baby we have lost, but so too for the emerging personality, the toddler, the little boy or girl whom we did not get to know and nurture. We may find ourselves imagining what our little lost babies may have been like as children and what energy, laughter and personality they may have brought to our family.

Miscarriage brings great panic, fear, grief and sadness and casts shadows of doubt over future pregnancies. As Ann illustrates, miscarriage can cause us to doubt our own bodies and ability to carry our baby safely;

"I had two early miscarriages before conceiving Ella. I found these devastatingly sad. It felt as if my body was failing me, or my womb was not a safe place to be. I had some hypnotherapy, which helped me come to terms with these losses and prepare to try to conceive again. When I became pregnant again (with Ella) it was pretty terrifying for the first few months, especially as I had some early bleeding. Hypnotherapy was useful again here, to help me to feel calmer. Thankfully it was third time lucky."

Ann, mother to Ella, 4

"Unfortunately I experienced two ectopic pregnancies, resulting in both of my Fallopian tubes having to be removed. My doctor dismissed my pains and concerns of my first (ectopic) pregnancy as being due to my belly button piercing, and due to this I continued with my ectopic pregnancy for three months. The pain became unbearable, I suffered extensive haemorrhaging and required emergency, life-saving surgery resulting in my tube being removed. Yearning to be a mother, I became pregnant again six months later and was devastated to discover once again this pregnancy was ectopic and my remaining Fallopian tube had to be removed.

These were dark times, my grief was immense, and I lost my father around this time too. What followed were intense years of grief, hope, and anticipation as we went through three rounds of IVF. The IVF cycle is immensely challenging, my body and mind were shattered and in need of deep healing, so unsurprisingly I was unable to hold on to the first two embryos and felt enormous grief for the loss of these babies and my hopes of becoming a mother. I so wanted to become a mother; I wanted to give love so much, I wanted it to be unconditional, to experience the gift of life and learn how to be selfless. After a period of rest, and much deep healing of my body and soul, supported through a deep commitment to Yoga practice, when offered a third round of IVF I was in a much better place, physically and emotionally, to approach this.

These were rocky times in my relationship with my partner, yet to my immense astonishment and relief this little mermaid was staying in. Although I couldn't relax until this baby was born, I steadied my tears and emotions through Yoga and acupuncture. I kept mobile throughout the pregnancy and allowed myself to enjoy every moment of it. The incredible transformation and growth occurring inside me was awe-inspiring and the love bond I was forming with my baby was so deep already I felt like a tower of strength and power."

Karen, Mother to Rosie, 8

Once again, we realise there are many aspects of motherhood over which we have little control; we can eat well, rest, exercise, take supplements and nurture the process in every way possible, yet ultimately, we cannot control the outcome. And it is worth reminding ourselves, in our darker moments, that there is nothing we did or did not do which could cause or prevent our miscarriage. Miscarriage research is underfunded, therefore, often, we do not know what caused our babies to be lost, making our coming to terms with the loss so much more difficult.

Milestones of empathy

Having not shared the news of pregnancy early on, many of us find it even more difficult to share the devastating news of miscarriage. This leaves us vulnerable and emotionally isolated. Like other experiences of death, our culture largely lacks the emotional language, skills and empathy to offer meaningful support.

"I think the silence and misunderstanding of miscarriage really add to the challenge of navigating the deep grief. The rule about not telling anyone you're pregnant until you're 12 or 14 weeks makes me so mad. It's fine if you never lose one, you get to come to terms with being pregnant and hope and plan, then tell people, perhaps with mild relief.

But if you lose babies at 11 and a half, or 10 or 7 weeks, the result of this crazy custom isn't comfort. It's culturally enforced silence.

It's not a relief that you didn't tell anyone, it's a burden that you have to carry all on your own. That your baby died and maybe no one, or almost no one, ever even knew about it."

Mary Ann, Mother to Edward, 4

"Miscarriage is another one of those devastating griefs women are quiet about. We put up with so much; it's a classic case of those who haven't experienced it not really understanding."

Ross, Mother to Charley and Chelsea, in their 20's

Whether or not we have experienced such loss ourselves, we can offer our presence and love to the grieving mother; we can hold the space for her to share her feelings and acknowledge her loss. We can listen and recognise her as a mother; a mother who has lost her child, her love, her hopes, her dreams.

Part of our transformation through motherhood is a deepening of our capacity for empathy and understanding of such losses and grief of others. And by speaking out and listening, really listening, together we begin to break the silence of this suffering, creating changes in the way we as women, collectively, experience and respond to pregnancy loss.

"The first flutterings, the scans, the worrying about movement, the worrying and kick counting. In the news a couple of famous Mums lost their babies quite late on in pregnancy and I was traumatised. I actually felt their pain, not that I'd experienced it, but I so knew, in quite a primeval way, exactly how I would feel if I lost my precious baby."

Shelley, Mother to Leia, 3 and Anya, 1

Shelley's experiences beautifully encapsulate our milestones of empathy. Having felt the awesome, gut-wrenching love for our own baby, we develop the emotional capacity to relate to others who we imagine have felt similar. Such empathy brings great potential for both individual and collective change.

We can have empathy for women who have lost their babies. We have the increased emotional capacity to appreciate her feelings. We can say we are so sorry for her loss with full authenticity, we are sorry that she will not get to meet and mother her baby and that we cannot imagine how sad she must be feeling.

We cannot change the situation or make it better, yet we can offer practical help with her home and other children, and we can empathise. We can let her know that we see her and her pain and not expect her to carry on as normal to avoid the discomfort of others. Miscarriage, like so much of motherhood, is something that each of us comes to terms with in our own way, yet the empathy and kindness of friends makes such a difference to our journey.

Deepening love, trust and spirituality
The process of loss can focus our attention more sharply upon life and death, we may begin to search for deeper meaning and find milestones, realisations and learning arise from our emptiness and pain.

We may feel a loss of trust in our bodies, yet when sitting with these issues, with reflection women explained how they went on to develop a deeper sense of trust in their body's wisdom and its knowledge of when to nurture life and when to let it go;

"Initially conception was easy – it happened quickly but then I miscarried at 11 weeks. That was a shock and also a period where I developed trust in my body, that it knew how and when to create or destroy life."

Mary Ann, Mother to Edward, 7 months

Some women speak of loss in a philosophical way, saying 'it wasn't meant to be'. Such an everyday, simple phrase may evoke trust and comfort for some, denoting that we believe that things have happened the way they were meant to, in terms of wherever we place our individual sense of meaning and belief, even though it is hard for us, individually, to bear.

"We conceived the first time, so very easily, despite being 40 and first pregnancy. Five months earlier I'd suffered a miscarriage which again had been conceived the first time trying, but sadly was not meant to be."

Deborah, Mother to James, 4

Women do not seem to need to hold particular spiritual or religious beliefs to come to this way of thinking. Perhaps it grows from milestones of acceptance and surrender and in realising that, ultimately, we do not have control and must place our faith and trust in something greater. Whilst such sentiments bring comfort to some, if we sadly go on to experience recurrent miscarriage, such sentiments can sound hollow and insensitive, holding little comfort or explanation for our devastatingly sad experiences.

Alongside pain, grief and sadness, miscarriage can also bring milestones of spirituality as can pregnancy itself. Miscarriage may inspire us to meditate and connect with the energy of our baby, and reflections upon our own emotions can deepen our connection with our heart centre and feelings of unconditional love;

"I've experienced four miscarriages. Alongside the grief and the awful sense of loss, I connected with the souls of the babies through meditation. It might sound strange, but I saw their reasons for coming, and their connection to our family, I learned about strength, and love, and it definitely brought me and my husband closer."

Faith, Mother to Dominic, 16, Stella, 4 and Emily, 2

Pregnancy is a unique time where our connection to the very

essence of life is tangible. We literally *feel* a new being growing within. We glimpse the intangible, ethereal aspects of life which we may overlook in our busy and outwardly focussed everyday lives.

Pregnancy and miscarriage can teach us that spiritual experiences do not have to be lofty, "out of this world" visions, but rather gentle understandings of the simplicities and connections within everyday human life. We awaken to the realisation that great love lies at the very heart of what we do, and that simple moments of feeling connection with our baby within our wombspace hold meaning and connect us to the awe of something greater than ourselves.

Any experience of pregnancy, be it for an hour, a day, a week or full term, is a coming together of our being with our partner and the presence of our baby. And whether or not our tiny babe makes it through to life in our arms and family, we are mothers and have connected physically, emotionally and on a soul level. Alongside the grief and sadness, such union can spark a search for greater meaning and connection, opening our hearts and inspiring journeys of compassion, love, empathy and understanding.

"After a previous miscarriage, the fluttering movements of another living being inside me were an amazing reminder of the life I carried and the unique job I was doing. I suddenly felt as though I had realised why I was on this earth and what I was meant to be doing, and that all the 'busy' stuff I'd filled my days with up until this point was really meaningless in comparison to this miracle of creating a new little person."

Fran, Mother to Emma, 35, Jack, 32 and Edward, 29

Mothering is a journey of love, yet at times this journey feels bitter, lonely and unjust. Through such hollowing-out experiences, we tunnel deeper into the truth of our being and deepen the spaces we hold for love, awareness and understanding. Certainly we meet milestones in times of pain and grief as we do in love and joy; we come to know more of life and what truly matters to us. Such experiences change us, bringing us deeper understandings of the complexities of mothering, grief and relationships.

Embracing pregnancy

As we come into the second trimester, for many of us, fears of miscarriage move to the back of our mind and we begin to enjoy more aspects of our pregnancy such as relief from nausea, our rounding belly and the spirals of movement within. For many of us, moments during our first pregnancy become some of our most treasured memories;

"I loved being pregnant, it was the most wonderful experience of my life. I did aqua yoga, swam with dolphins, wrote letters each day to my baby and each night would take a bath and play her a collection of beautiful lullabies. I don't recall any fears in my pregnancy – just ten months of love, ecstasy and joy."

Veronika, Mother to Bethany, 19 and Eliza, 17

"I was incredibly lucky with my pregnancy. I can honestly say it was one of the highlights of my life. I had no morning sickness and never felt or looked so fantastic. I hope I'm as lucky if any more come along! I loved it.

I was also not going to research too much. I was determined to enjoy feeling great and didn't want to weigh myself down with research telling me what I should or shouldn't be doing/eating/feeling. Apart from enrolling in an antenatal group (more to meet new mothers-to-be than anything else) I pretty much coasted through."

Melanie, Mother to James, 1

Alongside the joys, physiological changes can bring discomfort, uncertainty and exhaustion. So whilst we may certainly have times of joy, excitement and happiness, we may also find the experience draining and difficult. Here we meet another milestone of motherhood – that of contradiction.

How can we feel so loving, elated and happy, yet at the same time so anxious, drained and unwell? Through the years we can learn that one need not cancel out the other, but that we can expand to hold many conflicting emotions simultaneously. Our milestones teach us to fully enjoy the good times, and to hold and nurture ourselves through the challenges.

Sickness and intense nausea can make us snarl at the term "morning sickness" as such feelings zap our energy and appetite all of the time, leaving us debilitated and exhausted day and night, overshadowing any enjoyment of the early months.

When I trained as a doula with renowned obstetrician Michel Odent, he impressed on me the necessity of a shift of perspective, explaining that nausea illustrates high hormone levels and protection from consuming anything potentially toxic. He illustrates milestones of shifting perception and acceptance; how simple changes of mindset change experiences, help us to see things differently, and in a more positive light, and I endeavour to pass on this reassurance and shift in perspective to mums attending my Pregnancy Yoga classes. Yet we must be gentle on ourselves, for even though we may know such things intellectually, such knowledge does not always take away the intensity of such feelings;

"My sickness during the first few months was intense with nausea and puking many times a day. I put a mattress on the kitchen floor and just lay there waiting for the time to pass. I kept smelling strange smells in the house and failing to remove them, sometimes I spent the night on the balcony. I was worried it was the smell of paint and that it would hurt the baby. It got me stressed at first, but later that got less."

Hanneke, Mother to Vita, 2

Extreme sickness, pain and complications can make it more difficult to enjoy pregnancy. Similarly, difficult living conditions and uncomfortable or unresolved feelings can mean that some of us do not enjoy pregnancy as much as we may like. Yet even within these difficult experiences, women spoke of moments of happiness and joy as they connect with their baby and feel excited, highlighting milestones of contradiction as opposing feelings co-habit;

"I didn't enjoy pregnancy overall, and I'm not sure how much our difficult living circumstances impacted on this. There were lodgers living in the house with my parents and communal space was always busy. I struggled to keep my emotions in check as hormones surged and we carried on with little space of our own to adjust to this new development!

I think mentally, I fought the changes to my body as the pregnancy started to take over – I missed being as agile and feeling free. I felt sluggish and heavy and really struggled to sleep. I walked a lot, and enjoyed that. I also had chronic heartburn from very early on. Saying all this, I remember magical moments – the first kicks, scans, the excitement, lovely moments with my husband musing over who our baby might be and discussing how we couldn't wait to meet her."

Zara, Mother to Izzy, 4

Feelings towards our baby

Intrinsically connected to pregnancy are our feelings towards our babies, and experiences of this fledging love are as individual as we are. For some this love appears as huge surges of powerful emotion, and for others it is a more gradual, tentative presence; sometimes constant, sometimes fleeting. Sometimes it feels instant and easy, enfolding us in its warm presence, and other times eludes us, leaving us somehow anxious and unsure.

It can help to know that many of us have uncertainties about our feelings towards our babies both in pregnancy and beyond. The transition to motherhood is a time of such change, letting go and renewal, and our feelings are part of this process. Whatever our feelings during pregnancy, as time goes on and we get to know more of the little person our baby is becoming, our feelings grow, change and develop as do we as mothers.

Loving our children is deep and complex, yet thankfully mothering is a journey of *learning* to love. These are complex, tender issues, milestones we return to again and again through the years;

"I could not comprehend the impact the little life inside my womb would have. I loved him immensely from the very beginning."

Deborah, Mother to James, 4

"I felt a deep and consuming love from conception each time I've been pregnant. All the clichés I found to be true – that love grows so there is enough for everyone, is not finite and does not have to be divided between children."

Jenny, Mother to Matthew, 3 and Lucy, 14 months

Below, Jane illustrates the complexities of our emotional landscapes; we can feel uncomfortable with some aspects of our pregnancy or situation, yet we have a palpable bond of love and connection with our growing child;

"I always wanted children. I could always picture myself surrounded by children. I never met someone to have those children with. I became pregnant during a casual relationship and knew during the pregnancy that I would be a single mother. This made for bittersweet feelings all the way through.

I loved feeling my daughter move, but I felt so alone, even with family and friends around me. But I knew this was how it was meant to be... Seeing her for the first time felt like a small part of me there looking at me. It wasn't a rush of love; that love had always been there. This was just how it was, me and her, together, we would be fine, we would do what was needed, and we would manage."

Jane, Mother to Sarah, 8

We come to know and love our children in our own ways, and through so doing, embark upon another milestone of motherhood; we grow into our own authenticity, and come to know ourselves more deeply. Loving our children teaches us to grow into ourselves, to deepen into our own experiences and carve our own paths driven by our own feelings of inner truth.

Yet this is not always a smooth or easy process. Difficulties in our relationships or living situations, depression, anxiety or illness exert additional pressure, leaving us feeling physically and emotionally drained. Yet as Rebecca illustrates, whilst our path may begin as a difficult one, mothering is a *constant* journey of growth. Through the necessity of having to nurture our children, with time, we find our feet and discover our own authenticity and ways of mothering;

"I find it quite hard to talk about my pregnancies, and even to think about it. My partner didn't want kids, and I felt nervous and worried about a lot of things. Looking back it wasn't a good experience, things were really hard, and it was hard when they were babies too. But it's great now. I love them so much and I love being a mum, things are so much better."

Rebecca, Mother to Sasha, 6 and Josie, 5

Pregnancy emotions are varied, contradictory and intense, yet as a culture we expect pregnant women to be happy, rosy and blooming, joyfully anticipating the arrival of their baby, all of the time. Therefore it can feel like there is little space for expressing our darker, more ambiguous feelings.

Women spoke of their fears around motherhood, doubts of their ability to care for and love for their babies, and how they kept such thoughts to themselves for fear of being judged and shamed by others. Underlying all these emotions is the fear of being cast as a "bad" or "unfit" mother, and of our babies being taken from us. Yet by talking with a trusted partner, friend, relative or supportive midwife, doula or counsellor, relief can be found as we explore our feelings and receive affirmation, reassurance and support.

Milestones of body image

As women and girls, for many of us, our bodies have become the landscapes upon which we have judged ourselves and felt judged by others regarding our appearance, attractiveness and acceptability. The relentless industries of "beauty", fashion, marketing and media project falsified images of body shape and appearance to which we are told we should conform and aspire. Yet rarely do they speak of the strength, power and wisdom of the female body and psyche.

Pregnancy can, unexpectedly, bring about milestones of acceptance and positivity surrounding body image. The experience of our baby growing within leads many of us to look at our bodies in an entirely new way, with a greater sense of confidence, respect and awe. It can be deeply empowering when we peel away the shallow, negative messages of the "beauty" industry and instead glimpse the strength, power and innate wisdom of our body and its ability to create, nurture and sustain life;

"My experience of becoming a mother gave me a new found respect and confidence in my body for having nurtured this wonderful being within."

Margaret, Mother to Leon, 20 and Rebecca, 17

"I logged into a baby site and it sent me messages telling me how my baby was growing – it was so exciting and I learned more about the human body in those first few months than I ever did at school.

I was in awe – not only of our baby, but of my body – it just KNEW exactly what to do and when. All I needed to do was eat and drink well. It felt like a miracle."

Shelley, Mother to Leia, 3 and Anya, 1

As we walk the path of pregnancy, birth and nurturing, we have the opportunity to grow more deeply into our own strength, knowledge and wisdom. Milestones of truly knowing and embodying our inner strength and trust in our feminine body wisdom develop over decades, yet we begin to glimpse just how wise and powerful we are as we feel those first flutters of movement beneath our skin. Milestones of faith in the nurturing abilities of our body can evolve into positive expectations at our ability to birth, breastfeed and nurture.

Loving the bump – embracing our changing shape

There remains remarkable pressure on women and girls to be thin.

Yet skinny, flat-stomached models sit alongside adverts for heavily processed, health eroding food products whilst obesity statistics skyrocket; clearly there are deep complexities and stark contradictions in the messages we receive.

Yet pregnancy can be a breath of fresh air amidst this contradictory cultural overwhelm; for perhaps the first time in our lives we are able to relinquish entirely the pressure to be thin. Instead we can take the decision to eat well for the combined health of ourselves and our baby, and welcome and embrace our changing shape as a sign of health and wellbeing.

Women spoke of mid-pregnancy being a time when they began to feel comfortable in their own bodies, perhaps for the first time ever. They were able to embrace rather than resent their rounding tummies, and could feel happy and proud of themselves physically, with no pressure to be in any way different to how they were. Such milestones are truly liberating and empowering as we let go of inner criticism and begin to love and accept ourselves and our bodies for how, and who, we truly are;

"I loved being pregnant and I was so proud of my changing figure and round tummy."
Fran, Mother to Emma, 35, Jack, 32 and Edward, 29

"I loved being pregnant, it made me feel really special and when my baby started to move and kick it suddenly felt real. I loved watching my bump grow and the way I looked with it."
Charlotte, Mother to Raffy, 9 months

Pregnancy can sometimes bring surprising milestones surrounding body image and disordered eating. Whilst this is certainly not the case for everyone, for some of us this can be a time of unexpected positivity and release as we come to feel real freedom around our body and embrace our changing shape free from disordered eating, as was the case for Marty;

"In my late teens I'd been mildly anorexic; never a hospital case, but thin enough to lose my periods and with a fair selection of the associated obsessions and behaviours... In my early twenties I regained a healthy weight but never really lost the behaviours and thought patterns.

However as my pregnancy progressed, I continued to perceive

myself as perfectly formed while all those around me started to look increasingly scrawny! Some anorexics, even reformed ones, have a real struggle with pregnancy, but for me it was an almost complete cure; the behaviour patterns have only returned at those rare times when I've felt really, really cornered socially."

Marty, Mother to Jessie, 19 and Lizzie, 15

Mothering is a journey of opportunity and transformation; whilst aspects of the journey bring up our own pain and trauma, so too do they present opportunities for our healing, release and growth. As we learn to love and mother our children, so too do we have opportunities to discover those vulnerable parts of ourselves in need of our healing and our own mother love. Our milestones ensue as we bestow a little of that fierce, unconditional love we hold for our babies upon ourselves also.

Baby brain – how pregnancy changes our consciousness
Alongside physical changes and shifts in body image, pregnancy also brings changes to our mind. We forget things, become more sensitive and emotionally centred and develop a greater capacity for empathy. At first this can be disconcerting, especially as our culture does not understand the significance of such hormonal shifts, and instead writes us off as "hormonal", "ditsy" and "on another planet";

"My early memories are of the strange thing that happened to my brain and my ability to focus and think. Words like 'bovine' and 'baby brain' suddenly had meaning! I turned inwards and ceased to worry about the busy world out there – a big change for someone who always wanted to be a career woman."

Fran, Mother to Emma, 35, Jack, 32 and Edward, 29

Whilst it may be disconcerting to witness our ways of thinking altering of their own accord, as Fran experienced, these changes in mindset serve a purpose; they loosen our focus on the outer world, encouraging us to connect to our heartspace, guiding us within to focus upon our babies and inner landscapes.

Our complex hormonal systems are responsible for this overhaul in preparation for motherhood; we are being transformed; rewired and reconfigured in preparation for motherhood. Without such a shift, we could carry on as before, busy and engaged in the outer world, unprepared and unable to make the huge inner and outer changes necessary for our baby's nurturing. Yet at the time it feels disconcerting and we worry we are losing ourselves.

Obstetrician Michel Odent teaches that such changes are *integral to a woman's safe passage through pregnancy, labour and birth.* He urges midwives and doulas to protect pregnant and labouring mothers from interruption by the outside world, from observation and questioning, to enable them to fully experience these hormonal shifts which, he argues, orchestrate labour, birth, breastfeeding and bonding.

As newly pregnant women we have a foot in two worlds; our pre-pregnancy world of work, social life, relationships and the things we used to think about, and simultaneously we are stepping into a new inner world of nurturing and motherhood. A world we know little about and explore through our bodies, feelings, intuition and connection with our baby.

Yet how we bridge these two worlds is rarely straightforward; we lack the words to describe our experiences, feel disconcerted at the mental changes, and are, as yet, unaware of the deep transformations to come as we are re-formed into mothers. We begin to sense we are losing something of our former selves, and often we cling on, unaware as yet of the deep treasures to come as we journey forward.

Busy lives, careers, financial pressure and the expectation to carry on as before can make these changes difficult to assimilate. We are carrying on in our outer lives, often unable to find the space to navigate and understand the changes within;

"The first months of pregnancy were hard, I was constantly sick. It didn't help that I was working full time and doing a college course. Sometimes I felt I didn't have the time to enjoy pregnancy as much as I would have liked."

Alicja, Mother to Rozalia, 3 and Konrad, 1

"I just remember conception being nothing and everything. Feeling like everything had changed but everything had to somehow go on as if it hadn't."

Lizzie, Mother to Izzy 6, James 4, Lloyd 1

I see many women struggling with this transition in my Pregnancy Yoga classes, so we dedicate part of the class to sharing experiences of shifting emotions. This is a valuable time as there are few spaces women can share such inner struggles, feelings and contradictions as we journey from one world to another with others who understand.

In doing this women create connections and friendships, and empathy and understanding is increased amongst the group. We truly are upon a journey of shared inner discovery as we come to uncover new parts of ourselves as we make space for our baby and motherhood in our inner and outer lives.

Let us recognise and welcome such milestones of change. Rather than dismissing ourselves as "hormonal", let us instead perceive ourselves as becoming *heart-centred*, *nurturing* and *empathetic*, coming to life upon our inner landscapes. Let us begin to *welcome* such changes as valuable qualities on our journey to becoming responsive, connected mothers. Such a shift sees the emergence of the milestones of *value* and *recognition* as we begin to see the immense *worth* and *value* in the work of mothering.

It can be difficult to value such inner shifts when we are still carrying on at the same speed as before, expected to give the same amount of time and energy to our work despite the huge physical and emotional changes of pregnancy. Little time to slow down and care for ourselves can leave us stressed, exhausted and anxious. Everyone's circumstances are different, yet making time to care for ourselves and embrace our pregnancy can be very positive;

"After our long and challenging journey to conception, what followed was a fantastic first few months of pregnancy. I had time as I wasn't working to enjoy being pregnant, to rest and dream. Just wonderful. I would recommend a non-working pregnancy to anyone lucky enough to be able to afford it! I was so comfortable and content with being pregnant, the feeling of growing a new life was one that was so much more than I'd even dared to imagine whilst wanting to conceive. I loved it, every moment, from my first morning sickness to the fluttering kicks to almighty footprints and body rolls!"

Marie, Mother to Jean, 11 and Lewis, 9

"Due to the re-organisation of my company I was lucky enough to opt for a redundancy package, so was able to cease work when I was only a couple of months pregnant. This was the best thing that could ever have happened as I was able to relax and really enjoy my pregnancy."

Melanie, Mother to James, 1

Pregnancy is a journey in its own right, yet also it is a journey of preparation. We prepare our homes to welcome our baby, and our minds and bodies are readying themselves for labour, birth and mothering.

Chapter Two
Journeys of Labour and Birth

Birth asks us to let go in order to receive; to receive strength, trust, love, support, and our babies. Birth calls us to let go of our whole selves, then, as we claim our babies, to rediscover ourselves, as mothers. Through the great intensity of birth the pieces of ourselves are blown apart. We must then put ourselves together in a new way, and this takes time. For now we are not only the woman we previously were, but also we are mothers.

We put the pieces back together differently, incorporating our baby and our newly emerging *Mother Self* into the picture. This is a long process, and there are many times along the way where we feel raw, vulnerable, lost and at sea. Indeed, we will dissolve and re-form ourselves many times further throughout our journey and it is this dissolution, discovery and re-forming which forms the very essence of our transformation.

Birth calls to us to let go of fears; fears that we cannot do it, that we do not have the strength, fear of what may happen, of receiving intervention, of not receiving intervention. We must let go of control, release resistance, surrender to the intensity and allow it to flow through us, however our baby's birth unfolds.

Releasing self-doubt and discovering strength

Most women who have had a baby can recall times during labour when they thought *I can't do this*. I remember feeling like this at times with all three of my children's births. With my first daughter, whilst I was generally positive about the idea of labour, there were times where I really believed that I could not do it, although part of me hoped I could, and I was absolutely amazed when she was born.

With my second daughter two and a half years later, I had learned much more about the birth process through my training and teaching of pregnancy yoga. This time, around transition, as the sensations of doubt flooded my mind I said to my partner, 'I'm saying I can't do it, but I know I can. I just need you to tell me I can!' This reassurance worked, and soon enough my daughter moved down and was born into the warm water of the birthing pool.

Once again my resolve was put to its test when my third baby was ten days overdue and we were receiving frequent evening phone calls from community midwives saying our home birth was cancelled due to staffing shortages. I meditated, tuned in to my baby and asked for all to be well. The anxiety surrounding his "lateness" and the availability of on-call midwives for home birth was hard to deal with, but I went within, calmed my inner space, meditated and received the clear message that I must *let go and have faith*.

Once again I was learning my own milestones of motherhood. And sure enough, that night, contractions began, midwives attended and eventually he was born. Being a whole 3 lbs heavier than our second baby, this labour was less about self-doubt, and much more about journeying deeper within to unearth greater strength to deal with the intensity.

Like much of the mothering journey ahead, we find ourselves in a spiralling rhythm of strength and self-doubt. Yet as we let go of our fears and doubts, even for a moment, we gain a little more strength in the belief that *yes*, we *can* do it. And it is this strength, and fleeting moments of belief and determination, that strengthens our resolve, increases our energy, and gets our babies born. We experience glimpses of how strong and powerful we can be. Such flickers of insight into this power can remain with us for life, resurfacing and reminding us just how strong, wise and powerful we truly are.

Mary Ann recalls how the intense second stage of her son's birth caused her to doubt her ability to carry on, yet with good support she was able to continue and birth her son;

"I don't know how many times I said, 'I can't do it, it's too painful.' My waters broke in the pool but eventually I had to get out and push 'on land'. It felt excruciating in my back but eventually, almost three hours of intense pushing later, my baby's head emerged, followed, in the next contraction, by his body.

Rene (my Independent Midwife) unwrapped the cord, which was wrapped twice around him and passed him straight to me. I looked straight down and saw he was a boy. My placenta delivered itself spontaneously during the next twenty minutes as I cradled my son in my arms. I was exhausted but euphoric, and began to feed him."

Mary Ann, Mother to Edward, 7 months

Letting go into trust
Fear of letting go into the unknown holds us back in many aspects of life. Yet in labour, we do not let go into nothingness, rather we go deeper into ourselves, discovering deeper strength, trust, power and wisdom.

If the conditions are favourable, we can experience such letting go into the deep power and intensity of contractions, of the flow of natural, primal energy, the sensation of our breath or visualisations. We realise we cannot control the intensity of the surges, nor hold them back, so we must go into them and beyond, trusting they have an important, deeply purposeful job to do. We trust that our body knows how to birth our baby, that we hold within us such innate wisdom, and that likewise our baby knows how to be born.

As we let go and cease trying to resist or control the labour, we are more likely to be then able to *welcome* and *embrace* the sensations and experiences, knowing that each and every one is bringing us closer;

"The midwife interrupted me, worried about how long I was taking and if I didn't hurry up she'd think about transferring me. When she went out of the room I spoke to my baby: 'Hello my darling, we need to get you born...' and then there was a sinking sensation in my belly and the waters broke... I felt a powerful need to push.

It required a complete letting go of all resistance. So if there was anything I was still hanging on to I had to let it go now! On later reflection I sensed I'd been holding on to self-control because I was so used to this way of being. In the last hour or so the pushing was quite amazing and full on, like riding luxurious wild waves. It requires the same letting go and expansion like having an orgasm – you cannot hold on in fear and have a whole body orgasm.

Nature is so much larger than we are and the energy is abundantly available for us to tap into during labour. We are invited to dive into the sensations we described as pain and surrender to this powerful energy, otherwise it will become about the pain and not about the flowing process. We need to deeply trust our instincts and override the cultural conditioning that teaches us to mistrust them."

Alex, Mother to Jude, 9 months

When we feel our labour has gone well (which depends on many factors, especially our babies being ready, and being in an environment which enables us to feel safe, have low adrenaline, feel calm, listened to, warm, loved and unobserved) the intensity of this experience can stay with us for life, deepening our sense of confidence, empowerment and trust as we awaken to the raw power, wisdom and miraculous beauty of our body's ability to bring forth life;

"I wanted to give birth at home and hypnobirthing really caught my eye. There were no classes locally so I improvised by recording my own affirmations and self-hypnosis tapes and listening to relaxing music to train myself into deep relaxation.

My waters broke with a gush and I started with regular surges, I lay in bed and listened to my birthing recordings. I went into my own little world, I rarely opened my eyes or spoke and my husband found it hard to notice when I was having a surge as I breathed my way through them.

I got into the pool at 5–6 cm dilation and things really intensified. This felt uncomfortable, the speed everything changed really threw me. It took a while to realise I was in transition and to calm down.

Her head started to come down and it was frustrating to feel it sliding back up each time I was determined to push her out. With a big push she slithered out and I caught her.

We unravelled the cord from her neck, I put her to my breast and she began to suckle. I look back on her birth with such fond memories, when I put my birth music on it really chills her out and takes me back to how calm and peaceful I felt labouring in the bath.

Her birth inspired me to train as a Hypnobirthing instructor."

Jenny, Mother to Annabelle, 7, Nieve, 4, Chloe 1

As well as feelings of peace and relaxation, as Kelly illustrates, the physical power of birth can teach us of our great strength and inner knowing and be deeply empowering;

"Arriving at hospital with intense contractions, I explained, 'I just need someone to look because I'm sure this is what it feels like for a person to come out of you!' They cocked their head to one side and said, almost patronisingly, 'Is this your first baby?'

Imagine my delight (and smugness) to be told that the baby was RIGHT THERE. I'd described the contractions from the journey as: 'I haven't been pushing but my body is just DOING IT!'

Turns out I didn't need the snacks and reading material after all. A short and agonising hour later the midwife explained my waters hadn't broken and it was putting extra pressure on me. The midwife offered to break them as I gave a final push, and there at 3.25 a.m., on the bed upright on my knees and cheered on by my now very pale faced husband, she was born.

Screaming her first breath, she was passed to me and I held her as close to my chest as her short cord would reach. I realised in that moment I was completely naked, covered in blood and sweat and my voice was hoarse. I didn't care; I'd just birthed a baby! I ROCK!"

Kelly, Mother to Nell, 4 months

Letting go of our plans

For so many of us, we invest a great deal of time, love and energy during pregnancy in planning for birth. And whilst we know, intellectually, we cannot control what happens on the day, we still really want things to go as we hope. For many of us, this is a "hands-off" natural birth, often in a pool, with the desire to meet our baby in an environment of calm and loving excitement. Yet for so many of us, birth begins to teach us about surrender and letting go as we are confronted with situations which ask us to change or let go of our plans of how we hoped birth would unfold.

Having to let go of our plans is undoubtedly hard, however, unfolding issues with our pregnancy or concerns about our baby can cause caregivers to suggest intervention. And it is at this point that our experiences of the birth may change; for some of us, we may come to view these interventions as necessary and lifesaving, then looking back feel gratitude for the help we received and feel relatively at peace with our birth story. Yet for others of us, we may resist such changes and interventions and begin to feel disempowered, as it feels as if our birth is being taken out of our hands.

As Ronne explains, whilst a Caesarean birth was not how she had hoped her baby to be born, being able to grieve for the birth she had envisioned allowed her to let go and accept the change of circumstances as being necessary for her baby;

"When I was 5 days overdue, I went for my regular antenatal appointment. The doctor was concerned that baby's head was still not engaged, and sent me for an X-ray which showed my pelvis was tilted. She said if I was allowed to go into labour naturally, there was a danger he would get stuck, so recommended a Caesarean.

That wasn't what I'd expected or planned, and fortunately she let me and my husband have a few private moments together – I wept with disappointment and frustration at my body letting me down. My husband reminded me that what was important was delivering our baby safely. So the op was scheduled for the next morning. I stayed in hospital while my husband went home to get my bag and have something to eat. Just before he returned my waters broke, so they prepped me to have the baby that night.

59

Daniel was born just after 11 p.m., and his dad saw him before I did. I felt very present for the birth – and I'd started having a few contractions by the time I was wheeled down to theatre, so felt I'd experienced something of labour. I heard Daniel crying before they even took him out of my womb, and when the midwife showed him to me, all I could say was, 'He's so beautiful.' I loved him instantly."

Ronne, Mother to Daniel, 28

Deborah spoke of her decision to birth her son via Caesarean as a welcome and necessary solution to the long, painful and distressing hours she had endured synthetic induction. Rather than resisting the decision, Deborah felt intuitively induction would not work for her and was relieved to opt for a Caesarean birth. Her words illustrate the significance of our involvement in the decision making process during labour, both in how we experience events at the time and how we feel about things after;

"I prepared for a natural birth and never even considered reading literature on Caesareans. I enjoyed being pregnant and stayed active up until birth. The due date came and went, I didn't want any intervention, but two weeks passed and still nothing, so I was advised to go to hospital for induction.

Nothing happened for the first three days and I was feeling tired, it was impossible to rest; I was moved around constantly and monitored through the night. On the third day when all else had failed I was administered with the drip to start contractions and within 30 seconds I started to feel very ill. This was the worst part of the whole pregnancy. I had intense contractions every 30 seconds and was left like this for six hours.

I knew this wasn't going to work and could tell my body was saying no. After hours of waiting I was very happy to say yes when offered a Caesarean.

I made peace with how things were going to be, I felt relieved to be off the drip, and began to walk to theatre with a feeling of calm excitement, knowing I was going to meet my baby very soon. So much of this is how your mind is; it wasn't what I'd initially hoped, but it wasn't a terrible thing to go through. The anaesthetic was a lovely sensation, like a warm river running through my body; I found the anaesthetic to be relaxing and calming, just the opposite to the induction."

Deborah, Mother to James, 4

Deborah illustrates how acceptance can become a significant milestone of birth. Through making peace with the decision, knowing it was right for her at the time, although it was not what she had initially hoped, Deborah went into the situation feeling calm, excitement, relief, peace and happiness to meet her baby.

The ways in which we perceive such interventions are crucial to how we experience birth. If we welcome the interventions as being necessary, feel listened to and involved in decision making, and are treated with dignity, kindness and respect, we are likely to feel less trauma. Yet if we feel excluded from decision making, not listened to and experience interventions as physically and emotionally painful, disrespectful and invasive, we are more likely to experience birth as disempowering, stressful and traumatic.

Holding space for difficult birth experiences

However we bring our babies into the world we are expected to move forwards happily and enjoy new motherhood. Yet birth is not always straightforward, and many of us are left with intense feelings of shock, anger, grief and trauma. There exist few safe and tender spaces within which women can speak openly and honestly about such difficult and traumatic experiences. Instead we tend to keep such things to ourselves; memories and feelings are pushed inside as we carry on, surfacing instead through silent tears, uncertainty, anxiety, fear, depression, guilt and anger.

Beginning motherhood in this way is tough and feels deeply unfair; we are experiencing pain, confusion and trauma across our physical and emotional landscapes alongside the intense learning and constant, exhausting care our newborns require.

Zara had anxiety about birth and felt a hands-off birth would suit her best. She was fearful of interventions, and especially wanted to avoid instrumental delivery. It is clear to see how devastating and anxiety-inducing it was for her when, at 39 weeks, she was diagnosed with a condition which ruled out her plans of an intervention-free birth and suggested potential complications with her baby;

"I was sent for a scan at 39 weeks as my bump was so tight the midwives couldn't tell whether our daughter was head down or breech. The scan revealed I had Polyhydramnios, a condition where there's too much amniotic fluid around the baby. In 50% of cases there is no reason for this – in the other 50% it can mean there's something wrong with the baby.

At this point we were told (not asked) by a consultant that I'd be monitored daily and booked in for the next available induction. This was a shock and we were devastated.

I really didn't want an induction and tried from the start to get into labour naturally, but it didn't work and before I knew it I was on the drip. From not being in labour at all to aggressive contractions in the space of a couple of hours was beyond intense and I soon asked for an epidural. I knew the implications of having an epidural, but I think in my heart I'd given up – labour had been taken out of my hands and I knew I was now having a 'medical' labour and was 'on the clock'. I was so tense and scared – a million miles away from the natural labour we hoped for.

Being told I was ready to push but unable to feel a thing was surreal and frustrating. After two hours of pushing I felt panic in the room – I'd been pushing for too long with no progress and the midwives were getting worried. A doctor was brought in and he performed an episiotomy. I heard the word 'forceps' muttered and although exhausted I felt something primal in my heart and pushed my 9lb 3oz daughter out before they could get them!"

Zara, Mother to Izzy, 4

When we are induced we are monitored constantly, and this can restrict our position and movement (although this is changing amongst midwives who value active birth, and in hospitals with equipment available to support mobile monitoring). Induced contractions are intense and do not tend to build gradually. Neither do we have the endorphin release which accompanies spontaneous and gradual labour which helps us cope with the intensity.

Whilst initiating contractions which dilate our cervix, our experience of induction is very different to spontaneous labour both physiologically and emotionally. Induction, whilst effective for many women, can be painful, stressful and traumatic for many others. Accompanying the intense physical pain of the contractions are concerns about the wellbeing of our baby, the uncertainty of whether or not the process will enable birth or whether further interventions will be necessary.

Induction may leave us feeling labour has been taken out of our hands and our choices limited. Contractions are intense, immediate and unrelenting, and we may be vulnerable to a further cascade of interventions, depending on how things progress.

Yet amidst the anxiety and intensity of her labour, Zara recalls how she became aware of new inner depth and power – 'I felt something primal in my heart' – and she found new strength and determination to birth her baby. Even in the most traumatic and disempowering of situations, we can receive glimpses of our strength, instinct, power and wisdom and such insight remains awoken within us for life.

This was certainly the case for Marie where events of her daughter's birth took her beyond her understandings of her limitations and capabilities and taught her a great deal about her own strength, willpower, instinct and determination;

"After a long journey to conception and a fantastic pregnancy, the last few weeks weren't so much fun. I had mild pre-eclampsia, fluid retention and a split and tilted pelvis. I was enormous and in lots of pain. I spent a fair bit of time in hospital and the decision was made to induce four days early. It turned out this wasn't a day too soon!

Labour went well for the first 20 hours and it was expected my baby would be born quite quickly. The last few hours didn't go so well, my baby wasn't expected to be quite so large and getting her into this world was not going to be as easy as we thought.

Past the point of possibility to go for a Caesarean, things started to go very wrong. I soon realised that in order to get my baby out in a state that was positive I had to work harder than I ever imagined possible!

My baby was too big, her shoulder was stuck (shoulder dystocia is the technical term) and the cord was tangled around her neck. I'd read about problems at this stage but never imagined it would happen to me. I knew there was a limited time where the baby would be okay, I also knew from the reactions and faces of the staff and my husband that this was serious.

In those last few minutes I surpassed anything I thought I was capable of and pushed so hard, during and between contractions, because I knew if I didn't get her out she wouldn't survive much longer.

Eventually, 7 minutes after her head came out, her body followed! She was blue and grey and her Apgar score was 2; she was shown to me and taken to Special Care.

Amazingly she didn't have brain damage or any damage really, as would be expected from such a birth, and only spent the next 24 hours in special care. I was taken straight to theatre as I was losing so much blood.

I knew during those last few weeks of pregnancy that my baby was big, even though it was my first, the staff hadn't listened to me and apologised after they weighed her and she was ten pounds, five and a half ounces. This was why we had struggled so much! I'd been through both the best and worst experience of my life and learnt so much about myself and my inner strength."

Marie, Mother to Jean, 11 and Lewis, 9

The events of baby Jean's birth were undoubtedly traumatic, severe and distressing, yet so too does Marie share her milestones of learning, awareness and transformation as she deepened into her inner strength, instinct and intuition. Marie goes on to explain how these events were life changing, taking her beyond her limitations, initiating her into motherhood and teaching her of its value and importance;

"Fast forward a few days. We were home and I've loved being a Mummy ever since. The experiences of Jean's birth made me realise just how fragile life is and how, when life demands it, it is possible to rise to any situation if your will and determination are strong enough.

It changed me forever. Being a mum is what I was meant to do, and I was, and am, determined to enjoy it."

Marie, Mother to Jean, 11 and Lewis, 9

Enduring distressing experiences, Alicja describes milestones of deepening love unfolding alongside feelings of trauma;

"At 41 weeks my daughter was born by Caesarean. The birth was harrowing and traumatic. It was three days of labour, two hours pushing and an unsuccessful use of forceps. I was rushed for an emergency Caesarean and given an epidural, this failed; I could feel everything through the whole operation, and I'm not sure they believed me. The pain was severe as the operation had already started. I was told they'd need to put me to sleep with a general anaesthetic, but before I allowed a member of staff to put that mask on my face I was told I have a daughter.

Hours later I finally met my tiny daughter. A nurse pushed the bed into a room, and there she was. My husband was holding her, standing next to a window. He was crying saying how lovely she is.

I was numb. I didn't feel a thing. I was shocked. I expected I would just love my baby, that it would be natural, but I couldn't feel anything at all.

I took a couple of deep breaths. I looked at my husband, all the love he already felt for this tiny human. I took her in my arms for the first time and started feeding. I started talking to her and I knew everything will be fine. I just knew that I will get there. I know now I was really traumatised after the Caesarean. The love for my daughter was growing every minute and every hour. But for months after I had nightmares and flashbacks."

Alicja, Mother to Rozalia, 3 and Konrad, 1

Alicja's experiences are deeply moving and provoke feelings of sadness and anger that women endure such events at such a vulnerable time. Yet what Alicja shares is that whilst such events undoubtedly leave us numb and shocked, so too can we discover the capacity to open up a new space within our hearts. We can begin to feel the stirrings of love for our baby and nurture this love alongside our feelings of trauma and devastation, and help it to grow little by little, day by day.

Alicja shows how our partners can be instrumental in providing us with support and protection in situations like these, creating a safe space for us to begin to love our babies. Alicja's husband had already begun to love and take care of their baby whilst she was in recovery, and his love became her love as she slowly began to hold, feed and talk to her new daughter.

Alicja's story is both inspirational and distressing; women should not have to endure such trauma in the arena of birth, but what Alicja teaches us more than anything is that whatever our experiences, we still have the potential to begin to love. The power, strength and healing inherent in our emerging mother-love is deeply inspirational and is truly what will carry us through such difficult times. Such love has the potential to save, heal and repair ourselves as well as our babies.

Below, Harriet illustrates how we discover new elements of our *Mother Selves* when our babies are born; for Harriet this was her awakening mother-protector instinct. Whilst part of our conscious self may be experiencing shock and trauma, our emerging *Mother Self*, focusses upon our baby, taking practical steps to care for and protect him;

"The natural birth I'd hoped for wasn't to be and I ended up with a C-section. It was so surreal and I just wanted it to stop. But when my son was born my mother 'protector' instinct came out. I remember telling my husband to shield our baby from the bright light of the theatre while I was getting stitched up.

They thought we were mad standing with our hands shielding his eyes. It just felt so bright for his first moments in the world. I longed for it to be a cosy, warm, welcoming atmosphere for him, but I was glad he was healthy even though I was sore and traumatised."

Harriet, Mother to Riley, 4 and Leon, 1

Amy recalls how the events of her son's birth left her with feelings of deep sadness, resentment, and a void. And whilst she felt happy and elated after the birth, and loved her son deeply, the difficult feelings remained;

"My first son was eventually born via C-section. I had a long labour and had been pushing for a long time without seeming to make much progress, then people realised his head was stuck. I didn't feel I'd received good support or been listened to when I'd had concerns, I was exhausted and didn't have the energy to push any longer, so he was born by emergency Caesarean whilst I was under general anaesthetic.

I've always felt a deep sadness that I didn't see him being born, and sadly, my second son was born whilst I was under general anaesthetic too. I do still feel deep sadness and resentment around their births, and only have hazy memories of that time.

Yet once he was here I was surprised by just how much I loved him. I stayed in hospital for seven days, and had really good support. He took to breastfeeding really well and I was determined to do this. I refused drugs for the pain as I wanted to be capable for feeding him. I had a team of people supporting me and felt happy and confident."

Amy, Mother to Simon, 25 and Edward, 19

Like Alicja, Amy illustrates the contradiction of traumatic birth; on the one hand we are deeply injured physically, mentally and emotionally, yet simultaneously we discover a whole new landscape within our hearts as we begin to feel a deep, protective love for our baby. For some of us this love flows easily, strongly and is at times overwhelming, and for others of us, we feel so locked in hurt, anger, trauma and resentment about the birth, that we can feel numb, foggy and disconnected, and it takes time for tender feelings towards our baby to emerge.

Similarly, we may find it difficult to feel a connection with our baby as we were not awake for his birth, and may have seldom-voiced doubts that he is, indeed, ours. Yet as Amy and Alicja illustrate, whatever our experiences at the beginning, the potential to begin to love lies latent within. We may be traumatised on a very deep level, and like others whose births were distressing, we may not, as yet, have found the times or spaces in which to share, process and come to peace with such feelings.

If this is your experience, do consider seeking support from sensitive and experienced people. They can meet you in tenderness and understanding and hold a safe space for you to speak of your experiences, supporting you to move forward. Requesting an appointment with a midwife to review the notes from your birth can be supportive and informative, as can sharing your experiences and feedback with your local Maternity Voices Partnership which feeds back women's experiences anonymously with the aim of improving maternity services.

"You should just be grateful you have your baby"
There is little space and time given to the sharing of difficult and traumatic birth experiences, and surprisingly less sympathy and understanding for such experiences.

Indeed, for some of the mothers responding to the *Milestones* questionnaires and taking part in interviews, this was the first time they had spoken of their birth experiences in years.

Some hospitals do offer a postnatal listening service where women can meet with a midwife and go through their notes and review the events of the birth from what is recorded. For many women this is a useful thing to do, for it brings more clarity and understanding as to why things unfolded as they did. Yet what seems to be lacking for many of us is wider recognition and understanding of the *mental and emotional* impacts of traumatic birth. Rather, women speak of being told, implicitly or explicitly, that 'such things happen in labour, you have your baby – just get on with it'.

Of course we are thankful and grateful to have our babies in our arms, yet reading the experiences of Zara, Amy, Alicja and others, we can see too, how birth can be a hugely traumatic event which brings immense post-traumatic stress. Despite the love we feel (or wish we felt) for our babies, trauma remains; such mental and emotional injuries are real, valid and insidious; not easily forgotten or swept from our minds;

"I don't think I'll ever completely overcome the trauma of my first birth. It was three days of labour followed by two hours of pushing, use of forceps and emergency Caesarean with failed anaesthetic. It is still there in my head, it comes back in nightmares, I'm terrified of giving birth again."

Alicja, Mother to Rosa, 3 and Konrad, 1

Hazel speaks honestly about the way her son's birth unfolded and how these experiences carried over into early motherhood;

"I'd hoped to give birth in a midwife-led unit but because of medical history ended up in a consultant-led unit. Nothing that happened that day went as I expected – although with hindsight I realise that even if everything goes according to 'plan', I still don't think you can anticipate what labour and birth will be like.

As a first time mum I'd expected to be in for a long haul – but in fact Barnaby was born less than 11 hours after my waters had broken. Sadly he turned back to back and I wasn't able to push him out – after two hours I ended up with a ventouse delivery.

Meeting our baby really was an amazing moment – he looked into my eyes, gave a cough, then opened his mouth wide and started to yell! Who can blame him, after arriving the way he did. Shortly afterwards I had to go to theatre for stitches and he was left with his daddy; this was an amazing opportunity for them to bond and is something I know my husband remembers fondly.

Looking back, to be honest I feel sad, and maybe even traumatised, by the birth. I wanted a water birth, but when I was offered the chance to get in the water I was having contractions so thick and fast I couldn't make the decision for myself to move rooms to get in the pool. I wish I'd managed to get myself in there as I think that might've helped enough with the pain to enable me to push the baby out without help.

I also wanted to be mobile during labour but ended up on my back on the bed – I struggled to tolerate any other position with the continuous back pain of a back to back baby – but again I think if I'd got in the water things could have been different.

As for a ventouse delivery – 'brutal' was the way my husband described the process of inserting it – which had to be repeated several times as the suction hose kept disconnecting. I'm sure this contributed to the fairly severe tearing I suffered. Even now I feel horrified at the thought of it and I do believe my feelings about the birth contributed to me feeling very anxious as a new mother and not relaxing and enjoying the early weeks and months as perhaps I could have.

Having said all that – it was overall a very happy time and I particularly remember the first few hours in the delivery room. My husband and I took turns holding Barnaby, touching him and looking into his beautiful eyes, absolutely in awe of what we'd created!"

Hazel, Mother to Barnaby, 15 months

As new mothers these are complex landscapes to navigate. On one level, we *are* deeply thankful for the lifesaving interventions that have brought forth our babies, yet as Hazel and Alicja so bravely share, so too are we traumatised, distressed, injured and frightened physically, mentally and emotionally.

The sentiments that 'these things happen', 'birth can be unpredictable', 'the interventions saved your life' and 'you should just be grateful you have your baby' whilst, perhaps, intended to be reassuring, and said with a view to helping us move forward, do feel dismissive. Instead, they serve to invalidate and sweep away women's experiences of such events. We are expected to *just forget about it*, and to get on with being happy caring for our baby. It is as though society has closed its ranks on us, and we are left to navigate our way through the physical, mental and emotional trauma all on our own.

Telling us to be grateful is not a particularly helpful suggestion; such messages infer we should not be feeling anger, grief, frustration and sadness, or that we should not grieve for the birth we so wanted for ourselves and our baby. Rather, it invalidates our experiences, which, for many of us, causes us to push such feelings and memories further within, locking them away. Yet doing this only gives them the potential to resurface in all manner of anxious feelings later on.

Emotions of mothering are intricate, complex and multifaceted. As new mothers, we are capable of, and entirely permitted, to feel immense relief and gratitude that our baby is here, yet equally to hold feelings of great anger, grief, frustration, sadness and injustice about how the birthing process unfolded. Seeking support from an experienced and understanding therapist can help us to navigate these feelings of post-traumatic stress and anxiety.

Re-envisioning traumatic birth; the mammalian perspective
Such landscapes can feel bleak and isolating, yet if this has been your experience it may bring comfort to know that many women find it immensely helpful to view and understand their birth experiences

from the perspective of mammalian birth, and this is part of the approach I use in Birth Trauma Healing Yoga Therapy sessions. Such perspectives, as pioneered through the work of obstetrician Michel Odent, teach of the great importance of the birth environment and how such conditions influence the ability of physiological birth to occur unhindered.

When we feel safe, warm and unobserved and are in a quiet, dark and uninterrupted space, our mammalian brain senses safety and signals to our nervous system to cease producing adrenaline (a stress hormone which inhibits labour) and instead secrete high levels of oxytocin, one of the hormones necessary to dilate our cervix and bring our baby forth. If our birth did not flow and progress as we believed physiological birth could, it can be of use to reflect upon the conditions we found ourselves in and ask whether or not these were conducive to us feeling safe and unobserved on a deep level.

The part of our brain which orchestrates labour may perceive the presence of strangers, bright lights, people coming in and out of the room, questions, noise and chatter, an unfamiliar environment with unfamiliar sounds and smells, the rustle of gloves, packets and instruments, the feeling of being observed, touched and examined as a situation of *immense threat and grave danger*, rather than safety.

Therefore, rather than releasing hormones to dilate and birth our baby, instead our birthing hormones act suddenly, and in our baby's perceived best interests. They send messages of danger, halting birth hormone production and reprogramming our nervous system with fight or flight hormones of adrenaline to stall dilation and keep our babies safe within our bodies until the perceived threat has passed and we are once again in a place of safety and quiet in which to receive our baby.

Certainly, intervention is necessary at times and undoubtedly saves lives, yet so too can we see how the environment in which we labour influences the behaviour of our sensitive nervous system and hormonal secretion. Understanding our fundamental needs as labouring women helps us to perceive the behaviour of our bodies in new ways. Rather than feeling we ourselves failed as 'Failure To Progress' is scrawled across our notes, instead we can understand that our deep body wisdom sensed danger from the modern, medical birth environment and was doing its utmost to protect our baby, keeping him safe within until the perceived risk had passed. From here we can experience milestones of deepening understanding, trust and acceptance of our body, its sensitivity and wisdom.

It is only through women sharing our emotional and physical

experiences of birthing in different environments that we can begin to draw comparisons and deepen our understandings of our own experiences and the wider birth culture;

"As I recovered, Rene, my midwife, explained the cause of my pain. It turned out my son had emerged back to back – rather than back to belly – and he also had his head at a slight angle making it even more difficult for me to push.

I knew immediately I'd achieved, with her support, something I'd have almost certainly failed to achieve at hospital; the unassisted delivery of a long laboured, back-to-back birth. I felt elated that it had been possible for me to have my son in the comfort of my own home. Amazingly I didn't need any stitches and my body healed quickly."

Mary Ann, Mother to Edward, 7 months

Similarly, I remember the home birth of our third baby, a nine-pound boy, ten days overdue. After a night of intense contractions where I moved in and out of the pool and up and down the stairs, he took some time to descend, and then more time again for his head, and then shoulders to be born. It was intense to say the least and I still recall the irksome sound of my pelvic bones shifting to accommodate his passage. Yet once he was here, a little later the student midwife exclaimed she was surprised to see a big baby born by himself, and was happy to see it could happen.

She remarked that if his birth had taken place in hospital, she imagined it would have unfolded rather differently; suggesting I would have been placed on continual monitoring which may have restricted free movement and changing position, as well as ruling out use of the pool. It was likely he would have been a ventouse delivery due to his size and the time he was taking to descend.

Whilst we talked later about the benefits of free movement, changing position, pregnancy yoga, being unobserved and how I had felt the supported squat position both made space in my pelvic outlet and allowed gravity to assist during his slow emerging, I also recall feeling sadness. Such experiences illustrate how vulnerable we are as pregnant women to the birth environment, the availability and expertise of professionals and dominant medical cultures and protocols.

As we grow in awareness so we deepen in milestones of understanding; from here we can feel greater compassion towards ourselves; we can see that our body did its best within the surroundings, and that those supporting us were also doing their best

– yet from within the framework and regulations of our healthcare system, which is by no means a perfect system.

Our milestones and healing come as we hold ourselves, as well as our babies in love, gentleness and protection. We can accept that we have been deeply hurt and traumatised, and that our experiences have left us damaged on a deep level and hence have an impact on our experience of new motherhood. It is a milestone when we allow ourselves to feel as we do, and surrender the idea that we have, in some way failed or are in any way to blame.

We grow as we let go of pressure and expectations that we should only feel gratitude, and in doing so, create space, permission and validation for feelings of anger, grief, sadness and injustice. It can bring great comfort to have the support of others, be those partners, friends or professionals, as we explore and express our feelings and begin to move forward.

Meeting our baby

Meeting our baby is a surreal and sacred time, a time which evades description and explanation, where time itself stands still. We find ourselves in another world, overtaken by the awe, wonder and somehow unreal experience of being face to face with this little person, who, in some ways, we have known intimately for a long time, and who, in some ways, is wholly unknown to us.

These are special moments of peak experience, far removed from our usual state of being; in these precious moments, the physical, emotional and spiritual culminate as this complete little person, who began in our dreams and then our wombs, emerges whole and complete.

There exists the pervading cultural idea that as our babies are born and we hold them for the first time, we will love them instantly and immensely; yet as mothers come to realise, loving our babies and children is a hugely tender, tentative and individual journey. For some of us, the rush of intense love is overwhelming and instant; yet for others of us, there is more of a recognition and gentle knowing of the companion who has been with us for some time. And for others of us, we feel little at first, perhaps we even feel fear or numbness; our birth experiences can play a significant part in this, and our journey to love develops over the days, weeks, months and years ahead;

"I had no idea how I'd feel about meeting my baby for the first time, I didn't know whether I was carrying a boy or girl and didn't really have any strong preference. But when she was born and I looked at this red-faced, screaming, funny looking little thing with a shock of black spiky hair I fell in love instantly and knew that this little girl was exactly what I wanted."

Fran, Mother to Emma, 35, Jack, 32 and Edward, 29

"When my first was born I was totally besotted and held and stared at her for hours – instant love. Unbelievable!"

Ross, Mother to Charley and Chelsea, in their 20's

"When Izzy was born I just remember thinking she is the most beautiful thing I have ever seen. Looking back at photos, she is bruised, squashed and puffy, but I didn't see that at all. Lots of people had warned us we might not love her, not right away, and that was okay. But no one had warned us how strongly we might love her, the intensity of the emotion was totally overwhelming."

Lizzie, Mother to Izzy, 6, James, 4 and Lloyd, 1

"Caesarean births can be very intimate and special experiences. We brought our camera and captured the operation (photos for us only!) and my husband held my hand. The sheet was lowered as Skye was born, and my husband cut the cord. For the rest of the operation I snuggled Skye across my chest and in the recovery room, 45 minutes after she was born we had skin-to-skin and tried breastfeeding."

Michelle, Mother to Skye, 3 and Oakley, 1

"I remember lying in a hospital bed, exhausted, yet unable to sleep, feeling like I'd been in a boxing ring, but gazing at the most perfect pair of huge blue eyes I'd ever seen. She was everything I'd imagined, and at the same time nothing like I'd imagined. I knew her – and could feel she knew me too. Spending those first few days with her in hospital was such a magical time. I couldn't look at her enough – she was perfect. Relief and happiness washed over us after all the last minute worry about the Polyhydramnios, and we felt so blessed and lucky to have a healthy baby girl."

Zara, Mother to Izzy, 4

"Meeting my first child, I remember having a deep feeling of knowing her. When I looked into her eyes for the first time, I knew that I knew her. She felt right in my arms, and me holding her. I was aware she and I planned this dance before."

Violet, Mother to Sasha, 10, April, 9, Sam and Josh, 7 and Isaac, 2

Michel Odent speaks passionately about the time after birth, this *magical first hour*, a time where hormone levels peak and foundations for bonding are at a lifetime high. 'Don't wake her up,' he urges, calling those working with birthing women to protect them from disturbance, interruption, chatter and questioning at this crucial time. He explains that as new mothers, we inhabit a different zone; we are wholly focussed upon our baby and, in the right conditions, do this instinctively. We coo, stare, repeat simple words, stroke their skin, stare into their eyes and soak up their presence;

"I vividly recall the moments after birth, standing up in the bath. It went so smoothly, I felt hot but very fresh, my mind was awake. The feeling in my lower body was so interesting. Special. It felt like I'd come from an enormous adventure.

Then understanding there is a baby. All the time through childbirth I thought, if these few hours of labour is all you have to do to spend a lifetime with your baby, it's really nothing.

After birth I was in this magical space which I created during birth. It started from about half way into the actual delivery. I got stronger in my body while sounds and consciousness seemed to fade. You get into a rhythm. While I still heard everything, also I was away. That feeling continued for days. It was sacred. There I wanted to stay."

Hanneke, Mother to Vita, 2

As Hanneke's experience demonstrates, these powerful and transformative qualities of birth can occur if we are able to go within completely and find our own space, and rhythm of mind and body. Yet, however our birth has unfolded, meeting our baby is intense, emotional and surreal. As Eleanor illustrates, as connected as we may have felt to our baby during pregnancy, the reality of coming to hold them in our arms can leave us feeling shocked, elated and in an altogether different space;

"I remember reading a birth preparation book towards the end of my pregnancy that referred to how I felt about becoming a mother, and thinking to myself really I was a mother already. I felt so fiercely protective of this creature inside me, and so sure I already knew him, that the work was done before he was out.

Still, on meeting him I was astonished. I remember saying, 'It's a baby! It's a baby!' (As if it might have turned out to be a puppy!) He was just so complete, such a whole thing."

Eleanor, Mother to Thomas, 3 and David, 10 months

Lona, too, recalls the surreal qualities of this time, yet talks of how it is also a time of uncertainty; we are as new to mothering as our babies are to the world, they seem so fragile and delicate. We may feel unsure how to hold this tiny new creature, overawed with emotion, strange otherworldly sensations and the enormity of responsibility. Surroundings seem vivid, surreal and somehow magnified as our perception is sensitised and disorientated through intense hormonal peaks. For many of us, this creates a contrast of fuzzy, hazy feelings, blanks and strong, vivid memories;

"I have an image of seeing my baby for the first time lying on the floor, realising it was a boy and saying, 'Hello Tom'. I remember his eyes being a surprising dark blue colour and feeling I was face to face with someone who I'd been with constantly for months, but who I was only now going to start to get to know.

I tried to pick him up, but wasn't sure how. He was slippery and seemed so delicate, so the midwife passed him to me.

I remember drinking cold, black Earl Grey tea and cold, dry toast thinking nothing had ever tasted so good!"

Lona, Mother to Tom, 4

Our fledgling *Mother Selves*
Lona reminds us of our newness and fledgling inexperience as mothers. Just like our babies, we too are beginners; uncertain and inexperienced, yet eager to learn more. And it is from these first times together, and the hormonal exchanges we share, that we begin upon our shared journey of learning to love, connect and understand one another.

Similarly, in these moments, we can learn immensely what it means to be a mother, lessons which, at the time, are simply part of our experience. Later, we can reflect upon them and find great wisdom and understanding within. After a long labour and transfer from home to hospital, my first daughter was born and placed on my belly. Time seemed to pause somehow and nothing else in the world existed apart from this tiny creature.

She lifted her head and stared straight at me – wide-eyed and alert with intense expression. I was captivated by her alertness and sustained eye contact and the effort at connection she was making. As

I cooed 'hello' to her and gently stroked her body, she lurched upwards, crawling towards my breast. She continued staring, and of her own accord found her way to my breast, latched on and began to feed. I was amazed; I had not expected her, as a newborn, to be so active and competent.

Whilst at the time this was a magical and beautiful experience, a wonderful beginning to our journey, over time I realised what a lot I could learn. Through being there, still and available, she found and met her needs from my presence. Similarly, I did not need to "do" anything; but the events unfolded from my being and presence. Here, I had an early initiation into the milestone of *shifting from doing to being* which characterises so much of our early mothering journey, our experiences of breastfeeding, and the evolution of our *Mother Selves*.

I became inspired to trust *her* innate wisdom, instinct and knowing, coming to feel that it is my job to protect the space for her to unfold into, rather than direct her behaviour and development. Such reflections of her moments after birth continue to deepen my understanding of the mothering process decades later and remind me, always, to trust, to be, and to listen.

Transformation and identity

How our babies are born defines neither our identity nor our paths as mothers. Rather, like all experiences upon the mothering path, it simply brings us opportunities for deepening into love, connection, understanding and surrender. Our milestones unfold as we enfold both ourselves and our babies in the power, strength and tenderness of our unconditional mother love and begin to move forward, creating shared moments of connection each day.

As much as we heal from birth, birth itself can be healing and transformational. Through the depth and intensity we come to know strength and vulnerability like never before. We experience deep feelings of empowerment or disempowerment depending upon how our birth unfolded, and, more importantly, how involved we felt in the process. Like our wombs, our old selves have been opened wide as we let go of our past identities and usual ways of being, and opened ourselves up to immense strength, power and emotional intensity, which introduces us to new aspects of our being.

Birth, in all of its forms, changes us fundamentally. It opens us up so wide – physically, emotionally, mentally and spiritually – that we are unable to go back to how we were previously. Yet I believe this is the way things are meant to be. Birth is meant to be so powerful and overwhelming that it shakes us from our usual state, clearing all previous distractions and pre-occupations, breaking us wide open, transporting us to a new place of being, far from our normal ways of thinking and feeling. And it is into this new way of being that we receive our baby.

If birth was less intense, less dramatic, somehow smaller, perhaps our transition to motherhood would not be so great. If we could simply acquire a baby with little process we would not be so fundamentally altered, and in a place where we are able to let go of all we knew previously. It is this alteration that allows us to willingly give so fundamentally of ourselves in the ways mothering a newborn requires.

Labour as labyrinth

A labyrinth is a sacred, geometric spiral of winding concentric paths which lead us back and forth, round and round until we reach the centre. The inward journey often feels confusing, as if we are moving forwards, only to reverse and backtrack in the opposite direction. All we can do is trust the layout of the paths, and continue to walk, following our breath and observing our thoughts and feelings.

Already we can see the parallels with labour; sometimes we feel we are going forwards, contractions are strong and regular, then things slow down and tail off. The head descends, then moves upwards once more, leaving us frayed and confused. Like the labyrinth, all we can do is stay present, breathe and trust the process; there is no turning back.

As we reach the labyrinth centre, we feel peace and relief that we made it through the journey and our self-doubt. Meeting our baby parallels the arrival at the centre; the confusing, hard work and self-doubt is behind us, we pause in stillness, cocooned from the outside world, holding our baby at the centre of our universe as all else fades into insignificance. At the labyrinth centre we are held by the swirls of the paths, and held in birth by our hormones and the enormity of finally coming to meet our baby. It is from this place of deep stillness and magnified intensity that we begin to bond, form our deepest memories and are, ourselves, born as mothers.

As we begin our walk outwards from the centre of our labyrinth of birth and into our lives, we navigate these paths more slowly, for we have our baby in our arms now, and what was once familiar territory now seems so different. Everything is new, everything is changed, for we are looking at the world now not only as the women we were previously, but as mothers. We carry the intensity of our experiences along with our baby, and with the enormity of our caring responsibilities we take tiny, uncertain steps into our new terrain. Things have shifted fundamentally, we are vulnerable and uncertain and it can take time to find our feet and make sense of our new reality;

"Birth definitely took my body to its limits. I experienced feeling more vulnerable and at the same time more physically powerful than ever before. It was like the realms of my experience were widened. As a result the world seemed bigger and more scary all at once. In the end I felt more responsible (since I now had someone small and vulnerable to take care of) and at the same time less confident that I could 'control' things around me – I was learning about 'going with the flow.'"

Mary Ann, Mother to Edward, 7 months

Opening our body – opening our heart

Birth is a journey of opening. We open our bodies, hearts and minds to bring forth our babies. In an environment we perceive as safe, we are likely to feel empowered and positive, yet when we feel vulnerable and our opening is rushed or forced, we can be scared and traumatised. Yet however birth unfolds, it is this opening which is key; for it is within such a state of vulnerability and openness that we find the deep tenderness into which we receive our baby.

Our openness, shock, vulnerability and heightened sensitivity bring us far from our normal, intellectualised ways of being. Our hearts, as well as our bodies are opened wide, and it is into this vast lovescape which we receive our babies. We welcome them through our bodies into our open arms and bring them up to lie against our warm breasts and tender hearts.

We are raw and primed for great sensitivity through the hormonal intensity of labour and it is from such heights that we are able to receive our baby deeply and connect with him through every cell of our being. We are in a hugely receptive state, and it is in such a state we claim him as our own. We are vulnerable, sensitive and quite literally "out of our minds". We have been blasted into a much deeper, primal, heart-centred part of ourselves, and it is from here that we let him imprint upon us.

And it is from this place of intensity and unfamiliarity that our new journey must begin, and with much less guidance than our

78

labour. We must find our way back from this deepest part of ourselves, back into new everyday lives, and this can leave us vulnerable and unsteady.

Yet such unsettling postnatal feelings of shock and vulnerability are a crucial part of our journey. The intensity blasts away our previous, comfortable and familiar existence; all our pieces are separated and floating in the air, momentarily suspended, awaiting collection and reconfiguration. And our path continues tentatively as we gather them together and create ourselves anew.

Yet such re-formation does not happen instantly, and for many of us, it feels as if our pieces are scattered and misplaced for some time before we gradually bring them back together, in a new order. So much of our transformation, growth and learning through motherhood has its roots in our experiences of pregnancy, labour and birth and this putting-back-together process.

Such intense opening, in a safe and sacred space, has the potential to be enormously healing. The intensity which feels like it dissolves or destroys us brings with it the potential for transformation; for us to bring ourselves together in a new and altogether different way, to take full ownership of our body and our power, and in doing so, can bring unexpected healing;

"I hadn't realised until afterwards, but my first daughter's birth in a pool enabled me to greatly heal a childhood of sexual abuse. When a woman opens to give birth, she is at her most vulnerable: physically, emotionally and psychically. To be in a safe space while this happened, was incredibly empowering and life changing for me. There is no therapy in the world for that sort of abuse quite like an empowered birth."

Veronika, Mother to Bethany, 19 and Eliza, 17

Birth as an empowering process

I became pregnant with my first baby during the fourth and final year of my yoga teacher training. I felt very blessed to share the company of a number of women who had recently given birth during the course. Polly, a fellow student had recently given birth to her daughter. Reflecting on her experiences, she stated that no matter what support you have around you, it is down to *you* to give birth: 'You have to do it yourself,' is what she said, 'no one else can do it for you, not your partner, doula, midwife or homeopath, it is down to you, it comes from inside yourself.'

During the intensity of contractions, I came to realise what she meant. Regardless of the support and activity around us, it is down to ourselves to breathe, to keep our focus and to use our energy, intensity, strength and surrender to bring our baby forth. Only *I* could keep my inner focus calm, and consciously take my breath to a place deeper than the intense sensations. In doing so, and in keeping my focus on the interplay between my breath, the contractions and the downward movement of my baby, I found a powerful, yet meditative place, within which I could be consciously present and powerful during labour and birth.

Hanneke's experiences resonate as she shares how birth introduced her to the enormity of her inner world;

"Birth was magic. I delivered in the bath, at my mother's home. It was harmonious, meditative, sacred and impressive. I loved the time with myself. I realised after, even more than before, that there is really nothing to search for outside of you. It's all happening inside. It is about the possibility to open, to let go."

Hanneke, Mother to Vita, 2

My friend Polly got right to the centre of why birth, when it happens in a way where we feel safe, heard and supported, has the potential to be so empowering. Giving birth in such a way takes us to our limits and vulnerabilities, then gives us the opportunity to move far beyond. We let go of anything we have been holding onto and allow ourselves to be opened up entirely to the greater power of the flow of life surging through us. We become awakened to a searing force of deep inner strength, innate trust, power and ancient, Feminine biological wisdom.

We realise, either at the time, or with reflection, that if we are experiencing such sensations, then they must reside somewhere deep within us *all* of the time, and we have the capacity to connect with them. The power, wisdom and ability to create, hold and bring forth life reminds – or introduces – us to the power, wisdom, strength and capability we hold within. Coming into contact with such power can enable us to draw upon such qualities more often in our daily lives. Such experiences can change us forever, and awaken us to a more full expression and embodiment of our true power, courage and wisdom;

"As for how my birth experience has changed me; I've always been a quiet and shy person. Since being able to experience the birth I really wanted I now feel more confident in myself and more like I can take on anything!

I'm so proud I managed to have the kind of birth I so desired despite lots of people doubting my views and having to overcome obstacles. When I look back on that day I still can't believe I managed to do it the way I did.

It has irrevocably changed me forever."

Charlotte, Mother to Raffy, 9 months

Experiencing the transformative, empowering energy of birth can ignite passion and motivation to dedicate our time and energy to working to create change. We may feel called to support other women so that they too may experience the potent transformative experiences of an empowered birth. The intensity of our experiences can motivate us to become birth campaigners or advocates, to train to become a doula, antenatal educator, pregnancy yoga teacher or hypnobirthing instructor. We may feel drawn to write or create art around pregnancy and birth with the intention of inspiring others.

Equally, we may have felt so utterly traumatised and disempowered that we are motivated to learn widely about the subject. Our anger and growing understanding may cause us to piece together what happened to us, and learn how things could have been different so that we can strive to make them so for our second birth. We may feel motivated to help other women avoid such distress so that they are able to experience birth as an empowering and positive event.

Birthing teaches acceptance

Alongside empowerment, birth can bring precious milestones of acceptance. Whilst feelings of empowerment may be felt in the immediate period after the birth and remain with us into the future, our experiences of acceptance are more likely to be milestones we experience with retrospect. I now look back and feel at peace with how all my children's births unfolded, whilst at the time there were issues I felt unhappy about and wished could have been different.

Yet with time and reflection I grew to realise that birth can act as a mirror reflecting where we are in our own growth, learning and empowerment. Our experiences can bring milestones inviting us to go deeper and grow beyond our current experiences and beliefs. Such growth takes time; we may experience many months of sadness, disappointment, grief and frustration before we begin to move to a place of greater tenderness towards ourselves.

Celebrating birth as valuable and precious

So often our fundamental experiences of Femininity, our menarche (the onset of our periods), menstruation, fertility, sexuality, miscarriage, stillbirth and menopause are unspoken, hidden and overlooked. Similarly, the birth of our children is so rarely spoken about as a life-changing, powerful experience; rather it is discussed in terms of pain, pain relief and management, and kept hidden from the wider culture.

It is simply something we are expected to get on with and get over. Rarely do we hear of birth being spoken about in terms of its potential transformational power. And, sadly, this is much the general attitude to our experiences of mothering and, in wider terms, Femininity. Their potential for awakening is often overlooked.

Yet as we individually and collectively come to recognise menstruality, conception, pregnancy, birth and mothering for the powerful, transformative events they truly are, we begin to reclaim some of our Feminine strength and wisdom. And as we begin to recognise the meaning and value inherent in pregnancy and the bringing forth of our children, so too do we blaze the way for our mothering work, ensuring that it is seen, valued and celebrated.

Chapter Three
First Times

The first days with our newborn are surreal; time takes on a strange, less clear quality, and we can feel dazed after the intensity of birth. Our bodies feel like nothing we have known before, and we may find ourselves in the unfamiliar environment of a hospital. Whilst our body took care of our baby's needs during pregnancy, now he is in our arms it is our job to care for him. We must learn to meet his needs for food and comfort as he adjusts to life outside our womb.

"I spent 3 days in hospital while they monitored my healing as I'd needed stitches after his somewhat speedy entry into the world. The first day passed in a daze as I'd been up for pretty much 24 hours before he was born, so the first day was spent watching, cuddling, feeding, changing nappies and drifting in and out of light sleep. All the while feeling slightly amazed that finally this had all come to pass."

Melanie, Mother to James, 1

If we have given birth in hospital, a memorable milestone is coming home. This feels momentous; for in hospital we had help and support and were not really "on our own". Whilst we are usually keen to get home, there are also the accompanying feelings of responsibility – now it really is down to us to look after our baby!

"From the moment we bundled our first baby into the car seat for the short journey home from hospital and listened to his delicate cries in the back, we looked at each other and it dawned on us just how much responsibility we now had."

Louise, Mother to Flynn, 3.5 and Rowan, 10 months

Coming home is, for many couples, a momentous milestone in their partnership. In hospital, fathers and partners can feel less involved and more like a visitor. As Melanie recalls, once at home, dads and partners can become much more involved;

"By day three I was desperate to go home, although I was a little nervous about leaving the expert advice.

The first few days were quiet, my son slept a lot and I was able to catch up on sleep too. My husband was tremendous support in allowing me to stay in bed for another 3 days, really allowing my body to recover from the trauma it had been through."

Melanie, Mother to James, 1

Time can take on a different quality with a newborn; the first night at home without the backup of hospital staff can feel daunting; it is solely down to us to care for this tiny creature and so many things run through our mind;

"After a long first night at home I felt huge relief that we'd got him through that first night and he was still alive as I didn't trust my mothering abilities at that stage whatsoever!"

Louise, Mother to Flynn, 3.5 and Rowan, 10 months

In the beginning we are so new to mothering; few of us trust ourselves and may not yet see ourselves as having "mothering instincts" or abilities at all. Yet when we look back from further along our journey, we can see just how great a journey we have been upon; from fragile, unsure new mother, bewildered and anxious about picking up our babies, to confident women who know and love our children and know we will competently rise to whatever challenges come our way.

Yet we do not know this at the time, we don't have the gifts of hindsight or experience, just as we do not know the extent to which we will grow, deepen and learn through learning to love and care for our baby. So it is into the unknown we must walk, feeling and fearing our way, moment by moment, as we learn, on the job, how to care for our babies.

We may well be shocked at how our body feels after birth. We bleed for a number of weeks; this bleeding, known as lochia, is a combination of blood, mucous and tissue which our womb sheds as blood vessels previously supplying the placenta are restricted and our womb replaces its lining post-pregnancy. Our belly remains swollen and we may feel incredibly tender and sore. Pain may restrict our movement and changes in our breasts take us by surprise.

"How did my body feel after birth? I remember having my first shower and hardly recognising what I saw. The description that sprang to mind was 'hobbit' for some reason! I hadn't grown hair on the soles of my feet... but I just looked small and baggy and not like myself anymore.

The day my milk came in I remember being amused that my torso was half Pamela Anderson, half deflated bouncy castle... but I didn't care."

Hazel, Mother to Barnaby, 15 months

Yet birth is not the only way we become mothers; a parallel journey is meeting our children through adoption. Tess speaks of the uncertainty and anxiety, practical planning, excitement and contradictory emotions of meeting your adopted children, simply having to feel your way, day by day;

"I can't describe what it's like to meet your three young children for the first time. We had nothing to compare it to and no real way of preparing ourselves. In the January we'd decided on a group of three siblings based on a small A4 information sheet and a grainy photocopied photo. In the May we went to meet them for the first time, spending a little longer with them each day in their foster home until they moved in with us a week later.

Driving to the foster home that first morning was so strange; it felt like being on the moon or underwater. A real *terra incognita*. But I didn't feel too anxious, just strange.

Walking up the path to the front door of the boy's foster home, the twins answered the door saying, 'Hello Mummy and Daddy.' That was pretty unexpected! The rest was easy – they were adorable, they obviously loved their foster carers to bits but equally they seemed more than ready to come to their forever family.

We spent the week getting to know them, in theory, but it was difficult because they were in their foster home and we were very much visitors. We felt desperate to have the boys come to us so we could start getting to know them properly.

When the boys moved in a week later, things really started to go smoothly in terms of us becoming a family. There were some tantrums and some anxious moments, but it was quite clear from the start that things would be OK.

A couple of times in the evenings, after the boys were asleep, I did have fleeting moments of almost panic when I thought 'I don't even know who these children are and now they're with us forever!' but I think I just didn't have a moment of thinking time in the day, and it was anxiety slipping out when I had a minute to think."

Tess, Mother to Adam and Aidan, 8 and Shaun, 6

However we become mothers, there are always times we feel

excited and confident and times we are anxious and unsure. We so hope we will be good enough, and strive to do our best; we hope to hear the call of our instincts, to overcome anxieties and come to feel what is right for our babies and children.

Unearthing our instincts

Generally, as adult women in a Western culture, we tend to be comfortable in the realms of intellect and rationality. Our lifestyles and careers largely mirror our culture, focussing upon intellectual and practical capabilities, yet pregnancy, birth and mothering call us to awaken to deeper parts of ourselves and to act from a place of instinct. People begin to talk about "mothering instincts" and "mother nature", and whilst this may feel comfortable for some, others may doubt the presence of such instinctive feelings. Even if we do accept the notion of mothering instincts, we may have little idea of how to tune into that wisdom.

If mothering is an instinctive journey, we may feel we are poor contenders, with little hope of finding such instincts which will justify our involvement. Discovering instincts and hearing their message is one thing, yet having the confidence to trust and act upon their guidance is another journey entirely. Yet as many of us recall, the journey is rather different from how we imagined. We do not have to worry about *how* we will find our instincts, as rather they find us. It can be a rather strange feeling, especially when we are so used to relying on what we have learned intellectually, to awaken to deep instinctive feelings erupting from within, urging us to care for and protect our baby in a clear way.

"I was terrified of taking her home after a week of help in hospital and really felt I didn't have a clue – my degree and previous career no help whatsoever!

But the unconditional love I felt for her was immense and my protective instincts kicked in."

Fran, Mother to Emma, 35, Jack, 32 and Edward, 29

Our instincts are as old as humanity, and although we may doubt their presence, they are hardwired within. For millennia an infant's survival depended upon closeness to his mother. Such closeness provided nourishment, immunity, warmth and protection. Whilst the way we live has changed, the way our bodies behave and our baby's biological expectations have not.

Far from being "clingy" or "irrational" for wanting our babies close, rather we are reacting to instinct as mothers of all mammalian species have done through time. People speak of bonding as an emotional thing, but listening to new mothers talk, many of us experience this as a primal, intense, powerful physiological force.

Needing baby close

The first night in hospital with my first baby, the midwives asked to take her so I could sleep; I didn't really want them to, but didn't feel confident saying no, so agreed, asking them not to give her formula. I duly lay down trying to sleep, but despite being exhausted, adrenaline raced through me and my mind and body screamed for her return. I couldn't think of anything else, I was stressed and wanted her back immediately. So I listened to myself, let go of feelings of being seen as irrational or silly, and pressed the buzzer saying that I would like her back with me.

This was a big milestone on my journey; I let go of what I thought others may think and listened to myself and what felt right for my baby. As soon as she was back, cuddled across my chest, the adrenaline and stress dissolved and feelings of peace returned. Despite tiredness, the peace I felt was deeper and things felt right again. In that moment, I knew I could listen to myself, and trust that, step by step, things would be okay.

Instinct seems to speak to us simply and clearly; things simply feel right, or very wrong. When she was away from me, everything felt wrong, and intensely so to the point I could barely think, and when she was back, everything felt calm and right. We can see the huge role our hormones play in orchestrating our feelings and influencing behaviour.

Melanie describes her experience of awakening protective instinct and the way we develop feelers which extend beyond ourselves;

"The one thing that MAJORLY changes when you have a child is you discover your 'spider senses' so to speak. You're always listening out for a change in breathing or snuffling – you are hypersensitive to the slightest thing, even when you're sleeping, you're constantly alert."

Melanie, Mother to James, 1

We certainly become hypersensitive; using our entire body to *feel* for our babies, sensing their breathing, hunger and needs. We can see that by having our babies close, our instincts are able to develop unimpeded. Yet if our babies are not with us we can see how what may arise as feelings of maternal protection can soon become feelings of anxiety, as we are unable to do what our hormones and instincts are urging us to do; we are left battling intense feelings and rising hormonal reactions.

"Although Izzy had been born, she still felt very much part of me. On day 8 I went out without her, just for a couple of hours, and it felt like I'd left an arm at home. I couldn't stop looking for her."

Lizzie, Mother to Izzy, 6, James, 4, and Lloyd, 1

In a culture which does not currently recognise or value maternal instinctive behaviour, it is easy to see how our feelings can be seen and labelled as "irrational", "hormonal" and "oversensitive". We may be told to take some time away from our baby, perhaps criticised or teased, called "possessive", "jealous", "clingy" or "anxious" for wanting our babies close. How different things would be if such judgements and misconceptions were understood as our *awakening to the powerful call of instinct* which guides us in the care and nurturing of our child and the development of our *Mother Selves*.

Rather than internalising this cultural misnomer, as mothers we can recognise the great *value* of listening to this inner call, and instead congratulate and encourage ourselves and each other for listening to our inner voice. Through doing so, we come upon a valuable, repetitive milestone; we recognise what skilled and important work we do and come to *value* our mothering work. We need no longer feel silly or apologetic for loving our babies wholeheartedly, but rather *proud* to do so as we understand the great value, meaning and worth our actions hold.

"It's a scary time being confronted with looking after a baby when you've never held one before. But I think women come equipped with instinct that kicks in soon after birth – the snag is listening to it instead of all the other advice!"

Ross, Mother to Charley and Chelsea, in their 20's

Recognising and understanding our instincts develops as we journey further along our mothering path. We learn through experience; as we see that things are going okay, we learn to trust ourselves and our babies, and from such trust we grow in confidence and inner strength.

Loving our babies

Our feelings and love for our babies are as unique as we are. Some of us feel such love from the moment of conception, even before, and feel close and connected to our babies throughout pregnancy, and this love continues once they're in our arms. For others, we feel huge surges of love when we meet them for the first time and hold them in our arms. Yet for others of us, love develops over time, more slowly, as we get to know them in the weeks and months that follow. We may not remember feeling a huge surge of love at birth, but rather a continuation of the companionship we felt all along. And for others of us it takes time to begin to discover feelings of love and connection;

"With both of my children I wouldn't say I fell in love with them straight away, but felt like I wanted them to be with me all the time and to take care of them. Love didn't come strongly until a few weeks after when I'd got to know them a little more and studied their faces for hours on end."

Harriet, Mother to Riley, 4 and Leon, 1

"In a diary entry to my son I wrote: *I read somewhere that being a parent is a job for a woman and a hobby for a father. I now understand this. I always thought I'd be a wife predominantly, but I'm a mother to you first and foremost. I cannot allow myself to think just how much I feel for you – I would simply give up my life for you.*"

Corrine, Mother to Henry, 3

"I had to spend two nights in hospital after giving birth waiting for my blood pressure to sort itself out. I hated this! The ward seemed busy, disorganised, and I just wanted to get out and feel fresh air on my skin. The morning after we got home, I remember feeling such relief at hearing rain pouring down. It felt like I was in touch with nature again after an incarceration. I remember sitting by the front window while rain poured outside, holding my new baby in my arms and feeling the most intense wave of love I'd ever known."

Ann, Mother to Ella, 4

"Love is an interesting one for me. On paper I wasn't 100% sure I'd love my three adopted children, either initially or in the long run! I kind of hoped my instincts would kick in but I also felt there was no guarantee. I'd had plenty of private conversations with myself where I assured myself I'd make the most of it and be a good mother to them come what may, to the extent that I eventually stopped worrying about whether I'd love them or not.

As it turned out, it wasn't an issue. Meeting the boys for the first time was so intense, strange and fast-moving that I barely had time to think, we just 'went with it'. The only shaky day was the one day we had at home on our own, after having spent a week near the boys' foster home – Social Services gave us one day to clear our heads and prepare for the boys moving in to our house the following day. My husband went into a very strange zone, looking back it was probably a kind of nest-feathering equivalent – mowing the lawn (which he never usually does!) doing bits of DIY (ditto).

As soon as the boys were in our house, I felt I loved them and would look after them forever. I even felt this in the very same moments when I found myself thinking 'I don't know who these children are!'"

Tess, Mother to Adam and Aidan, 8 and Shaun, 6

Early motherhood is an intense, up-and-down experience and it is easy to make incorrect assumptions about how it is for others, especially when social media seems to share only the positive, smiling pictures. We all come to love our children in our own way. None of these are the *right* experience, and no one mother's experience of loving her child is any greater, or lesser than another's. There is no *one* way to love, and no *right* way; love is not something which follows rules set out in books nor conforms to plans or expectations. Our feelings are simply our feelings. We learn to love our children in our own way, and many of our personal milestones lie in the discovery, deepening and expansion of this love.

Landscapes of love

If we imagine the elements of our mothering landscape – great mountains and valleys, diverse geology, forests, vegetation and climate – let us envision love as the fundamental element of water. Our love brings life through our landscapes and carves unique features of our terrain.

Like waterfalls cascading down a mountainside and curving through the valleys, love for our babies finds its own way. It takes its own time and carves a unique route. Sometimes the water is still and crystal clear, beautiful and reflective; we are calm and things feel balanced. Oftentimes it will be gushing, raging, sometimes overpowering, like a river bursting with monsoon rains. We become flooded, swept away and overwhelmed by its intensity, crushingly aware of the vulnerability of our children and ourselves.

Sometimes love may be hard to find, as in a drought. We know water is there, somewhere, deep below the surface or in another place, and that rain will pour and rivers flow one day. And so it can be with loving our babies; at times we fear love is absent from our landscapes. All we can do is carry on, caring for them, keeping a lookout for signs of love upon our horizon.

If this resonates, reflect on the water analogy; just because water is obscured from view, it has not left the ecosystem. It cannot leave the ecosystem. It lies beneath the surface, waiting for a time to rise up; it lies further ahead, just around the corner, waiting for its presence to be discovered. Love is always within us; only sometimes it takes a little time to surface. Mothering is a long term game, and changes come as we find our own ways of connecting with our babies.

"After a shaky start in pregnancy, not sure I wanted to be a mother, a difficult labour and emergency C-section, things changed so much when he was finally here. We got on really well with breastfeeding. I stayed in hospital and had good support. He took to it really well, the midwife said he was like a duck to water and this made me feel good, confident. I remember feeling so close to him and wanting to spend all of my time with him, holding him and breastfeeding in the chair. I really enjoyed those early times, I was very happy, so attached and content."

Amy, Mother to Simon, 25 and Edward, 19

Perceiving Amy's story through pregnancy, we may have imagined it difficult for her to adjust to motherhood and feel such easy love for her baby, yet love emerged upon her landscapes. As new mothers we are vulnerable and not in conscious control of the feelings we experience; we may choose how we respond to our feelings to some extent, but our feelings arise of their own accord. Any of us can feel any type of emotion, and fluctuating hormonal levels mean we do so with great intensity.

A milestone for many of us is recognising our vulnerability and the fluid nature of our thoughts and feelings, and understanding that feelings change over time. Through recognising our vulnerability and incompleteness we are better able to cultivate an attitude of love and gentleness towards ourselves. We can take care of ourselves, allow ourselves to rest, seek and accept support and feel our feelings and know with time they will pass. We can remind ourselves that we are beginners at the very start of a long journey; that we have much to learn, and to trust that we will grow in skills and confidence with time.

The impact of birth experiences

Feelings towards our babies are often entwined with experiences and emotions of birth. It can take time and much reflection to begin to see these as different aspects of our emotional landscapes, and to begin to unravel and separate out the different threads and feelings. However birth unfolded, receiving our baby is intense and life-changing. The combination of intense, and sometimes traumatic, physical and emotional experiences, along with hormonal flux, and the realisation of the enormity of new responsibility, means we feel hugely different to how we feel normally. Whilst this seems like a rather obvious thing to state, it is a hugely overlooked aspect of early motherhood. We are so changed, so fundamentally altered on every level, and yet, simultaneously, we must begin the constant work of baby care. There is so little time and space to recognise, explore and begin to process our feelings.

We may be experiencing a combination of trauma and elation, numbness and confusion, profound happiness, shock, joy and deep responsibility; yet when we are asked how we are feeling it can be difficult to answer, and, anyway, attention is focussed on the baby, so even if we are asked, we simply say, 'Fine'. Whatever our birth experiences, we are expected to put this behind us, get on with the tasks of baby care, receive visitors and *get back to normal.*

Yet there is no going back. Since becoming mothers, we are fundamentally changed and our lives will never be the same as they were previously. Yet lack of cultural recognition for this immense change can leave us flailing, attempting to suppress waves of panic and anxiety as we feel so out of our depth, physically weak and drained, so emotionally high and low and so utterly lacking in support and understanding.

Our feelings towards our baby are but one aspect of a huge spectrum of emotional, physical, hormonal and psychological transformation and so often we are left alone, restless and exhausted, to comprehend these vast inner changes alongside caring for our baby once our partner returns to work.

When we feel birth has gone well, we can feel we are riding high on a wave of soaring love hormones. This oxytocin-fuelled sense of power, love and strength opens us up to deeper elements of ourselves. We move forward emotionally flying, feeling strong and deeply empowered. I remember feeling like this with my first daughter and memories of these positive, hormonally induced peaks never really leave you.

Yet what we are feeling are the experiences of our hormones; the conditions of our birth allowed our bodies to behave at their optimum and release huge levels of oxytocin and other hormones which kickstart physiological transformation, reforming our inner landscapes with our full quota of hormonal help.

Yet hormonal systems are extremely sensitive; if our birth process was interrupted, if we felt observed or unsafe on any level, we may not have received such hormonal help. We can see just how vulnerable we are as birthing women, not only during the birth itself, but in the time after. We may be rushed through the first minutes and hours with procedures and room transfers taking precedence over quiet, uninterrupted time of inner awakening. And if birth has been traumatic, we have to get to know, love and care for our babies upon landscapes of conflict, shock, pain and physical and psychological healing;

"My son was born by C-section following a long labour; I felt very sore and tender, I couldn't walk, was exhausted, weak and dizzy, I felt as though I'd been torn apart.

I was mentally exhausted, confused, not understood and vulnerable. I felt disconnected from my baby, scared and opened-up.

I'm very sensitive so I don't think everyone feels like this after a C-section, but for me personally I found it very hard, and what followed were some really difficult weeks of anxiety and depression. I did put this down to the way my son was born, but then I felt like this with my second baby who was born vaginally, so now I think it's my hormones and how I'm going to feel for a while after giving birth. Although it's awful, I know much more how to care for myself now and know I won't be like that forever."

Harriet, Mother to Riley, 4 and Leon, 1

The impact of traumatic birth can carry over into early mothering, casting a shadow of doubt, anxiety and depression. Yet it is not always this way; a difficult and traumatic birth can become a catalyst to transformation, urging us to become stronger, more determined and empowered.

We read previously about Marie's experiences of a difficult journey to conception, and then the birth of her baby being complicated by shoulder dystocia. Marie explains how such experiences led her to discover strength, power and determination within. She explains how *from* her experiences she found her mothering instincts, and this birth defined her path as a strong, determined and resilient mother;

"Probably as a result of the start we had, I was determined and very definite that I wouldn't be told what to do with my baby. I was going by my instinct, after all, that's why she was here and that's how we would live from now on!

I listened to people's opinions, then did as I felt was right for me and my baby. I asked advice from my Mum, who gently guided and supported me, but Jean and I very quickly learnt to enjoy each other's company. I breastfed when she was hungry, cuddled her for hours, gazed at this miracle that my body had produced and truly enjoyed our new lives together."

Marie, Mother to Jean, 11 and Lewis, 9

Hazel spoke previously about the distressing experiences surrounding her son's birth, and made the link between those experiences and her feelings of sadness, trauma and anxiety in the early weeks. So many of us have these feelings, and like Hazel, we rarely feel we can put them into words and share how we are feeling with anyone, even those close to us;

"I was very anxious, I didn't feel confident handling this wobble-headed little thing and was in awe of my husband who was so natural with him. Looking back I realise how anxious I really was. I remember going out with Barnaby in the car on my own for the first time when he was 3 ½ weeks old, and I was terrified. I just didn't feel confident that I could cope on my own, although I don't think I voiced that to anyone, not even my husband."

Hazel, Mother to Barnaby, 15 months

Strength of feelings, strength of fear
Whilst it was likely that we would've been expecting to feel overwhelmed by the intensity of birth, we are often less prepared for

the power of emotional surges as tides of vast, intense and contradictory feelings sweep across our inner landscapes.

We are overawed by the strength of love for our babies, yet so too do we realise how incredibly vulnerable they are. Our urge to protect them awakens within us and suddenly we see just how many potential risks and threats exist. Whilst such thinking can be understood as our newly emerging *Mother Self* risk assessing our environment to maintain safety, a practice expected and commended in the workplace, as new mothers such feelings can be overwhelming;

"You cannot prepare for the strong emotional and irrational feelings that come about once you become a mother. James often woke sneezing in those early weeks and I felt so sad and tearful about this. I caught his leg while putting him in the car seat and was so upset and worried about my mothering skills. Eventually I think you just learn to run with these irrational feelings and see them for what they are. I still have them even now."

Deborah, Mother to James, 4

"The world felt like a dangerous and threatening place. Although we'd had a tough time in late pregnancy, with worries about his growth, I knew he was fine, and that he was all mine to nourish, build and protect. Suddenly he was out there in the world, so separate and self-contained... I had to work out how to get food into him, transport him and soothe him; it was so much harder."

Eleanor, Mother to Thomas, 3 and David, 10 months

Mothers speak of the intensity of the bond and how life seemed irrevocably changed forever. Such feelings were less of a gentle, balmy kind of love as portrayed through soft focus media images of mothers and babies, and more a guttural, physical urgency for them to be safe. Such feelings speak of power and instinct; of *needing* to be together, less from a perspective of choice, and more from a perspective of biological survival;

"I always knew a mother and baby bond was strong, but I was shocked to realise just how strong. To physically feel pain and panic when she cried and I couldn't get to her. To worry that, 'if I fall here what will happen to her'; not 'oh that would hurt me...' These are all very intense feelings."

Marie, Mother to Jean, 11 and Lewis, 9

"So many times in the early weeks, I found myself feeling we were still attached, that there must have been something wrong in the cord-cutting process. If he cried when someone else was holding him my body twisted and cramped, howled out to get him back, as if I could put him back inside me."

Eleanor, Mother to Thomas, 3 and David, 10 months

Eleanor puts into words the gritty, urgent, primordial emotions we feel when we physically experience our mothering instincts calling us to reclaim and protect our babies. A huge milestone at this part of our journey, but one many of us do not come to recognise until sometime later, is that as new mothers we *do* have instincts, and we are feeling them from the beginning. Yet at the time we may not experience them as this, but as intense, overwhelming, confusing emotions. We may perceive ourselves as anxious, overprotective or fussy, labelling ourselves with the negative and dismissive judgements society tends to cast upon mothers following instinct and intuition. Yet as we progress we may look back and see those intense, gritty feelings as the awakening of our raw, and as yet unrefined, instincts.

The first days and weeks are physically, mentally and emotionally tough. Our babies need us pretty much constantly; we are recovering from the huge physical expenditure of birth, and hormones overhaul our inner landscapes and physiology. Intense feelings of danger can provoke bone deep anxiety; we may become overwhelmed with fear of what may happen and find ourselves feeling frightened and isolated;

"I found the first weeks tough. I was sore, could hardly walk, breastfeeding hurt (but I was determined to keep going) and was terrified to be by myself with my son.

I loved him and wanted him near me but felt overwhelmed with exhaustion and suffered with postnatal anxiety – everything around us seemed like it could be a danger to him, I couldn't get it out of my head. I now know this is quite common and they are just thoughts, you just need to find ways of dealing with them."

Harriet, Mother to Riley, 4 and Leon, 1

"A few months after having my daughter, some great things started to happen in my career. I never felt quite in touch with it though, it felt quite small in comparison to the overwhelming feeling of being a new mum. I was trying to navigate both, on little sleep and energy. As soon as our daughter started to sleep longer, I started suffering from severe bouts of insomnia and postnatal anxiety. I was being pulled in so many directions without the space to breathe. The love I felt for her was overwhelming and caused me to start to panic about losing her."

Zara, Mother to Izzy, 4

"One of the major changes to my nature is that I'm absolutely terrified of anything dire happening to my son. What if he were to get really sick? What if someone snatched him? There is a whole host of horrors I really have to switch my mind from thinking about otherwise I'd drive myself mad.

I've spoken to my mother and friends about this and they all assure me this is a natural part of being a mum. It is tough though sometimes and I do fret 'is it natural to be this scared?' To which, so far, any Mum has always answered a resounding 'YES'!!"

Melanie, Mother to James, 1

We can come to understand these feelings as our instincts urging us to protect; we are realising our vulnerabilities and the fact we have less control over life than we would like. Deep down we fear something bad happening, and deeper still, know we have little control over such events. Such realisations are difficult to bear and rising anxiety can feel as though it is taking over our inner landscapes, affecting our mood and behaviour. We can reassure ourselves knowing that with time such feelings pass, and that as we gain more experience so too will we grow in confidence.

A key milestone of coping with anxiety is talking to others and reminding ourselves to stay in the present moment; to become aware of our thoughts as being only thoughts, perhaps exploring yoga breathing, meditation, relaxation or mindfulness practices and trying to stop our mind projecting forwards so that we can keep ourselves anchored in the present moment with our baby.

If this is your experience, know you are not alone, share your feelings, tenderness and vulnerability, and allow yourself to be supported. Seeking support from friends, your midwife, GP or a counsellor can provide a safe space to help you navigate these intense emotional landscapes.

Journeys through depression
Alongside anxiety and exhaustion there can be frequent feelings of

low mood, sadness, low confidence and feelings of isolation and detachment which may be symptoms of postnatal depression. Whilst awareness of PND is increasing, it is still something few of us feel able to talk about, at least when we're experiencing it most severely. Our silence means we experience these feelings alone, contributing further to our sense of isolation, failure, detachment and perceived inferiority as we compare ourselves to others who, we assume, are doing so much better than we are.

Some mothers spoke of a connection between traumatic birth, anxiety and depression, and when babies were born under general anaesthetic some women shared unspeakable fears surrounding their struggle to bond, questioning if this baby was actually theirs. Yet others, like Alicja and Carol, explained that whilst birth was traumatic they found great relief in being able to finally care for their baby themselves. Birth experiences led some women to experience post-traumatic stress, whilst others, like Marie, described how traumatic circumstances led them to discover stronger and more determined parts of themselves. Motherhood is deeply transformational, introducing us to previously undiscovered aspects of ourselves, some of which are immensely joyful, and others intensely challenging.

Like Ronne, we may find ourselves overwhelmed, exhausted and falling into a difficult emotional place. Whilst it is upsetting to read how Ronne felt at the beginning of motherhood, through bravely sharing her story she brings hope and inspiration; we can see through seeking help she was able to overcome her depression and go on to discover deep joy and happiness in caring for her precious son Daniel;

"I loved my son deeply but was exhausted by waking to feed him several times each night. I felt myself falling into an emotional pit. I worried constantly something awful would happen or there was something wrong with him. When he got a cold at six weeks, I became frantic. I began neglecting myself and feeling unable to go out... I felt overwhelmed and cried often and copiously. I saw other mums in my postnatal group coping much more competently (or so it seemed to me), and felt I was hopeless.

I felt myself being overtaken by all-too-familiar feelings, as if I was being encased in darkness.

Because I had a history of depression I'd been referred antenatally to a wonderful doctor who looked after women with postnatal depression. She arranged for one of her team, a community mental health nurse, to visit me once a week after Dan was born. The nurse, Mo, proved to be an important source of support. When she spotted the signs of postnatal depression, she took me to see Dr Oates who decided it would be best if I went back on medication.

It was the right decision. Within about a month, I began feeling better and started positively enjoying my beautiful little boy."

Ronne, Mother to Dan, 28

It is incredibly difficult to share such feelings at a time when society expects us to be joyful. We fear we will be judged and deemed unable to care for our baby. Yet as Ronne illustrates, seeking help usually creates networks of support to hold and guide us through our vulnerability.

Milestones through depression include accepting our feelings and embracing our vulnerability. We can accept we are struggling, that we do not have to be perfect, and that it is okay for us to speak to others and accept help. Seeking help is a milestone of courage, as well as a sign of our strength and ability to care for our baby;

"I remember feeling stressed and worried, snapping a lot at my partner. I put this down to the huge life changes; moving house, having a baby away from the support of family and friends, the ongoing stress of work.

Yet even as things settled down, I was still struggling and finding things hard. I began to think that maybe I had postnatal depression as I'd been feeling this way for some time. I went for an appointment with my GP, and she arranged some appointments with a counsellor.

From just a couple of appointments where I was able to talk about my feelings with someone who listened and understood I felt a big difference. It helped me to see things more clearly and I started to feel less worried."

Elsbeth, Mother to Rowan, 6 and Evie 2

Milestones of understanding

Much of our work as mothers revolves around physical baby care, and for most of us, this is entirely new. *So* much is required physically and emotionally; we are beginners, as embryonic in our mothering as our babies are to the world, we grow and learn as they do. We may read about parenting and hope instinct will guide us, yet there are times we simply do not know what to do. At first it is hard to even pick up and hold our tiny, wobbly headed infants, let alone know how to feed, nurture and comfort them. Few of us grew up in extended families or communities, and for many of us the first baby we hold is our own. Vast parenting literature exists but how do we know which books to choose, and whether or not the advice is right for *our* baby?

It's little wonder that many of us, like Shelley, feel confused and isolated as we find ourselves far removed from our previous, familiar lives, at home with our baby and surrounded by advice yet unsure which path to take;

"The early weeks and months were hard. No matter how you prepare yourself, reading, advice etc., when it happens it's a shock. It's like nothing you've done before. You're a mum 24/7, 365 days a year f.o.r.e.v.e.r.

Suddenly you're responsible for this tiny human and sometimes you have the answers and sometimes you don't. There are all these hormones whooshing round your body. You stare for hours in wonder at your baby and cry with love, happiness, hope, worry, doubt and confusion."

Shelley, Mother to Leia 3 and Anya 1

Yet within this *not knowing* we experience many tiny milestones which become our growth and wisdom. We may have an intellectual approach in mind, yet it is only when we are with our babies, without experience, not knowing, that we *learn*.

We become mothers through mothering. Slowly we begin to recognise his signs and bring him the love, food, warmth and comfort he seeks. This isn't always easy. There are many times we fear we're failing; our efforts seemingly making no difference at all; he may cry for hours, refuse to feed, his little body writhing in obvious distress, and we feel utterly lost.

All we can do is continue trying; pick him up again, lay him down, take off his nappy, wear him in the sling, sway, offer a feed, a different position. Eventually, something brings the comfort he was searching for, or perhaps he just felt better and fell asleep, exhausted from his efforts, leaving us with a heady mix of distress for his distress, relief that he is sleeping, scared to move in case he wakes, needing to eat, drink and wee, emotional, exhausted, overawed by his breathtaking tenderness and beauty.

'I never imagined it could be so hard...'
We learn that there are lovely, joyful times and times we find

everything challenging, exhausting and utterly overwhelming. Yet we carry on, sometimes not even because we want to – we are so exhausted – yet we carry on, simply because we have to.

When nothing we have read seems to work we just have to get through it our way, using the energy and resources we have in that moment. And in doing so we discover strength, energy and tenacity we did not know we had. Amidst the exhaustion and frustration of pacing the floor with our colicky, desperate three-week-old through the long hours of the night we may stumble upon a place of stillness, a deep love which moves us to tears. We gaze at this tiny, helpless, strangely captivating creature and our heart opens; we deepen into milestones of uncomplicated mother-love as we are overcome with tenderness, exhaustion and emotion. It is as though the intensity of labour was a forewarning, a preparation for new depths to be discovered;

"It was extremely challenging at first. Having very little sleep and coping with a screaming baby when you really don't know what's wrong is awful. There were times exhaustion threatened to take over.

The worst time was when my son had colic. He went through a period of non-stop screaming when I tried to get him to sleep. Nothing worked. As he was so young, there was nothing I could give him. I just had to pace the floor with him. And pace. And pace. I remember the feeling of frustration because I didn't know what was wrong and the uncharitable feeling of just wanting him to shut up. This passed thankfully and calm resumed."

Melanie, Mother to James, 1

As our inner and outer landscapes of mothering are so rarely discussed, when we are struggling we often feel as though it is we, ourselves, who are failing; we doubt our capabilities and lose confidence. We may not have expected it to be so hard, for our baby to need us quite so much, and for it all to be so chaotic, constant and exhausting;

"Looking back at our first weeks, I was miserable. Life was chaotic. I felt tired all the time. I felt I'd made a terrible mistake in having a child – that I just wasn't cut out for Motherhood, that I was too old to make a good job of it, I was 36.

I didn't understand no one was supposed to carry on life just as they had before. I felt a complete failure because everything was so difficult. In reality it was so difficult because I was so tired, but neither I nor my husband had bargained on that.

Then I got sick, some kind of chill, and felt even less able to cope. I had no one to reassure me that this chaos would pass in a matter of weeks. I really felt this was what life would be like for the next 20 years. In reality I was expecting too much of myself."

Alison, Mother to Callum, 23

As Alison so rightly concludes, before we have children we cannot comprehend what it will actually be like; we expect it to be perfect, joyful and loving, something we've looked forward to for so long. We have no frame of reference to perceive the tiredness, no idea how we can get through it, or even the knowledge that it will not be like this forever!

The problem lies with our expectations of ourselves and lack of recognition of the steep learning curve of early mothering. We grow to realise it is not our baby which needs to be fixed but our expectations which need to shift. Our milestones come as we shift our attitudes and become a little more gentle upon ourselves.

Starting to understand baby's needs...
We may have read many parenting books, yet funny as it sounds our babies have not read these books themselves! They are coming to us raw and ready, with biological expectations of us meeting their needs as they arise. Books, forums and advice from all philosophies can share ideas, tips, and introduce us to new ways of thinking, yet they are not written about *our* baby. The only person who can really tell us what to do is our baby himself. For it is only he who knows how he is feeling, when he is ravenous for a big feed, and when he would prefer snuggling and a little milk for comfort and to soothe him into sleep.

Whilst he does not tell us in words, we slowly learn to understand through watching him, holding him, listening and being attentive and close. Once we begin to see our parenting as meeting our children's needs, whatever these may be, parenting becomes simpler. Our milestones may come as a letting go of expectations and rather looking at the little one in front of us and asking, *What does he need in this moment?*

"I'm a midwife so maybe I have some knowledge or instinct about those early weeks. I don't remember ever feeling nervous about what to do or confused. My style, if there is one, tends towards an attachment/continuum approach. My job was to meet her needs as best I could. She joined my life, came with me wherever I went. I didn't adapt so much as she just slotted in like a jigsaw piece. I feel I'm still that kind of mother though now she is 8 her needs are different."

Jane, Mother to Sarah, 8

Once we learn to see behaviour as communication and begin to recognise cues, we can begin to respond with more confidence. We mostly do this without being aware of it, but these are very significant milestones; tiny moments when instead of feeling confusion, or not even noticing our child's cues, we think, for example, *Ah, he usually does that when he's getting hungry, I'll see if he'd like some milk.*

We are learning to *recognise, understand and respond,* and through these milestones we deepen into trust of ourselves and our babies. We trust him to communicate his needs and ourselves to recognise and respond. This way mothering becomes a cycle of positive reinforcement; as we respond to his needs (even if we don't get it exactly right all the time) he trusts us more and continues to communicate, and we continue to learn his language and become more refined and accurate in our responses.

When my son was a baby, before he started to rub his eyes or cry, he would play with his earlobe. He only did it on one side, squeezing his little ear between his finger and thumb. I don't know how I recognised this, but I noticed he did it when he was getting sleepy. If I stopped whatever we were doing and snuggled him up with a feed just as he was rubbing his ear, he'd fall asleep easily, but if I left it longer, he would cry and be more unsettled. It's amazing how we notice these tiny, seemingly insignificant actions, yet as we get to know our babies, we realise such actions hold the key to greater understanding and connection. However, this is not a linear process! Just as we think we have it sorted, they reach a new stage, have a growth spurt or bout of illness and we must once again begin to observe, listen and comprehend the new information conveyed.

'It's different when it's your own...'
To an outsider the repetitive tasks of bathing, feeding, changing, settling and soothing may seem endlessly dull. And certainly many of us feel this way some days. Yet this is looking at mothering from the outside, judging from the practical landscape only, and those times when we are exhausted and the joy is lacking.

Interactions across our inner landscapes bring these tasks to life as we experience meaningful love and connection. It is through these tasks of baby care we discover love and joy; how he curls his hand around our finger, his soft skin, big, eager eyes locking into ours, holding our hair as he feeds, the satisfied, milky smiles; it is here we build connections and grow to know and love him more. We love him not as *a* baby, but *our* baby.

"Before I became a mother I wasn't interested in babies and did wonder how I'd occupy myself being at home with two little ones. Would I find it interesting? Would it be enough for me? Yet it's so different when it's your own, it's the emotional experience and the connection that makes it so. You LOVE them, they're yours and you WANT to nurture them.

There's a huge inner shift which takes place as you become a mother and care for your babies. And it's this shift, this desire to nurture them, to be there for them and meet their needs even though you're exhausted which makes it purposeful. And this must be part of nature's plan, for without this desire on our part they wouldn't thrive and grow."

Natalie, Mother to Sam and Oliver, 2

Much transformation occurs at this interface between our practical and emotional landscapes, and shifts in one sphere create shifts in another. Gazing at his fluttering eyelashes as he sleeps, we feel a deeper sense of tenderness and compassion; as he wakes we are less likely to be cross at the disturbance and more willing to meet his needs and hold his little body in love as we bring him to our breast for the eighth time that night. We are learning of *love in action*, not just blissful, euphoric happiness, but our dedicated, constant attention as the physical manifestation of our love.

'They all seem to be doing so much better than me...'

When we are struggling it is easy to compare ourselves to others; to judge ourselves harshly, assuming others are coping better. We may meet other mums at parks and playgroups and instead of feeling supported, feel inferior. They do not seem as flustered, tired or overwhelmed as we do; we imagine their babies sleep soundly whilst ours scream for what feels like hours. We imagine they left the house smoothly, after having a shower and doing hair and makeup whilst we hunted for cleanish clothes after the last feed was brought up over us once again.

"I missed the antenatal reunion at 6 weeks because I was too tired to leave the house, this reinforced the sense that everyone else was coping and I was a total failure."

Alison, Mother to Callum, 23

"I made some new Mum friends from classes at my local Sure Start – some were great in the way they were honest about their experiences and could talk about things, but there were others who I now see were not so honest, and when they talked and made comparisons they made other mums feel a bit crap – like we were the only ones feeling like this, we were doing something wrong. It took a few years to get to the stage where I was brave enough to stop hanging round mums that were competitive. I spent more time with mums who were like-minded."

Shelley, Mother to Leia, 3 and Anya, 1

It is easy to make snap judgements, yet we are only seeing that mother, and she us, in that moment. We judge based on a tiny fraction of our lives. And this is only in our imagination and more often than not, this is not an accurate reflection of the other's reality. For as we connect and begin to talk and listen, we realise everyone finds aspects of baby care difficult and has hard days feeling exhausted, overwhelmed and covered in milky vomit.

Our milestones here lie in *empathy*; learning to let go of judgements, both of ourselves and others, and beginning to recognise what a big job mothering is and what a lot it requires from us. Cultivating an attitude of kindness, friendliness and gentleness, to ourselves and other mothers we meet, regardless of parenting approaches, has the potential to change our day, our outlook and our experiences. Friendships with other mums are a great source of fun and companionship and we grow in empathy for ourselves and each other as we realise that we are all simply doing the best we can to get through the days and nights and care for our babies as well as we are able.

'We're getting there…'
After a few weeks, mums speak of a shift where things seem to 'click' and make more sense. It feels as though we are in a different place to the intensity and confusion of the early weeks. Interestingly, this shift occurs not in our baby, but in ourselves and our perceptions. We have come to realise what motherhood entails and the extent to which our baby needs us.

For Harriet, her baby did not begin to feed less or behave differently, rather *she* came to realise her baby was just fine as he was and it was okay for her to let go of her expectations and meet his needs for milk and cuddles. The milestones we encounter are those of *acceptance*; an acceptance of our baby and his needs, rather than our expectations of how things should be;

"At five weeks everything clicked. Although my son still fed all the time, breastfeeding was more comfortable and I relaxed into sitting around feeding all the time. I started going out and about and started to enjoy my new life as a mother.

The first few weeks with your first child is an initiation. It's bloody hard work getting used to nurturing another human being 24/7 and it's massively changed me as a person. I know now I had no need to worry about being a bad mum as I had in pregnancy. No mum is perfect but as long as you try your best to nurture and guide your child and let them know they're loved then all is well."

Harriet, Mother to Riley, 4 and Leon, 1

A new normal
As we come to understand our baby's cues, things begin to feel a little easier; he still needs us enormously, but anxiety and confusion from the early days diminishes as we adjust and grow in confidence.

Yet mums spoke of discomfort around feeling it was okay to fully meet their baby's needs. There remains an insidious cultural warning from parenting paradigms past against "spoiling" babies by giving them too much attention and meeting their needs as they arise, urging us not to "give in" and let them "manipulate us". Imagining a tiny, dependent baby is manipulating us when he expresses his biological needs of hunger is seen by many as outdated, yet such messages persist, and we can receive such advice from well-meaning friends and relatives. A significant milestone alongside recognising our baby's needs, is feeling it is okay for us to meet them wholeheartedly.

Many of us reach a place of acceptance where we are able to say, 'Yes, this is how things are, this is what my baby needs so this is what I am doing.' We have found our feet as mothers, found a new normal and our fledgling confidence emerges. We now know it is normal to feed often, day and night, knowing this is simply what he needs at this time of development. That's not to say there are not still times we feel frustrated, overwhelmed and exhausted, yet what tends to shift is our perception; we no longer resist his needs even though we may still find them draining sometimes.

We deepen into *value* and *recognition* of the immense worth of what we are doing, realising that caring for our baby is *the most important thing that we can be doing.* Similarly, we deepen into *acceptance* that this is what our baby needs at this time. As we accept rather than resist the length of time and the pace at which babies need to be nurtured, we can let go of frustrations and deepen into love, joy and connection in the present moment.

Our milestones come as we realise that this is exactly what we need to do at this time. We can let go of notions that we ought to be doing "something more" and give ourselves permission to really *enjoy* the time we spend loving, nurturing and holding our baby. This surrender is such a joyous and liberating milestone, it introduces us to the shift from *doing to being* where we come to value and understand the quality of *being* with our children, present and connected, as central to our work as mothers;

"The first months were hard, as they are for new parents. After my husband went back to work I was on my own all day. But I was happy, looking after my daughter. She was feeding for hours, so I just sat in my chair, tried not to think about chores and fed her. I bought a sling when she was two months and that helped a little. But my little one was just on my breast constantly for the first four months of her life."

Alicja, Mother to Rozalia, 3 and Konrad, 1

Journeys of sleep

One of the most challenging aspects of the first weeks, and for many of us, the first years, is sleep, or lack of it. Sleep and feeding dominate our landscapes; we are prepared for the fact our babies will wake through the night, yet it is not until we feel the physically, mentally and emotionally draining effects of constant night waking, we realise just how challenging this can become.

Sometimes, no matter what we do, our little ones do not sleep, or rather they sleep in our arms or across our chest, but not for long stretches through the night. Indeed, nighttimes may be far from peaceful for our babies as they writhe in distress, unable to settle to sleep. Sometimes, whatever we try, be it rocking, carrying, bathing, feeding, nothing brings them comfort. Their pain becomes our pain and we can find ourselves feeling hopeless and helpless. Once they have finally drifted off, we know it is only a matter of time until they wake once again.

It takes time for their circadian rhythms to mature and although we may not realise it, they *are* comforted by our warmth and presence. Feeding often through the night helps meet their nutritional needs and informs our milk supply to meet their requirements.

"Those first few days looking after a squally, constantly demanding newborn flew by in a hurricane of breastfeeding, nappies and soothing hugs. Night blurred into day and day into night, as my usual eight hours was shattered into two hour shards, making me feel as if my tiredness would end me. Or at least I wished it would. The relentlessness and intensity of labour contractions were, I suppose, a forewarning of what looking after a newborn is like. Bedtime was no longer a pleasure but a snatched creep beneath the duvet until the cry for milk was heard once more."

Corrine, Mother to Henry, 3

So many of our struggles lie in perceptions and expectations of what motherhood *should* be. In the beginning I had little idea of what my baby would need regarding sleep; we simply imagined we would feed her, cuddle her and put her down to sleep. How wrong could we be! She was content when feeding or sleeping in my arms, yet when we attempted to put her into her cot she would cry immediately.

We found this disconcerting and wondered what we were doing wrong; was she ill, were the bed sheets cold or too scratchy, did she need to be propped up higher with pillows under the mattress? We tried it all. It seemed that what she really wanted was to be asleep, upright, on me, or to be feeding. I received the advice that she was manipulating me and I was spoiling her, yet how could I leave her to howl, cry and vomit? She seemed to need us immensely, to be close and held, so why, I wondered, was I fighting this?

I did not believe in the "spoiling" philosophy, could not leave her to cry, so my growth came as I resolved to love her, hold her and carry her for as long as she needed, and let go of others' expectations. I explored how to co-sleep safely, and happily welcomed her into bed with me during the nights where, after feeding, she seemed to settle to sleep with ease. And although she still woke often to feed, in accordance with her biological needs, the whole process became less fraught, stressful and exhausting. Through the daytime I carried her in a sling which helped with reflux, and my milestones unfolded as I learned to recognise her needs, explore my own feelings about meeting these and let go of any resistance or values which were not my own.

As challenging, frustrating and exhausting as they can be, these times don't last forever. Hazel illustrates we truly can carve our own path through the difficulties of newborn sleep and deepen into love, contentment and connection as we go;

"Barnaby never settled well in his Moses basket, either during the day or at night, so I held him a lot. I can't say I found this a chore in any way, although I suppose at the time I thought it would be useful sometimes if he could snooze for longer than ten minutes so I could eat a meal or have a shower.

If I had the time again, I'd wear him in a sling for those times when I really needed to get something done, but I didn't really find out about babywearing until he was a few months old, and as he was a very sicky baby I struggled a bit even then because he always managed to be sick on me when I got him in the sling.

Mostly I just enjoyed spending a lot of time holding him, I have zero regrets about it. He's 15 months now and still takes lots of his daytime naps on my lap, and I cherish the closeness, because I know in no time he won't want to cuddle up to his mum anymore. (I'm choking up thinking about that!)"

Hazel, Mother to Barnaby, 15 months

'Is he sleeping through yet…?'

I lost count of the times I was asked this anxiety-inducing question about our first baby. Sleeping through! She was barely sleeping at all apart from on me, feeding. The comments and enquiries from others can feel challenging, yet with hindsight we can see these are usually well-meaning attempts at connection. Yet at the time we may not feel this way, instead feeling judged, criticised and sensitive about our parenting, feeling we are doing something wrong and somehow failing.

Our milestones come as we deepen into our heartspace and responsibility, let go of outside expectations and decide how *we* would like to care for our baby through the night. For me, this was the decision to hold her, to feed her as much as she liked and to co-sleep to save me from sitting up in a chair for hours and falling asleep with her on my lap. In his book *Nighttime Parenting*, William Sears explains that babies are not faulty, manipulative, or in need of fixing, rather they simply need us, as much if not more, during the dark of the night as they do in the daytime. Looking from our baby's perspective, nights are long, dark and quiet; they may feel particularly alone, frightened or disorientated, and need our comfort and reassurance.

Milestones evolve as we learn to look at things from our baby's perspective, let go of external expectations and learn to listen to our inner landscapes. Melanie reflects on her journey through nighttime parenting; how she came to cast off comments with strength and humour and find truth, strength and trust in doing things her way;

"I battle with chronic fatigue as my son is not a good sleeper, at 15 months he still wakes for a feed at least once, on a good night and up to three times on a bad night. Some nights I can get him back to sleep quickly, sometimes it takes two hours. Because there is no real routine to this nighttime nightmare, my body clock is shot to pieces.

This is the hardest thing to cope with. There have been times when I've wanted to cave in and listen to those who advocate 'sleep training' and getting my son off the boob at night, but I've read the research on how damaging it is to leave babies crying and also I just can't do it.

My son does not have the luxury of language yet – the only way he can tell me something is wrong is by crying and a mother's natural reaction to a crying child is to comfort it. It is a basic instinct and who am I to go against nature? So many people have told me I've got to 'stop' and the old chestnut 'you are making a rod for your own back' but I say PAH to them all. My son needs me. End of."

Melanie, Mother to James, 1

Yet alongside the overwhelming exhaustion, sleep can be the source of some of our most treasured memories;

"I remember my husband and I in absolute stitches at his startle reflex – how his arms would suddenly shoot up, and then sink back down soooooo slowly, all while fast asleep."

Hazel, Mother to Barnaby, 15 months

"As I was tired very much of the time, I often had a nap with him in our bed with him cradled in the crook of my arm. It was a blissful feeling and he must have enjoyed it too because he was always very peaceful. I felt paradise was 'having a small, soft body snuggled up beside one', it was such a relaxing, happy experience."

Alison, Mother to Callum, 23

'Is he in his own room yet...?'

Knowing where our babies should sleep can be a source of confusion and anxiety. Everyone has an opinion and it can be challenging to find a way through the advice. Yet as with many aspects of parenting, there often isn't an objective "right way". The best place for you, your partner and baby to sleep is the place or places you feel most safe, comfortable and able to meet your baby's needs (though adhering to UNICEF/WHO guidelines when it comes to safe sleeping arrangements is absolutely essential).

Some of us choose to co-sleep, others prefer to use cots, and for many of us, we find our own combinations which evolve with baby's development.

"My husband didn't want our baby in bed with us, so we developed a routine that suited us as a family. Whenever my son woke at night, I found it easier to get into his bed beside him, that way he went straight back to sleep. Usually I'd get back in my own bed a few hours later.

At weekends my son and I shared the family bed and my husband slept in his bed. That way my husband was able to sleep in undisturbed on weekends and it was a treat for my son to be able to sleep beside his Mum all night."

Alison, Mother to Callum, 23

Natalie shares her journey of becoming happy and confident with nighttime parenting, and how trust in an unfolding process played an important role in her evolution;

"Before children I loved sleep and didn't think I could cope with getting up through the night. I find it amazing that now I can cope with being woken several times a night to breastfeed the boys, it's taken me a while to accept this and let go of the worry of not getting sleep. I've learned to put the needs of my children first and compromise my own in the short term.

Having twins was a real shock at first. By far the most difficult part has been sleep. We all slept in the living room for the first few weeks as getting up and down stairs with everything was difficult. I'd be woken constantly through the night as the boys wanted milk. It has been, and still is exhausting, but I want to do it.

It has been hard and I still complain, but I don't want to stop or receive advice, I just want someone to listen and to understand, this is the benefit of having like-minded friends.

Right now I'm trusting that night feeding is a phase in their development. I realise it won't always be this way, this is just a stage, and with time it will change and I'm sure we'll have different worries. Now we have broken sleep for a physical reason – their neurological need for milk, but when they're teens I may be awake worrying about what they're doing. It's about acceptance that life has changed.

That's not to say I always feel this relaxed about it. I adjust and then have relapses. I move forward to acceptance of how things are, then find myself relapsing back and struggling. I might read something, forget to trust myself and them, then look for advice when I'm feeling weaker, I worry more, but come back to trusting myself."

Natalie, Mother to Sam and Oliver, 2

Natalie brings insight into the spiralling inner journeys we make; oscillating back and forth between trusting ourselves and our children and looking outside for information and support. Neither place holds all of the answers all of the time, and our milestones come as we listen to guidance from others, to our baby's needs and our own inner voice, then feel our way forwards, step by step. As we grow in experience, we learn to hear the feedback from our inner compass, bringing confidence to trust ourselves more deeply.

Trusting her instincts led Natalie to make changes regarding where her boys slept. Rather than trust being linear, instead we see how it is a sensitive and spiralling process as we move back and forth between our anxieties and the quiet call of our instincts. Natalie's milestones included an *inner shift* where, rather than solely making decisions intellectually, she listened to her inner compass, heart or intuition and *felt* how such changes may be experienced by her babies;

"Early on the boys slept together. At around six months we agreed that Sam would sleep better in his own room, as he was sleeping well, but being woken by Oliver who still woke a lot for milk. So we kept Oliver in with me and moved Sam into his own room.

Yet as the nights went by, I didn't feel comfortable with one in my room and one out. I struggled with it for a while, then decided to bring him back in, and that night he was back with me I felt so much better, so much more settled emotionally. I feel at ease now, knowing exactly where he is. I remember falling asleep happy thinking, *That's right now.*

It's been a transformation; it meant listening to myself more, then making changes to put things right, even though it may be different to how other people do things. Some people feel sleeping together is strange, and the mainstream doesn't seem to go that way, but the most important thing is feeling right yourself.

We had reasons for putting him in his own room, but they were intellectual reasons. Within myself I felt it was wrong for him to be there, and it goes back to what I was saying about listening to your heart or intuition, the feelings that arise within – these are your instincts, and sometimes it takes a bit of time for your mind to catch up! That night he came back into our room I felt relief."

Natalie, Mother to Sam and Oliver, 2

Mothering is a journey of deepening trust. In the beginning everything is new, yet we continue, gain experience and begin to understand. Trust deepens through many small milestones; we stop doubting ourselves so much, anxiety diminishes and we begin to find our inner confidence and authenticity. So too do we begin to recognise and value the immense work we are doing. We realise that all the feeding, holding, rocking and loving, whilst undoubtedly challenging, is meaningful, valuable and precious work, and we become inspired to continue with confidence, doing the very best we can with the energy and capacity we have available.

Chapter Four
Breastfeeding Journeys

As individual mothers coming to hold our babies after birth, nothing feels so personal and intimate. Yet we seldom realise we are mothering in times of unprecedented social change. Sustained historical and continued influence of cultural, political and economic forces have combined to all but decimate collective social and biological wisdom regarding nurturing infants. Beginning to understand these influences helps understand our individual breastfeeding journeys.

Just as birth has become a controlled, medically managed affair, with knowledge and skills taken out of women's own hands and communities, so too have we all but lost sight of our collective wisdom for feeding and nurturing our babies.

For the greatest part of human history, breastfeeding is how infants were nurtured. Children grew up seeing women of their families and communities nourishing babies at their breast, and such skills were embedded within the culture as simply how things are. Yet from the 18th century medical professionals extended their reach into infant feeding, suggesting alternative food sources as being superior to a mother's milk.

Over time, such influences became widespread and established, undermining breastfeeding as the optimal way to nourish and care for babies, dismantling collective skills and wisdom. Over the last century, formula companies have become highly lucrative and powerful corporations that profit from the decline of breastfeeding. Such financial, and hence political clout, is powerful and widespread, influencing medical research, training and professional practices alongside aggressive global marketing, despite the World Health Organisation's recommendations for exclusive breastfeeding for six months, and for breastfeeding to continue for two years and beyond.

Over time, such forces have skewed our ideas of infant feeding, undermining breastfeeding as the norm. Science continues to discover health-promoting qualities of breastmilk for physiological, immunological, emotional and intellectual development alongside numerous health properties for mothers, yet it does so in a culture so pervaded by corporate interest that much misinformation and misunderstanding cloud the breastfeeding process.

Therefore much advice we receive from those around us, however well-intentioned, is often unknowingly influenced by scheduled formula feeding and usually undermines the breastfeeding process. We find ourselves holding our babies, beginning our journey unaware of the many ways these invisible corporate, political and social landscapes undermine us. Such influences surround us and can take root within, ebbing away our confidence as we wonder if *we* will be able to *do it*, if we should *give it a try*, and whether or not our milk will come in.

"In our antenatal breastfeeding session, the midwife asked how many of us were 'going to try' breastfeeding. Most of us put our hands up – me included. Then she asked how many 'were going' to breastfeed – that really made me stop and think. She explained the percentage of women who can't make enough milk is vanishingly small, yet so often you hear women saying they couldn't breastfeed because they didn't make enough milk, whereas more likely with the right support and confidence in themselves, they could have carried on.

So even before our babies are born, we're undermining ourselves with thoughts that it's difficult, it might not work, and so on. I resolved that I was going to breastfeed – I would make it work."

Hazel, Mother to Barnaby, 15 months

If we face difficulties, as many of us do, and the support we receive does not resolve our difficulties, rather than seeing our experiences stemming from vested economic interests, instead we blame ourselves and internalise feelings of guilt and failure. I hope this brief introduction illustrates breastfeeding is about so much more than what we do with our own babies. Understanding the cultural background helps reframe our personal experiences within the wider economic context and Gabrielle Palmer's *The Politics of Breastfeeding* is an excellent resource for further understanding.

Beginnings
The journey begins, for many of us, before our babies are born. For some mothers, breastfeeding barely features on our inner landscapes; it is not something we have seen much of and feels unknown and uncertain, so we go with formula as this is what we know, can access most easily and feel most comfortable with. Yet a great number of mothers would like to breastfeed. Of that number, some want to give it a try, and for others, there is an awakening within and they know it is what they will do.

"Before I had children I knew I'd been breastfed and knew if I had a baby, the next thing to do was feed it. When Jean was taken to special care they said they wanted to feed her a bottle. My response... 'No you don't.' I was so determined no bottle teat would go in her mouth, I got them to cup feed her my expressed milk. The early days were difficult but I wasn't going to give up; near constant feeding followed for a while. It became easier and so convenient, no bottles to worry about, milk on demand and tailor-made nutrition."

Marie, Mother to Jean, 11 and Lewis, 9

"I was always going to breastfeed. I'm sure there's an element of luck, as in most things with parenting, but I also think there is an element of attitude and expectation. Mindset plays such an important role. My daughter latched on early and stayed there for a number of hours. The tone was set for our breastfeeding journey. It always felt very instinctual. We co-slept and I carried her. She fed as and when she needed, through illnesses and wherever we were."

Jane, Mother to Sarah, 8

"Breastfeeding was something I was going to 'try' and it was hard work at first. Seeing her cues, positioning her wriggly body and trying to get her to latch on was tricky, but when we got it, it felt great."

Shelley, Mother to Leia, 3 and Anya, 1

In the middle of my first pregnancy, a friend gave me a copy of La Leche League's *The Womanly Art of Breastfeeding*. Until this point, I thought I would breastfeed, but gave little thought to what this might entail. This book opened my eyes to the many ways breastfeeding supports health and development of both babies and mothers, and introduced me to ideas of responsive, on-cue feeding and gentle attachment style parenting. I eagerly read about the supply and demand process in which feeding baby at the breast for as long and as often as they like, builds and establishes our milk supply.

This preparation soon came into its own, as from her very first feed my daughter, whilst latching on and feeding well, struggled to keep her milk down. Yet thanks to my reading, I wasn't put off; I continued to feed as she indicated and held her upright after a feed, which seemed to help with the posseting. I had no experience with breastfeeding, yet had developed a belief and trust in the process. Had I not had this information behind me, I would have felt much more worried about her bringing back her milk and been vulnerable to advice which could have undermined our fledging breastfeeding relationship. Certainly, trusting the process was a milestone and preparation during pregnancy was key.

As we learn, so too do we come across the feelings and experiences of others. We soon realise people have differing views, and hold many opinions which undermine breastfeeding's supply and demand process. We see the embedded normalcy of scheduled formula use and how this has become entrenched within beliefs, experiences and opinions;

"I never considered not breastfeeding. It wasn't until a friend said I 'might not be able to do it' or it 'might not be for me' that I realised how many women don't breastfeed. I guess with my own mum and aunties breastfeeding it was the norm for me. I feel lucky to have that as it must be harder if friends and family don't value it."

Harriet, Mother to Riley, 4 and Leon, 1

So much of our journey is influenced by what we see around us. If we have grown up seeing breastfeeding, it is more likely to be the norm for us and may not feel like such a remarkable decision to make. Yet the opposite is also true and it is here, in our subconscious observations of life, that the invisible influence of artificial feeding takes root as the way to feed babies.

"I think my decision to breastfeed, and the perseverance and strength it demanded feeding twins, came from my personality, maturation and background. Growing up on a farm I see it as the normal thing to do, growing up seeing animals feeding their young. But perhaps if I'd grown up in a city I wouldn't have that vision. Perhaps people don't see it at all, let alone see it as normal."

Natalie, Mother to Sam and Oliver, 2

Certainly our background influences our experiences, yet as emerging mothers, we create our own path, weaving threads of our past along with hopes for the future. It is this path of *creating* our mothering style which is rich with potential for growth, learning and transformation, and breastfeeding provides rich terrain for such growth.

Beginning the journey
In the beginning we have much to learn, we must become competent

in holding our newborns as well as deciphering a whole new language of non-verbal communication. This is intense and all consuming; we experience many tiny milestones as we go from being unsure and tentative to confidently scooping our babies close to feed them. Yet in the early days, everything is new, we are flooded with uncertainty as we wonder: *when to feed? How to hold her? Is she on properly? Has she had enough?*

First, we must learn the mechanics, the positioning; how to hold baby and bring him to our breast, and then how he opens his mouth, 'latches on', and begins to suckle, known as attachment. Leaflets illustrate positions and we learn that babies need to open their mouths wide and take a good mouthful of the surrounding breast to extract milk effectively.

It sounds simple, yet real babies are small, wriggly and have their own preferences. And as so few of us grow up seeing breastfeeding we lack experience of the subtleties of the process and can be unsure as to how things should look and feel. Simply learning how to hold our baby, bring him into a comfortable position and sustain an effective latch can take a lot of practice and patience and many thoughts of, *Am I doing this right?*

"I was surprised how hard establishing breastfeeding was. I naively thought because it is natural it should be easy, but how wrong I was. Getting my son to open his mouth to latch on in the early days wasn't easy. I found it especially hard to find a comfortable position and spent many days propping various parts of us up on cushions."

Charlotte, Mother to Raffy, 9 months

Milestones of the early days revolve around finding positions we can hold and feed comfortably and feeling baby latch on comfortably. Whilst this sounds straightforward, lack of normalcy of breastfeeding means we rarely have images of what this looks like, meaning we must discover this afresh for ourselves. We must step into the unknown and begin to explore what works for us and our baby.

"I was induced at 42 weeks, went into hospital on the Thursday and she wasn't born until Sunday. I barely slept and felt utterly exhausted when she finally arrived. I struggled to feed in hospital.

The midwives showed me how to hand express and we tried feeding colostrum from a syringe. It was painful, frustrating and unsuccessful. During her first night, Lucy cried a lot. I was in a curtained cubicle on a ward with several other babies who were wakeful and crying so neither of us were getting much sleep. I remember pacing around my bed holding Lucy trying to stop her crying. Whenever I tried to breastfeed she seemed unable to do it and would cry again. I was so tired, I remember my legs giving way and knew I couldn't stand any longer.

I thought to myself, *Well I've got to lie down as I'm too tired to sit or stand. I will just try feeding her lying down.* At that point I'd never heard of anyone breastfeeding lying down and I didn't really think it was the correct thing to do. I remember finding it quite a funny idea through my very blurred state of mind. Anyway, it worked! I don't know if Lucy fed much on that occasion, but within a couple of minutes we were both asleep, and in the moments before I fell asleep I remember thinking, *It's working!* and was quite pleased with myself.

That was a memorable moment for me.

It makes me laugh now to think it never occurred to me women can breastfeed lying down. Since then, I have spent countless hours doing so with both children."

Catherine, Mother to Lucy, 3 and Tess, 20 months

Catherine illustrates the impact of the invisibility of breastfeeding and how deeply such a lack of images penetrates our experiences and expectations. As women growing up in a bottle feeding culture, we come to breastfeeding blind, if we come to it at all. Yet we have our instincts, and our baby's biological expectations to guide us, and it is through learning to listen to those instincts within and letting go of culturally dominant messages, that we begin to experience confidence, transformation and empowerment.

"I definitely thought it was going to be easier than it was. I studied the theory a lot, but it's one of those things you've just got to do to learn how. I don't think anyone can really teach you how to breastfeed your baby."

Lizzie, Mother to Izzy, 6, James, 4 and Lloyd, 1

"One of the reasons I imagined breastfeeding would be easy was I (wrongly) assumed it would be easier with larger breasts – actually it turned out that wasn't the case – partly because my nipples point down rather than out, so advice about positioning seemed difficult to follow – also I couldn't see whether my son was properly latched on as my breasts were in the way!

I'm glad I persevered through difficulties and the support from my Independent Midwife made all the difference. I'm so glad to discover this amazing capacity of my body and I'm in awe! It's been an amazing lesson in 'practice makes perfect' seeing as you so quickly have to start doing it so many times a day."

Mary Ann, Mother to Edward, 7 months

Sometimes sticking with it, especially at first, can be challenging. Yet as Deborah found, there is no *one* way or *right* way, but rather the way or ways that work for you;

"James would only breastfeed lying down, no other way, and as time went on would only feed from the right breast, totally rejecting the left. So this is what we did! I fed him on one side and this worked for us."

Deborah, Mother to James, 4

No two mothering paths look or feel the same; our milestones come through recognising and embracing our individuality. Being guided by love and compassion to do what feels right for our baby with the support and capacity we have at each moment, we make decisions and move forward. For some of us this will be continuing to breastfeed, sometimes smoothly, sometimes with difficulty, and for others of us, the best path feels like letting go of difficulties and switching to formula, and as Michelle illustrates, we can create our own path combining both approaches;

"Breastfeeding was difficult, after much expressing and delight at filling a 5 ml syringe, taking drugs to help my supply... all the time my daughter being hungry, we took the decision to bottle feed. After two weeks with a small milk supply I tried my best to breastfeed but she was having none of it. The frustration for both of us was having such an impact on new family life, I switched to expressing with formula top ups, and this worked well for us."

Michelle, Mother to Skye, 3 and Oakley, 1

Milestones of Motherhood sets out to lessen the gulf between different experiences of early motherhood and instead seeks to recognise the shared path upon which we all walk and the wider landscapes influencing our journey. However early motherhood evolves, we all experience great transformation through learning to love and care for our babies. Let us recognise the similarities of our experiences; our tenderness and vulnerability, and have empathy for ourselves and each other.

'He wants to feed constantly...'
Alongside learning how to physically hold baby, so too are we learning to recognise when to feed. Unlike formula feeding, breastfeeding does not work effectively by following a timed schedule. Rather, we need to follow our baby's cues, feeding him when he indicates a desire to feed, as this is how our milk supply builds. This requires fathoming a whole new language of communication through movement, gesture, nuance and emotion and requires our astute observation;

"I was recently looking back at videos of my eldest son in his early weeks and one stood out for me. He was lying in his basket displaying EVERY classic feeding cue – twisting his head, licking his lips, reaching his fist to his mouth... and I was, at the time delightedly recording it as 'baby does cute stuff'.

I laugh now at how obvious his messages were, if only I'd been able to read them. I think I learned this stuff pretty quickly, although there were still many occasions in the early months when I found myself asking, 'What do you want?' when I felt I'd tried everything."
                    Eleanor, Mother to Thomas, 3 and David, 10 months

As we come to recognise his feeding cues – turning his head, opening his mouth, bringing his fist to his mouth – we quickly realise just how often he seems to want to feed. For many babies, milk and suckling meet their needs for comfort, closeness, interaction, reassurance, calming and soothing to sleep, alongside nutrition and immunity.

Alongside practical learning unfolds the growth within our inner landscapes as we struggle with, and eventually accept and even embrace the amount of time they do indeed need to feed. Often this requires a *huge* inner shift in how we perceive what we do and how we spend our time. We come to realise just how much our babies need us and how intense the work of mothering can be. So many of us struggle with feelings that we are constantly feeding and *getting nothing done*. Our milestones lie in learning to rediscover the great *worth and value* in our time spent nurturing, connecting and feeding.

"The first 14 months were a bit of a blur, mainly because of lack of sleep. She seldom had a daytime sleep and never went more than 3 or 4 hours through the night without a feed. I was determined to breastfeed on cue rather than regiment feeding to every 4 hours as was the 'done thing' in those days.

So I spent most of my time with her attached to my breast or crying and was exhausted. The reality of having to put another's needs first, 24/7, was quite a shock initially, and a wake-up call that life had changed irrevocably.

But I persevered and I'm proud of myself for that. In the scheme of a lifetime, 14 months is not so long really. I was there for my baby whenever she needed me day or night, and breastfed for 14 months until she decided to wean herself. That coincided with the first time she slept through the night. I woke in shock that morning thinking she must be dead... but she was fine and so was I. We had survived phase one together!"

Fran, Mother to Emma, 35, Jack, 32 and Edward, 29

Fran recognises a significant element of our transformation, and one which many of us struggle with – putting our baby's needs before our own, day and night, at least in the beginning. And when we realise these dependent little ones have needs pretty much constantly, we begin to realise just how much our lives have changed. This adjustment can be tough; it can be hard to give so much of our selves. In addition, so much of the time and energy of mothering is rarely recognised, let alone valued, by the wider culture which prefers to focus upon our return to "normal" and return to the workplace.

We are embarking upon the milestone of surrender; as we surrender to our baby's needs, so too do we open the door to feelings of deep love, connection and joy. We open ourselves up to loving and mothering and the process transforms us. Mostly it feels we are doing this blindly, feeling our way through doubt and exhaustion, yet our milestones come as we listen to the call of our inner landscapes and develop tentative confidence that we are doing okay.

"Before becoming a mum I was into sports and the outdoors and was used to pushing myself. These experiences helped with breastfeeding as feeding two was a huge physical challenge. The pure amount of time involved is immense, and it takes a big emotional commitment to commit to feeding them fully, and long term.

I was feeding pretty much constantly. It took a huge amount of commitment. But it was, and is worth it; it was through this intense time of feeding I learned about truly being there for them, being present and meeting their needs."

Natalie, Mother to Sam and Oliver, 2

Slowing into acceptance

Certainly we *do* a great deal for our babies and children, yet mothering is about more than the things we do. It is an *attitude*, a *commitment*, a *sense of being with* our children; present, available and welcoming. We resolve to be there with them and for them, not always *doing*, but sharing time and space, *being* together. And it is through the many hours spent feeding them we discover this milestone.

Our babies need to feed an enormous amount, yet so too do they need us to observe them, to hold, carry, cuddle, soothe, connect, change and care for them. Through being together they signal their needs and we respond. So whilst we are constantly engaged with our babies, busy on our inner landscapes reflecting and connecting, and busy on our physical landscapes feeding, holding, changing and keeping ourselves fed as we can, still many of us have this overwhelming feeling that we are "doing nothing" and "getting nothing done"!

Prior to motherhood, many of us were busy; we are brought up encouraged to be busy and doing "something productive". After the anticipation and intensity of birth, we can find the constant days of baby care a very different pace; things are slow and repetitive, yet constant. And whilst we are constantly busy, probably more so than before, we often feel exasperated, wondering *What have I achieved?* or *Why can't I get anything done?*

This is a vulnerable, yet profound time of transformation; yes, our frustrations may highlight the tasks we are not completing, or even getting round to starting, yet what we are learning is the very *essence* of mothering; *being there* for, and with, our babies, connecting, understanding and meeting their needs. We shift from *doing to being*, recognising mothering as a *constant process* rather than a distinct task, and feeding, in all of its intensity, is a wonderful teacher.

Valuing mothering work

Babies are designed to feed frequently; their stomachs are tiny and our milk is easily digestible and uniquely tailored to their developmental stage. Our milestones come as we begin to understand

and accept their intense need to feed as normal development. Then we can begin to really *value* the time we spend feeding as time well spent, an investment in our children's health and wellbeing, yet this does not mean we will not find it tiring and frustrating at times;

"I realised early on it was my job to meet my baby's needs. Needing frequent breastmilk is part of their neurological development; would it be better to say 'no' and deny their needs? Of course it wouldn't.

I see my job to continue to meet their needs, but more so I want to meet their needs. It's that inner shift which occurs as you become a mother, you know things intellectually, but emotionally, you feel like you want to be there for them. I find it hard, and tiring, feeding two through the night, but I want to do it."

Natalie, Mother to Sam and Oliver, 2

A significant milestone for many of us is casting off the cultural paradigm of "spoiling" babies, and instead deciding to meet their needs fully. We journey through our own resistance, as well as society's outdated expectations, into understanding, accepting and embracing our baby's physiological needs.

Far from *doing nothing* we can re-envision time spent feeding and soothing as vital mothering *work*. And as we learn more of the lifelong health properties of breastfeeding, we can marvel at the physical, intellectual and emotional nourishment our babies receive. As we come to think in this way, even though at times we can still find it difficult, constant and demanding, we can *enjoy* what we are doing, *embrace it*, and recognise it as worthwhile and valuable.

Milestones come as we value time spent *being together*, making the shift from *doing* to *being*. As we give ourselves permission to rest, slow down and enjoy our babies, many of us experience spontaneous moments of love and happiness amidst exhaustion and overwhelm. To onlookers nothing may be noticed, yet as mothers, holding and connecting with our baby we can feel bliss, closeness and waves of love. These are milestones many of us come to appreciate again in retrospect once our children have grown. We look back at the baby days with memories of love and simplicity.

"I loved breastfeeding, I loved the enforced pauses, just having to sit and cuddle close, for hours each day."

Lizzie, Mother to Izzy, 6, James, 4 and Lloyd, 1

We begin to realise that time spent sitting, lying, cuddling and feeding is dear and precious, especially as we notice how quickly time passes. Bonding is not something that happens only in those moments after birth, but rather takes place with every interaction. Each time we look at her, as she meets our gaze, each time we touch her warm skin, talk and sing, each and every one of these interactions become the tiny threads which, woven together, become the fabric of our lifelong relationship.

Emergence and formation of our *Mother Selves*

The slow paced, intense and constant nature of responsive feeding serves another purpose; it gives us time to think, read, reflect and consider our evolution into motherhood. With my daughter in my arms, as she fed, slept, woke and fed, week after week, I found myself reading, thinking and also *feeling* a great deal about motherhood; my *Mother Self* was coming into being.

It is not just with our intellect that we mother, but also with our awakening instinct and intuition which shape our approaches and guide decisions. Time spent feeding gives us time to deepen into our inner landscapes, an enforced pause to explore, feel, reflect and deepen into our mothering identity, hearing the whispers of our awakening *Mother Selves*. It was through these times I resolved I would not leave her to cry; I realised my personal priorities at this time were meeting her needs then preparing healthy food to nourish the family.

I felt my *Mother Self* forming and emerging more strongly alongside the realisation that things wouldn't be this intense forever. This milestone – of recognising the transience of breastfeeding – can help immensely with the frustrations, exhaustion and intensity of early breastfeeding as we realise this is but one short period in our lives together;

"When my daughter was born I had no idea how to properly latch her on, my nipples were sore and bleeding. I was lucky to spend 5 days in hospital and eventually got support. For four months she was constantly on the breast, then one day she fed for fifteen minutes and was done until she was ready for her next feed.

I was astonished.

I was so proud I managed to get through those first months, mastitis, sleepless nights, sore nipples. After that initial time, I started to enjoy breastfeeding. It wasn't painful, I was giving my daughter the best food and I was feeling proud of myself as a mother.

I couldn't give my daughter everything, I failed to give her the birth I wanted but at least I managed to give her the best food."

Alicja, Mother to Roza, 3 and Konrad, 1

Just as the heat of the furnace removes impurities and melts solid ore into pure molten liquid ready to be cast into a new shape, our time submerged in the constancy of responsive mothering burns away our rigidity and expectations. This overwhelming intensity changes our being, from the inside out. We become molten, letting go to be re-formed, fit for a new purpose. We emerge as mothers with a deeper understanding of what our baby needs and the capacity, strength and willingness to respond.

When breastfeeding is challenging

Certainly, there is happiness and relief as we get to grips with feeding, and become more confident getting out and about with our baby. Yet it takes time to find a new rhythm. Alongside the general exhaustion and overwhelm, breastfeeding difficulties can make the early months incredibly stressful.

Some of us might find our nipples tender as we adjust to the sensation of feeding, and there can be an intense feeling as the baby draws the nipple deep into his mouth, but feeding itself should not be painful, as babies suckle on the less sensitive breast tissue, not our nipples.

"I thoroughly enjoyed feeding once the pain of engorgement had passed. It was painful as he first latched on, like an intense electric shock, but it only lasts a minute or so then it's fine."

Amy, Mother to Simon, 25 and Edward, 19

If we only experience a short burst of sensitivity as our baby latches, and our nipples adjusted quickly, we are likely to feel we got off to a good start. Yet for some mums, breastfeeding is acutely painful throughout the entire feed; our nipples become sore, cracked and bleed and the whole experience becomes painful and stressful. Our babies may seem unsettled and hungry, we may see blood in our milk, experience pain and mastitis and receive well-meaning advice which suggests moving to formula. This may feel like the best option if we do not have accessible, friendly and effective support to help navigate these difficulties and it is for such reasons many women switch to formula.

Sadly, good breastfeeding support is not always easy to find when we need it most and as new mums with extremely painful, bleeding nipples and a screaming, hungry baby, we are vulnerable. We may blame ourselves rather than seeing our situation within the wider politico-economic context.

If we do seek support, often the first thing we'll be advised to consider is our baby's latch; does he seem to take a wide mouthful of breast as well as the nipple, or does it look like he is only suckling on the nipple? If he doesn't manage to get our nipple drawn back past his hard palate and instead suckles on the nipple itself, it can cause pain and he will be less able to extract milk effectively. For some of us, receiving help that shows us how to encourage him to open his mouth wider helps navigate this early problem and we move on to pain-free feeding.

Yet sometimes problems can be more complex; it may appear from the outside that baby *is* latching on well, yet pain remains. Our nipples become damaged, baby does not seem to be feeding effectively and weight gain may become a concern; we can feel alone and frustrated, anxious that help is not yielding a solution.

We may eventually conclude that it is we who are to blame, that we do not have enough milk; that the process is not working. Such feelings undermine our confidence as we struggle with sadness, anger, frustration, injustice and disappointment, unsure as to why breastfeeding is so challenging. If this is your experience do consider calling one of the breastfeeding helplines – the National Breastfeeding Helplines run by the Association of Breastfeeding Mothers, the Breastfeeding Network, La Leche League or NCT, as well as continuing to seek help locally.

Could it be tongue tie?

Tongue tie describes a condition where baby has restricted movement of his tongue due to the membrane beneath the tongue (the lingual frenulum) being too short or too tightly attached to the base of the mouth, restricting free movement. Baby is unable to extend and move his tongue sufficiently well to effectively withdraw milk, meaning he latches on too shallowly causing pain and reduced milk extraction. Once diagnosed (based on both the appearance of the tongue and an observation of how a typical feed goes), tongue tie can be treated simply and breastfeeding can continue, and in most cases, improve.

Whilst this may sound straightforward, the experience of feeding a tongue-tied baby can be distressing; we may experience intense, prolonged nipple pain, babies can become distressed, feeds might be long and difficult and we can have concerns over milk supply and weight gain. Sadly, there is vast geographical variation in expertise, diagnosis and treatment, meaning this distressing, yet rectifiable condition is often overlooked. Yet if our baby's tongue tie is recognised and treated early on, in the first hours or days after birth, issues can be resolved quickly and breastfeeding can improve dramatically;

"We spent a few hours together before he was whisked away, he wasn't feeding well and blood tests showed problems. It turned out he was tongue-tied and after snipping his frenulum he fed better and thrived.

In the early days I had lots of problems with engorgement and sore nipples. I remember breastfeeding with tears flowing down my face because of the pain, but after a few days at home these difficulties passed once he got the hang of feeding."

Sharon, Mother to Christian, 3 and Jessica, 6 months

"After the first 36 hours I was in excruciating pain. Luckily I had an Independent Midwife who diagnosed tongue tie and performed a minor operation to fix it. It wasn't immediately easy to feed again, he lost 10% of his weight and having been born at the 75th percentile, dropped to the 25th – I was worried initially but in time saw he was slowly gaining weight."

Mary Ann, Mother to Edward, 7 months

Even when tongue tie is diagnosed and treated quickly, it takes time and perseverance to find a new breastfeeding rhythm as baby must relearn the mechanics of feeding with increased tongue movement.

Many issues with pain and poor milk transfer can be addressed with careful attention to positioning and attachment, helped by a skilled supporter. But undiagnosed tongue tie is another reason women experience pain and find breastfeeding does not seem to be working as well as it could. Tongue ties are by no means uniform and they can be hard to spot even by professionals. Becoming informed about this ourselves, and seeking out specialised breastfeeding expertise from a lactation consultant or breastfeeding counsellor, can bring fresh insight and change things enormously. Yet finding the time, finances and energy to do so can be incredibly difficult alongside the tiredness, anxiety and constant work of early mothering and breastfeeding.

Even when we seek help, we may not immediately receive the expertise we require. We may be advised to switch to formula, and may face a long and arduous journey where we struggle for weeks and months before either finding appropriate help or working things out ourselves;

"Breastfeeding was so hard at first. There was so much pain, and I was so ignorant – on his second day he went seven or eight hours without a feed and it didn't occur to me this might mean there was anything wrong. We narrowly escaped a hospital admission for jaundice, but then had a huge hill to climb with diagnosis and treatment of tongue tie.

I hadn't realised how certain I was about breastfeeding until it proved hard. This was when I saw I had to carry on – I was hating it, but couldn't stand the thought of giving him anything else. This slightly negative motivation saw me through three solid months of whole evening cluster feeding whilst in a lot of pain.

I wish I'd had the confidence to trust my body and my ability to read my baby and meet his needs. I spent hours making charts of times between feeds, expressing milk in the hope he'd take a bottle, second-guessing milk production and worrying whether I could manage discreet enough public nursing.

Starting to feed without pain, after about three months, was glorious, as was the first day when every feed was comfortable.

Second time around this has been so very different. I love the frequent feeding, have no idea how often he feeds, and will do it anywhere – such hard-earned but precious confidence."

Eleanor, Mother to Thomas, 3 and David, 10 months

"Breastfeeding; the best and worst of times. The major milestone for me was unthinkingly bringing baby to breast without wincing, curling toes, examining the position and trying to remember what the textbook said.

The process took too long with both babies as I agonised over whether I was doing it 'right' – pointlessly as my babies struggled with undiagnosed tongue tie – and again after treatment when it took time to learn to feed with unrestricted tongues.

And wow it was messy.

Supply was never my problem, I was praised in hospital for how much I could express, I was told it was great my baby had gained weight, then felt like a cheat when that couldn't be maintained at home as I knew I couldn't keep syringe and cup feeding and had to see why attachment wasn't working.

Diagnosis and treatment of posterior tongue tie (in both babies) was a huge relief and starting the breastfeeding journey again gave me trust in my body."

Jenny, Mother to Matthew, 3 and Lucy, 14 months

Diagnosis and treatment for tongue tie varies enormously area to area. An independent midwife, doctor or lactation consultant may be able to diagnose and treat tongue tie at hospital or in your own home in one area, whereas mothers living elsewhere may need to travel large distances;

"I'm proud to live in a country that provides the NHS but feel very let down by the lack of breastfeeding knowledge and how clinical systems and targets get in the way of supporting mothers.

I felt ashamed to pay for private help but so incredibly relieved that someone listened, observed and understood, looked, touched and felt to understand my babies' mouths, provided a procedure that worked and finally made me feel like I wasn't going mad. I'm sad for all those mums who think they can't feed because they don't receive good support."

Jenny, Mother to Matthew, 3 and Lucy, 14 months

Receiving a diagnosis of tongue tie is a milestone in itself and may come at the end of a difficult journey. It brings relief and explanation for why feeding has been so difficult; the frenulum can be snipped and often we can continue feeding with lessening pain. Yet, sadly, not everyone receives a correct diagnosis, or if they do, they still may lack the support to work on positioning too, and breastfeeding continues to be fraught and painful.

We may continue to receive guidance which fails to bring improvement and are often told to supplement with formula. This may feel like the best path given the extent of our pain and the impact of stressful feeding on our physical, emotional and mental health and enjoyment of mothering. Yet sometimes this is not the path we feel able to take as it goes against our deep desire to breastfeed. This leaves us in a difficult and isolated place; we feel compelled to continue, yet it is painful and complicated and external help fails to yield improvement;

"I had a lot of pain for the first three months. I tried everything, saw several breastfeeding counsellors and read everything I could. We were both treated for thrush, tried nipple shields, nipple creams, different positions, expressing, part bottle feeding. You name it!

Nothing seemed to work and I found myself crying in pain every time she latched. It was awful. I was so upset because I kept thinking I'd just have to stop when I really didn't want to.

I'd been looking forward to this aspect of having a baby for a long time, although I don't think I realised this until I was faced with not being able to breastfeed.

No one ever gave me a diagnosis for the pain, but eventually I think my body just got used to it and gradually the pain began to fade away. It had taken three months of discomfort but I got there in the end and was so pleased I was able to continue.

I couldn't believe Lucy then breastfed until she was about 15 months old. After such a difficult start, I felt I'd achieved a lot in being able to keep the breastfeeding relationship going for such a long time. It taught me a lot about my own strength and determination as a mother."

Catherine, Mother to Lucy, 3 and Tess, 20 months

Seeking experienced help can rule out tongue tie, so it is always worth persevering in asking for support, yet if such help does not bring a clear solution, we can feel it is up to us to take stock of the situation and make our own decisions regarding moving forward. Catherine illustrates the potent transformation held in such times as we learn more of our depths, values and determination.

Milestones of strength

Experiencing challenges feeding her son, Louise found herself on a difficult journey, yet the help and support of her partner made a world of difference. So often the importance and role of our partner is overlooked, yet their attitudes, help and availability has a significant impact on our breastfeeding journeys. For Louise, her partner's love and support provided space for her to find and trust her instincts and persevere through challenging times, emerging as the strong, confident and loving mother she is today;

"Difficulties unfolded with our first baby who struggled to keep milk down from day one. He appeared to be in constant discomfort, vomited a large amount of most feeds and slept very discontentedly.

Breastfeeding was a nightmare for ten weeks. My nipples were ripped, cracked and bleeding and the infant feeding advisor said they were in the worst state she'd seen in her career.

I cried, or fought back tears at most feeds, stamping my feet to try and manage the pain without letting my baby see me upset. He fed every half hour for months, cried before and after feeds and pulled off suddenly, ripping my nipples.

I expressed with a hospital machine to give each breast a rest every few feeds and had mastitis five times with a raging temperature requiring antibiotics despite my aversion to them.

However, I knew instinctively breastfeeding was important to my baby, and after ten weeks things started to settle down, my breasts healed and feeding became comfortable thereafter, despite being very frequent.

I'm so glad I persisted, and couldn't have done it without the full support from my partner. Breastfeeding provided essential bonding and comfort for my baby and I during the difficult months that followed, and due to my son's emerging difficulties, became his only source of nourishment way beyond the usual 4–6 months.

Neither myself nor my partner were breastfed as babies, so we had little support or understanding on that front. I am now so proud of myself that I was so stubborn in persevering.

It's something I enjoyed for 2 years with my first child once we got through the initial hurdles until he self-weaned, and have now enjoyed every feed for 10 months with my second. It brings a huge sense of contentment, in part from the hormones released and in part from the feeling of achievement, knowing my baby enjoys it and doing something great for my baby's long term health. I realise breastfeeding is only one of many things a mother may do for her children, but in my case, it is an essential source of bonding."

Louise, Mother to Flynn, 3.5 years, and Rowan, 10 months

Anyone reading Louise's story – and unfamiliar with breastfeeding – could easily think she was doing herself a great disservice by persevering with something causing such pain and suffering. Yet when we see her struggle was motivated by love and a strong instinctive knowledge that breastmilk was what her baby needed, we see a powerful example of how love and instinct intertwine, helping direct sustained determination to ensure the wellbeing of our child. Louise's son went on to develop severe and multiple food intolerances. For many challenging months, breastfeeding was an invaluable part of his nutrition and recovery.

Louise's milestones speak of strength, grit and steely determination. Whilst these may not be the pretty side of motherhood, they are essential and awaken us to the deep, primordial strength we hold within. As mothers we come to realise that on the one hand we possess great love, nurturing and gentleness, yet if times are challenging, we may discover indomitable resolve, strength and power. Our *Mother Self* is gentle and loving, yet so too is she tenacious, fierce and single-minded in our children's nurture.

Some of us are introduced to such strength during labour, and for others, it emerges as anger and passion at not having the birth we hoped, yet it emerges, one way or another. This may not be the beautiful, graceful imagery of motherhood we expect, but rather a powerful strength enabling us to unearth new will and determination. As mothers we learn to embody these seemingly opposite elements of the Feminine; gentleness, love and nurturing alongside immense power, grit and unwavering tenacity.

We learn to walk a dual path; strength guided by wisdom and love. The world can learn much from a mother's inner journey; for great strength can lead to great accomplishments, when tempered with great wisdom and love.

We experience such love, power and instinct in different ways; for Louise and Catherine it brought energy and motivation to continue with breastfeeding, yet for others, instinct guides us differently. Our strength and love hold us as we decide to let go of breastfeeding despite this being what we so dearly wanted. As Ronne, Alison and Zara share, struggling with breastfeeding pain without effective support or hope things will improve is incredibly challenging.

Whilst moving to formula is not what many women want, a practical, survivalist part of ourselves awakens, saying this may be what *needs* to happen at this time. Once again we are reminded how so much of our journey is about deepening into love for ourselves and our babies, surrendering, and deepening into love once more.

When it feels impossible
Sometimes, breastfeeding isn't the beautiful, nurturing experience we'd hoped for. Instead, it may be fraught with difficulties. Pain, the rapidly deteriorating state of our nipples, high levels of anxiety and concerns about weight gain mean continuing feels impossible and counterproductive. Also, we may encounter the little-known condition of Dysphoric Milk Ejection Reflex (D-MER), which means

that rather than experiencing feelings of love and satisfaction when feeding, we feel uncontrollable waves of anxiety and overwhelming sadness and negativity each time our milk lets down. Whilst there is excellent support "out there", this is not always within reach when we need it most. Many women ask for help many times yet the help does not always bring forth effective solutions and again illustrates our collective, systemic loss of breastfeeding knowledge.

"Breastfeeding issues clouded our first few weeks. Despite mine and the midwives' best efforts, she refused to latch on for more than a few minutes and would howl in frustration and misery when she kept coming off again. I was in agony and took paracetamol with codeine before every feed, which would usually be a high stress ordeal lasting about an hour and a half as she clamped on then kept coming off, screaming hysterically.

She would scream, I would sit there quietly sobbing, biting a pencil between my teeth to handle the pain.

We got further advice from midwives and health visitors – nobody could explain why she still hadn't got the hang of it or why my breasts were still so raw. I was so determined to feed her myself – in the end we got two electric pumps and I pumped both breasts when she woke for a feed while my husband bottle fed her the breastmilk from the pumping session before. It meant we were both up for night feeds but it was the only way we could keep up my supply to her demand, and my husband was amazingly supportive.

I kept that up for about five months until we switched to formula, as my supply started to dwindle. Pumps are no substitute for the real thing – but it was the only way I could feed her for as long as I did. I felt so guilty switching, but also relieved; I was no longer tied to breast pumps, I got my energy back and best of all, I was finally allowed the luxury of feeding my daughter myself.

I always felt awful when we were out and about and felt I was getting judgemental glances for feeding her with a bottle – sometimes I wanted to scream to people to listen to the journey we'd been on. A couple of people said, 'It's a shame you're not feeding her yourself.'

As I'd been so passionate about breastfeeding, it was particularly hard to take."

Zara, Mother to Izzy, 4

"I was sent home from the Maternity Unit using a nipple shield and my baby wouldn't feed without it. This slowed down the amount of milk he was receiving, so feeding took longer. Friends advised to 'starve' him into being willing to take the breast without the shield. I felt that was too cruel, I couldn't do it.

I was so tired, I was falling asleep sitting upright feeding him – that was scary, waking up to find 20 minutes had passed without being conscious.

Then at about four weeks he began to lose a tiny amount of weight and my Health Visitor suggested switching to the bottle. This broke my heart but I knew I couldn't let him lose weight.

Even when I switched, things weren't much better; he wanted 8 smallish feeds a day rather than the usual 6, so I was constantly sterilising bottles and feeling terrified I wouldn't have sterilised them correctly and would poison him."

Alison, Mother to Callum, 23

Alison and Zara illustrate that when breastfeeding feels more difficult than positive, our anguish to do our best for our babies intensifies and we become increasingly fragile and vulnerable. When support fails to bring improvement, it can feel heartbreakingly disappointing to have to let go of breastfeeding, yet such decisions are motivated by intense love and compassion for our baby, even if this goes against what we would ideally choose.

Realising such decisions arise from *love* and the desire for our baby to be well-nourished can help us to perceive feelings of guilt from a new perspective.

"Breastfeeding began well – but didn't proceed smoothly. Within a couple of days my nipples cracked and bled; pain every time I fed was intense. The breastfeeding support nurse was on holiday, so a variety of people tried to show me how to hold Dan and get him to latch on properly... I felt bombarded by different approaches, rather than supported.

I felt pressured, still in pain from the C-section, my hormones were all over the place, I felt completely overwhelmed. Hospital nurses offered nipple shields and UV light therapy, neither of which made any difference. All the while I was battling 'baby blues' (I cried at the drop of the hat). I began expressing milk which was laborious and made me feel like a cow.

By the time we came home, I'd been persuaded to supplement with formula, so once again felt like a failure. I hadn't been able to give birth naturally; now I couldn't feed my son properly. One midwife who came to check my scar said smugly, 'Well, I fed all four of mine no problem. Some can do it, and some just can't.' I don't know if she meant to make me feel completely inadequate and incompetent, but that was the effect her words had.

More tears. More feelings of failure.

I kept trying. My nipples kept bleeding. When I expressed there was blood in the milk. Daniel didn't sleep much, I was completely exhausted. Neither I nor my husband had any family nearby; we were relatively new in the area so I hadn't had a chance to make friends locally. I felt alone, overwhelmed by despair and desperation, going rigid in anticipation of pain every time I put my son to my breast.

Eventually my health visitor persuaded me that feeding should be relaxing and pleasurable for both of us, and if that meant giving him formula, it would benefit us all. So, reluctantly, but with some sense of relief, I switched, telling myself I had done my best. The health visitor was supportive and caring – the closest thing to a mother I had – assuring me my baby would thrive, and I was doing what was best for him. He did thrive, but I felt I'd failed in some very fundamental way.

I still feel that even now, nearly 30 years later. The deep sense of longing, and the pain of loss I feel when I see a woman breastfeeding is hard to articulate."

Ronne, Mother to Daniel, 28

Ronne's story is so incredibly tender; yet we can see that the failure and inadequacy is not hers at all, but rather lies in the lack of effective breastfeeding support. As breastfeeding knowledge has all but disappeared from our communities, we tend to look to medical experts, many of whom have no personal experience of feeding, hold differing opinions and whose training and practice is often unknowingly coloured by the influence of the formula industry. It is difficult as new mothers to see the wider political and economic factors influencing our situation when we are tense, emotional and exhausted. Rather, we perceive it as our failure, and internalise much guilt and distress within our inner landscapes.

If we had to let go of breastfeeding, we simply have to find other ways to nourish and nurture our baby. Whilst breastfeeding is one expression of love, mother love is deeper, more resilient and more encompassing than any single action. We must find new ways forward; news ways to nurture, nourish and love our little one. Little by little our fledgling relationship develops, we bond, love and nurture, and find new confidence to move forwards;

"So I fed my baby from a bottle, and we bonded – at first it was through the constant repetition of the daily routine of feeding, cuddling, washing, dressing, nappy-changing... over and over... with each bath, nappy change, feed, we were looking at one another, I was talking and singing to him – and felt the surge of wellsprings of love I did not know I contained. It was deep and shook me to my roots, in a good way. I remember the first time he smiled at me – at about three weeks old, when I was holding him and singing to him. I felt everything inside me melt."

Ronne, Mother to Daniel, 28

Ronne's words are of vital importance; we are more than the sum of our parts and the actions we take. Our love is strong and infinite and comes from within. Regardless of how our babies are born and fed, by far it is our love and sustained presence which nurtures their early experiences of life. We can hold them close to our hearts, be caring and responsive to their needs, stroke their soft skin and talk to them softly, letting them know how very loved, wanted and safe they are.

Weight gain, growth charts and 'Is he getting enough...?'
Another manifestation of the cultural dominance of formula feeding is the question of how much milk baby receives. Formula feeding has all but eroded the collective sense of trust in a baby receiving the perfect amount of milk to satisfy his needs via the supply and demand mechanism of breastfeeding. Instead, a culture has evolved which focusses on measuring amounts of milk in fluid ounces. This serves no purpose when breastfeeding, rather creating much anxiety and undermining trust in the process. One of the most significant milestones we encounter is letting go of the need to *know how much* baby has had, instead learning to trust the process of supply and demand and recognise the signs that he is receiving plenty.

If breastfeeding begins well we are more likely to feel able to trust this process;

"I'm so glad I haven't had any major problems with breastfeeding and have been able to trust myself and my body to feed my newborns exactly what they need, without measurement."

Harriet, Mother to Riley, 4 and Leon, 1

Yet where concerns are raised about weight gain our journey

rapidly becomes stressful and arduous, at times feeling like a journey of doubt and despair rather than love and trust. Yet such difficulties can become fertile ground for awakening us to deeper aspects of our strength and instinct;

"My resolve to breastfeed was tested pretty soon because Barnaby lost 12.5% of his bodyweight in his first five days and we were packed off to see the paediatrician. We got off to a slow start with breastfeeding – it was 48 hours before he got interested in feeding, but as far as my husband and I were concerned, we were doing all right.

Barnaby was a 'happy spitter' – regurgitating seemingly huge volumes of milk after every feed, although fortunately he was never upset or in pain with it – he was feeding every couple of hours and wasn't unhappy. I remember the midwives asking what my supply was like and if my milk had come in, and looking back now I don't feel they helped the situation. I knew my milk had come in but I was never one of these women who was painfully engorged and leaking milk all over the place. So I didn't answer those questions the way they expected I don't think.

I remember being in the car on the way to see the paediatrician thinking this was going to be the first test of my mettle as a parent – if they told me to supplement with formula, was I going to have the guts to say no? I was determined I would – I had already begun to trust my instincts as a mother – but happily I never had to find out. The paediatrician could see he was strong, healthy and happy, so we were sent home and told as long as he started gaining weight within the next three days, they'd be happy. He did – and never looked back... this made me enormously happy and proud, and amazed at what my body could do."

Hazel, Mother to Barnaby, 15 months

"The early days of breastfeeding were a struggle for me. Not because it hurt but my son just didn't really suckle. Trying to ensure he was getting what he needed was the absolute worst part in the really early days.

I tried to express, but failed dismally. It's an awful process and when you only get a dribble it gets incredibly disheartening. My health visitor told me to stop as it was only discouraging me and making me feel worse. I was advised to top-up with formula.

I remember feeling really aggravated because my latch had been assessed at hospital, with the midwife at home and health visitor; all of whom said my latch was perfect. And it was. It was just that the little so-and-so didn't get the whole sucking thing. It's very hard to explain.

He must have been getting something as he was having wet and dirty nappies, but his weight dropped a couple of times which had the midwife and health visitor on high alert. Unfortunately my son was weighed after a day of non-stop screaming where he would not take the breast and also refused to take the bottle. I know now babies can drop (and put on) weight very quickly. My midwife told me if his weight dropped again he'd probably be taken to hospital, which put me in the state of a near nervous breakdown. I remember my husband being furious with her.

It was at this point I nearly had a meltdown, as the midwife told me she would be back to weigh my son the next day. I remember being up all night getting my son on the boob every hour on the hour determined his weight should pick up. I was terrified my son would be taken away.

I remember the midwife coming back and my son's weight had picked up. I remember telling her his weight had probably dropped as when she weighed him last he'd had a day of not drinking anything as he hadn't been well. This seemed to fall on deaf ears. The outcome was I was monitored very closely and had health visitor visits for weeks.

My son is a very bright, alert boy and even the health visitor had to concede to this, although he never regained his birth weight percentile, something my health visitor couldn't believe.

Eventually I got signed off from the health visitor and heaved a huge sigh of relief. I knew my son was fine, even if his weight curve was two lines below where the health visitor thought it should be. The upshot was I rarely went to weigh-in clinics as I felt really aggravated by the whole business.

I was so worried at one point I booked an appointment with my GP who told me to ignore the weight charts, I had a perfectly healthy, happy baby.

The thing about being a new mum is that it really is a voyage of discovery and if you are told something by your midwife or health visitor you take it to heart. Throughout all of this, the biggest thing I learnt was to trust my instincts. I am a good mother. I know when my son is ill and when he isn't.

A big milestone for me was to accept that it is okay to know that I DO know what is right and best for my child.

I'm glad I persevered with breastfeeding. I thoroughly enjoyed it.

So much so that I'm still feeding him at 15 months. My next huge milestone will be when to stop. I'm dreading it!"

Melanie, Mother to James, 1

Melanie illustrates the intricacies of our learning; the physical skills of feeding alongside understanding what is normal and what may be of concern. Such experiences lie at the heart of our transformation. We begin by hearing the whispers of our instinct; that all is, indeed, well, or that something may be amiss. Yet then we must develop the trust to listen, and the confidence to act upon our inner knowing. Being in close connection with our baby supports this unfolding process;

"With blossoming pride I carefully transported our six-day-old to his check-up. The midwife asked how things were going, to which I replied fine, and she asked to weigh him. I confidently stripped his clothes and nappy, hoping he wouldn't wee, and she placed him on the scales. Checking his birth weight she calmly informed us he'd lost a lot of weight, far more than expected in the first week.

She asked to show her how I fed him, and my unease grew as I tried to breastfeed. He didn't suck very well at all. She could tell I had the right position, but he wasn't doing his part. My heart was already beginning to make its way up to my oesophagus when she said we need to take him to hospital; I felt an all-consuming guilt.

My precious boy was not a week old and I'd unwittingly let him go hungry. The guilt suffocated my heart.

On the drive to hospital I cried. On arrival I was sodden and heavy with emotion. Flicking through that day's copy of *The Sun*, I failed to see the funny side of staring at a pair of perfectly formed mammaries whilst my own breast was violently pumped by a machine.

We were admitted to the maternity ward, hours passed yet my tears and increasing hysteria did not.

Once alone in the room, I closed my eyes, took a deep breath and gave myself a talking to. My own mother's stoic influence on my subconscious reminded me there was no more time for tears. I sternly told myself I am his mother, and it is my responsibility to see he is well. I reassured myself I was not a failure because I couldn't breastfeed him properly, and wrote in my diary, *As long as he was eating something, I didn't mind.*

No longer was I the irresponsible twenty-something. No longer could I just cry and wail and expect others to sort things out for me.

This calmness and clarity of thought soothed my previous guilt. I am his mother. Yes I gave birth to him, and became his mother physically, but it was not until I was faced with a crisis, both of my competency and his health, I realised my responsibility to him. I was his mother and had a job to do."

Corrine, Mother to Henry, 3

Weight gain concerns are common in the early weeks, bringing intense anxiety and foreboding. We know our baby needs milk to survive and when feeding seems not to be going well it shakes us to our core.

Corrine's story brings a powerful insight into our shifting perspectives and growth through motherhood; in passing through vulnerability we connect with deeper parts of ourselves and emerge stronger, wiser and more experienced, able to move forward with clarity and confidence. At times we may feel we are drowning in guilt, anxiety and overwhelm, yet as Corrine illustrates, we cannot stay lost in our inner landscapes for too long; we have to awaken to the here and now and meet our responsibilities. Our baby is much more helpless than we are and needs us to find a way forward. And it is this necessity to carry on from which we grow. He knows not of our ideals or inner struggles, only that he needs us and feels safe in our arms.

Measuring milk

Many times at our breastfeeding group I remember mums having detailed discussions about how much milk their babies had taken. I remember feeling astonished, overwhelmed and intimidated by how much information they held about the amounts their babies were consuming. I never felt I could join in these conversations as I truly had no idea how much milk my daughter received. I just knew she fed often, posseted sometimes, drank more, fell asleep, drank more through the night, was putting on weight and filled her nappies. I even stopped counting how often she fed and took the clock out of our bedroom as it really didn't help with tiredness. Instead breastfeeding became a journey of trust, surrender and acceptance that she knew what she was doing and was receiving enough to meet her needs.

Many of us have our babies weighed and their growth plotted on percentile charts. This can be reassuring and useful, giving us and our health visitors an overview of our child's growth, yet if our babies do not follow the growth projections, these weigh-ins can become a source of great anxiety. Some babies continue to follow their percentile line of birth but for many others growth patterns vary. The charts act as a safety net to identify feeding difficulties or underlying health problems, yet for many babies, growth simply occurs at their own rate according to individual and hereditary metabolism, appetite and personality. It can be hard to work out when there is a real problem behind slow growth, and when it is just that our baby is "finding his line" on the chart – and sometimes those telling us to ignore the charts can be giving us false reassurance.

At first we may not recognise this individuality and if our baby's growth does not concur with the chart projections, the early months can become overshadowed with anxiety, doubt and comparison. Far from trusting the process, we begin to desperately calculate amounts of milk which may lead to expressing, measuring and bottle feeding, often further complicating breastfeeding. Once again we see how the dominance of formula feeding continues to erode the breastfeeding process and the trust we place in it.

"My baby lost 10% of his weight in the first few days, I was worried initially but in time saw he was slowly gaining weight.

I've since begun to feel the obsession with weigh-ins and percentiles is uncomfortable for me. I actually haven't weighed my son since week 8 as I feel he is developing well and the exact weight doesn't seem important. I have noticed it becoming a source of stress and worry for other new mothers and I think that's a shame."

Mary Ann, Mother to Edward, 7 months

Finding our own way
Much advice, whilst well-intentioned, is based on scheduled formula feeding and undermines breastfeeding supply and demand. Scheduled feeding, supplementing with bottles, making baby wait for breasts to "fill up", and sucking on a dummy all reduce time suckling directly at our breast which causes milk supply to diminish. We must pass such comments through our inner compass, discerning what is useful and what is not. Once again we are called to learn, understand and listen to our inner knowing then find the confidence to act accordingly.

"Despite having every intention to breastfeed, it wasn't easy at first. I was in agony every time he fed and couldn't believe how much he fed. I had people telling me he fed too often and I should leave it longer between feeds. But I refused to listen, not sure if it was my stubbornness or listening to my instinct. I kept feeding him on cue and I cried lots!

My husband said he thought putting him on bottles might not be such a bad thing if I was so stressed. I said 'no way' and would give it until five weeks, which I did, and everything clicked into place. My nipples didn't hurt anymore and I'd accepted how much I needed to feed."

Harriet, Mother to Riley, 4 and Leon, 1

"I know it sounds bad, but I was lucky I didn't have family close by. If I did I wouldn't have had the physical strength to carry on breastfeeding. Every time I called my mum or sister I heard I should give my daughter a bottle, that she's not gaining enough and is hungry. But I could just put the phone down and carry on."

Alicja, Mother to Roza, 3 and Konrad, 1

"The health visitor was concerned about one of my twins, saying he wasn't putting weight on and had dropped more than 10%. They threatened me with hospital and wanted to put him on a feeding regime, but this went against what I felt was right for him.

He was a little jaundiced, his birth had included forceps, so I imagine he had a sore head, and was more sleepy so wasn't feeding as well as his brother. I was totally committed to breastfeeding and knew I could do it. He didn't need hospital, he needed a calm, quiet home and to be able to feed as much as he wanted.

I'm sure my personality beforehand helped; I was used to overcoming problems and barriers and had the self-confidence I could overcome this. I trusted myself and my body and see breastfeeding as the normal way to feed a baby.

Being a health professional I knew how things worked, I knew he wasn't malnourished and they would have to have my consent to admit him; I knew they couldn't just take him into hospital, and I knew he just needed some time to settle and to feed in his own way and this is exactly what happened."

Natalie, Mother to Sam and Oliver, 2

Natalie illustrates how our experiences of mothering and breastfeeding are not standardised, but rather draw heavily upon our previous life experiences, knowledge, perceptions and beliefs. We can remember this is also the case for those offering advice; we can explore where suggestions come from, and often discover they lead back to past personal breastfeeding difficulties and a formula-dominant culture.

Night feeding can attract particular attention, as this can be something we find especially challenging and may share feelings of exhaustion and exasperation with others. Yet much advice is, once again, ignorant of the hormonal supply and demand system of breastfeeding. We may be advised to 'give him formula to make him sleep through' or 'put him in his own room', not respond, let him cry, or 'self soothe'.

Night feeding can be exhausting at times, yet as we come to understand more of the breastfeeding process, so too do we realise how it is a crucial element. Hormone levels governing milk production are higher during the night, so night feeds help establish and maintain our milk supply, and feeding, suckling and closeness are essential comfort to babies through the dark hours of the night.

Rather than following advice which undermines supply and demand basics and dismisses our baby's needs for milk and closeness, many of us look for other changes we can make to improve quality of sleep. For me, after some weeks of feeding in a chair then attempting, always unsuccessfully, to put her into her cot asleep, I brought her into my bed, fed her lying down and co-slept.

This felt like a wonderful revelation as I no longer needed to sit up in the chair and struggle with her waking constantly as I lay her in the cot. Rather she woke, we fed, then we slept. Co-sleeping is an arrangement many families come to, from desperation as well as choice, and when it is set up safely can make responsive nighttime parenting much simpler. It also happens to be the normal nurturing practice for the majority of the global mothering population!

"Breastfeeding led to bedsharing for us. Barnaby fed every two hours from birth, I just couldn't sustain that night after night if I was getting up and sitting in a chair. Something bad would have happened – at best I'd have dropped him.

So into the bed he came, and at 15 months he's still there. To be honest I didn't want to bedshare, because I was worried about how we'd ever get him out – and my husband is ambivalent about it too – but I simply did what I had to do to survive.

Only now is he beginning to sleep slightly longer stretches (sometimes 3–4 hours, hurrah!) and hopefully if that continues then we'll see about gentle ways of encouraging him to sleep independently. I'll miss the cuddles in the end though!"

Hazel, Mother to Barnaby, 15 months

Sharing feelings and experiences with like-minded mums can make a world of difference. We can share feelings of exhaustion and mammoth night feeding sessions and be met with empathy rather than advice to go against how we wish to nurture. We can share tips for getting through the tiredness and talk about different sleeping arrangements. Such friendships can be a breath of fresh air as we realise we are not alone, that others feel this way too, and understand the reasons we want to nurture our baby at the breast despite the tiredness.

"I looked on Facebook for sites locally that supported my parenting style, it was great being with like-minded mums and sharing, growing and supporting each other. We met up and became really good friends. We organised an event called The Big Latch On locally. An international event where mums latch on at the same time to raise awareness for breastfeeding.

We organised a fundraising festival for families with money going to the local NICU. It felt great to do something that gave back and be part of something supporting other mums."

Shelley, Mother to Leia, 3 and Anya, 1

Beyond babyhood

Once difficulties have been overcome, breastfeeding can become one of our most valuable elements of mothering. We deepen in understanding of the immunological, emotional and physiological benefits and the tender connection reminds us just how precious and fleeting these baby times are;

"I love breastfeeding my son, it gives us such closeness and will always calm him whenever he cries. He's nine months now and I plan to keep feeding him as long as he wants and needs."

Charlotte, Mother to Raffy, 9 months

"Especially now, as my daughter grows and starts to show her character, the difference between her as a playful, aware child and a child on the breast is beautiful. Her eyes instantly switch to dreamy, trusting mood. It's complete comfort, for her and me. She recently discovered laughing on the breast, it's so sweet.

In some moments I find feeding exhausting, when it's taking a long time, is all I can do, or when I'm sick or need sleep. But overall it's one of the things I love most. Connecting to my child in silence. It calms me on busy days, and she's so happy and relaxed from feeding and touching my skin.

Hanneke, Mother to Vita, 2

As Hanneke illustrates, breastfeeding continues to be a source of connection, nourishment and nurture as children grow. Observing and understanding the comfort and benefits, many mums choose to continue feeding alongside introducing solid food, and WHO guidelines recommend for breastfeeding to continue for two years and beyond. My first daughter loved breastfeeding alongside the new world of food, so we carried on; breastfeeding remained a time of connection. Like many toddlers and young children who continue to enjoy their time at the breast, she would return for a feed and a cuddle at those times she needed comfort, reassurance, a nap or respite from frustrations.

"I'm preparing to start weaning and can't imagine I'll stop breastfeeding anytime soon – I really can't see why I would as it now feels like the most natural, simple and efficient way to nourish my son as he starts to explore food."

Mary Ann, Mother to Edward, 7 months

For busy toddlers there is great intensity in the world around them and across their emotional landscapes. The availability of the breast provides a form of "reset" for their little bodies and emotions, soothing them as they feel tired, frayed and overwhelmed. The combination of physical closeness, suckling reflex, milk, emotional connection and time where they can completely let go and be held physically and emotionally is a *wonderful* mothering tool. It supports them in regulating their own emotions, contributes to our ongoing positive relationship and provides support through illness.

Whenever my toddlers became overstimulated, ill, hurt or upset, they'd crawl into my lap to feed and cuddle. Within a few minutes their bodies relaxed and they softened in my arms, their previous intensity dissolved away. This biological "reset" offers them a way to let go of turbulent emotions, and reconnect and recentre in a way they've been doing since birth. Once calmed and comfortable, which often only takes minutes, they are off playing, chatting and exploring once more.

My milestones surrounding sustained breastfeeding (in which children breastfeed until they no longer have the need and wean in their own time) was to let go of critical comments from people who had no experience of this kind of long term feeding. Instead, I deepened into trusting my instincts and my children. In doing so I continued our journey of instinctive, responsive parenting where my children enjoyed the comfort and immunological support of breastfeeding through the years of their early childhoods.

We also discovered tandem feeding, where an older sibling continues to feed alongside a newborn, and created some beautiful memories of babies feeding alongside older siblings, little hands clutched together. Over time, breastfeeding became less important as they outgrew their need and gently expanded into further independence. Now these intense years are behind us, I've forgotten the exhaustion and frustration at not being able to "get stuff done"; rather I look back with warm memories of the seeming simplicity of my younger children at the breast and am reminded of just how precious this time was and how quickly time passes.

"I never planned to breastfeed more than six months to a year but it just kind of happened, I ended up nursing my eldest until he was 3 and a half. Then my second was born and I plan to let him self-wean also. I think it's so beneficial for the children and makes your relationship so close.

If you're going to breastfeed full term it's nice to have friends who are doing the same. There are phases when your child is, say, over 2 and wants to feed all the time and most people think it's weird, but then it's nice to have someone to talk to who can say, 'Oh yeah mine did the same at a similar age, they'll grow out of it.' It's good to have someone who understands why you are doing it and doesn't try to persuade you to wean when they aren't ready."

Harriet, Mother to Riley, 4 and Leon, 1

We may still face challenges feeding older babies, yet at this stage we are so much more confident and established in ourselves as mothers that we simply see these as issues that can be overcome, rather than – as in the early days – intense and possibly insurmountable challenges;

"I had a lot of discomfort early on, and the constant regurgitation was soul-destroying. Then we hit our stride for a few months, until Barnaby started getting teeth and turned into a Biter. With a capital B.

There were some days I was getting bitten at every feed; whatever I tried didn't seem to stop it. There was never mischief in his eye – I genuinely believe he was in pain and that was how he dealt with it. But I shed a lot of tears and there were times I felt angry for the pain he caused me.

It got to the point I seriously considered weaning him – but by this time I'd read quite a lot about breast milk and came to the conclusion that however hard it was, I wanted to just grit my teeth and get through it. I wanted to do the best for my baby.

Eventually the biting got less – although even now I get the occasional nip, but usually when he's asleep or just nodding off – and I feel like we're in our breastfeeding groove again. Since he turned one I think I'm enjoying it more than ever – perhaps something to do with him being mobile now and also me going back to work – we're not in contact as constantly as we used to be, and breastfeeding is such an easy and enjoyable way to reconnect.

I want to get to two years, in line with the WHO guidelines, and maybe even beyond, depending on how much he's feeding at that point."

Hazel, Mother to Barnaby, 15 months

Amidst the busyness of the toddler years, perhaps when we're back at work or having a particularly hectic day, breastfeeding provides an oasis of calm and quiet in which we can return to each other, relax and reconnect;

"I returned to work part-time when she was 8 months old and expressed at work for a further 18 months – that milk was taken to our childminder. I stopped expressing at that point as I seemed to be getting less off. But she fed as much if not more when we were together."

Jane, Mother to Sarah, 8

"Ella is now nearly four and a half and still has a very loving relationship with the boob! When we started I had no idea we'd still be going strong now. She tells me she will 'just stop one day as a surprise'. Part of me is SO ready to finish, but another part will mourn the end of this aspect of motherhood. You get the best cuddles ever at the boob!"

Ann, Mother to Ella, 4

Certainly, a milestone is breastfeeding coming to an end. For some of us, this happened earlier in our journey than we would've liked, perhaps in circumstances beyond our control and against our wishes. Sometimes, we feel very ready to move on, yet at the same time, feel the mourning of the passing of this intense stage of mothering.

"As for breastfeeding milestones, my biggest was stopping feeding. It was heart-wrenching, but I fed each one until they were ready to stop, but I was very sad to be losing that most intimate of times with my babies."

Marie, Mother to Jean, 11 and Lewis, 9

"Breastfeeding was never an easy journey but I fed James up to his second birthday at which point he was feeding less and just stopped. I would have preferred to feed him for longer but accepted his decision and focussed on the fact that despite difficulties, we'd shared that special time for two years and both done our best."

Deborah, Mother to James, 4

Often with child-led breastfeeding, weaning does not occur as a significant milestone, but rather happens almost without our noticing, slowly and simply as part of their unfolding development. We won't know it is their last feed until they don't ask to come to the breast again, as simply, that need has been fulfilled;

"She slowly self-weaned. I don't remember when exactly but it eventually became only at bedtime when she fed. After age 7, it wasn't every night, it just slowly stopped, completely on her terms."

Jane, Mother to Sarah, 8

Joy, awakening and transformation
Breastfeeding can awaken us to deeper truths surrounding our power, wisdom and Femininity. Merging the qualities of love, gentleness, nourishment and perseverance across our emotional and physical landscapes teaches us of the intricacies of our Femininity and is worlds away from the tabloid portrayal of breasts as sexualised objects.

A positive breastfeeding experience can transform how we view our bodies, breasts, and experiences of Femininity. Such a transformation can be profoundly healing; inspiring new trust, confidence and self-esteem. Such shifts create positive ripples throughout our landscapes which we can pass onwards to our daughters and sons;

"I had big hang-ups around my boobs as a young woman, I had a large bust and was very uncomfortable with this. Yet after exclusively breastfeeding my daughter, continuing for nine months, things totally shifted. The breastfeeding experience gave me a different sense about what my boobs are for; I see them in a different way now. I see what they have given her. This hugely increased the confidence I had in my body, and became a positive spiral for me to feel more confident and positive about myself in other ways.

I saw how society is, how it sexualises the body, and through my breastfeeding experiences, this all melted away. It's nonsense. I see what my body is really for and how strong and nourishing it has been for my children. This brought deeper confidence in myself and my body which I want to pass on to my daughter."

Margaret, Mother to Leon, 20 and Rebecca, 17

"I had no trust in my body. I blamed it for my miscarriages and letting down our babies who didn't make it into the world.

When I had my amazing babies I needed my body to be useful and nurturing, and breastfeeding was the way we achieved this."

Jenny, Mother to Matthew, 3 and Lucy, 14 months

Breastfeeding can bring a deeper dimension to our perceptions of body image. We can see weight gained in pregnancy as purposeful, for milk production, and imagine it fuelling our baby's development. We can find beauty in our new and changing body, coming to further love, accept and embrace ourselves for who, and how, we are as we deepen into love for ourselves and our babies;

"Continuing to breastfeed, and now enjoying it, finding a way of ease reminded me of the amazing power and efficiency of my body – the fact my son has been entirely fed and nurtured through my body seems amazing. It's something I feel positive pride about."

Mary Ann, Mother to Edward, 7 months

"The all-consuming need to nourish my babies overshadowed any conscious thought of how my body looked post-pregnancy. In fact I recently came across a picture of my pale, wobbly self skin-to-skin with my son in the early days and felt I was beautiful in that time.

The intensity and emotion (even as I write), swamping rational thought, has only happened like this since becoming a mother, and it feels wonderful."

Jenny, Mother to Matthew, 3 and Lucy, 14 months

Such experiences are nothing short of revolutionary compared with the mainstream messages urging mothers to "take control", diet, exercise and "regain their pre-pregnancy body shape". Once realising the great effects of breastfeeding for ourselves as well as our baby, many women feel an uprising of passion and energy, becoming inspired to help others as Mother Supporters, Peer Supporters or Breastfeeding Counsellors for breastfeeding support charities or the NHS.

Connection and awakening spirituality

Through breastfeeding we become more aware of our shared experience with mothers through time and place. In our busy, individualised lives, we tend to feel distant and separate from women around the world whose lives seem worlds away from our own. Yet through feeding and nurturing our babies we may reflect, perhaps in the quiet hours of the night, how there are millions of others who are also, at this moment, and across time and space, quietly loving and feeding their babies just as we are;

"I've never allowed myself to feel uncomfortable feeding in public; I'm just doing what is normal in the majority of the world."

Louise, Mother to Flynn, 3.5 and Rowan, 10 months

Natalie describes how an awakening across her inner landscapes led to profound empathy and connection with animal mothers;

"Surprisingly, I've been feeling more connected to animals through breastfeeding. I remember taking my sons to a wildlife park and seeing a gorilla with her young. The baby was having a cuddle and suckling, then holding on being carried around. I felt a real connection to that gorilla. It sounds funny but I realised, 'I'm just like you; I understand how you feel.'

I saw a pig lying down feeding her nine piglets. I felt that connection again, compassion, really strongly. I realised we felt the same. It felt amazing to know how that pig was feeling! I realised just how close we are to other mammals, that we are all connected, that we are not, essentially, different, but the same."

Natalie, Mother to Sam and Oliver, 2

Breastfeeding speaks to us of our connection with other mothers – be they human or of a different mammalian species. All of us are striving to nurture, protect and care for our young. Despite our differences we are reminded that mothering is part of something much greater than solely our own baby; we are contributing to the nurturing and continuation of all life. The flow of milk and mother-love connects us all. Breastfeeding speaks of the abundance of nature through the process of supply and demand. If we take time to reflect and muse over such truths, breastfeeding can be a catalyst for awakening greater spirituality, connection and understanding of the wisdom of nature.

In the small hours of the night, alert to the stillness and quiet suckling of our baby, we can experience an intense connection with them, and an expansion of our consciousness. Our somewhat altered state of mind, through exhaustion and hormonal surges, can awaken us to feelings of love, wonder and realisation.

We may feel something deep, meaningful and poignant, that this, being here, holding our baby in the dark of night, is somehow as right as life can get. And although we may not be able to put this into words, or even remember much of it in the morning, we may feel touched and deeply moved, as though, through our love and softening frame of mind, we have glimpsed a deeper truth beyond the frustrations and day-to-day exhaustion. We are awakened to places deeper than the busyness of our thinking minds – to our inner landscapes, the terrain of heart and instinct, of love, wisdom, intuition, power and deep Femininity.

Chapter Five
The Mothering Path

We learn to be mothers through mothering; we are constantly learning and engaged across our inner, emotional and outer, practical landscapes. Whilst busy across our practical landscapes, meeting the needs of our children (as well as attending to other commitments), an equal amount of mothering work occurs across our inner landscapes. We do not only perform a practical action, like making lunch or feeding a baby, rather, accompanying our actions is a parallel investment of constant thought, planning, research, evaluation and emotional labour, investment, connection and contribution.

Such inner work of mothering is diverse and constant; intellectually we find information and make decisions regarding how we hope to meet our children's needs, nurture their health and respond to their emotions. We give to our children emotionally through every interaction. We are *constantly* scanning the environment, processing information and emotions whilst maintaining an invisible thread of connection with our child. Such work would be highly prized in the professional employment arena yet remains mostly invisible in the context of mothering.

Our inner landscapes are multifaceted terrains, and alongside our processing and evaluation of our mothering tasks we experience our own feelings. We feel great tides of emotion, responsibility, guilt, frustration, exhaustion, overwhelm and tenderness alongside whatever may be unfolding within our physical bodies. Much of what we feel is heightened by hormonal reconfiguration, priming our being for optimal bonding, nurturing and connection.

"Some days I just get on with the day-to-day stuff of being a mum, then it would hit me what a huge responsibility I have; all the decisions I make will affect my baby. The choices and the way I parent will shape her. I had this huge swell in my heart and the enormity of it all felt like so much pressure – I have to get this right. The thing is we're humans, we make mistakes. Sometimes we don't get it right. Then the worry and the guilt..."

Shelley, Mother to Leia, 3 and Anya, 1

We invest great time and energy in researching what is best for our children's wellbeing, in terms of health, diet and discipline, as well as choices around childcare, education and other activities. In every form of business such research and risk assessment is established professional practice, yet in the realms of mothering, our efforts are rarely recognised as valuable. Incredulously, we are mocked, dismissed and labelled as "anxious" and "fussy". Yet again we see how mothering and the wellbeing of babies and children is undervalued by our wider culture.

It is through our constant observation, reflection, action and evaluation that we become experts. Far from "flapping" or "fussing" about whether our little one has his gloves and hat, has had a snack and has spare clothes, we are performing important work. Through knowing our child, we know that getting cold hands on a walk rapidly leads to discomfort, and taking him out without having eaten enough does not give him the best chance to enjoy being with friends. Knowing him, we realise he will find social interactions harder and may end up distressed more frequently than if he had eaten prior to the outing.

Through paying attention to detail, we nurture the process; we give our children an optimal chance to learn, grow and thrive, experiencing themselves at their full potential. Despite lack of value and recognition by wider society it is a milestone to recognise and value our mothering work in this way. Our milestones are entwined with how we value ourselves and our mothering work. Let us not trivialise our work by saying that we are "fussing", but rather, let us recognise the *worth and value* of the thought and physical work we put into caring for our child.

Certainly, these are small and constant tasks, yet it is all of these small things which lead to our children feeling, and being, loved and well-nurtured. Each time we meet their needs, we contribute to their feelings of self-respect, trust, belonging and self-esteem. We lay the foundations for their future happiness, emotional intelligence, positive relationships and intellectual and physiological development. Let us recognise this essential work and know its worth and value.

'Cherish the moments and the years will take care of themselves...'
This simple sentiment holds much wisdom and is so relevant to the parenting journey. At the beginning everything is intense, and we wonder how we will sustain it; how can we cope with months of continuous feeding and years of broken sleep. The path ahead, and weight of responsibility, feels insurmountable.

"I woke every time he cried, I remember one night, coming back to bed after feeding thinking, 'This is it for the next 20 years – him completely dependent on me.' I felt trapped – it didn't matter that I loved the little person trapping me beyond anything I'd ever known. In fact, that made it harder, because I knew I could never leave him. It was a staggering realisation."

Ronne, Mother to Dan 28

The constant, repetitive care of babies requires us to give more than we have ever given before, from the very core of our being. Their needs are immense and immediate, and mothering calls for us to give of ourselves deeply and constantly. And often we struggle, physically and emotionally, with repetitive daily tasks of changing nappies, mealtimes, bedtimes, getting them dressed and clipping them in and out of car seats.

Prior to becoming a mother, we may have felt organised and effective. Yet we soon learn that simple activities with small children can be overwhelming. Attempting to leave the house to get somewhere on time with a baby, who may, at any moment, need more feeding and nappy changes, can leave us overwhelmed and stressed before we even manage to gather together everything we need, find our keys and get out of the front door. As a mother in the house alone, managing to have a shower and make lunch amidst frequent breastfeeding, we realise just how many demands there are upon our time, and how limited, at times, our resources become.

Whether or not we return to paid employment, preparing meals, keeping on top of laundry and housework alongside keeping our children safe and stimulated is huge and constant work. And whilst our society has changed since the days of our grandmothers, and domestic work, food preparation and childcare is no longer seen as solely "women's work", all of these tasks still need to be done, and we must work out, within our relationships, how we will do this, and, often, how to balance this with paid employment. And in truth, women still carry out the majority of this work the majority of the time *alongside* paid work and other responsibilities.

Thinking of the whole is overwhelming; parenting spans decades requiring great responsibility and emotional and practical investment. Milestones come as we bring ourselves back from the overwhelm, back into the present moment, and remind ourselves to find the joy, love and simple pleasures of what we share with our children now. Let us consider the shift from *doing to being*, and see our constant interaction with our children as valuable, rather than measuring our worth in completed tasks and productivity.

Connecting with our children in the moment and realising mothering is much more a process than a task to be completed helps us release constant worry and future projection. We give ourselves respite and come to find joy and contentment in the small moments. We come to realise that indeed all we really *do* have is our connection with our children in each moment and this is both a mothering and spiritual milestone indeed.

"I cut out pictures from a catalogue and pasted them in a scrap book; then we looked at it together and he learnt the names of items. I just showed him the pictures and to my delight he was interested."

Alison, Mother to Callum, 23

Connecting with our child in the present moment is the *essence* of our mothering work. Once we begin to understand the value of connection, we realise it is the seemingly small moments which constitute our journey. Mothering is not a task completed, rather it is a mosaic or tapestry, built day by day, handcrafted from all the experiences, activities, emotions, love and connections we share.

As we come to realise the value of being present, we come to cherish the sweet, snugly, beautiful times; those moments where we stroke smooth skin, and hold warm bodies close. We can give ourselves permission to fully enjoy these lovely, fun and wonderful bits, for they are our treasures alongside the struggles and frustrations. We can let go of the need to know how it is all going to turn out and simply enjoy what we have now, in our arms and our hearts. For it is such moments which replenish our inner landscapes, giving us energy, strength and motivation to carry on.

'It goes so fast...'

We may find ourselves anxious, exhausted, overwhelmed from teething and growth spurts, wondering where we have lost ourselves. Suddenly we look at our baby and realise just how much he has changed. We realise, in an instant, how incredibly fast he grows and how quickly time passes. Like snowflakes melting though our fingers, we realise this process is beyond our control; we cannot pause time and keep things as they are. We realise these moments are incredibly fleeting and the old sayings are true; they are not babies for long and they do indeed grow so fast;

"It's the little things that make me realise my boys are growing up.

My eldest, aged 4.5, had quite long hair, but I decided as his hair grows fast we'd go to the barbers and get a shorter cut.

He enjoyed it and was chatting away to the barber. Afterwards he looked like a new boy, I felt quite emotional; he looked so grown up! I need to keep reminding myself this is going to happen often, things don't stay the same, they're slowly growing up.

My youngest is just starting to walk; he's toddling along, wobbly, getting steadier day by day. My baby is walking! How did this happen! He's not a baby anymore!

Again it feels strange, him growing to a different stage, leaving behind the baby stage, but it's exciting, and I need to keep reminding myself to enjoy each moment and embrace change!"

Harriet, Mother to Riley, 4 and Leon, 1

"I will always try to do my best and help my son in every way. I love him beyond words and enjoy all our time together. Even moments that are difficult or I feel tired, I remind myself that one day I'll wish I could have those moments back again. Children grow so quickly. Everyone tells you this, it's so true."

Deborah, Mother to James, 4

As our babies grow, we notice that things we once found difficult and worried over have melted away and we find ourselves facing new challenges. Rather than fearing we will be woken through the night *forever*, (although it certainly feels this way at times) or that difficult, challenging times, arguments, tantrums and strained relationships are the way our family has become, we can remind ourselves that these times, too, will pass;

"I always say to myself 'it's just a phase', or 'it will pass' when I'm finding things difficult or challenging. I think with each of our child's phases we have an opportunity to learn about ourselves, how we can transform and grow."

Harriet, Mother to Riley, 4 and Leon, 1

"Ella will start school soon. Part of me is ready for a change and new opportunities. But I know it will also be sad – the end of a magical and infuriating time.

Motherhood is sometimes enormously difficult. I find some things very challenging, such as what to do when Ella repeatedly will not brush her teeth or get dressed. All small stuff, but it can be very stressful! I've found I have to develop new reserves of calm and creativity to find my way through these phases, I find it amazing how you can love someone so deeply yet also find them immensely irritating (temporarily!) all at the same time.

Love is a complex thing. And I know that these challenges of early childhood are just the beginning. What is tooth brushing compared with broken hearts?"

Ann, Mother to Ella, 4

Valuing presence and relationships

Once we begin to understand the fleeting nature of childhood from the perspective of a parent, we value time spent with our growing children all the more. Although the early years can be incredibly challenging, rather than seeing them as something to simply get through, we come to see them as the gold dust of our parenting journey. We recall the exuberance of our kids splashing in puddles, purple-faced from foraged blackberries; stories they told us as we were trying to cook tea and just wished for half an hour of peace; pictures scribbled on walls; long, drawn-out bedtimes and early morning stories and cuddles. It is these moments that become the memories of their childhoods.

Anna, mother of six, reflects with tenderness upon the importance of the small, seemingly everyday moments, the things we would not necessarily recognise as special at the time;

"Now my children are adults, it's not the big milestones I think of most often but the ordinary, everyday things we took for granted. I think of the children jumping into our bed, walks backwards and forwards to school, long summer holidays playing in the garden or walking to the library coming back eating ice lollies. I think of winter evenings playing games, snowball fights. I think of them running around at the park or the beach.

Our silly little family rituals come to mind. Jumping in pillowcases on Christmas Eve, singing carols with someone playing recorder. I think of the Easter egg hunts, how when we came in from a day out Daddy always had to make beans on toast. I remember watching them unobserved as they sat and played or as they slept at night and bursting with love. I think of the times when some silly game made us all fall about laughing and the silly song we always sang on the way back from holiday.

These things didn't always seem like fun at the time. I remember sighing when they wanted to wash their dolls' clothes or help with some household chore that I hoped to get done quickly. I was irritated at times by having to listen to them chatter on about something when I really didn't have time. Now I would love to go back and enjoy those moments instead of wishing them away.

There were hard times, with tears and arguments and misunderstandings, illness and anger. But what I wish I could remember better are all those everyday things that, in retrospect, were not so everyday after all. At the time they were just part of the fabric of everyday life. They didn't stand out as any sort of milestone, but were the cornerstones of childhood. I realise it is these cornerstones that meant the most, and wish I'd appreciated so much more."

Anna, Mother to four daughters and two sons, all now adults, and grandmother of four

Anna is so right; it truly is the small things, time simply spent together, which we come to realise matters most. We can become so distracted by the seemingly bigger things – work, financial worries, the constancy of everyday tasks – that we forget the real value of simple connection; the seemingly everyday moments, cuddles, talking, nothing special, big or expensive, which we come to look back on as being most important of all. No doubt we will look back and cherish these moments when our children are far from our laps and our dinner tables, yet if we can learn to love, cherish and value the importance of these moments at the time they take place, we empower ourselves to feel the joy, beauty and absolute perfection of our family life, whatever form it takes, alongside the times we are struggling and things are not as we hoped.

Reminding ourselves to be emotionally present brings our family journey alive; we can shake ourselves out of just going through the motions, wishing they would be quiet so we could get on with something else, or wishing we were elsewhere doing something more necessary. Our awakening through intense years of mothering alerts us to the fact that time does not stand still, and that the importance doesn't lie elsewhere, but is here, right in front of us, in the connection we share with our children in each present moment. We can grow in gratitude as we realise just how blessed we are to have our children and our family life, no matter how imperfect or difficult it seems at times.

Lizzie puts into words the *shift from doing to being* which we experience as we grow from predominant focus on *doing* and productivity, to realising the importance of *being present* with our children.

"My focus shifted from productivity and the need to have 'achieved something' to having quality time and relationships."

Lizzie, Mother to Izzy, 6, James, 4 and Lloyd, 1

Mothering is a *quality of being*. It is about being responsive and connected to our children, sharing joys and supporting them through challenges. Understanding this helps us value what we do as mothers, especially when it is mostly invisible to others.

Often both as a culture and individually, we judge our worth and value on the "results" we achieve – what we have produced, what can be counted, seen, quantified and rewarded with pay. Yet as mothers, so often we feel we have little to show for what we have done that day, despite having not stopped for a minute. We may look around after a drawn-out bedtime and sigh at our messy house, sink full of dishes, the scattered muddy boots, wet coats, toys, pens and the like, and feel a sense of despair. Yet as we come to perceive our work from milestones of *valuing relationships*, *being present* and *recognising the immense worth* inherent in spending time with our children, we begin to see the value within our work.

Yet this is not a straightforward journey, for as much as we may value mothering, we still have to find ways of managing the practicalities alongside caring for our children and any other work and activities. For many of us, it *is* a struggle to keep on top of our homes, laundry, employment, shopping and preparing food alongside responsive baby care, school runs and a home filled with the joy, challenge and creativity of energetic children. Most of us are still struggling to figure out how to do this, often single-handedly.

Catherine speaks of adjustment and reflection and how she ultimately came to see the toys, felt pens and playdough accumulated through the day, not as a sign of her failure, but as evidence of the joy, fun and creativity she facilitated and shared with her children. Her story is testimony to our transformation; changes on one level effects change throughout our landscapes.

"There are many times when I stand in the middle of the house and look around feeling a real sense of despair. I'm naturally a tidy person so it drives me mad to be surrounded by a mass of strewn toys, piles of laundry, just stuff everywhere. In the past I've wasted energy tidying up in the middle of the day when I'd have to do it again in the evening anyway. But even knowing this is not always enough to stop me trying to regain some control of the house.

In having children you inevitably lose a lot of control over your life – like when you can sleep, go out etc. I think trying to keep the house tidy is quite significant for me in that it represents one area in which I can have some control.

Over time I've definitely become more relaxed, I had to. I still hate the mess; the food thrown on the floor, endless spillages, but I accept it now as part of the fabric of life with children.

Sometimes I'm even able to like it a little and have a slight feeling of pride that I'm able to let my children be children and make a mess. I guess in that respect they are actually teaching me to be a bit more relaxed and less controlling, which is good! I have started to try to look at the state of the house at the end of the day as a representation of what I, and my children, have achieved that day.

If the playdough is still out on the table, and there are pens and paper lying around, and jigsaw pieces and Lego, then I can look back at the day and think, 'Yes, we did all of those activities today.' I now have to scrape playdough out of the carpet and clean felt tip off the table and pick up Lego and jigsaw pieces, but at least I know the children experienced all those activities today.

I try to look at all that has gone on around the house as a constantly changing patchwork of our day-to-day routine. It's always messy, but it makes me feel proud that I'm here to be part of that picture in my children's lives."

Catherine, Mum to Lucy, 3 and Tess, 20 months

Over time Catherine came to re-envision her mothering on a deeper level; whilst being messy, her house reflected times of shared creativity, play and connection. We may not see the immediate benefits of love, connection, creativity, listening and reading stories being assimilated into our children's psyche, forming the bedrock of their self-esteem and emotional wellbeing, yet we have the material reminders from the times we shared. Such a shift in perspective can help us value what we do and bear the years of mess and chaos.

Devoting ourselves to parenting... for a while
Knowing the benefits of our presence for our children, and how time passes quickly, can help us become more willing to be present with

our children. We can let go of resistance to be elsewhere and allow ourselves to meet our baby's needs completely. We can become more comfortable to give of ourselves fully for we know it will not be like this forever. We only have to look at the bags of outgrown baby clothes and developmental stages passed to know how quickly time passes. Rather than rushing to get our own life back on track, we can accept how life has changed, embracing the intensity of early mothering and the new directions it heralds.

"As someone fully committed to attachment parenting, I was there 100% for my children. They are now young women, and as I do things for me, I smile and think: those years flew by, it really was no sacrifice to give of my time.

The early years were intense. My daughters are 22 months apart and there were many times I felt I was in a straitjacket. What it did do for me was make me appreciate the moments of time to myself as they grew older. I came to really appreciate the pressure cooker years, and now the way I use my time is incredibly productive."

Veronika, Mother to Bethany, 19 and Eliza, 17

Rather than seeing mothering as something which "takes over our lives", robbing us of our freedom and independence, we can embrace the intensity of the experience and meet new milestones of perception, value and acceptance as we do so. We can grow to re-envision this time as a different season of life. Yet initially, this is a difficult milestone to realise, as culturally, we have little framework from which to take inspiration. The predominant model seems to value striving to get *back to normal*, back to work and generating income, with little voicing of the transformative path we have embarked upon and the new potentials it offers.

There *are* some voices inviting us to be there fully for our children, including the instinctive voice within us, yet these voices are not loud or mainstream. No wonder many of us find ourselves feeling lost during maternity leave, trying to claw back time from our children to regain our previous selves and sense of place and identity in the world. Yet if we had other models to follow, would we still feel this way, or might we embrace mothering as a worthy and valuable element of our life journey?

"I became pregnant in Bali; the Balinese culture upholds pregnancy and mothering as a spiritually revered and valued element of

Femininity. Such perceptions are embedded within the art, culture and social structure. If women continue with work, they work slowly, at their own pace. Mothers and children are at the centre. Becoming pregnant in Bali gave me a deep sense of wellbeing, positivity and happiness to trust pregnancy and motherhood."

Alex, Mother to Jude, 9 months

As we embrace how life is changing and open ourselves up to new landscapes of learning and connection with our children, we begin to awaken parts of ourselves long forgotten, or not yet discovered. Louise explains how through letting go of expectations she discovered a new sense of wonder and simplicity as she spent time getting to know her children and experiencing the world through their eyes;

"We love to explore the world, and assumed we'd be off to Mongolia in a rusty camper with our small children! We considered big trips, but if the kids are happy we're happy at the moment, so tend to do things that are least stressful and most fun overall.

Through being a mother I've learned how to enjoy the smaller things in life, which I previously didn't appreciate enough. Watching my 3-year-old be chuffed he can climb higher in the playground, seeing my baby beam on his first go in a swing, enjoying a short walk and picnic together, making sandcastles, throwing stones, watching butterflies and bees, making things out of playdough or cardboard and seeing my little boys delight in what they've made; being able to enjoy a nice sunny day because I'm off work and not stuck in a grey, stuffy office as much as I used to be.

So many things that before becoming a mother I either couldn't experience or took for granted. We hope to do the bigger things in the future, but plan to wait until both boys are older to appreciate and remember."

Louise, Mother to Flynn, 3.5 and Rowan, 10 months

Amy recalls experiencing a similar shift in wanting to be there for her children and not seeing this as a sacrifice of her time, but as something she inherently *wanted* to do. This resonates with the *inner shift* Natalie spoke of earlier; we intrinsically *want* to care for our babies, tending not to see this as a "chore" or "inconvenience". Although we are tired, we still *want* to do it because we want to meet their needs. Interestingly, Amy recognises the role of our shifting hormones in cultivating such feelings;

"The hormones women experience through pregnancy, birth, breastfeeding and mothering helped me enormously to bear the housework, time with the children and to be there for them 100%. This was what I wanted to do, I wanted to be there with them as much as they needed me, this didn't bother me at all, they need you, and you do it, I had no resentment for the housework at all, yet now everyone is older, and I'm working too I feel it shouldn't just be me who still does it all."

Amy, Mother to Simon, 25 and Edward, 19

Amy raises interesting issues regarding how, as times change and children become more independent, the role of the mother is perceived by others and the expectations which may still be projected onto us despite the needs and capabilities of everyone in the home having changed enormously.

Embracing ourselves, nurturing change

We may value gentle parenting and respectful communication yet there are likely to be times when exhaustion and frustrations get on top of us and we mother less well than we would like. Such times present milestones of opportunity; experiencing ourselves behaving as we *don't* want can bring us great insight.

We can learn more about the causes of our anger and frustration and identify areas where our own needs may be overlooked. We can see our anger or frustration as a gift; we can see it as an instruction to take care of ourselves, to listen to our own needs as well as meeting the needs of everyone else. We return to the elusive, recurring milestone of caring for ourselves as lovingly as we care for our children.

Rather than blaming our child or shutting out those aspects of ourselves that we don't like, instead we can look within with love and gentleness. We can listen to the parts of us which are hurt, excluded and angry, and rather than judging, we can be kind. We can recognise we too are learning, we can ask ourselves what we truly need to be able to care for ourselves and our children as we would like.

Recently, I shouted at my youngest as we were rushing his sister to her trampoline club. In the minute I was completing a form for a new library card and gathering overdue books he poured water over himself and turned on the computer. This meant I had to take time to turn it off as well as get him fully changed, and still return the books and get to the class on time. I felt frustration rising as I screeched, 'I've just put your shoes on!'

As I set about finding new clothes and yelled at the girls to stay in the car and stop arguing, I saw his little face crumple. He began to sob. My frustrations shifted, and in their place I felt a well of guilt and shame as I saw things from his point of view: he wanted to watch a cartoon and loved pouring water. My heart opened to him as I saw things through his eyes and I felt awful for rushing him and making him cry. I reflected on all this and made an effort to be more connected to him, to say sorry for shouting, to have fun with him at the park whilst his sister was at her club, realising that I caused much of the stress by trying to cram too many things in and rush him along to keep up with the pace of other family members.

This became an important milestone for me; I realised I can get frustrated if I'm rushing and trying to do too much. It helped me to understand that I need to give myself and the children more time for certain tasks, and reaffirmed my belief in peaceful, respectful communication. It reinforced the importance of making sure that I look after myself and am not overwhelming myself to the extent that I snap and shout at my kids. Whilst it is easy to say *we need to take care of ourselves*, sometimes it can take us *not* doing so, becoming out of balance, feeling the results of exhaustion, frustrations and frayed tempers, to motivate us to breathe deeper and make sure we *do* give ourselves the space, support and rest we need, enabling us to meet our little ones more often with love and less often with frustration.

"One of the greatest lessons I keep living over and over is to take care of myself. I learned that if I'm going to take care of them, I have to take care of myself physically, emotionally and spiritually."

Violet, Mother to Sasha, 10, April, 9, Sam and Josh, 7 and Isaac, 2

Unfolding empathy

Seeing how our needs being unmet can spill over into frayed tempers and tense communication enables us to develop empathy, understanding and compassion towards ourselves and others. When we see another mum shouting at her kids in a supermarket, the looks of judgement on the faces of passers-by are clear to see. Yet knowing how we, too, can feel and behave when stressed and exhausted, we can see this mum through eyes of understanding and compassion. We can empathise, knowing no one gets it right all the time; we do the best we can with the reserves of energy and patience we have left that day.

None of us start the day planning to shout at our kids, yet tiredness and the strains of the day combined with whatever else we may be holding across our landscapes, can leave us with less patience, tolerance and understanding than we would like. When we or others are struggling, rather than being judgemental, let us be empathetic, offering kindness and compassion to the other mum, or parts of ourselves, which are struggling.

Alongside the cultivation of empathy and compassion we learn to practice and model apologies, reflection, self-awareness and moving through conflict. Rather than ploughing on in our bad mood, continuing to blame others, too ashamed or angry to admit we are wrong, we can use these outbursts as opportunities.

We can show our children that if our feelings and frustrations cause us to make mistakes, we can get through this with love. We can explain our crossness is not their fault; that we love them and that we are sorry.

We can use these situations to show that no one gets it right all the time, and that when we behave in ways we wish we had not we can repair relationships. We can embrace all aspects of ourselves, take full ownership of our behaviour and love ourselves more deeply. Through doing so, we share with our children valuable illustrations of how we, as families, can move through times of tension, conflict and big emotions.

We can take time to reflect and explore arising feelings, memories and thoughts; journalling is a useful tool for deepening such emotional awareness. We can develop deeper understanding of what causes us to feel upset or off balance and commit to meeting our own needs.

Developing awareness of our menstrual cycle and how we feel different at different times of the cycle is a valuable practice in increasing our self-awareness, recognising our needs and caring for ourselves more fully, as well as modelling more positive relationships with our body and cycle to our children. *Wild Power* by Alexandra Pope and Sjanie Hugo Wurlitzer is an excellent resource on cycle awareness and conscious menstruality.

Pressure of perfection

As mothers we feel immense pressure to be perfect. We know good nurturing is important for children's physical and emotional health; we want to get it right. Our babies are just so precious, *they* are perfect, and we want to give them the care and nurturing they deserve. And whilst mothers through time are likely to have felt this way, such pressure seems magnified today as we are deluged by the sheer volume of parenting information online and via social media.

We all have ideals of how we would like things to be; such visions keep us on course, encouraging and inspiring us to do the very best we can each day. Our commitment to good mothering combined with love motivates us to get up, day after day and night after night, to feed and comfort our children. Our resolve to validate their emotions and parent them respectfully reminds us to take time to listen to why our children started fighting or arguing, to hear both sides and hold the space whilst they talk, rather than responding only with punishment.

Yet there are also times when things are not as we hoped. We may struggle to realise our ideals amongst everyday practicalities or our partners may hold differing views, necessitating the need to compromise. We learn, grow and evolve as we balance our ideals and values with our practical resources each day. Perfection exists in our minds only; what is real are the needs of our babies and children and our varying capacity to meet such needs each day.

"I had to learn to compromise on things I previously thought important, sometimes because things are different to what I expected and sometimes because my partner and I have different views. I thought I'd dispose of television completely, but found I can minimise it to 20 minutes for my little boy whilst settling my baby for a nap."

Louise, Mother to Flynn, 3 and Rowan, 10 months

"I've put pressure on myself to be perfect 100% of the time – unrealistic. I want him never to be hurt – unrealistic. I want him to be happy all of the time – unrealistic. I wish I could keep him a small child and always with me – unrealistic."

Deborah, Mother to James, 4

Finding authenticity

Our aim is not to be perfect, but to learn day by day how to create a life whereby we live, as much as we can, in alignment with our values whilst growing to understand and meet our children's needs. With experience we come to know more of the reality of parenting and reach milestones of authenticity as we come to understand what feels right for ourselves and our children.

Through knowing and accepting ourselves and our children we become more able to find greater happiness and contentment. We create family life in our own ways and are more able to let go of the debilitating pressure of perfection. And this is where the alchemy unfolds; once we cease striving to be perfect, we are able to experience the healing balm of unconditional love as it weaves its way through our days. We create our own, individual, imperfect, authentic, family life, learning to do things our way and be okay with that.

"I was a better mother before I had kids! I had this lovely, but completely unrealistic picture in my head of what having children would be like. Of course, there are the lovely moments, but everyday life is hard work.

Today my little boy decided to spit up food on my arm while my two-year-old had a meltdown needing attention. I was weed on and woken every hour of the night, but I wouldn't change it for the world.

I love my kids, make many mistakes, but try to be as good a mother as I can."

Alicja, Mother to Roza, 3 and Konrad, 1

As Alicja illustrates, by accepting the chaos of our days and connecting to the core love for our children, we free ourselves from the crushing pressure to be "a perfect mum", instead giving ourselves permission to be *our baby's mum*. Our children love us far beyond our flaws and just want us to be with them. As we become gentler upon ourselves, we can reflect upon where we struggle; we can see that sometimes we take on too much and have unrealistic expectations of ourselves. It is these unrealistic expectations and comparisons with others which can make us feel as though we are not good enough;

"My mother was registered blind and I used to take her out once a week. Once my son began walking it was incredibly difficult to look after a blind person and a toddler intent on running away. I used to 'lose the rag' with him and looking back feel mortified at what 'the public' must have thought of me. I should never have attempted to look after them both simultaneously, but hindsight is a wonderful thing."

Alison, Mother to Callum, 23

As we grow to understand more fully the needs of our children and our capacity to respond, we become more realistic in our expectations. Mothering *is* immensely hard at times, yet a milestone is to do *our* best, rather than striving to be *the* best.

"I'm always honest about my motherhood journey. Sometimes it's not been pretty, sometimes it's been damn hard, but it's always completely worth it; each day is a learning day and I try to be the best mum I can be. I've learned that 'normal' can be a pretty large spectrum."

Shelley, Mother to Leia, 3 and Anya, 1

When things are flowing smoothly it is easy to feel the love and feel good about ourselves. Yet when we face difficulties and feel ourselves floundering, this is the time we really need to love and embrace ourselves, to listen, learn, grow and care for ourselves more tenderly.

Mothering and creativity

As mothers we are creators. From the very beginning we are the energy which animates childhood. Working across our physical and emotional landscapes, we weave threads which become the rich and well-worn fabric of family life. Often, we perceive creativity in terms of art or music, yet creativity lies at the very heart of mothering; through many small, repetitive, seemingly insignificant actions, we bring into being our families and the days of our children's childhood.

We cook meals, pack lunches and picnics, pour drinks into sippy cups, wipe faces and bottoms, buy, wash and fold clothes, hold hands, dry tears and little bodies after baths, soothe feelings, trapped fingers and cut knees, read stories, listen to dreams and imaginary tales, working constantly across our landscapes to create and maintain the substance and quality of family life.

Once we begin to perceive ourselves as *creators*, we can become more focussed and discerning about *what* we create. We can evaluate what is nurturing and what is depleting *for us*, observe actions, feelings and relationships and choose what to cultivate and what to let go of.

Mothering and creativity may not seem an immediate pairing, especially in the early years when we are so whacked with exhaustion that the very idea of being "creative" may be far from our energy-zapped mind and body. Yet what I am speaking of is not creativity as *separate*, but rather creativity as *central* to mothering. Through our physical exhaustion and mental haze we create ways to carry on, ways to love, nurture and connect.

"I'd nap with my son when he was little as I was exhausted too. He loved this and was always peaceful as we fell asleep together.

When he became a toddler we developed a game where I would lie on the couch and he would run his toy cars over me for hours. We called this game 'hills and valleys' and it meant I got a rest and knew exactly what he was doing."

Alison, Mother to Callum, 23

"Feeding both was constant work; I managed by feeding them at the same time but logistically this took a lot of getting used to. I'm an Occupational Therapist so perhaps work experience helped; after wrangling with cushions and blankets we saw positions that worked best and tailor-made a feeding cushion I could prop them both up on and feed simultaneously. I took this everywhere so I could sit and feed them both comfortably. It was about learning to recognise new needs and adapt to meet them."

Natalie, Mother to Sam and Oliver, 2

"I'm a naturally creative person (I certainly love to write and draw) but it's when I sit at the dining table with my husband and two children, sharing a meal I've cooked and talking about how our day has gone, that I'm the most proud of what I've helped to create: a family."

Teika, Mother to Rebecca, 12 and Jerome 9

Alongside creating family life, we may feel an awakening of creative energy which may have previously lay dormant or unexplored. Lucy Pearce explores this renaissance of creativity through motherhood in her inspirational book *The Rainbow Way*.

The family culture we create
We may daydream in pregnancy about meeting our baby and holding her in our arms. Such humble musings hold deep significance; we are dreaming up the images we hope to manifest. We bring substance to our visions, reading up on different parenting approaches and forming stronger ideas of what resonates with us and how we would like to respond to our babies.

"An important part of my journey is my evolving ideals about parenting. I hadn't given much thought to what sort of parent I wanted to be. Like many first-time mothers, I was engrossed in pregnancy and preparing for birth.

Since having my son I read and learned about gentle and attachment parenting, and try to parent along those lines. I try to model behaviour I want my son to learn, treat him with respect, meet his needs and try to understand things from his point of view, to work with him rather than trying to control him. It's challenging, I definitely have my off-days, but hope I'm on the right track."

Hazel, Mother to Barnaby, 15 months

We listen to our instincts, such as not wanting to smack or leave baby to cry, then explore information aligned with our values. But even then we do not simply implement this into our mothering; rather we read, reflect and pass ideas through our inner compass, taking on what resonates, creating interactions which honour the uniqueness of our family. As we become clearer about how we would like to parent we are more able to cultivate the qualities that enable these ways to unfold. We access our transformational potential and create inner change to manifest the interactions we desire.

"I didn't want to smack, I definitely didn't want to do Cry It Out – so I read up on different parenting styles and we do a blend of gentle and natural parenting. Cherry picking the main ideas and ethos, but not doing everything. My own journey is continuing with attempting to stop shouting. I don't want to be a shouty Mummy, so I try to do what I can to control my temper and show patience."

Shelley, Mother to Leia, 3 and Anya, 1

"I tried hard to give him explanations as to why I wasn't pleased with his behaviour or why I was forbidding something. It was important to me to be firm but not authoritarian. I loved thinking about the 'psychology' of raising a human being. As I reflected and researched different issues my confidence and wisdom grew."

Alison, Mother to Callum, 23

"Motherhood has definitely made me more conscious of environmental and health issues: especially what we eat and clean with. I don't always live up to my ideals, due to lack of time and money, but I keep trying."

Ann, Mother to Ella, 4

"When I started having children I was a working mom. I thought that what made me a good mom was going to work then coming home to clean and do things. I've realised however, over the years that what makes me a good mom (for me) is my presence. Paying attention to their needs and helping them understand themselves and the world around them is what's important to me now."

Violet, Mother to Sasha, 10, April, 9, Sam and Josh, 7 and Isaac, 2

Shifts in our insight and perception inspire us to create afresh, so that new chapters and ways of being can emerge. Transformation occurs as we listen to our hearts and intuition and dare to create a family lifestyle which reflects and resonates with our inner values.

Balancing lifestyle and finances

An element of family life, often in conjunction with our partner, is working out how to support our family financially. This is different for each of us as we come to motherhood in different situations, careers and values. Due to the fundamentally transformative nature of early motherhood, lifestyle choices we envisaged during pregnancy may not feel right once our baby is here. Milestones come as we figure out what is right for our family and create lifestyles which reflect our evolving needs and values.

"When my son was 5 we were rapidly going broke. I was a stay-at-home parent and didn't want it to be any other way, so this was tremendously worrying. I was really concerned that having to get a paid job would compromise my ability to be the kind of Mother I wanted to be.

I managed to find a job delivering catalogues and taking orders for a homewares company. I was able to work evenings and weekend afternoons so my husband was available to care for our son. I was working for a pittance but it was enough to keep us afloat until Working Tax Credit was introduced about 18 months later."

Alison, Mother to Callum, 23

We must create and recreate our family lifestyles time and again as needs and circumstances change and these are rarely straightforward decisions. We find ourselves pulled in competing directions; we may have found our job interesting and inspiring and not be ready to let it go, yet similarly feel drawn, and deeply so, to being with our babies on a full-time basis. It can be daunting to give up one income if we are used to living with two.

The desire to be with our baby is strong for many of us, and like

Charlotte, can motivate us to explore new options as to how we may care for our children as well as contribute financially;

"I always wanted to stay at home with my children. I'm now at the point of deciding what to do about my job. I know I don't want to leave my baby to go back to work, but I hate the thought of leaving a job I love. I also worry if I leave my job, but find we need extra income, I'd have to find a new job I may not enjoy so much.

I'm exploring new ways to make money from home. I've completed a proofreading course and hope to be able to find work using these skills to allow me to work during evenings and nap times."

Charlotte, Mother to Raffy, 9 months

"It was a milestone for me when I decided not to go back to work and to set up a business from home. Being a mum turned into a way of life and I knew I wanted be there for my son when he needed me. I'm so glad I did that and although it was a large step, it's the best decision I've ever made.

I feel blessed to be able to wake up with both my children every morning and have relaxed mornings together. We don't need to rush to get anywhere and can enjoy a wholesome breakfast together.

Mealtimes are a big part of our family life and most days for breakfast, lunch and dinner we sit around the table. My husband can now join us for most lunches and dinners as he also works at home which is lovely. I enjoy making food to nurture my family and taking the time to sit and connect with each other."

Harriet, Mother to Riley, 4 and Leon, 1

We may wonder how we can create family culture in line with our values alongside practical and financial requirements. Different things work for different people, and it can take time, often years, to reach a place where we feel everyone's needs are balanced. Yet with vision, perseverance and understanding of what is important to us, we *can* find balance and create lifestyles which work for our family;

"We have a lovely balance these days, my daughter spends two and a half days a week at nursery, the rest of the time I'm with her and she spends a short time with my Gran so I can work three days a week. I love our dedicated time together – she's responded really well to the routine and knows what's happening each day. We meet up with friends, go for walks and an art club together. We're closer than ever, and I put that down to me having relaxed, recovered from postnatal anxiety and really having taken stock of what's important."

Zara, Mother to Izzy, 4

Zara illustrates that growth and progression really does evolve through reflection and transformation across our landscapes. By having time and space to reflect and heal across her inner landscapes, Zara was able to come through postnatal anxiety and deepen in enjoyment in her relationship with her daughter. Through doing so, she became clear in what brought her true depth and meaning – her relationship with her daughter and partner and her creative work – so, with time, was able to arrange her days to reflect this.

It takes time, dedication and courage to discover ourselves as mothers, create relationships with our children and carve out lifestyles which honour everyone's needs. Yet with vision, time, and perseverance we *can* get there, and as Zara and Harriet illustrate, it feels good when we can live authentically and with gratitude lifestyles which resonate with our inner landscapes.

Strength and change
Sometimes, creating change feels scary. At times, we may feel the need to adjust aspects of our lives or respond differently to our children's changing needs. Recognising the need for change is one thing, yet creating it physically requires courage, strength and perseverance.

Perhaps we realise our full-time work is placing too great a pressure on family life, maybe we are unhappy as a stay-at-home mum, or our marriage has issues we need to address. Recognising these changes upon our inner landscapes is certainly a milestone, yet bringing them into reality requires deep transformation as we gather strength, trust and courage to create new ways of being;

"I've tried to keep to my 'gut feeling parenting' approach through the years. I've fallen foul of following society sometimes when I should've followed my heart. These times have been relatively few, but unfortunately they were the 'big' things like schooling. Time passed and those mistakes have been rectified by home schooling. Decisions were hard as extended family generally follows the path most taken.

Now I have the strength of mind to say to people, 'This is right for us so please respect that.' I think I'm only able to do that because of my experiences of being a Mum which have taught me that I am strong enough to rise to the needs of the situation.

School never felt right for any of us and eventually we made the decision to home school. I now wake up in the morning content in the knowledge that we got it right in the end. We are repairing the damage and are much less vulnerable than we were in those early home schooling days.

I'm back to going by my gut feelings, and with extra strength I've gained over the years I'm able to lead my little brood on our lives of discovery together."

Marie, Mother to Jean, 11 and Lewis, 9

Sometimes we stray off our path a little and face challenges which awaken us to look within, connect once again with our instincts, gut feelings and inner knowing. Through getting bustled along with social expectations we may find ourselves feeling lost or facing difficulty as the path we find ourselves upon does not feel right.

By getting lost then finding ways through, we discover strength, courage and clarity and grow in confidence. Such experiences propel us forwards in a positive spiral; we grow to trust ourselves more deeply, know we *can* trust our intuition and create change enabling us to live with greater authenticity.

Such awareness never leaves us; it remains within like tree rings depicting our growth through the seasons. At times I have felt anxious, afraid to make changes and doubted my inner strength. When giving birth I felt hugely capable, in touch with the powerful energy of the Feminine. When I find myself lacking courage now, I remind myself of this. I go within and connect once again with those deep feelings of strength, empowerment and Feminine knowing. Connecting to these experiences reminds me of my true power and capacity, even though the actual experiences were some years ago. Through reconnecting with such qualities, we can once again draw upon their strength and wisdom, helping us find new ways forwards.

Changes as they grow
In the beginning it can feel as though we are swamped by motherhood and an early milestone is the recognition of how fast time passes. Alongside valuing being with our children lies the discovery of newly emerging elements in our relationships and new opportunities as children grow.

"From about age 3 I enjoyed the fact he was that little bit more sensible and aware of his own safety. This made taking him on holiday in a caravan much easier, we could let him run about and keep an eye on him from the window.

He was a very active wee boy and my life developed in the direction of getting him out of the house every single day, rain, hail or shine, so he had the opportunity to explore.

As we were able to tackle more complex reading material, I found reading him bedtime stories more and more enjoyable. I was always looking for material that was more unusual, as well as the usual stories about teddy bears and animals.

I remember absolutely loving ages 6–7, he was still so cute, but also old enough to do much for himself. We had such great fun. Every evening I set aside one hour before bed when he had my undivided attention – we played all kinds of games as well as reading books.

We joined a short tennis club and went to the cinema as his attention span increased. We experimented going to a musical as he enjoyed the tape music. A whole world of possibilities was opening up for us. As he grew I was always on the lookout for new experiences to broaden his horizons, but having to bear in mind we were limited financially."

Alison, Mother to Callum, 23

Alison captures the feeling of excitement and adventure as we realise our child is no longer a tiny baby whose sole focus is milk and sleep. As Alison recalls, *A whole world of possibilities* opens up for us as we realise we are able to explore the world together. The milestones we encounter may be of potential; of realising how things are changing, how time is moving on; possibilities of new adventures and the potential of sharing things we enjoy with our children.

"We've reached the stage where I can share some of my own passions with him, particularly music and words, but also patterns and visual imagery. A wonderful experience most days is starting to sing a song and hearing my three-year-old joining in from the other room. We have whole conversations in song, and this always lifts my heart, because music brings me such joy, and seems to for him too."

Eleanor, Mother to Thomas, 3 and David, 10 months

Eleanor identifies the excitement inherent in the realisation that we are able not only to rediscover some of our own life passions, but to share them with our children. Mothers spoke with happiness how, as children grew beyond infancy, the flow and pace of life changes and we are able to rekindle previous passions and interests alongside our children. After years of practicing yoga with my babies on the mat beside me, then having them climb on my back through the toddler years, they now come and practice postures with me, teach their friends and ask for a relaxation to settle to sleep.

Women spoke of taking their young children hiking, walking and camping, cycling, and being able to go at a slightly faster pace as their kids rode their own bikes, rather than trudging along carrying a toddler, a toddler push along bike and a changing bag. Parents spoke of playing football and rugby together, of watching films, reading books, playing games, painting, skiing, travelling and listening to music; all exciting milestones in themselves as we realise the pace of life is changing, and potential opportunities for sharing more experiences with our children are opening up with every passing year.

Just as activities expand, so do our relationships evolve and mature. In the beginning we are all-consumed by the constancy of mothering a newborn, yet with time things shift and change. New elements of ourselves surface and previous ones re-emerge, yet this time we can share more of ourselves with our children. We grow through mothering, and although we may feel we lose aspects of ourselves at first, in the long run we can see how we deepen, develop and assimilate our experiences, evolving and unfolding into more of the woman we have the potential to become.

"I've gained confidence to be myself with my children. I'm very close to my own mother, and the only thing I'd change about the way she was with us growing up is she didn't let much of herself show – I think she believed there should be some distance between mother and children.

These days she and I share our vulnerability and it's a wonderful thing – so I wanted to start this early with my own children. I tell them when I'm feeling sad, angry or tired, explaining how this affects what I want to join in with. It's had a fantastic effect on my three-year-old, who has an incredible vocabulary of emotional words and concepts so can always explain himself, and he's learned about patience and the give-and-take of relationships. It also means he spontaneously tells me he loves me, just as I do him – I believe he understands those words.

When he chooses books he will introduce them as, 'This is one you really like,' (or sometimes, 'This is one you said you never wanted to read again.') and I love it that he has identified my feelings and is acknowledging them."

Eleanor, Mother to Thomas, 3 and David, 10 months

Trusting the unfolding process

The opposing forces of control and surrender are issues we return to again and again. We may first experience this duality at the very beginning in our experiences of fertility; whatever our plans (or lack of plans), we soon realise conception is not something we can control. These milestones continue through pregnancy, culminating in labour and birth, and continue to unfold through mothering as we find ourselves learning just how little control we have, and how much we really do have to surrender each step of the way. This is a journey of relinquishing our need for certainty, deepening into trust and learning to nurture, rather than control, the unfolding process;

"A recurring theme has been control, or lack of it, or letting go of it. I wouldn't describe myself as a control freak, but I like to have as much information as possible and make informed decisions.

In the early days I remember agonising to my mum about whether I was doing something right or could be doing it better, and she said the problem was I wanted certainty, and I wasn't going to get it with a baby (or indeed for the next 20 years!).

She was right and I realised I needed to try to relax and trust my instincts more. That has come and I've settled into being a mother."

Hazel, Mother to Barnaby, 15 months

Our desire to control stems from the deep desire to do what is best for our child, to make things as positive as we can with the resources we have. We want things to be right, nay perfect, yet try as we may to parent as we feel optimal, time and again, we are reminded we are unable to control the entire journey. What we can do is to *nurture the process*, and trust and embrace our children for who they are. Whilst we can do a great deal to influence their lives, it is our acceptance, trust and unconditional love, rather than control, which makes the most difference.

"I think because our children are adopted and from a background of chronic neglect, we've been able to let go of a lot of the controlling impulses we might have had if we were the boys' birth parents. We've had to work with what we've got in terms of the boys' needs and issues, we've had to be relaxed and selective in terms of what we try to control.

In truth, I've often thought this has helped quite a lot and made me a better mother than I would've been otherwise. Very often I've been in the company of other mothers who have worried so much about really minor things. I know I would've been the same, had I been a birth mother, but instead I've had to operate along the lines of 'what is, is'.

My boys have another mother, their birth mother, which I've had to accept. They also have five other siblings, and a foster carer whom they love very much. They're not 'from' me or my husband, or from our town. They may well want to hook up with their birth parents or their siblings when they're older, which would be understandable and we'd want to support them. All of these are things I've had to process, and as a result I've been able to let go of a lot of the controlling and perfectionist tendencies I know I would have had otherwise!"

Tess, Mother to Adam and Aidan, 8 and Shaun, 6

For Tess, parenting has been a journey of reflection, trust and surrender, all of which has led to shifts in perception and a deepening into acceptance rather than control. Tess goes on to explain how *trusting the process* developed through her professional practice became a source of strength and guidance;

"The practical side of parenting has always been a weak point for me – I'm not a practical person, nor organised or tidy for that matter, and I'm fairly absent-minded. From the start I've known I wasn't great in this respect, but at the same time, I think my training as a psychotherapist really helped. I'm so used to 'trusting in the process' and I've found this immensely useful in parenting, especially with adopted children where I wasn't able to rely on natural bonding from birth.

Because of the nature of adoption, my husband and I have always said regarding our children that we need to make sure they feel safe and that they feel loved, and that we won't worry too much about anything else. I think this has served us well, helping us stay focussed."

Tess, Mother to Adam and Aidan, 8 and Shaun, 6

Tess shares valuable milestones; we can let go of control and surrender ideas of perfection and through doing so we release pre-conceived ideas and welcome and embrace the children we have before us. Rather than controlling their environment and behaviour, instead we can focus on creating a nurturing environment within which our children can grow and unfold.

Journeys of understanding

Once we surrender control, we begin to understand more of who our children are and what they need from us. So much of learning to mother is learning to understand, and understanding awakens transformation. Indeed, it can be our *lack* of understanding and the ensuing struggles, frustration, resentment and confusion which ignite our journey of deeper understanding. So often it is through the times of struggle, of miscommunication, clashes and disharmony that we yearn for greater communication, and henceforth create deeper compassion, empathy and understanding.

If, early on in our journey, we are told our baby is manipulating us by crying for attention, we may follow advice to leave him to 'cry it out' and resist urges to comfort him. Yet if we begin to look from our baby's perspective, we see a tiny, helpless human, utterly dependent on us for his very survival. We are his world since his life began in our womb; our touch, smell, presence, warmth and heartbeat comforts him and we bring food and reassurance. From such shifting perception, we may come to see his crying as communication rather than manipulation.

Such shifts are significant milestones and can change how we care for our children. As we see the world from our baby's point of view, our connection, compassion and empathy increases; we grow emotionally, becoming more responsive. Our relationship deepens.

"Time played a vital role in helping me cope and learn how to look after and care for my children. I've learned that getting to know your child doesn't happen overnight, it takes time, patience and learning."
Francesca, Mother to Emily, 4 and Ashley, 1

Time spent together gifts us with insight into how they see the world, which is invaluable for communication. We come to see what is, for them, precious, meaningful or frightening. Whilst something like a broken stick or a feather lost on the wind seems trivial to us, once we come to see things through our child's eyes, we see the meaning and value they invested in this object. We begin to understand why they are so upset and why they won't be placated with another stick from the beach.

Since we understand what is happening for them, we are able to validate their feelings and support their emotional development rather than denying or dismissing their feelings. Such recognition honours their experience and brings a sense of being heard and understood, which is worlds away from being told to 'stop being silly'.

Deepened understanding can help us handle challenging situations with greater insight and confidence as, despite the intensity, we at least understand some of what our child is going through;

"Our daughter has a pretty challenging personality – she is highly emotional with big highs and lows. She has always been very quick to get upset, and the switch from zero to meltdown can happen in seconds. She is extremely independent and will resist suggestions for the sake of it, even if it is of benefit to her, but her need for independence is something we're proud of as well.

Whilst she still takes us by surprise, we've grown much better at recognising the situations that trigger a tantrum, and as she has grown and become a little more rational, she's become better at making herself known, and we've become better at negotiating, and accepting her need to make her own choices!"

Zara, Mother to Izzy, 4

We learn to mother by mothering; Zara and her husband have come to understand more about their daughter through being with her through the highs and lows each day. Through observing, communicating, listening and reflecting they gained insight beyond their daughter's behaviour and grew to understand the needs and feelings she expresses.

It is through such interactions that we trust and observe, reflect, then try something different, that we come to understand with greater depth and clarity. From such understanding, and a willingness to understand when we do not, trust develops and our children feel more comfortable sharing more of themselves. We come to see the feelings behind the behaviour and together find ways forward.

We further our own growth as we let go of being the "expert" and open our minds and hearts with willingness to learn from our children. What follows are milestones of acceptance, surrender and respect, as we come to understand, then accept, more of who our children are. Such acceptance becomes unconditional love in action; for the more we understand them, the more we are able to accept and love them for who they truly are.

Understanding ourselves

Mothering brings opportunities to understand ourselves more deeply. We walk a new terrain, unearthing parts of ourselves which have never before received our conscious attention. With consciousness and self-reflection we learn a great deal about our capacity to love, to care, to let go of past hurts and persevere.

"Over the last four years I've gone through a tremendous evolution into motherhood, through physical and emotional challenges, revelations of what being a parent really entails, testing my own understanding of my strengths and weaknesses and revealing a level of love and commitment I didn't previously think possible."

Louise, Mother to Flynn, 3.5 and Rowan, 10 months

We cannot gain such understanding or knowledge through reading alone; it is by going through it, by loving and mothering our children day in day out, come what may, that we learn of ourselves, our strengths, weaknesses and capabilities. We gain deeper self-knowledge through gritty experience which brings with it well-deserved, hard-won confidence; a confidence from which we are better able to go forward, trusting our own abilities and capabilities as women and mothers.

"No one told me how lonely it would be, how there would be days I would feel I disliked my kids. And it would be okay because they were the only humans around me and that the feeling would vanish, but I would need to acknowledge it. I didn't know that sometimes you dislike someone, for a moment, then bounce back to loving them.

I didn't know lack of sleep would seriously affect my judgement, and worst of all, I didn't know how to direct my sadness. Yet through loving my babies, and responding to their needs, and reading about mothering, I eventually found a way through, found my purpose as a mother, and created a place where I belonged."

Vanessa, Mother to Lilo, 10, Boo, 8 and Sammy, 1

Vanessa reflects upon her inner landscapes and what a deep, and at times lonely, journey mothering can be. Yet with time, and *through* mothering, Vanessa found herself. She emerged stronger with a sense of identity, place and confidence. Let us recognise the changes and emotions we experience, and give ourselves the space, time, love and gentleness to explore, understand and welcome our journey.

"I feel we go through enormous metamorphosis as mums. Everything we thought we knew of ourselves before changes; our lifestyles and routines, our bodies and emotions, our priorities and perspectives. This is a monumental time of change and transition when everything you thought you knew and understood about yourself is suddenly under question. But it's not something much talked about.

One of the hardest things you have to deal with is the sudden vulnerability you experience through your child. It was so unpredicted. And it was almost contrary to the confidence parenthood gives you – parenthood is an enormous dichotomy, full of charm and desperation, fullness yet fear. Pride, yet anxiety. I felt both complete yet fragmented by the pull of parenting."

Ross, Mother to Charley and Chelsea, in their 20's

Ross recognises the constant dichotomy of parenting; protection and surrender, strength and vulnerability, loving and letting go. These mazes of motherhood produce a mass of intertwining, contradictory feelings across our inner landscapes, sparking contemplation, compassion, transformation and deep understanding.

"I surpassed difficult times by turning within. Regarding children's behaviour, I tuned into myself and began learning to understand where their behaviour began. I realised the behaviour patterns they have are a direct result of my reactions to them. I learned to use anything and everything that was going on as a step to understand what was difficult and learned to use the difficult situation as a stepping stone to move to the next level."

Violet, Mother to Sasha, 10, April, 9, Sam and Josh, 7 and Isaac, 2

As Violet so wisely illustrates, understanding is key. Increased awareness gifts us with knowledge and compassion, enabling us to deepen into acceptance, trust and unconditional love. We can be more loving, compassionate and gentle with ourselves and nurture our tender, struggling parts. In doing so, we heal ourselves a little more, deepening our capacity to love, connect and communicate more authentically.

Through knowing our own struggles, we come to see each mother is walking her own path, discovering her own capacities and vulnerabilities, no doubt loving her child as much as we do. We walk a shared journey; we all struggle with day-to-day practicalities, feelings of love, overwhelm, tenderness and vulnerability. We love our children beyond words, yet snap when we are tired and stressed. We all fear something dreadful happening so pray for their safety. And, no matter the struggles of the day, we think they are sweet and beautiful as they sleep.

Chapter Six
A Mother Again

Becoming a mother for the first time brings sweeping change across our landscapes. Our bodies, hearts, minds, homes and relationships rearrange to make space to nurture our baby. So we may expect that as we welcome another baby there are less adjustments to be made. And in some sense this is true; we are familiar with mothering and our routines and relationships now accommodate children.

So too have we developed knowledge, understanding, confidence, tenacity and the practical and emotional skills of mothering. Yet a new pregnancy calls us to rearrange our family landscapes further to make space to welcome and nurture another baby. Many of our challenges, milestones and transformation lie in the necessity to meet the needs of our newborn alongside continuing to mother our firstborn.

We may wonder, and worry about, how we will care for our newborn whilst continuing to respond to the needs of our first child. And this time there are few dreamy imaginings, for we know exactly just how much love, care, time and energy babies require. So too are we familiar with the intensity of labour and the overwhelming, all-consuming love babies evoke. We are less likely to worry about how we will handle daily practicalities; what may concern us more is whether we will be able to love another child as wholly as our first.

A new pregnancy

The overarching theme of second pregnancies for many of us is just how different it is to be pregnant alongside caring for a child. There seems to be so little time to connect with and enjoy pregnancy the way we did with our first, and the months seem to pass by so fast. We can feel pangs of guilt as we forget we are even pregnant, and our first child's energy, excitement and constant need for us can become more challenging as we feel pulled in new directions; wanting to be there for our child whilst feeling the presence of pregnancy though our bodies and emotions. We abruptly discover the new direction our growth and transformation is heading in as we learn and struggle to balance the practical and emotional needs of more than one child.

"I took my first pregnancy very seriously, doing everything I could to look after myself and my unborn child: pregnancy yoga, pilates, aqua-natal, Daisy Birthing, antenatal classes, birth plans, pregnancy books and so on and ate the healthiest diet I'd ever eaten.

Second pregnancy I was drawn to eating lots of carbohydrates and natural sugars as I was exhausted and struggling all of the time and it seemed to be what my body was craving to get me through.

I like to feel in control of things and well prepared. Hence, during my second pregnancy felt much more anxious as birth drew closer, feeling that with having a toddler to look after and my job whilst suffering from painful, debilitating Pelvic Girdle Pain for 7 months, that I couldn't pay proper attention to preparing physically and mentally for birth."

Louise, Mother to Flynn, 3 and Rowan, 10 months

Second pregnancies can be challenging, especially when exhaustion, nausea or pelvic pain restricts our normal activities. We feel torn and upset we are unable to be as active, available and energetic with our first child whilst simultaneously feeling guilty for not giving our second pregnancy the same care and attention we did our first. We stumble against milestones of deepening transformation, often with discomfort, as we learn to share and expand our mothering energy.

"My eldest was 18 months when I fell pregnant; second time round there's no napping because you have a toddler to entertain. The second pregnancy flew past so quickly and it was hard to enjoy it. The labour was quicker and I gave birth in the pool with my other half delivering the baby."

Shelley, Mother to Leia, 3 and Anya, 1

We learn to alter our perspectives; we can only do what we can do, we cannot be *everything to everyone, all of the time*, as much as we may wish and try to be. We realise the necessity of caring for ourselves so we are able to care for others. Such experiences prepare us for mothering two as we learn of the necessity and challenges of balancing multiple needs. Alongside the challenges, sharing pregnancy with our child introduces a new element of love and excitement to family life and nurturing our child's curiosity and relationship with the baby is a beautiful element of this time of change;

"My belly grew and the boy inside danced, he amused his sister by pressing his body against my belly as she sang to him. He loved her and she loved him."

Vanessa, Mother to Lilo, 10, Boo, 8 and Sammy, 1

"Jessie was there for the home birth and saw exactly where her new sister came from, which I feel was a great benefit for her."

Marty, Mother to Jessie, 21 and Lizzie, 16

Alongside concerns of coping practically, we often feel concerned about what is happening upon our inner landscapes. *How will love for our new baby unfold? Will we know them in the same way as our first? Will we love them? Will it be the same? How can it be?* In the quiet moments, such questions inspire doubt and worry; *what if we do not love them in the same way?*

Our relationship with each child unfolds differently, although, at the time, we may not know or even want this to be so, feeling we should love and mother each child in exactly the same way.

Every pregnancy, birth and mother-child relationship is unique and ever-evolving. A valuable milestone at this point is deepening into wisdom, love and acceptance; trusting each relationship will develop along its own lines, realising that when experiences are different with different babies, this does not make them greater or lesser, only different, though equally valuable and authentic. We have to trust that love finds its own way.

Approaching birth

Approaching birth once again brings back experiences and memories with our firstborn, and these may be treasured or traumatic. Yet reflection on our first child's birth can bring clarity to how we would like our second to unfold. Motherhood is *immensely* transformative; we are not the same women we were as we approached the birth of our first baby. Through the days, weeks, months and years of mothering our first child, whether we realise it or not, we have grown immeasurably and are approaching our second birth with greater awareness, confidence, knowledge and empowerment;

"Labour and birth with my first daughter were horrendous and the trauma remains with me; forceps, C-section and failed anaesthesia. But becoming a mother of another was so much easier. The labour was easier, I didn't get the VBAC I wanted although I negotiated for this and laboured for some hours, but the C-section was fine this time and I had the honour of being there to hold my baby as he was born."

Alicja, Mother to Roza, 3 and Konrad, 1

"The birth of my first daughter had been a protracted and stressful experience. The induction had taken a long time, and I ended up with the opposite of the drug-free, pool birth I hoped for. I felt physically drained and very uncomfortable for quite a while after.

In contrast, with my second daughter I went into labour naturally. I felt completely in control, calm and unworried, managing labour on my own, sending my partner off to bed. We were at home and it was a beautifully warm August night. I was in increasing discomfort but managed it fine and felt calm throughout.

I was so focussed on managing the labour that we left it very late to get to hospital and Tess was born within five minutes of being there. I felt incredibly proud of myself, I had the best labour I could have wished for; it felt like an achievement."

Catherine, Mother to Lucy, 3 and Tess, 19 months

Birth is transformational and holds the potential to awaken us to previously undiscovered inner strength, focus and power. Once we touch upon such places, this knowledge never leaves us. It remains within, providing sustenance, trust, strength and nourishment.

"I found a new trust and respect for a woman's body after the birth of my second daughter. My first delivery was highly managed with induction, long labour and eventual C-section. I didn't feel down about it, even though I wouldn't have chosen it that way.

But then I had not yet experienced the thrill and exhilaration of natural childbirth – indescribable. I felt amazing and able to take on anything; a great confidence boost and adrenaline high to get through the first few very long days and nights."

Jenny, Mother to Matthew, 3 and Lucy, 14 months

After a traumatic, difficult or challenging first birth, or a birth which unfolded differently to how we hoped, having a more positive birth experience with our second baby can be remarkably healing. Yet our emotional landscapes are complex places where profound love and responsibility can lead to complex, contradictory feelings. For all the joy, love and healing our second birth brings, so too may we harbour guilt and discomfort, for as much as we are jubilant our second baby received such a birth, we feel upset this was not the case for our first.

What we experience are milestones of acceptance; of holding these feelings, accepting the way things unfolded and doing our best to care for and love ourselves and our children each day. We can reflect, understand and let go, yet most of all we can deepen into love and compassion. We can find strength and comfort in the knowledge that we did all we could in the situations we found ourselves in, with the resources, support and knowledge we had available. Similarly, we can recognise all of the ways our children are thriving now, and cultivate a wider perspective, understanding that as intense as it may be, birth is but one element, one day, of this lifelong journey.

Beacons of transformation

Births become markers along our mothering journey, mirroring our continued change, growth and transformation as we assimilate previous learning and experience. This was certainly the case for Francesca who began motherhood within the chaos of alcoholism. Motherhood became her catalyst for change, where she found the motivation, strength and determination to seek help and begin recovery. With great determination and commitment to her daughter, Francesca changed her life and found this reflected in the pregnancy and birth of her second daughter;

"In comparison to my experiences with my first daughter, pregnancy and birth of my second child was completely different. A lot of this is to do with my state of mind and how much I learned and grew as a person and a mother.

By the time I got pregnant for the second time I'd been sober nearly 3 years so this was a significant factor in why it was so different and so much easier. Also, I'd done it before so it wasn't as alien as the first time round. I was so much more confident, my life was already changed in the sense that there was no longer just myself and my partner to worry about as I'd been caring for my daughter for three years.

My second pregnancy was planned and I couldn't have been happier when I found out. When I look back to this same moment with my first, I just want to hold myself and tell myself that it will be alright. I really feel for that sad, messed up girl I was, but at the same time I'm so grateful to be where I am now and accept that was just my path.

Through having my first child I met a lot of like-minded mothers and they were a huge factor in why my second pregnancy and labour was so different. The support, guidance and wisdom I gained from these women is second to none; they were, and still are, a great comfort, bringing much courage and strength. These women empowered me and taught me about natural home births, which I went on to do and found it one of the most empowering, wonderful experiences of my life, something I will carry with me and draw strength from always.

During labour with my first child I was filled with fear, panic, pain and self-doubt, whereas with my second I trusted everything was as it should be. I remained calm, was able to practice yoga and hypnobirthing which helped immensely, and most of all, believed in myself and knew I could do it."

Francesca, Mother to Laura, 4 and Ashley, 1

Francesca speaks with milestones of tenderness of how she can look back at her younger self with kindness, compassion and acceptance. Mothering is a journey of love, yet it is not only our children who flourish within the unconditional love mothering awakens, but ourselves also if we allow ourselves to be embraced by it.

A new breastfeeding journey

As we saw previously, breastfeeding first time round is an intense learning curve. We must learn a whole new language of communication, master numerous practical skills and come to terms with the time investment required. As Margaret illustrates, breastfeeding difficulties with our firstborn can cast shadows of guilt and failure across our inner landscapes. Yet if we choose to try again, this time bringing learning and confidence accrued through mothering, breastfeeding our second baby can be different, becoming a positive, healing and enjoyable experience;

"I'd not had a good start with my first baby; I felt anxious during pregnancy, had an emergency Caesarean and lost a lot of blood. I wanted to breastfeed, but it was difficult for us both. I gave up after seven weeks and this left me in a low way, with lots of self-criticism and judgement.

With Rebecca, my second, I decided I would just see how it went. There are five years between them, and looking back, I'd grown in confidence a lot, both in myself and as a mother. I was able to accept myself as things were, and fed her exclusively. We carried on for nine months!

This was a very positive and healing experience. I found a new confidence in myself and a real shift in how I felt about my body and breasts. Also, it showed me just how much I'd healed and grown over those five years."

Margaret, Mother to Leon, 22 and Rebecca, 17

As Margaret illustrates, if we give ourselves time to pause and reflect upon our mothering journey, we see just how far we have come. Rather than judging and criticising ourselves for not getting it all right in the beginning, we can cultivate an attitude of love, tenderness and compassion, realising we have been doing our best to learn and love with the knowledge and resources we have.

Through mothering our first child we develop knowledge, skills and confidence, and these become the foundation for mothering our second. Through feeding our first, even if this was not a straightforward path, we have experience, confidence, understanding and tenacity to bring to our journey;

"After our experiences with number one (extreme breastfeeding difficulties and food allergies), I became uncompromising in following my instincts with number two. I carried my second baby in a sling most of the first 6 months as he's a very sensitive person who hated being put down. I responded to him quickly, not leaving him to cry to 'get used to it', breastfed exclusively on cue for 6 months before introducing any solids, feeding in the night as much as he wanted.

Breastfeeding and weaning second time around have been easy and natural, with no issues, proving to me once again that doubts I had about myself were unfounded first time round, and issues with weaning were simply due to health problems, not my inability as a mother, which I was constantly made to feel whether through well-meaning but unhelpful comments or my own thoughts. I've enjoyed trusting my instincts and ignoring traditional Western protocol this time, (at least as far as is practicable) and know that, in our case, I'm doing the right thing for me and my baby."

Louise, Mother to Flynn, 3 and Rowan, 10 months

Reclaiming our instincts

Louise's story brings home the fact that, as mothers, our instincts are not some wishy-washy emotions which have no place in the "real world", making us "clingy" or "irrational". Rather, they are deeply held expressions of wisdom arising from within and guiding us to what is right, and at times *essential* for our children's survival and wellbeing. Whilst it is certainly a journey to begin to hear, listen and act upon such knowing, especially as we are conditioned to value intellectual thought and opinions of others over ourselves, some of our most profound milestones occur through listening to, and allowing ourselves the trust and confidence to be guided by our instincts.

If breastfeeding did not unfold as we hoped the first time, many of us approach feeding our second with confidence and determination that this time, things will be different. Whilst we may not have positive experiences to draw upon, what we do have is the depth of growth and development motherhood has brought us. Similarly, as the mothering landscape is now well-trodden and familiar, this time we are less likely to be overwhelmed by the enormity of it all and are much more able to focus our efforts on relearning to breastfeed if this is where our passions lie;

"Going home after the birth of my first, I had two weeks before I had to decide if I was to finish my course and return to studying. Inside, I didn't want to leave her, ever. Inside, I wasn't strong enough.

She'll be fine, you breastfed her for three weeks, nowadays powdered milk is more than enough.

She was indeed, fine. I used the pump, left my milk and she spent mornings with daddy. He would take her to my mother's house (with extra bottles) where she would stay until I arrived with boobies and milk.

My mother did the one thing no one should ever do; she did what she thought was best and gave her formula.

And in a matter of days, even though I couldn't understand why, my sweetheart stopped wanting my milk.

Today, my mother defends that babies should be breastfed and I sometimes wonder if she forgot her past actions. My daughter has been through a journey of her own and we have the sweetest bond. Would I have changed the past? In a heartbeat.

Yet all I could do, and what I did, was to breastfeed my second for as long as he wanted, and prevent history repeating itself. Because we all make what we like to call mistakes, and yet, it is how we learn and grow, so they must happen.

My daughter was breastfed for less than a month, my son went on to be one and a half until he, on his own, moved on."

Vanessa, Mother to Lilo, 10, Boo, 8 and Sammy, 1

Being able to breastfeed our second baby can be a tender and healing experience as we come to terms with how events unfolded with our first. We may revisit previous emotions and feel sadness that things did not go as we had wished. Yet as Vanessa illustrates, we cannot change the past; what we can do is have compassion for ourselves and our journeys, look forward, and make decisions about how we would like things to unfold.

Rather than seeing past actions and events as failure and feeling guilty, we can instead see just how much we have learned and grown in strength, awareness, trust and intuition. We can transform feelings of guilt and upset into determination to move forward in the direction we want to go.

Trust in the process

Running in parallel to the confidence we have built in our mothering abilities is the growth of trust. By far the most fundamental aspect of my learning throughout the intense years of breastfeeding my first daughter was to trust her, myself, and the innate intelligence of the breastfeeding process. I learned to trust that my baby would know what to do, and my main job was to create and, if necessary, guard the space for her to be at my breast as much as she wanted. I learned to trust the supply and demand nature of breastfeeding, meaning I had to trust her to know when and how much to feed, and I had to learn how to recognise that she was receiving enough. Such trust and experience enabled me to persevere with getting breastfeeding started with my second daughter, which proved challenging.

After being born and placed on my belly, my first daughter had simply propelled herself upwards and begun to feed whilst I looked on in amazement. My second daughter, whilst being born smoothly at home, just did not seem to take to breastfeeding easily. She did try to latch on, but seemed to stick her tongue out, suckling before she was latched on properly. It was difficult to get a feed started, regularly taking around ten minutes of her trying to latch, becoming unsettled, me expressing a little milk and changing positions until she managed to open her mouth wide enough without suckling prematurely to latch effectively. We persevered; I kept calm, breathed deeply, and leant upon the trust accrued with my first daughter; breastfeeding would work, we just needed to stick with it, and give her the time and the space to work things out for herself.

I also had the unexpected benefit of tandem feeding my first daughter of two-and-a-half which proved invaluable; I would feed my first daughter for a minute or two, which would mean she felt happy and involved, plus my milk flow was stimulated and let down, then we would swap and continue to encourage the baby to latch on. This proved very useful as she got a little milk immediately and did not have to struggle and then be overwhelmed with the milk let-down. As she grew and developed she soon got the hang of it, albeit in a completely different way to her sister.

I felt immensely thankful for my learning with my first daughter; that breastfeeding had become a way of life and something I had come to trust innately and completely. Had I not had these experiences I could see how the whole process could have become fraught with anxiety and easily slipped away from us if effective support could not have been found quickly.

Whilst we do bring trust, confidence and experience to our second and subsequent breastfeeding relationships, we can also be in for a few surprises. Whilst we may think we know about feeding, what we learn at every step of mothering siblings, is how they are all so unique and express their individuality through all aspects of their growth and development.

Just as my first daughter loved to feed and it was her altogether favourite activity as a baby and toddler (in fact today she has a passion for creating and enjoying food), for my second daughter, breastfeeding was something functional and quick, her passions lying in exploring the world around her. For as soon as she was more aware of the outer world she would stop feeding and look around, stimulated and interested in anything and everything. As I realised this, I fed her in quiet, unstimulating places, like parked in the car before meeting friends. She is the same today; she will eat when she's hungry, and for as little time as possible, before returning to play and adventuring.

Lizzie recalls the differences in feeding her babies, as well as the blossoming pride, fulfilment and happiness at watching her babies grow knowing they are nourished by her milk;

"I was surprised how different James was from Izzy. He fed differently, desperately, as if he'd been told there was a shortage. I remember feeling totally drained. With both of them, I loved watching them grow and thinking 'I did that.'"

Lizzie, Mother to Izzy, 6, James, 4 and Lloyd, 1

"I had no sore nipples second time, I still feed my first daughter and my milk supply was already really good when my little boy was born. Plus, he was never one to feed for more than a couple of minutes. This time around the baby had to fit into our family, not the other way round, and he is thriving. I'm so much more self-confident as a mum as well."

Alicja, Mother to Roza, 3 and Konrad, 1

Pregnancy and breastfeeding combined

For some of us, breastfeeding is a significant part of baby's early months, becoming less important over time, and for others feeding continues to be a significant part of our child's life for many months and years. If our first child values breastfeeding into their first, second, third or fourth years and beyond, we may find ourselves becoming pregnant alongside feeding. Once again, our mothering path takes us into new, uncharted territory as we begin to navigate our way around this new, unfamiliar landscape.

Whilst sustained breastfeeding is not often visible in the mainstream, it happens for many families. We may be met with uncertainty, questions and comments from those around us unfamiliar with this way of nurturing, but at this stage of our journey, we are less unsure and vulnerable; we are likely to have a sturdy store of confidence, understanding and trust in the process.

Early pregnancy can make nipples incredibly sensitive and for some of us, such sensitivity and change in sensation makes feeding our toddler uncomfortable or unbearable, whilst for others it is less intense and is not an issue. Some of us choose to wean our toddlers during pregnancy and some little ones lose interest themselves as our milk supply changes. Others seem not to be perturbed by the changes pregnancy brings and happily feed throughout.

Whatever women around us have chosen to do, this is an incredibly personal decision, as what feels fine and natural to one is unbearable to another. Once again, we meet the milestone of discernment; letting go of advice and choices made by others and focussing upon what feels most nourishing for ourselves. We must make the choices that feel right for us, developing and diversifying the ways we nurture and connect with our children;

"The most significant symptom of early pregnancy was agonisingly tender nipples. Weaning Jessie completely from the breast became a priority. The process was guilt free as she was nearly five years old, but fraught because she could no longer be knocked out in minutes at bedtime, requiring instead to be cuddled by her father in front of the television for up to two hours."

Marty, Mother to Jessie, 21, Lizzie, 16

Whatever happens, our relationships change, as does the way we parent our firstborn, as we make space for their sibling and we develop new ways of connecting with one another as the family dynamic shifts. Continuing to feed our toddlers can become a surprisingly valuable mothering resource as we struggle in learning to balance the needs of our toddlers and newborns. Amidst the exhaustion and feelings of being torn between everybody's differing needs, breastfeeding can bring a sense of peace and relief.

Soon after my second daughter was born, our toddler returned from grandparents and was excited to see her new baby sister snuggled in, feeding. Tired herself, she climbed into bed with us, and began feeding alongside her sister, tentatively putting her arm around the new baby, stroking her face and watching as the baby curled her tiny hand around her finger. This remains one of my most tender memories of simplicity, love and connection. Norma Jane Bumgarner's *Mothering Your Nursing Toddler* and Hilary Flower's *Adventures in Tandem Nursing* are useful resources for exploring tandem feeding further.

Shelley explains how breastfeeding both daughters helped ease the chaos and struggles and brought a sense of love, calm and harmony;

"Second time round there was no napping when the baby naps because my toddler wanted to play, I was so knackered. I felt I achieved nothing. I'd be in my dressing gown, breastfeeding both the toddler and the baby. The house would be a mess and I'd think, *What are we going to have for tea?* I honestly needed to clone myself to get everything done and give each child 100%.

I felt guilty many times because I was juggling to meet each child's needs; the baby took priority as her needs were more, but feeling like I wasn't giving my all to each of them if I did puzzles with my toddler, my baby wasn't getting my attention, and if I was giving baby attention I wasn't with my toddler. In the end I wore baby a lot and tried to do things with them both.

The only thing I could do that I felt I did well was tandem feed. The little Mmmmmmmmmmmmmmm noises, snuggles and love made me feel great."

Shelley, Mother to Leia, 3 and Anya, 1

The duration of breastfeeding is another area where experiences with our firstborn pave the way for greater confidence with our second. Despite the World Health Organisation's recommendation to breastfeed exclusively for six months, then to continue breastfeeding alongside the introduction of solid food for two years and beyond, this is rarely mainstream practice in the West. Therefore, if we continue feeding beyond babyhood, we are likely to receive advice or criticism from those who have not experienced such a practice. Similarly, we may have felt pressured to wean our babies from the breast earlier than we hoped and with reflection wish we had been able to carry on breastfeeding for longer. Such experiences can give us motivation and confidence to meet our baby's needs the second time with less concern for the opinions of others.

Loving another

From pregnancy or even before, many of us wonder, and worry, about whether we will be able to wholly love another child. Being so fully aware of how much we love our first child, we worry about whether it will be possible to love our next baby in the same deep way.

Through mothering our first child we have already learned much about the power of unconditional love, yet what we are still to discover is how love expands and multiplies when shared. For most of us, as soon as that next baby is here, we are amazed at just how much we *do* love this baby, and how it feels as though a new place in our heart has opened with love especially for this little one.

Yet the love we feel for our new baby in no way diminishes what we feel for our first, in fact we may love them even more, and the way we see them can be suddenly transformed; they seem so large and grown up. We come to realise that love need not be divided nor diminished, but rather it multiplies, expanding to enfold everyone. If only the same were true for our energy, finances and practical capabilities.

"When it had just been myself and Jessie, I often felt enormous awe and wonder at how much it was possible to love this little person. I did worry during my second pregnancy that the experience had been a one-off. So it was a source of great joy after Lizzie's birth to discover how easy it was to love just as much all over again!"

Marty, Mother to Jessie, 21 and Lizzie, 16

Such depth of love can teach us a great deal about the abundant nature of life. Unconditional love is not finite; not limited nor dependent upon anything for its existence. Loving our children can introduce us to the profound depths of giving and receiving. And whilst many times over we become physically and emotionally drained and depleted, unconditional love is something *beyond* our day-to-day feelings and energy levels; it is a source of giving and replenishment we can turn to again and again, so that we can continue to nurture ourselves and our children with great tenderness. It is a space to which we can go to find relief, wisdom and the energy to carry on.

"Seeing both my daughters together made my heart swell, I have so much love for them it filled my whole body."

Shelley, Mother to Leia, 3 and Anya, 1

If we experienced postnatal anxiety or depression with our first, then concerns about feeling this way again may surface. We may fear we will not easily love our baby and be unable to cope, and such fears are grounded in reality rather than anxiety, for this was our experience previously.

This can be an extremely anxious and challenging time, even more so if we do begin to feel the return of familiar, uncomfortable mental and emotional states. Yet our experiences and learning means we are better equipped to recognise these feelings sooner than perhaps we did the first time. Similarly, we have more experience of knowing how to take care of ourselves and how to seek effective support.

"I experienced depression and anxiety after the birth of my first baby and at the time I put this down to our birth experiences – he was born by Caesarean after a long labour. So the second time around I did everything I could so birth would be different; I thought if he was born naturally I'd have more help from my hormones in adjusting to mothering him and would hopefully avoid becoming depressed again.

I hired a doula, practiced pregnancy yoga and negotiated for a home birth. I had a VBAC (Vaginal Birth After Caesarean), it was an intense experience, but even after this, I felt myself slipping into a dark and vulnerable way, and although I could see it happening, there was nothing I could do to stop it.

But this time, although the feelings are awful, I knew I'd been through it before, and that I could again. I did lots to help myself, and, with time, things changed. I found a way forward, love my sons immensely and am happy with life and mothering once again."

Harriet, Mother to Riley, 4 and Leo, 1

The practicalities
Whilst tender feelings for our newborns blossom, what is often more

difficult, is how we bring this love into action. We may lie in bed feeding our newborn with our toddler cuddled up beside us, feeling love and connection of universal proportions, but getting up, showering, getting everyone dressed, feeding the baby again, making breakfast, washing up, getting out of the house, getting to playgroup, then doing the shopping is quite another story. We may have worried about how we would love both children, yet once they are here and we realise our heart has ample space for both, we realise our immediate challenges lie in the practicalities.

I loved my second baby as dearly as my first, and rather than feeling love was divided, I felt it multiply, grow, and expand more with each child. Particularly tender were the feelings of seeing my babies and children love, and interact with, each other. Yet the same cannot be said for the practicalities of caring for them. What energy I did have had to be carved up and shared between them, in ever decreasing slices. Whilst I had great stores of love, the same was not true for time, attention, physical presence and the capacity to listen, at least in the beginning of mothering two.

I found it a huge struggle to give physical and mental attention to both, and struggled with much guilt and self-criticism, for I just wanted to be there 100%, responsive and present, for both of them. What I realise now, and have learned over the years, is that my milestones lay in learning to become a mother to my *family* at this time. My transformation required learning to balance needs, share attention and nurture relationships between us all, rather than focussing solely on one child as I had previously. In the beginning this felt virtually impossible; I wondered how on earth to care for a new baby as well as a toddler, who, before the baby came along, took up all my time anyway.

So whilst we are familiar with baby care and meeting the needs of our older child, unless we have excellent support or are able to clone ourselves, we have to learn how to do both things simultaneously. Slings, wraps and baby carriers can become a lifeline for keeping baby close and held whilst we interact with our toddlers. Yet as mothers alone with our children for many hours each day, there is much to learn and at times we have limited practical and emotional capacity. We can feel extremely sensitive about the impact our new baby will have on our firstborn, and worry about how our precious relationships will fare;

"The hardest thing having a second child has been the feeling of splitting my time between the two of them and not having the energy to dedicate as much quality time to my eldest as we did previously.

I take control of almost all the care of our baby, which I think I need to rebalance a little as he gets older so I can spend more uninterrupted time with my first boy. As a mum of two, there is suddenly less time to spend on the quality extras with either child and time becomes a juggling act focussed more on practical necessities. I always used to have a lovely time with my first boy at bedtime, feeding, reading stories and singing. Now, my partner puts him to bed as it happens at the same time as our second needs breastfeeding and settling to sleep. We haven't yet found a way of altering this without a lot of crying from number 2, so I try and find time during the day to do those things instead."

Louise, Mother to Flynn, 3 and Rowan, 10 months

Whilst we may not find the perfect way, for that surely exists in our minds only, what we do find, is our way. We have babies and children depending on us for food, comfort, holding and love; we have to simply carry on, doing the best we can with the time, love and energy we have available, and it is here that slings, wraps and carriers can be invaluable.

Certainly, these are milestones of balance and expansion, enabling us to blaze a trail into previously uncharted territories of emotional and practical capacities. Change can be uncomfortable. We are forced out of our comfort zone, and at times we feel unable to give as much as we would like. Also, there is little time for ourselves and our partners too.

"I do feel more confident handling a baby second time around, but on the other hand, he suffers sometimes, I think, from not getting the devoted attention my firstborn did. I'm so keen to make sure the big one doesn't feel pushed out that I sometimes almost consciously inhibit the joy I let myself feel in the small one.

I was also sure I couldn't love number two like I did number one. It has come harder – he is bewitching and delightful, but also very high-need, and he's diluting my time with the big one, and there have been times I've resented him for this. And of course babies don't give back to you in the same ways as energetic three-year-olds do."

Eleanor, Mother to Thomas, 3 and David, 10 months

Our emotional landscapes are complex places; we so want to do as good a job with our second baby as we did with our first, whilst still continuing to be responsive and connected with our older child. At this time of challenge and growth where we often feel stretched and compromised, we can reassure ourselves that love finds its own way; that each relationship will develop in its own time and in its own way. We need not, indeed cannot, attempt to replicate the relationship with our firstborn, as we cannot go back in time to there being only the one baby once again. Rather we must move forwards, embracing our new family circumstances, giving ourselves permission to get to know and love our second and subsequent babies for who they are, and develop new, altogether unique, relationships.

"I soon discovered that being a mother of two was more than twice the work of being a mother of one because of the way they fragment your time; for example, when the little one has finished feeding there is likely only to be a uselessly small timeslot available before the big one has to be escorted to or picked up from somewhere.

In contrast to all of the reading I did during Jessie's babyhood, half a side of A4 became information overload. For four years all I basically did was get through from one end of the week to the other."

Marty, Mother to Jessie, 21 and Lizzie, 16

However, as Marty goes on to illustrate, we do indeed learn a great deal with our first child which gifts confidence to mother both through the challenges we encounter;

"However, there were big positives. First, of course there was the joy of watching my two daughters grow and develop, not just as individuals, but in their relationships with one another. Second, I threw away the advice of all the parenting gurus to whom I paid such attention first time around; their perspectives all seemed too narrow now, one way or another. And third, I did manage to cling on to one of my voluntary roles. I repeatedly considered giving it up, but it was one in which I had really acquired the capacity to help people, and being able to do so helped me to face my own problems constructively."

Marty, Mother to Jessie, 21 and Lizzie, 16

"Having a second baby was a totally different ball game. Having one child was a picnic, our time was luxurious. Parenting a new baby with a toddler in tow was a shock to my system.

Medical mismanagement of her birth left my husband and I in absolute shock. I suffered postnatal depression, though didn't recognise it for what it was until sometime later.

Life came to a standstill. The new baby was such a shock for my first child, and her sleep patterns went out of the window. They both required me in bed for hours every night. My idea of a night out with my husband was him ordering an Indian takeaway and us eating by candlelight at the foot of the family bed.

I was the perfect mother when I had one child. I was the world's worst when I had two. At least that's how it felt. I'd gone from all the time in the world to enjoy one-on-one time with my daughter, to splitting myself in half to meet the needs of both. I felt a failure at times. Regardless, I carried on and every day was a new day to start again."

Veronika, Mother to Bethany, 19 and Eliza, 17

"I was nervous having a boy, I knew girls, I am one, but how could I be close to a boy? Yet the same strong emotion took hold as soon as he was born. He was in special care and I ached for him. I was too weak to walk but I told them I had to see my baby."

Lizzie, Mother to Izzy, 6, James, 4 and Lloyd, 1

As Lizzie illustrates, despite our initial worries, love and instinct emerge and guide us forward in growing to love and understand our children. At the other end of her parenting journey, Jane acknowledges the differences in her relationships with her sons and daughter, reinforcing the fact that whilst differences may exist in relationships, love remains constant;

"I have to be honest and say there are differences in my relationships with my sons and daughter. I know how a female mind works. Males are a mystery at times. I would like to think I haven't treated them any differently, but I probably have, with all the best intentions. What is no different is how much I love them, am proud of them and will always be there for them whatever happens in their lives. I will continue and will always be their constant."

Jane, Mother to Aleisha, 24, Richard, 18, Sam, 15 and George, 9

Many of us do not have daily support from extended families, making this an intense time practically and emotionally. Our milestones call to us to let go of notions of perfection, of there being one way of doing things. We come to realise that now things are different, compromises must be made. We may not be able to do all of the same things with our second baby which we did with our first, just as we may not be able to carry on mothering our eldest as we did previously.

We must adjust and realise that although our children's experiences of infancy and childhood are different, this does not necessarily make them any less. We can begin to see that although each child may lose some focussed parental attention, they gain in other ways – the presence of a sibling, the widening of social circles, the experience of evolving love;

"I did feel guilty I wasn't giving Lizzie, my baby, the attention I'd given Jessie in her early years; I seemed mostly to be dragging her round like baggage in the wake of her sister's hectic social life! But I later reflected that her life was no less rich, it was just rich in different ways, in particular involving exposure to lots of older children, which I think allowed her to grow up with great social confidence."

Marty, Mother to Jessie, 21 and Lizzie, 16

The feelings of being torn between both children are present whatever our children's ages, for a new baby requires a constant investment of attention. Faith had her second baby when her eldest son was 11. Whilst she found balancing the needs of her newborn and her son different than it would have been had her son been a toddler, she still found herself struggling, feeling torn at times;

"Dominic was 11 when I had Stella. Up until having her I still read to him at night, I tried to keep doing this, but in time it fell by the wayside. I was tired in the evenings, and spent much time feeding my baby. But the reading would have changed with time anyway; he wouldn't have wanted this to carry on as he grew older and spent his time doing different things.

We also used to co-sleep, not all the time, but occasionally. I remember him telling me he did feel upset I didn't still sleep with him, as by then I had my new partner. But again, this is one of those things that would have stopped in its own time.

When we've had family crises, or something bad has happened in his life, he has come back in with us occasionally. I did find a few things difficult in sharing my time and attention between them both, and I have to say this does feel difficult sometimes even now as I want to give my son the time and attention he needs for what is going on with his life now, and feel I struggle to do this as well as I would like due to the constant needs of the little ones."

Faith, Mother to Dominic, 16, Stella, 4 and Emily, 2

Evolving relationships

One of the most joyful aspects of nurturing two are the budding relationships between children. For just as we have been rearranging our inner landscapes to welcome the new baby, so too has our first child. Witnessing our first child, in all of his innocence, begin exploring and expressing interest and love for his new sibling can be a tender and beautiful element of this time;

"It's been wonderful watching our two boys growing to care strongly about each other; this relationship is developing as our baby learns to crawl and wants to join in with whatever our three-year-old is playing."

Louise, Mother to Flynn, 3 and Rowan, 10 months

"Reflecting on my journey as a mother, I've felt a deep and consuming love from conception each time I've been pregnant. All the clichés I've found to be true; love grows so there's enough for everyone, is not finite and does not have to be divided between children.

I've never been happier than hearing 'I love you mummy, and daddy, and Lucy' as part of my son's daily chatter, unprompted. Our home is full of affection, kisses and cuddles."

Jenny, Mother to Matthew, 3 and Lucy, 14 months

Witnessing such expressions of love from our first child is truly beautiful, and indeed reassuring, as certainly it is on our mind how our eldest will adapt. *We* know we love him just as much as we did previously, but often worry he will feel left out, or somehow less loved. And for many children, adjusting to the shifting dynamics is difficult at times.

It can and does take time for a gentle and loving relationship to develop between siblings; older children can find it incredibly difficult adjusting to a new baby in the house; a baby who seems to take up so much (of his) time, space, cuddles and attention. This can be extremely challenging, especially as we come to realise we cannot always be everything to everyone.

"Becoming a mother of two was a lot more challenging than I thought. I had a big bond with my eldest son and things changed greatly since the birth of my second. The main thing I found hard were the attacks from my eldest to his baby brother. He had found it hard to deal with and felt angry towards his brother. But recently it changed and I've found moments where he's told his brother he loves him, or I found him helping him out. This makes me smile, as I know (or hope) eventually they will be best of friends and play together."

Harriet, Mother to Riley, 4 and Leo, 1

When difficulties for our older children arise, we realise what a truly big job mothering is. We need to be there for our new baby, whilst simultaneously supporting our older child to express his emotions, anger and sadness, much of which is likely to be directed at us and the baby. We learn milestones of empathy and compassion as we try to hold him, guide him and love him through these difficulties alongside the practicalities of parenting. Our milestones come with reflection; we know it will not always be like this, that this stage will pass, they will grow and things will change.

Shifting dynamics with partners

Just as our relationship with our first child, and then second, evolves, so too does motherhood herald shifts in relationships with husbands and partners. This is certainly a broad issue, and deserving of discussion beyond the scope of this book, yet here we listen to women's reflections on romantic relationship changes as we rearrange our inner landscapes to encompass loving our children;

"Far from the second child making the first feel usurped, I think partners must feel usurped as soon as the first comes along. I feel for them too as I felt I just couldn't cope with loving a partner as well as a baby. Thankfully I had a wonderfully loving, understanding partner, who must have taken a back seat for a while, but who was also besotted with the baby, so that surely helped."

Ross, Mother to Charley and Chelsea, in their 20's

"Becoming a family is an ongoing journey. Sometimes things seem plain sailing and sometimes they don't. I think that the adaptation to parenthood can be a massive challenge to a couple, even when it's planned. I don't think that you can truly prepare for the new people that you become, and the new order (or disorder!) your life takes on!"

Ann, Mother to Ella, 4

"'How are you deciding about things?', 'Are your beliefs matching?' I found it quite hard to not understand each other in some points of child rearing. Although few, the differences were somewhat aggressive as they came from the core of us. You pursue your biggest truth for your child. The little time you spent with your partner gives hardly enough chance to vent and recharge."

Hanneke, Mother to Vita, 2

"At some point I realised that my son was more important to me than my husband. It felt like falling in love. I loved my husband, but he definitely took a back seat in my life now."

Alison, Mother to Callum, 23

Below, Eleanor speaks honestly about the unconditionality of the love we feel for our children, compared to the different kind of love we feel for a partner. Her depth of perspective brings insight into our inner landscapes regarding how, and more so why, we can and do love our children as we do, and are able to have such reserves of patience and energy to continually meet their needs;

"I do feel bad for my husband. I love him – of course – but the way I feel for my children is so different. I suppose it's about unconditionality; they can do preposterous things but I get over it so quickly, because they're mine, whereas the husband was just an addition to me. I could cast him off (not that I plan to) whereas the children are stuck with me.

They've taken his place, though, in my bed, in my arms... I do talk to them first, and defend them to him, and cook with them in mind, and make all my plans around them. It's because they're small and helpless and they need me, but also because of the pleasure and fulfilment in meeting their needs. And of course, because they're young there's no complexity to this, no difficult balance of 'I'll do this if you do that', no grudges or promises or tallies. I'm so orientated to their wellbeing and I'm sure there are times he feels that he loses out. I hope he feels it's worth it, and understands that it's an investment in our family as a whole, but I'm sure that at times he just feels pushed out, and pushed aside."

Eleanor, Mother to Thomas, 3 and David, 10 months

Eleanor's insights illustrate the deep and complex growth unfolding within as we unconsciously rearrange our inner world to become a foundation of unconditional love. It is clear how such a shift in our emotional and physical focus can be immensely challenging for partners, and how the constant tasks involved in caring for babies can mean there is little time to nourish ourselves and our adult partnerships.

Confidence is cumulative

Whilst there are without doubt practical and emotional challenges, what we do bring to mothering our second child is the wisdom of our previous learning. Whilst we may struggle with balancing everyone's needs, much of our path is smoother as, similar to the discussion regarding breastfeeding, we bring with us trust, knowledge, confidence and understanding born of experience;

"Through having my first baby, I learned to trust my instincts and believe in my own abilities; I became confident in myself through having dealt with everything that came up."

Amy, Mother to Simon, 25 and Edward, 19

When my first baby had a cold or cough which disturbed her sleep I remember worrying very much; I would read extensively and ask for advice. I sat holding her all night surrounded by bowls of steaming water, we put eucalyptus on the pillows and radiators. I worried about her breathing and we attempted to prop her mattress up to help her breathe more easily. I was tense and concerned, yet with my second and third babies, when they were snuffly I did not feel this sense of panic. I realised I had learnt what to do, felt I could trust myself to recognise when it was a normal snuffle, and when to be more concerned, and simply accepted that there would be a few unsettled nights, but with time they would feel better.

Coming to mother our second baby highlights the breadth and depth of our learning and transformation; we know, instinctively, and from experience, how to get on and nurture babies, identifying and meeting their needs. We can let go of anxieties more easily, trust ourselves more readily and, knowing how fast time really does pass, welcome a sense of being present and enjoying the time we share;

"It's different because I don't worry in the same acute, extreme way. I understand in my heart (rather than just knowing intellectually) that everything passes, and he'll be a baby for such a short time."

Eleanor, Mother to Thomas, 3 and David, 10 months

"In terms of mothering second time around, I can see I learnt from my first child how to tune into her needs. I was with her all the time and feel I can read her very easily. I know what will make her tired, how to respond to her in her difficult moments, when she will be feeling worried and need reassurance etc. Certainly, this did not happen from day one and I can see now what a steep learning curve it was.

But with my second daughter, I think I was more instinctively tuned into her needs from the start, because of what I'd learnt from Lucy. In particular, I'm much more relaxed about when and how things happen, like when and how to get her to sleep, how much she eats etc.

This is partly born out of necessity – I don't have as much time to devote to her needs now I have two children – but also because I know that ultimately she'll get what she needs so there's no point stressing myself out trying to force a routine if she resists it. With Lucy I got very wound up if I couldn't get her to sleep. With Tess, on the whole I'm able to let her shape her own routine and find I waste less energy on trying to make things happen in a certain way. This time around I feel like I know what I'm doing most of the time, and it feels good."

Catherine, Mother to Tess, 3 and Lucy, 19 months

As Catherine illustrates, mothering is a cumulative journey; our previous growth and past learning becomes the foundation for our future mothering and transformation. Similarly, when third and fourth babies enter our lives, the adjustment is less intense, as we simply know we will, somehow, expand across our hearts and everyday practicalities to create space to love and nurture them as required. We have already been forged as mothers – learning how to mother a family, expand, extend and balance differing needs – therefore we have much more familiarity and confidence upon the emotional and practical terrain of mothering to welcome further babies.

Some of us become mothers to two or more babies whilst for others our path continues as a mother of one. Sometimes this is through choice, and sometimes through circumstance;

"I remember when my son was around 2, I was just loving it, I found him so much more interesting than a baby, he seemed like a wee boy and was so much fun.

At this time I began to want another baby – previously I'd felt it would've been too much to cope with. Unfortunately, I was ill on and off for the next 4 years and on medication which made trying for a baby very difficult. I never managed to conceive again, which upset me greatly for a time, as I really wanted my son to have a sibling.

In the long run I came to terms with a situation that I had no control over and just concentrated on the pleasure from being with my son."

Alison, Mother to Callum, 23

"We never had a second child – my hormones went crazy, and when I failed to get pregnant after six months of trying, my husband and I both went for tests. It was a tense time for both of us. We discovered I wasn't ovulating, I was offered drugs to stimulate ovulation. After a great deal of soul-searching, I decided not to take them. I was 43, and had a very deep, gut feeling that if I was no longer producing eggs, nature had her reasons, and I shouldn't force things with drugs.

Yet again, though, I felt like a failure. This wasn't how I expected my body to respond, especially as I'd gotten pregnant very quickly the first time around.

When I was 45, I began having persistent and prolonged bleeding, and eventually had a hysterectomy – so there was no longer any chance of becoming pregnant again. I still feel I've not fully grieved for the loss of my womb, or for the loss of the second child I never had.

The child I did have, though, my wonderful son Daniel, has grown into an exceptional young man who still, at age 28, fills me with love and pride. He has been a consistent joy to me and my husband and has taught me about the true depths of unconditional love."

Ronne, Mother to Daniel, 28

Alison and Ronne illustrate that even in the most emotionally difficult times, the power of love and joy of connection we feel for our children can provide remarkable strength and motivation to continue. When we may be breaking across our inner, emotional landscapes, love for our child reminds us that there is part of life which is very valuable, requires our full attention and is very much worth living. This depth of love quietly whispers to our hurting parts, shifting our focus and gently encouraging us to carry on. As we encounter and grow through life's challenges, we come to understand, more profoundly, the depths of our own strength, tenacity, power, tenderness and capacity to love.

Chapter Seven
Challenging Times

All we encounter upon our mothering path brings opportunities for learning. Always we are called to deepen into ourselves and discover more of our capacity for trust, tenacity and unconditional love. We learn through joy and delight, yet so too do we learn through hard times and grief. Such learning is uncomfortable and hard won, yet with reflection we come to see how such times forged us, unearthing more of our capacity for strength, compassion and empathy.

Some of us are able to talk honestly about our feelings and difficulties and are blessed with supportive friends and family with whom to share. Yet a great many more women spoke of feelings of discomfort in speaking openly and the isolation this brings. Such isolation is especially difficult to bear when it arises from recurrent miscarriage, the tragedy of stillbirth, mental health issues, and the challenges of addiction. So often we feel we must put on a front, only showing the positive, happy sides of ourselves and this is exacerbated by the constant presence of social media portraying the simple, happy side of the family lives of others. When asked, 'How are you?' how many of us really feel able to express how we truly are? And where is the space for such tender and empathetic sharing amidst our busy days?

What follows are real, honest and powerful experiences of women's lives. We can draw strength from the women who walk before us, see that change *is* possible, and that we, too, are capable of finding strength, clarity and ways forward in even the most difficult circumstances.

Mothering alongside addiction

Let us begin with Francesca, a woman whose bravery and courage in overcoming her addiction, is remarkable and humbling. As Francesca illustrates, our path to motherhood may begin in difficult circumstances, yet motherhood is a powerful catalyst for change as we awaken to the great responsibility we now hold;

"I'm a recovering alcoholic and have been sober for nearly four years. I got sober around ten months after the birth of my first child, so becoming a mother and recovering from alcoholism have gone hand in hand. Therefore sometimes it's difficult to say whether it's solely becoming a mother that led to my change and growth, or my program of recovery. Both have contributed significantly, and to help you to understand let me briefly talk about my 12 step program of recovery.

My program has given me tools with which to cope and live a happy fulfilled life and my job as a mother allows me to put everything I've learnt into practice. My program of recovery is, in a lot of ways, a spiritual program which teaches me to trust a power greater than myself, which I now do. The program is all about learning how to live life on life's terms, changing, growing up, forgiveness, acceptance, letting go, tolerance, love and a million more things! It's been so important in my mothering journey, if I hadn't found this place and got sober, I most definitely wouldn't be the mother I am today. I'm so grateful I found the program; it saved my life and gifted me a life beyond my wildest dreams.

I will never forget the day I found out I was pregnant with my first child. It was around lunch time at the beginning of November 2010. I had a serious drink problem, which I was in total denial about, and was just about to get into the bath with a bottle of wine, but instinctively something told me to do a pregnancy test before I opened the bottle, and sure enough the test came back positive.

The emotions that followed were overwhelming. A mixture of panic, fear, joy, despair, happiness and sadness all whooshed together, spinning round my stomach. I felt crippled and consumed with anxiety and fear. I was still very much a child in an adult's body and certainly didn't feel like the image I had in my head of 'what a mother should be like', or capable of being responsible for raising another life.

I could barely look at myself.

My life was chaotic, a mess, but at the time I didn't see it that way. Almost instantly after seeing the positive result on the test I was longing for my 'old' life. I wasn't ready to give up the drink, the parties, the wild times. I was in the grip of alcoholism and was craving a drink, wishing the test had been negative so I could pop the cork off the bottle of fizzy wine and continue drinking 'guilt-free'. I wish I hadn't felt this way, but I wanted to drink more than I wanted to be pregnant. However, today I understand that that was due to my addiction, and not because I'm a bad person or didn't love my child.

Somehow, I managed to stay sober and thankfully didn't continue to drink during pregnancy (with the exception of twice when my addiction unfortunately got the better of me). A part of me knew if I was to take that first drink I'd lose all control over my drinking and could seriously harm this defenceless, innocent soul inside me. I would have done anything to get completely and utterly steaming drunk without harming my baby, but I knew that wasn't possible. I was never an ignorant person and knew the risks involved if I drank during pregnancy.

I'd started drinking from a very young age and had never gone longer than a week without a drink since I was 13 years old. I didn't know how to live a sober life. I white-knuckled it during pregnancy and hung onto the fact that I'd be able to start drinking again once I'd given birth. I grew very angry, bitter and resentful at my 'friends' who were continuing to drink as I wanted to and began to shut myself away from people. I also had resentments against my unborn baby for stopping me drinking. I remember finding pregnancy extremely difficult, longing for it to be over.

On the other hand, despite the cravings and desperateness I felt without alcohol, a bond and attachment with my baby began to form, I began to feel a connectedness to her. Every part of me wanted to protect this little person from danger and harm. I especially wanted to protect her from myself and my drinking.

Never in my life had I felt more protective over anything. It was as if something had changed within me and I would do anything to protect this person even if this meant putting my own needs aside. This feeling has never left me.

This is truly an enormous milestone; one of my very first milestones as a mother. Something definitely changed during pregnancy. The only way I can describe it is as though someone suddenly flicked a switch marked 'protector' from 'off' to 'on'. I would go as far as to say it was a magical experience like someone casting a spell over me. I had drunk the potion and been transformed from a scared, afraid coward into a powerful, fierce wolf who would attack if provoked in regards to protecting my child. It was this kind of animal instinct to protect that kept me away from the drink.

I remember desperately wanting to get to the next stage in pregnancy as this would give me comfort and reassurance that the baby was okay. When I was 4 weeks I longed to be 14 weeks as the chances of miscarriage significantly reduced. And when I got to that stage I wanted to be 20 weeks so I could get my scan and the professionals would be able to check and tell me if the baby was developing normally. I worried a lot about the baby's wellbeing and found that things like scans and midwife appointments helped calm me down.

Despite pregnancy being quite a negative experience, there were a lot of positive feelings too, more so as pregnancy developed and my fears over my baby's health and wellbeing began to calm. My bond with her started while she was still inside, I remember that being a great comfort, that feeling of the baby being so close, knowing that you and you alone are sustaining and growing a child is very empowering.

I didn't think about the birth because I was full of fear and dread at the thought. I did do some research and decided on a hospital birth with the hope of having the baby in water without drugs. This is a very lovely idea, but sadly my first child wasn't to be born this way due to unforeseen minor complications, she was instead born on the hospital bed while I was high on morphine and gas and air. This experience taught me a lot as a person, firstly that sometimes we have no control over situations and how things are going to pan out, and that we have to let go and trust that everything is as it is meant to be. Just because it isn't as I would've liked it doesn't mean it isn't what I needed. At the time I was very unhappy and angry at how the birth had gone, but today I don't feel like that. Becoming a mother and my program of recovery helped me grow so much in acceptance, strength and understanding I no longer carry resentments about the birth.

Once the labour was over I remember feeling euphoric. It was such an amazing, warm, happy buzz that swirled around my body. I was keen to have skin-to-skin which I got as soon as she was born. It was such an overwhelming experience when she was placed in my arms. I couldn't quite believe she was ours and that this incredible, perfect little person had been made inside my womb. I was so in awe of her and fascinated by the miracle of life I was holding so close to me. I remember being truly blown away and mystified by her.

Again though, fears crept in and I was soon desperate for reassurance she was okay. Once all the midwives had checked and they left the room and it was just me and my partner, that's when it hit me that there was really no going back, that we alone were responsible for the care and wellbeing of this little miracle.

In the first weeks I was in bits. My head and emotions were all over the place. Our families were unknowingly putting pressure on us to see the baby and I was putting pressure on myself, in a nutshell, to be perfect. I wanted to be content, happy and just kind of go with the flow, but I was fighting this new reality and was longing to go back to my old friend the drink.

During the first week I cried at least 4 times every day. I argued with family and struggled immensely with life in general. I felt frightened, alone (in the sense of the responsibility to look after my child even though I have a supportive partner and family), discontented and generally all over the place. I didn't have a clue how to look after, or even how to just be with, a baby. I remember having to ask the midwife how you changed a nappy. I didn't have much experience with babies and didn't have any trust or faith in myself. I remember thinking, *How am I going to be able to do this?* It was a very traumatic time and a very confusing one as I had this expectation that everything 'should' be amazing and happy, which in parts it was, but a lot of the time in those early days it wasn't.

As usual, my answer was to escape in a bottle. I wish I could say I never took another drink once my first child was born, but sadly, after her birth I still wanted to drink; I wanted my old life back; my old freedom to please myself, so when my daughter was about 10 days old I decided to go out for a work do. But it was different; I had this nagging feeling that I just couldn't shake that I shouldn't be doing this, and for the first time in my whole life was the first to leave the party after only having a few drinks. I had a terrible feeling that something wasn't right, that I needed to get back to my baby.

Sure enough I was right; on the way home my phone rang, it was my partner telling me he was at the hospital and that the baby had been struggling to breathe. It was the most terrifying experience but thankfully when I got there the baby was fine, it had been a false alarm. My partner had mistaken the mucus that most babies are congested with after birth as signs she was struggling to breathe. It was at this point I started to take a look at myself and my drinking. It forced me to look at myself and think about what kind of mother I wanted to be and what kind of mother I would be if I continued to drink as I had.

I pretended to everyone and mostly to myself that everything was okay. I didn't want to admit the truth, that I was finding it really difficult. I was unhappy, my self-esteem was non-existent unless I had alcohol in my system and even then it was still pretty low; at best I was arrogant. I was plodding on resentful, bitter and angry.

I felt like I was wishing my life away, wishing she would be older so I could get back to my life. Wishing she would be more fun, more interesting. I rushed her through all of her first times. I couldn't wait for her to smile, laugh, talk. I bathed her at one week old and uneducatedly filled it with so many baby products that she developed eczema. I believe this is what caused her skin condition. I know now how sensitive a baby's skin can be and didn't bathe my second child until about 6 or 7 weeks old. I had such an urgency with my first chid for her to do things. I'd get obsessed with reading all the different stages and things she should be doing and got worried when she wasn't.

In comparison, those early days with my second child are so very different indeed, all for the better. I've changed and grown so much since then thanks to my program of recovery and the amazing people I've met on my journey that I now don't recognise that person anymore. I feel like a different person. I trust myself, trust my children and accept things as they are today. I no longer have the desire to make everything as I think it should be, well, most of the time. I've been able to enjoy mothering so much more the second time around and haven't been in any hurry for her to grow, in fact I've found I'm now quite the opposite and almost don't want them to grow up.

I was lost with my first child. I didn't know who I was and felt like I didn't know what I was doing, but I was doing my best and looking back that is all that matters. I thought that to be a good mother I should be constantly doing things with my baby, offering her different experiences and I most likely overstimulated her as we never seemed to stop. I think this is also a reflection of how I was at the time.

I wasn't at peace within myself and always needed a distraction. I couldn't sit still so to speak, and wasn't able to just be with my baby in the house. Again this was due to my low self-worth; I didn't like myself and looking back I probably believed my baby wouldn't like me either.

In comparison, it has been completely different with my second, it's almost the opposite, I'm much more at peace within myself, I'm confident and now know my worth. I now know that there's no one in this world that my children love more than me. Getting sober and getting into recovery has helped me to become the person and the mother I want to be today."

Francesca, Mother to Laura, 4 and Ashley, 1

Francesca's story speaks for itself; her growth and transformation is intense and powerful, bringing her face to face with some of the most vulnerable aspects of herself, yet so too has it been a journey of love. Her immediate urge to protect her baby, even from herself, illustrates the power of instinct and unconditional love in action, and how such love can create profound clarity and shifts in perspective as our priorities sharply rearrange. Through learning to love her baby, Francesca began a journey of learning to love and truly value herself – and a large part of this was her commitment to overcoming her alcohol addiction. Ultimately, she shifted her inner landscapes from places of conflict and criticism to peace and self-acceptance.

For regardless of our outer work and the practical aspects of our lives, it is our inner, emotional reserves from which we mother and upon which we heal. When we are struggling and lacking self-love, we can find aspects of these early times challenging. Yet herein lies a gift; for in the beginnings of loving our babies, and sometimes struggling to love them, we are brought up close to elements of ourselves we may have been denying and turning away from. We are invited to look within, with honesty, and to embrace these hurting aspects, these aspects of ourselves of which we may feel ashamed. We can then create another way forward. For Francesca that way forward involved admitting her addiction to alcohol and embarking on a program to help her to overcome it.

It took great courage for Francesca to share her story, yet I am so very pleased she did. Her journey lies at the very heart of what *Milestones of Motherhood* is about and the transformation and growth motherhood can ignite. Holding ourselves in the same, fierce unconditional love and acceptance with which we hold our children is a key milestone of our journey. This is not a selfish journey; for the more we love, heal and nurture ourselves, the more our inner resources are cultivated and replenished, increasing the inner stores from which we can nurture our children.

If you are facing difficulties of your own, let Francesca's words speak to you. Connect deeply within yourself and uncover the strength and belief that you, too, *can* learn, grow and create positive change where necessary. Feel inspired that change *is* possible. Let the love you hold, or wish to hold, for your child nurture yourself and inspire your way forward.

Journeys through IVF

For some of us, becoming mothers is the most challenging part of our journey. Conceiving our baby becomes the journey itself, a journey of anxiety, anticipation, hope and devastation. Few women speak openly about their IVF experiences when they are going through it, meaning for many this also becomes a journey of loneliness and isolation. Emma chose to be open about her journey as a way of coping;

"Once we were married we started trying for a baby straight away. I came off the Pill, but after seven months I still had no cycle and no sign of pregnancy. A scan revealed I had polycystic ovaries (PCOS) and wasn't ovulating. This was a real shock, being told it could be difficult to have children. Since my older teens I'd been trying not to fall pregnant and now I was ready, I couldn't. It had never crossed my mind I wouldn't be able to have children; I was devastated at what this might mean.

My consultant prescribed Clomid, a fertility drug that stimulates ovulation. I felt hopeful that this would sort things out and I'd soon be pregnant. Yet this was not the case, each month the ovulation sticks showed I was ovulating, but I still wasn't getting pregnant; worry and frustration began to set in, and the doctors couldn't give an explanation as to why. I started having some vision problems, things started feeling very wrong with my eyes and I became very panicky as I'd always had anxiety about my sight. It turns out that as Clomid is a steroid, one of the side effects can be eye problems. I stopped taking it, I was frightened, terrified, I became fixated on it, worried I was losing my sight. I was trying to manage this, along with the grief of not getting pregnant alongside going to work; I fell into a very dark place of fear, anxiety and desperation.

Our next option was IVF, and as my husband already had a child, we would have to pay for it ourselves. We booked the consultation, I was terrified, I had no idea what to expect, the anticipation was very nerve-racking. Nowhere in our county does it, so each appointment was a long journey, which added to the anxiety. The initial tests confirmed the PCOS and revealed my husband had a low sperm count, which was thankfully righted through vitamins.

The IVF journey is intense; I was shocked at having to inject myself daily for up to eight weeks. I was so anxious about taking these drugs after what had happened with the Clomid, the first part of the process is drugs to shut down your system, then you take two injections to stimulate the follicles. I began talking to people about the IVF, rather than keeping it private as many people do, and I was met with horror stories. Also, around this time lots of friends were falling pregnant. I so wanted to be happy for them, but I wasn't; that's what infertility can do, it brought out this jealousy and bitterness which made me feel so low, angry and isolated.

Time went on, I was back and forwards out of the county to appointments. It wasn't working. My ovaries weren't shutting down, so I had to take the first round of injections for much longer. I felt so worried about the potential side effects. Plus it was the cost of paying for more medication. We didn't have the spare money, so friends and family paid. I felt awful. We were taking a large amount of money and it was a gamble. We didn't want to waste it, but at the same time were so desperate for it to work.

Eventually the drugs worked, my ovaries responded and I took the second round of injections to stimulate the follicles. Driving through to the hospital was agonising; my ovaries were so bloated and pushing on my bladder. Facing the next stage of the process, new fears surfaced; I'd never had medical procedures before and was terrified of sedation; I was getting so panicky and worked up and so desperate for it to work.

Fortunately the process went smoothly; I had twelve mature eggs, we were happy, but I was in so much pain. With IVF it is all the waiting and phone calls; each step, the anticipation, desperation and hope of getting to the next stage. We waited, they called, and out of the twelve eggs, seven had been fertilised. Now we had to wait to see how the cells would divide. At each step you expect the number of potential eggs to decrease. The best day to get to is day five after fertilization as this is the blastocyst stage, and there is a higher chance of successful implantation. We got the phone call on day three saying two had developed and they wanted to put them back in.

There is no dignity in the process.

Then you have to take daily pessaries internally to thicken the lining of your womb.

I didn't have high hopes.

Then came the two week wait. It's a horrific time. In two weeks you have a blood test and they ring you after 4 p.m.

I remember sitting on the sofa looking at my phone, knowing I was going to feel absolutely elated or totally deflated. I didn't think it would work, I was psyched up for a negative pregnancy test. I felt like a failure already. If it hadn't worked, what would we do now?

They phoned. It hadn't worked. We made an appointment to talk about it.

We chose to try again. We were warned of the risk of OHSS, overstimulation of the ovaries.

We had a holiday at the end of the summer. I was so deflated. Everyone knew about it and I felt like a failure. I'm a teacher and it is so hard to see families on their third or fourth child. My colleague was having IVF too, we were going through it together. Except that it worked for her and she was pregnant.

As a teacher I planned to have IVF in the summer holidays. So we waited, we planned to try again, and time went on. And lots of friends became pregnant. I felt so desperate, I was desperate to try again, but knew we had to wait until the following summer. Another year passed and I felt time ticking by, feeling pressure to be getting on with it.

This time I took the short cycle, two weeks of medication then follicle harvesting. I took a low dose and didn't produce many follicles. The eggs were retrieved and there was only one. One compared to twelve last time. I was so low and depressed, not in a good place at all and my body was struggling. We got the call that it hadn't fertilised so they wouldn't attempt to put it back in. We didn't even get the chance.

The resentment was coming now. Friends were falling pregnant, relatives who had only been with partners for five minutes. We had a family meal where a family member presented us all with their scan picture. No one knew what to do. It was so public. At the same time I felt happy, and horrifically heart-broken.

My niece was born. There was the dreadful jealous side. But I looked after her a lot and it helped me. We have a close bond and continue to do so. It did help and took my mind off things slightly.

Fast forward another year. More friends are pregnant. My best friend, the one whose shoulder I had cried on through the whole process, she was always there for me. She was pregnant. She told me she was terrified to tell me. I felt so bad. What sort of a person was I?

For me it was part of being a woman, to have a baby. My husband didn't feel like I did. He had a child already. He couldn't understand why I was so jealous; he didn't understand why I couldn't be happy for folk.

Another year went by.

I spoke to someone and they asked if I'd tried acupuncture. I'd already started yoga to help with anxiety and I loved the effect it has on you, it really helped and I started to feel different. I was under lots of stress with work, school, OFSTED, I tried the acupuncture and found it really relaxing. At the same time I was working on getting my stomach issues settled and had cut out gluten and dairy and was feeling in a better place physically.

We saved up for the third round for the forthcoming summer holidays. This time we had the short cycle once again, and I produced quite a few follicles. More than the second time. Something felt different. I felt okay, I'd already been through the sedation and knew what to expect. Plus I was in a much better head space. Fourteen eggs were retrieved, and they rang the following day saying twelve had been fertilised. Twelve! I felt really good.

They rang on the fourth day recommending a blastocyst transfer with three to four being frozen. This was brilliant news, getting to the blastocyst stage, it was the furthest we'd ever got. But it's always in your mind, saying not to let yourself get carried away. After all, with IVF there's only a 25–30% success rate. It's not high. For every success story there are many more couples it doesn't work for. You can hope, but you can't keep hoping forever.

We went for the egg transfer, and I had fertility acupuncture before and after implantation. It was a hatching blastocyst, it was doing all the right things and showed really good signs. We had the two week wait, and had booked Centre Parcs with family. It was an intense time. I bought pregnancy tests as well as being booked in for the blood work, as I felt so positive this time.

I took the first test on the Wednesday. It was negative. But it was early, probably too early, and I felt so positive, so we waited and I took another on the Friday.

It was negative.

My mum saw my face before I said anything. We were crying. The world collapsed around me. Everything had gone so right. I don't know what else I could have done. How could that test be negative? Everyone was crying around me, we were all on this journey together and I had let everyone down.

I decided I wasn't going to make the long journey to the hospital for a blood test that would be negative anyway. I booked one at my local surgery. I didn't want to speak to anyone. I was in the darkest place I'd ever felt. In my mind I couldn't imagine me without a child. I began to think about adoption and fostering.

My husband didn't speak. He just went to work. We were very low. He was like a closed book.

But the lining didn't come away straight away and I didn't start bleeding. My mum suggested taking another test. The blood test wasn't being done for a few more days. My mum bought a Clear Blue, one of the expensive ones. I woke on the Tuesday morning thinking I'd just do it as I hadn't come on since I'd stopped taking the pessaries.

I did the test and put it to one side. I thought if I didn't look it might work. I looked to the side and saw two lines. I couldn't believe it. The shock!! I ran to Lee and threw the stick at him. Is it a false positive?

It was too early to call my clinic, so I posted on some of the IVF groups, there were two strong lines. I called the clinic at 8 a.m. They told me not to get too excited, that it could be a chemical miscarriage.

My mum and dad were overjoyed, it was like they'd won the Lottery, they dashed through to join us. The staff at the clinic were matter of fact and told us not to get our hopes up. We had to wait for the results at 4 p.m. Now there were new things to worry about, what if the hormone levels weren't high enough and it was a chemical miscarriage?

The clinic phoned and said it was wonderful news. I don't even have the words to describe how I felt.

That weekend I realised I hadn't thought where our life was going. For the past six years everything had been consumed by fertility treatment, all of life was on hold, all our money was saved for the IVF.

But I couldn't start thinking about the future yet. At seven weeks I had a viability scan, it was nerve-racking, new fears were creeping in all the time. I was neurotic, I know you should try not to have stress during pregnancy, but I couldn't help it. I was so elated to be going through the pregnancy process, but at the same time, was terrified. At nine weeks I had a bleed, I called the GP who said it sounds like a miscarriage. I was devastated. But in hospital they revealed the heart beat was still there, it was a bleed behind the placenta. This stopped in a week. But I was tense, I was having vivid dreams and nightmares, with a terrifying fear of something going wrong.

But as I got into it, pregnancy ran smoothly, I started pregnancy yoga and this helped with the anxieties. I had no real pregnancy problems, I tried to enjoy it, but it was all about getting through the stages. At 24 weeks, the baby was viable. This was a huge relief. It was finally my turn. I could finally start thinking about having a baby and being a mum to a child of my own.

I felt so geared up for my labour, ready to use the breathing and positions I'd learned from yoga. It was a quick birth and here she was. I was in a very negative state about my body not doing what I thought it should, but in labour it did everything and more. It was amazing. I couldn't believe she was here. Our Sienna Hope.

A lot of anxieties followed as a new mum, I was in shock, it wasn't what I'd expected it to be like, I'd wanted it for so long, but I found it really difficult, but then there is the love. Nothing can describe that. And the bond we have is so strong. She is our little miracle, reminding us to always have hope.

Going through the process of IVF is tough, and it changed me a lot. It taught me to always have hope, for whilst it doesn't always work, sometimes it does. Infertility is nothing to be ashamed of, even though it does make you feel very ashamed and inferior to others, there's no point in blaming yourself. It made us much stronger as a couple, going through all of those emotions together, and made me much more resilient as a person. I've learnt not to put so much pressure on myself as to how I think things should be, and now try to go with the flow more in bringing her up. I'm so much more appreciative of every little thing, and I couldn't love her any more.

And now we're edging into that process again; I'm a bit disappointed I've not become pregnant naturally, as many people do after IVF, but we have some blastocycts frozen and are just beginning the journey to have them put back in. And we'll be back there, in that cycle of hope, fear, anxiety and anticipation, hoping to make it through each of those many stages and bring one of those tiny babies-to-be to life."

Emma, Mother to Sienna, 18 months

Emma's story brings to light the tremendously challenging journey conception can become. A journey like this changes everything; mothers are acutely aware that nothing can be taken for granted, and whilst moments of pregnancy can be joyful, the journey is challenging and different to those whose pregnancies were conceived more easily. The IVF journey, each day, brings to the forefront milestones of surrender. For this is a journey of hope and anxiety, a journey of many stages, a process which can be nurtured, but the outcome is beyond anyone's control.

This is a tough place to be, yet as Emma illustrates, this journey can evoke a deepening into one's self; the discovery of inner resources, grit, strength, determination and deepened emotional experience and capacity. It is not a journey easily chosen and, sadly, does not always have a happy ending. But when it does, the feelings of hope, awe and gratitude can create a new landscape within, providing ongoing support, trust and positivity.

Journeys through recurrent miscarriage
Women spoke previously of their experiences of miscarriage, the shock, grief and sadness, as well as the silence enshrouding miscarriage and the anxiety surrounding subsequent pregnancies. When miscarriage is followed by the birth of another baby, we can hold these desperately sad experiences within our landscapes

alongside focussing our love and attention on the child or children in our arms. Yet sadly this is not always the case. Mary Ann brings to light the rarely spoken about, devastating and isolating journey of recurrent miscarriage;

"The sonographer diagnoses a missed miscarriage, it's our third in a row, fifth in six years, it doesn't get less shit really. Every time I get pregnant we focus on being positive, on believing that this time it will work out. We allow ourselves hope, and then when we find out, that hope is dashed. It hurts.

Raw. Tears. Despair.

I'm wandering about the house like I don't know where I'm going, I'm beginning, very slowly and gently, to bleed. I know now that my body knows exactly what to do once my mind catches up. It's the weirdest thing, but once I know my baby won't live, it's like my mind let's my body allow it to die. I feel powerless to birth another living baby (another as we have one who is almost 4) and paradoxically, at the same time, so powerful in maintaining the illusion of pregnancy, I don't seem to miscarry until my mind has caught up.

Mine are always 'missed'.

I suddenly feel like I can't bear to tell anyone, can't bear to share the news that our baby isn't coming after all, as if, when I speak it, it will become real and break me all over again. Or as if they will judge me and try to find a reason or an explanation. Believe me, I've heard them all before. 'It wasn't meant to be', 'Maybe it wasn't the right time', 'Your body wasn't ready', 'They keep changing their mind about coming earthside'. Endless ways to explain away what feels inexplicable – that our baby didn't keep growing and won't live. That our grief is real.

It most definitely doesn't feel better the next day. It just feels like awakening to the confirmation of devastation. Like when someone dies. Which in fact, they have. We just never met them. It's happened again and the only consolation is that now there have been three in a row we might actually be able to get it investigated. We might get some suggestions or ideas about why this might be happening. Because one thing I'm sure of, none of the 'explanations' and suggestions apply any more after five miscarriages;

'The baby decided not to come'; what, five of them? There must be something wrong with me.

'Maybe your body is struggling to hold on to a pregnancy'; what, after four missed miscarriages where my baby died long before it left my body?

'Maybe the time wasn't right?'; five times? Then perhaps it never will be.

All the explanations and ways of trying to console and explain just seem so unhelpful after multiple miscarriages. Because they either stop applying, or make you feel like the whole thing is your fault. You are broken in some way. And believe me, I don't need any help with feeling that way.

And, to be honest, that is sometimes how I've felt in these past three years of a yearly miscarriage just in time for Christmas. Like I am broken. And whenever I see any kind of professional I dread the bit where they either sweep my pain under the carpet, 'It's very common,' or 'Just try again, you don't have all the time in the world,' or some explanation about fate or destiny.

I don't want any of them. I don't want to hear anything that in any way invites me to tip any more of the blame back onto myself. I didn't eat right, prepare right, move right, pray right, envision right, do it right, behave right or whatever.

Believe me. I'm doing all of those things to myself in my head, perpetually, and the biggest challenge is not to. To stop blaming myself for my body where babies struggle to live.

Over the weekend I miscarried our baby, as in the physical process happened. Letting this happen naturally has been a choice for me every time since the first miscarriage I had in 2013 where, when I got back to our flat after discovering our baby had died, I went into a mini-labour within a couple of hours and our baby left my body.

Although it was deeply sad, I was also left with a sense that my body knew what to do, so I've opted for 'natural management' every time since. I'm sharing this because, the first time, I was so shocked that a labour-like process happened. I had no idea a miscarriage could be like that and to be honest hardly knew anything about them. I think I assumed it was something that wouldn't happen to me.

This time it took longer, a whole week in fact. And, perhaps because it took a week, I've been really aware of the physical and emotional changes; I've been plunged into deep despair and grief. This time it has really got harder and I've been struggling to cope. I know this is part of the process but it's also hard, sad and so annoying for this to be happening again the week before Christmas.

I would actually love a Christmas without fresh grief, as our last miscarriage happened a year and a week ago, there is such a sense of déjà vu. And even the Christmas before that we spent praying a miscarriage wouldn't happen, only to find I was miscarrying on 1st January.

One of the things I personally find helpful about a natural miscarriage is that it means we're able to bury our baby in a simple way, beneath an apple tree we planted where our other babies are also buried. It helps me to have this memorial and a way to say goodbye.

I feel like it's all crushing in, like we might never have another baby despite all the hoping and trying to do the right thing, all the energy of hoping and praying. There's a glimmer of hope that we can finally get medical investigations now after having three miscarriages in a row, but it has taken us two and a half years of trying to get here. It feels like forever.

Our son is 4. I am 41.

After he was born I remember thinking I wanted to have another baby before I was 40. I'm more than a year late, and now I'm not even pregnant. Meanwhile everyone I know or see seems to have two, three or four babies. I know that isn't true, but that's how it feels. Everyone I pass, everyone I see. I have loved being a Mum to the one child I have so much that I imagine if I'd started earlier maybe I would have had four.

That thought causes me to burst into tears again.

I've been pregnant six times. After our son was born I remember thinking it wasn't very likely I'd miscarry again now I'd had a child that lived, even though I'd had two miscarriages before him. I was so wrong and it hurts. I know now for the next few months that everyone will seem like they have plentiful fertility and babies and it will be impossible to totally silence the voices inside whispering 'What is wrong with me?', 'Why can't I carry another child?', 'What did I do wrong?'.

We got a Christmas tree yesterday and our Son has been decorating it, it seems strange to be doing festive things when I feel so raw inside, yet what else to do?

We were both in tears again this morning. It's horrible to wake up knowing again. I have occasional fleeting thoughts that maybe the scan was wrong, maybe my baby is alive inside me. I'm not bleeding much yet so that helps entertain them for a second or two, until the crushing reality returns. No heartbeat. A baby cannot survive with no heartbeat.

A part of me doesn't want to let this baby go, even though it's no longer alive. A part of me just wants it to stay with me.

And please don't say, 'It wasn't meant to be.' How do you know? As far as I'm concerned it was meant to be, and something has gone tragically wrong. If someone dies you don't say 'It wasn't meant to be'. You say 'I am sorry for your loss'. My baby died inside of me. Please don't assume it wasn't meant to be. It feels like you want to sweep my pain away and make everything alright. I don't want it to be. Everything is not alright. I am in mourning and, for now at least, I want to be.

I still feel sick and so sad, but it has helped also to be sharing what is happening and not trying to hide it. Physically, I'm still pregnant at the moment, I've still got some symptoms, that's the oddest thing. But it helps me to be writing this, letting the thoughts, especially the darkest ones, pass and dissipate a bit.

There's part of me that doesn't want this process to end; that wants to hold on to my baby. And yet I know this part can't go on forever; that eventually my miscarriage will complete.

I feel comfort in the fact that we've made a tradition of burying our babies, however small, in the earth under the tree, that we've given them a shared resting place. I feel so grateful for this place and for the dear person who gave me the idea when I first miscarried. I know it's not what people usually do but it's brought us some comfort and I wanted to share it.

Even if people think it's strange you have every right to mourning your babies, however short the time they lived with you."

Mary Ann, Mother to Edward, 4 and the babies who did not get to grow up in her loving arms

Mary Ann chose to share her story as part of a commitment she made to herself of making miscarriage more visible. For as devastating as miscarriage and recurrent miscarriage is, what is equally difficult to deal with is the feeling that we must cope with this pretty much alone, and quickly, whilst pretending that everything is fine to the outside world.

This is a stark and devastating journey, putting us through cycles of immense grief and tentative hope against the backdrop of our menstrual cycle. Women spoke of miscarriage and difficulties with fertility bringing out the worst in them, making them become jealous, bitter and angry; wanting, but unable, to be happy for those around them who seem to conceive and birth babies so easily.

Yet these journeys of pain, loss and grief are most often journeys of isolation and aloneness; for whilst miscarriage is extremely common, with one in four pregnancies being lost, acknowledging miscarriage, and really talking about it, seems to be largely absent from our culture. People do not know what to say and the custom of keeping pregnancy quiet until after the twelve week scan shrouds us in silence, meaning few women, and even fewer men, feel able to share experiences and seek answers and support.

For most of us, it is not until we are in the surreal and terrifying place of feeling cramps, sensing some bleeding, or feeling the atmosphere change during a scan, that miscarriage really features upon our landscapes. And it is here that we reluctantly begin the unwelcome journey of pregnancy loss. We may have to go through physically and emotionally devastating intervention to remove our baby from our womb, or as Mary Ann shares, experience the natural unfolding of loss.

After a scan discovered my own missed miscarriage at eleven weeks, the doctor said I could either have a procedure to remove the baby, or go home and see what happened. I was not sure what this meant, but I wanted to avoid medical intervention if possible, so opted to go home. I had no idea what would happen, and as I began to bleed I imagined what was to follow would be like a period, for this was my understanding of miscarriage having not experienced one myself nor heard others speak of theirs.

In the early weeks, a miscarriage can seem like a heavy period with some cramps, indeed we may not even recognise this as the loss of a baby if we bleed close to the expected time of our period. Yet as Mary Ann illustrates, miscarriage occurring after those early first weeks sets off a kind of mini labour. As I bled and felt cramps I imagined this would be as bad as things got. I was desperately sad, frightened as to what might happen and I felt emotionally alone. Yet as the hours progressed, I began to experience what I knew to be contractions, after having laboured with my first baby two years earlier.

This took me by great surprise and I found myself on my knees hanging over the bath, swaying and breathing through intense surges. Being in unexpected labour, alone, knowing your baby is no longer living is a frightening, sad experience. Yet even this did not prepare me for the shock of my baby leaving my body. How are we meant to bear this as women, to know what to do, what to expect and how to cope when we have not grown up seeing and hearing such things, not understanding they are another manifestation of our Femininity. Alone, birthing, then holding the warm mass in my hands, feeling its weight and the grief and finality this brought was overwhelming, yet so too did it later bring a sense of deep trust and strength. I could get through this, devastating as it was, my body knew what to do.

And when women contact me about attending Pregnancy Yoga, then share the horror of what they experienced through miscarriage, I feel able to empathise, to share their grief, their shock at the physical nature of the experience, and the power of our bodies to create and release life albeit at the expense of our emotions.

Certainly, this is an uncomfortable subject. Yet what we are sharing here are milestones of empathy, knowledge and transformation through grief. For through the bravery of Mary Ann and others sharing their experiences, we are beginning to dismantle the social expectation of silence and invisibility which causes so many of us to experience and suffer the grief and shock of miscarriage alone. Through talking and sharing we are raising awareness and creating living milestones of transformation, for ourselves, for those women who have gone before us, and those who walk ahead.

If miscarriage is an element of your path, hold yourself with tenderness; do not try to hold everything together, but let all of yourself be heard. Create space for your grief, anger, tears and bitterness, and express your raw pain, tenderness and vulnerability. You are not alone. Whilst our culture has little space and sensitivity to respond to such losses, women are changing this, little by little. We can speak about our experiences, we can listen to friends and truly acknowledge the death of their loved, unborn child. We can acknowledge their loss.

Let us transform our individual, silent suffering into learning, re-discovery and education. As women *now*, we need to learn and teach, for no one else is doing this for us or our daughters and sons. Research into miscarriage, stillbirth, fertility, menstruation and menopause is sparse and poorly underfunded, so let us harness this power of raw emotion, grief and intensity and, in our own ways, let us rise; let us create new, shared knowledge, support and learning from our own experiences, unravelling the hidden silence around our Feminine experiences. Let our milestones of miscarriage, pregnancy loss and stillbirth bring truth, grief, recognition and acknowledgement of our losses. Let us deepen into empathy, compassion and communication, creating new ways of living, grieving and mothering for ourselves, our babies and the others who walk this path now and in the future.

Journeys of perinatal loss

Pregnancy and birth are not always straightforward journeys; for many of us there are the unspeakable fears that something may go wrong, that our baby may not live. According to the Tommy's website, in the UK 1 in every 250 pregnancies results in a stillbirth; this equates to around 8 mothers who lose their babies each day. In 2018, 2943 babies were stillborn, and there were 2,131 neonatal deaths (where babies died within the first 28 days).

Yet, as with recurrent miscarriage, our culture largely holds such experiences in silence, meaning most mothers, fathers and families are left to deal with tragedy and grief in near isolation.

All women, initiated into motherhood through conception and pregnancy, are blasted apart during the birth of a child. All of us find ourselves at the centre of a labyrinth, inhabiting a new, unfamiliar place from where it is impossible to return, and sometimes difficult to move forward. Our landscapes are in pieces and not yet formed, not yet together. But when our babies are stillborn, we do not have the privilege of taking our time postnatally to put ourselves back together in a new, vibrant way, with our babies at the centre of our new identity. Rather, we begin a difficult journey of grief; reconfiguring our lives as mothers where our babies live in our hearts, but sadly not in our arms.

We are mothering, living and grieving around the silent space where our babies should have been. Dawn, Roseanne's mother, shares her journey;

"Roseanne is my much loved daughter. At 7 lbs 7 ounces, she was delivered naturally and was perfectly formed. Roseanne's pregnancy was textbook; she was a little tinker at scans, hiding behind her hands, and loved rocking out to ACDC with her dad. She was already developing her own personality and character. She was our Rosie Bean.

We decorated her nursery and filled the drawers and cupboards. The theme was travel with hot air balloons, aeroplanes and a giant world treasure map. We intended the treasure map to stay with her throughout her days so she could plot and record her travels.

Two days after her due date I went into labour. A few hours later, during a routine check, nobody could find Roseanne's heartbeat. Her passing was confirmed with a scan. She was delivered peacefully and silently a day and a half later.

We spent that day with her. She was blessed in the chapel, a remembrance photography charity sent a photographer. We took hand and footprints. She was bathed and dressed. We held her and sang to her, read to her and told her stories.

We had a cuddle cot which allowed her to stay cool for the day; vital equipment we didn't even know existed. We had 24 hours to make a lifetime of memories.

We had to leave the following morning as we'd made the difficult decision to have a post-mortem carried out. We placed her in the Moses basket, wrapped in her christening blanket with her rabbit snuggle and all her teddies, her pink charm tied to her wrist; each of her immediate family have the same charm. I insisted the midwife take her in her Moses basket. Babies are transported in a metal box and I couldn't bear the idea of placing her in it and closing the lid down. I also would not walk away and leave her behind, she needed to leave first.

We held a funeral with only immediate family. She was dressed in her going home outfit, as she still was coming home. We had a balloon release at the seaside that evening and over 80 people came to celebrate her short life, even though none had met her outside my womb. She has a beautiful headstone that's always adorned with a balloon.

Shortly after, we decided we'd start writing her name wherever we travelled. We thought we'd still use her treasure map and place a butterfly everywhere her name went. I started an Instagram page Postcards to Roseanne to keep a record of the name photographs we took. We soon had others contributing and had her name printed onto cards with her footprints for people to carry with them and photograph. She's since visited Machu Pichu, Taj Mahal and hundreds of other beautiful places. Her name hangs in the dashboard of a car and the wheelhouse of an RNLI lifeboat.

The single most frightening thing to any parent experiencing the death of a child is that their child will be forgotten. The postcards allow people to show us that Roseanne is not forgotten. It allows people a tangible expression of their grief and love for us. It's a very practical way for people to help us and show their support, when there really aren't any words to make it better.

I speak openly and honestly about Roseanne because that's what she deserves. I know we continue to be surrounded by and propelled forward by her energy and memory. Recently, the media was taken with the mother orca that carried her dead calf for days. It was on TV and across social media until the mother gave up her calf 17 days later. The outpouring of compassion for the animal was palpable. Sadly, most people can't find the words when it comes to a human mother whose baby has died.

People are petrified to say the wrong thing so mostly don't say anything at all; this only increases the feelings of guilt, shame and isolation you already feel. It is very likely you know and could name at least a handful of people that have experienced a miscarriage in the first trimester. It's less likely you can name someone who's experienced the death of their baby in the latter stages of pregnancy or shortly after birth. Inevitably though, you will know people; 1 in 250 births, 15 babies every day, are lost to stillbirth or neonatal death. The most important thing is to be brave enough to speak their baby's name and say 'I'm sorry'. That's more than enough; and you'll never know how much this makes a mother's heart sing.

I believe Roseanne was sent to us for a reason; that we'd do something as a result of her death. Most bereaved parents need to help others or prevent others experiencing the same pain. Roseanne's post-mortem showed she was perfectly formed and healthy; her placenta had stopped working in the early stages of labour. Vital signs of placenta difficulties had been missed during pregnancy; steps that should have been taken were not. The truth is, Roseanne may have survived had these steps been taken.

We've since worked with local health services to ensure correct care pathways are followed, and shared vital research from Tommy's The Baby Charity with our hospital trust. I've trained to become a befriender for my local baby loss support group, Teardrop, and completed a sponsored walk for SANDs, the Stillbirth and Neonatal Death Charity. Each Christmas and Birthday we've provided books and furniture to the bereavement suite Roseanne was born in for other parents should they find themselves in the same position.

I discovered yoga as a strategy to manage my grief and trauma. Grief itself isn't something to be treated or avoided, it's simply an expression of love with nowhere for that love to go. It cannot be escaped, or solved, you must face it and walk through it, even make peace with it. But the symptoms of grief can be harmful and challenging and it's these symptoms that can be addressed, managed, and brought back into harmony so you may live a functional, and ideally, a fulfilled life.

I sought support from a local yoga teacher where I explained I needed to do something physical but needed various forms of support. After a full term pregnancy, long labour, and several months of grieving I'd moved very little except for walking the dog and my physical strength and muscle tone was lacking significantly. Grief is beyond exhausting; a type of tiredness and heaviness no sleep could ever fix.

I was extremely apprehensive; there has been a lot of work in the last few years to break the silence around baby loss, but I still felt anxiety about going anywhere new or meeting new people. At that point we still had no answers as to why Roseanne had died, so we couldn't answer that question for other people either. People find it difficult to hear that babies can just die for no medical reason.

Lucy held the space perfectly, she allowed me to talk about Roseanne, I shared some photos of her and Lucy shed tears and thanked me for sharing Roseanne with her. It has always been, and will continue to be, important that I'm given the opportunity to talk about Roseanne as anyone with living children would be given time to talk about theirs.

We explored some simple, restorative yoga poses and a yoga nidra relaxation. The yoga nidra was transformative. It was profound; for the first time I was able to stop racing and repetitive thoughts and bring awareness to my breath and body together.

Despite having never practiced yoga previously, I now see yoga as an integral part of my daily self-care routine and an important tool for managing my grief and processing the trauma. Significant anxiety and depression were mental difficulties triggered by my grief, they shifted and changed and needed to be managed on a daily basis. It became even more important to continue to practice when I returned to work some months later and had to rejoin 'normal' life.

After feeling how yoga supported me, I wanted to share this with others; I'm training to be a yoga teacher and hold safe, nurturing yoga sessions for bereaved mums and their families. Postnatal Yoga, Baby Yoga and Massage are ideal places to socialise with like-minded individuals, share tips and empathise with experiences, yet none of these places offer a held space for a mother without her baby to feel safe and nourished. Despite 1 in 4 pregnancies ending in loss, and 1 in 250 births resulting in stillbirth, there are few places for like-minded individuals to get together, empathise, share experiences and anecdotes of exhaustion and grief and swap labour stories. Postnatal aftercare following stillbirth and late miscarriage is notoriously poor; most will never be visited by a midwife or receive a six week check from their GP. Provision for this community of women is scarce and I personally am endeavouring to address this in my local area.

I believe this group of women, and their close family members, need particular attention and specific strategies due to the complexities of the circumstances. This is a multifaceted experience of grief and is often misunderstood and neglected.

The isolation all new mothers face is exacerbated by the silence around baby loss. This has certainly been my experience, and I'm acutely aware of the conversation stopper that is 'my baby died'. This led me to avoid situations where the need to share this could arise, or you may feel you're raining on someone's parade by speaking your truth.

The isolation is real and I wanted to create a safe, nurturing space for women who've experienced perinatal loss to come together. Holding a yoga space is a brilliant opportunity to form supportive community connections; to grow circles of empowered, strong women. I am a mother, it is part of my identity, this is so important for mums who have lost their babies, in the Teardrop group we acknowledge grief and our babies in the gentlest of ways, I introduce myself as 'Dawn, Roseanne's mam', leading the way for everyone to speak the names of their child when they otherwise may not have spoken them out loud that day or even week. This connection and empathy we share is one of the gifts we receive in our grief. We would not choose these gifts over losing our loved ones but we feel deep connections with others and are capable of great empathy and compassion, this is also a reflection of the power of women's circles.

Women experiencing perinatal loss will have difficult and complex relationships with their bodies, and in particular the womb, and the approaches of Uma Dinsmore-Tuli's Womb Yoga can provide support here. Feelings of failure and shame are interconnected with the physical trauma of birth and ongoing healing and pain. Many women feel anger and guilt that their body did not manage to do the 'job' it was supposed to. Many mothers will hope to become pregnant again very quickly but will not trust their bodies; at 25 weeks pregnant with her 'rainbow' baby, a friend actively disengaged with her baby to protect herself from a subsequent loss 'when it happens'; such is the mindset of pregnancy after loss.

Through my yoga study, I learnt that there is a bliss and inner joy which resides within us all of the time, we must only recognise it and it will come to us. This is a powerful message of hope when you are in a state of grief, typically a time where you feel hopeless and question your ability to love and feel joy again."

Dawn, Mother to Roseanne

Dawn expresses the process of grief poignantly; beneath the depth of emotion, anger, sadness, loss and all of the accompanying physical symptoms, Dawn teaches us that grief is *love*, with nowhere for that love to go. This love is not to be pushed away, hidden, buried, but as Dawn shows, it needs healthy routes for expression. This is our *mothering love* searching for purpose; for spaces to be expressed, heard, witnessed and received. Through following such love, Dawn grew to create beautiful, powerful healing spaces for others grieving their babies.

As Roseanne's mother, Dawn's mothering identity, milestones and instincts were awoken, and her path has involved working out how to channel these energies, to tend to herself, and later others, whilst still holding Roseanne in her heart, but sadly not in her arms. Through her volunteer befriending, contributions to her hospital trust and bereavement suite, and valuable yoga offerings, Dawn's mothering energy flows. She allows her powerful, unconditional Mother Love, awakened by Roseanne, to nurture and tend to herself as well as creating safe, empathetic spaces for other women to be held in all of their sadness, emotion and vulnerability.

Mothers who lose their babies experience an immediate shift in their status and identity; an invisible cloak of isolation, space and awkwardness redefines them, instantly changing their relationships, personhood, place, purpose and future. As with recurrent miscarriage, birth trauma, and other remaining taboos of the Feminine, let our journeys of compassion and empathy borne of the mothering path become the insights and energies to create new ways, places and spaces of reaching out, recognising and holding mothers whose babies reside in their hearts but not in their arms. Let us recognise that such losses may happen to any one of us, to any one of our babies, and *do* happen to many women throughout the world each day.

Certainly, journeys of maternal grief deserve exploration beyond the scope of this chapter, yet I hope this insight into Dawn's mothering journey ignites wider awareness and understanding around stillbirth, and brings about milestones of empathy, compassion and connection, sparking desperately needed wider cultural change. Reaching out to a mother who lost her baby, recently, or decades ago, does not remind her that her baby died, she has not forgotten this; rather it reassures her that her baby lives on in the hearts of others as well as her own.

Journeys through postnatal anxiety and depression

Postnatal anxiety and depression, often acknowledged only in retrospect, can cause great turmoil. Difficult feelings seep into our inner landscapes, clouding and controlling what we anticipated to be a time of great happiness and connection. Such experiences *are* widespread, yet it can be difficult to believe so, for they are rarely talked about openly. When women do talk, it is often in retrospect, once we have begun to feel differently and believe there is a safe enough distance between ourselves now and previous difficult thoughts and feelings. All too often, we experience our difficulties in isolation. Even when we see friends, rarely do we share our inner experiences for fear of judgement, shame and concerns about the consequences of speaking out.

Yet, through reflection, both alone and with the support of friends and professionals, we *can* gain greater awareness and understanding of our own minds, thought patterns and emotions. Through losing ourselves to our fears and vulnerabilities, we have the opportunity to rediscover ourselves anew, although this is neither a short nor easy journey.

"One of the biggest milestones for me was coming through a difficult time of anxiety after the birth of my second child. There was too much going on, too many life changes too close to his birth; I was vulnerable and sank into a dark time. I'd moved away from my little tribe of like-minded friends when my son was one month old into my in-laws, who were caring, but not on my wavelength. It was tough.

On top of my low mood, my elder son, who was three-and-a-half, was struggling too. To be honest, some days it was hard to keep going. Some afternoons I was just so tired and lonely and I couldn't wait for my partner to come through the door.

This time I never let go of hope. I've been through bad times before and knew that things can get better, even if it doesn't seem like it at the time. There are many things that can help; I read to get answers and inspiration. I spent time in nature and felt its healing force. I cried. I meditated. I let strong feelings flow through me. I used crystals and reiki and I took my placenta essence. I cuddled my baby and his peaceful nature inspired me to get through each day.

I pushed myself to go out and meet new, like-minded people because I knew, even though I didn't feel like it, this would be my saving grace. And it was. Once I met some lovely new mothers in my local area things started to get better. We made new friends which brought new excitement and joy into our lives again. Slowly but surely each day became easier and we found new ways of living.

I believe dark times, although hard and scary, are there to help us re-evaluate our lives, what is important and what we can let go of. If we let them, old hurts can heal and we can come out feeling more enlightened.

I feel very proud of myself for being strong and getting through such a time where I questioned if I actually wanted to be here. It definitely wasn't easy but it highlighted to me how vulnerable a new mother is and how important a like-minded support network is at this precious time."

Harriet, Mother to Riley, 4 and Leon, 1

Harriet illustrates that every experience, no matter how difficult, is of worth since it provides us with the opportunity to learn greatly about ourselves, giving us the chance to feel stronger and better able to cope with future challenges.

Fran, too, brings valuable insight into the inner landscapes of postnatal anxiety and depression and our potential for recovery;

"Becoming a mother has been one of the most challenging yet wonderful life-changing experiences. It has been filled with every emotion, at times leaving me at the depths of despair then giving me the chance to feel euphoric with just a look at one of my children. Part of this is because I have experienced postnatal depression and anxiety after both my children were born. I write this pregnant with my third child, nervous of those scary feelings returning once this baby arrives.

Postnatal depression stripped me of the connection I so desperately wanted to feel towards my children, and this was made harder due to how much I so wanted to be a mother. I put pressure on myself to be perfect – something you soon realise is not what you need to be, nor do your children expect it. Children can bring the absolute best out of you because you are their mother. They allow you to be a child again, seeing the world from their eyes, their innocence, their wonder, curiosity and amazement at the world around them.

Seeing them grow and being the main person who aids their development resolved so many of the negative feelings I experienced. Knowing you are everything they need and more, seeing their unconditional love as they look at you, their smile, their warmth in your arms.

Motherhood has changed me for the better, it has allowed me to take a step back, see the world around me, take a moment in the busyness of life – which can be so difficult to do. I've learned that you can recover from the depths of depression and anxiety that I faced after the children were born. I didn't admit how I was feeling the first time around, and this didn't help my recovery. After my second child was born, I was open and honest, and wanted desperately not to feel the way I did the first time. Talking about how I felt aided my recovery, as it gave me the opportunity to seek the reassurance I needed that I could get through it all again.

My children have not been affected by my experiences, in fact I think it has helped me form a stronger bond with them. I have grown to love them, rather than feeling that instant love at first sight which many people say they have as soon as their baby is born. I know this is a healthy way of experiencing motherhood, as my love has grown the more I have learned about them."

Fran, Mother to Joshua, 5 and Lily, 2

Fran describes so well how overwhelming emotions and anxious thoughts can become the dominant focus of our attention, robbing us of the easy connection we hoped to have with our baby. Yet what Fran illustrates is the way we can recover through time. By focussing on her children's development, being present alongside her challenging inner landscapes, and slowly getting to know her children and her own immense value in their lives, her landscapes began to shift. With time she saw herself becoming a capable, strong and loving mother, the world to her children, and it was this perspective which paved the way for her recovery and her evolving strong and positive relationships.

Mothering is a long game. There may be times when we are not enjoying it, when it does not feel easy or joyful, when we are physically present but struggling emotionally and mentally. What we can learn from the experiences of others is that many, many women go through similar challenges on their mothering journey. We can learn that this is okay, that reaching out to others, talking about how we feel, and getting the support we need, alongside continuing to mother our children each day, are all milestones of strength. We can let go of feelings of shame, regret and isolation, and instead reassure ourselves that with time things will change. Our feelings will change, as will our situations, our children and the ways in which they need us. Mothering is ever-evolving, and our mothering journey will not always look or feel this way.

"Things with my first son were incredibly challenging, he developed severe eczema and food intolerances. When he was five and my second daughter was 3 months, my own mam died. I was pregnant with my third baby. It was such a hard time. Losing her changed everything. She'd always been there for me and helped with the kids.

When my third baby was about six months, I started to get what I now think of as some form of anxiety and depression. I was neurotic about stuff and became obsessed with head injuries. Ozzy, my eldest son, despite the extent of his eczema which covered all of his body and caused him to wake and cry every night, was still an active, physical child. He'd climb everywhere and everything, and like all children, would fall and bump himself.

Rationally, I knew all children fall and hurt themselves, have accidents and get poorly, but at that time I couldn't distinguish illness; in my mind they were either well or they were going to die. It was terrifying. If he bumped his head I was convinced it was serious and he would die.

Looking back now I can see that it was probably to do with losing my mam, and the other difficult circumstances we were living in, it was probably some kind of post-traumatic stress, but it was a long time before I got myself out of that. And I've had another phase of it since, when my last two children were younger. Looking back I can see it's probably triggered by pregnancy hormones and is something which changes with time.

I felt ill a lot of the time and it did take a long time for things to change. I got through it by pure determination. It was so hard, I had to carry on and wanted to, to be able to care for my children, but that was the source of my anxiety. It was a gradual thing, but I did it by talking to myself; really looking at things and talking to myself rationally.

I did go to a counsellor and spoke to people about it, I was offered medication too, but I strongly felt that I didn't want to mask my feelings with this. But I discovered that no one else can really help, for as much as they try to reassure you and tell you it is okay, it actually made it worse, as I thought 'but you don't know that it is'. So I just tried and tried to rationalise it in my own mind.

I was lucky to have really understanding doctors, I would take my son and they would do the tests etc. which I thought were necessary, this would reassure me a bit, but I would still panic. Looking back, I had trained as a nurse before becoming pregnant and in a way this helped, especially in caring for my son and his skin condition, but on the other hand, having worked with children I also knew what could happen, so it was a double-edged sword.

But that was a long time ago, my eldest is 23 now, and now I know the signs. I know it comes on with extreme tiredness, and if I'm not giving myself the time I need to look after myself. For a lot of years I felt really guilty if I was giving time to myself and wanted to be giving it to my kids and really being there for them. But now I know I've got to give myself the time, to be who I am as well as caring for them. I don't mean I need lots of time away from them, or to have put them into childcare when they were little, but giving myself time out.

I've done it all myself and had little support from partners, and when my mam died I felt I had to take on the role of being her, of being there for everyone in the family, taking care of all of us. When you no longer have that person, that role model to turn to, you have to be that person for yourself. For such a lot of years I felt I had to do everything, as I really didn't have the support. But I remember my health visitor explaining that if I wasn't well, and wasn't 100% myself, then I couldn't give 100% to my children.

It's taken me years to really understand and realise this. My eldest is 23 and my youngest is 8 now. But recently I can do this, now the one thing I've realised is that I do need to give myself time out. I don't mean leaving the kids to go to the pub as a lot of people think time out means, but rather giving myself time to read a book, have a bath, socialise. To keep in touch with friends as they can really be your rock when you're struggling. It is something that has taken me years to be able to do, but now I understand just how important it is, and feel so much better for it.

Now I'm able to handle the anxiety. I take myself away from the situation and look at it rationally. If my daughter wakes up with a temperature, I do worry, but then I look at it rationally, I look after her and I don't go into a panic thinking she's going to die of meningitis which is exactly how I used to feel.

Feeling neurotic has been really challenging, but having been through it, and knowing how to handle it and prevent it, I feel strong now. Also, when others around me are feeling similar, I feel really able to help them. When friends, or my kids, or kids at school tell me they're feeling anxious and worrying about things, I understand what it's like for them. Rather than dismissing it, I make the time to talk to them, and to listen, I can empathise as I've been through it myself."

Angela, Mother to Ozzy, 23, Amelia, 18, Marianne, 17, Aeryn, 10 and Willow, 8

Angela provides a detailed and insightful account of transformation within her inner landscapes. Through inner reflection, and self-awareness, day by day she created new ways of thinking and perceiving situations. With commitment to simply carrying on and loving her children through the difficult times she created and sustained change through her inner and outer landscapes. Angela developed deepened trust in herself and gained hard-won knowledge of how strong she can be.

She also came to truly understand and accept the necessity of caring for herself as well as her children. Her great love for her children, her deep capacity for empathy, as well as a personal understanding of how challenging mothering can be means she provides genuine support, help and understanding to the children and families she works with today.

Angela's journey illustrates the full circle of unconditional love; through wanting to be there, 100%, for her children, she learned the necessity of giving *herself* this same love, care and acceptance. For it is only when we ourselves are replenished and nurtured that we are able to sustain our mothering through the intense decades of our children's growth. Understanding and accepting the necessity of self-care is a milestone we come to, forget, and are reminded of, time and again.

Yet by committing to love and nurture ourselves we are making a lifelong commitment and investment in our family. Caring for ourselves does not necessarily have to be large periods of time away from our children, if this is not what we want or have the support to do. It can begin with the recognition that we too have needs and finding ways of meeting these within everyday life.

Let us be ever mindful of the health of our bodies and our minds; giving ourselves the time to eat nourishing food, to sit down and breathe steadily, to exercise – whatever is necessary for our overall good health. We can meet our needs for rest and sleep by resting when we get the chance, and asking for help and support when we need it. We can be gentle upon ourselves and develop an attitude of compassion, letting go of the need to be perfect. We can hold ourselves in love, recognising how well, and how much, we *are* doing rather than criticising ourselves for what we are not getting done. And as we care for our bodies and minds, nurturing our inner resources, we develop greater, sustained capacity to care for our children. Those times we feel endlessly depleted, anxious and overstretched, can become reminders to turn within, to look at our own needs and remember to bestow upon ourselves the same fierce care and unconditional love we bestow upon our children.

Unconditional love brings awareness and healing

Unconditional love brings with it a kind of magnetism; something powerful and alchemical. As our hearts awaken to new depths, such love brings with it a resonance, alerting us to anything within which does not resonate in this same vibration. This explains why we can find ourselves loving our babies wholeheartedly, then being taken aback as we find ourselves suddenly experiencing emotions and memories of feelings and times in our lives which were painful.

Yet unconditional love is a magnetic, powerful force for healing and transformation, herein lies the essence of our transformation through mothering: unconditional love shines a light on the darker areas of our inner landscapes, allowing us to explore those areas. This, in turn, can bring about healing and change. And as Francesca reminded us in her account of battling her addiction, we are motivated to love, heal and better ourselves for the good of our children, as well as ourselves.

This process of surfacing memories is not something which only occurs during our children's infancy, but rather throughout our lives as mothers. Whatever stages our children and teens are at, if we have unhealed memories and emotions from such times, feelings can arise within, bursting into our awareness as strong emotional reactions, causing irritation or conflict. Often, we feel it is our child and their behaviour which is causing our reaction, and certainly at times it may well be, yet with awareness and self-reflection, we can embrace these experiences as invitations for further inner growth, healing and transformation.

"Having Izzy made me face some difficult issues surrounding my relationship with food; I've always struggled with over or undereating and body image. I found weaning her really hard, I was so anxious not to pass on my own anxieties about food and body image. I remember talking to a friend about the issues we were having with Izzy eating and her saying, 'This isn't about Izzy, it's about you, isn't it?'

Having Izzy has forced me to work through things, I'm still growing and it's up and down. Just the other day I felt another wave of freedom; I don't have to be thin, I don't want Izzy to think she has to be thin, I want her to be healthy and strong."

Lizzie, Mother to Izzy, 6, James, 4 and Lloyd, 1

Introducing her daughter to food, Lizzie became again reminded of the trauma and difficulty of her own relationship with eating and body image. Driven by love and so wanting things to be different for her daughter, Lizzie turned her listening inwards and explored what lay beneath years of buried feelings. She reflected on past experiences and allowed the transformative nature of unconditional love to create change, bringing forth waves of freedom, insight and new ways of being. As parents we think we must be in control and teach things to our children, whilst this is true in many respects, as Lizzie illustrates, our children, too, offer opportunities for us to learn and heal.

Journeys through overwhelm

Some of our most intensely challenging times lie in the daily and nightly care of children. We are learning to understand, meet and balance multiple needs, constantly, often on limited emotional, practical, energetic and financial resources. We become exhausted from the night waking, the crying, the everyday, constant multi-tasking and the many repetitive jobs to be thought through and done for each child. This is as much mental and emotional work as it is physical and we may well wonder how we are going to get through the day let alone the year.

It may sound trivial to those who have not lived it, but meeting the constant needs of our babies, toddlers and children can leave us feeling desperate. Of course we will not feel like this all of the time, but when we do, we imagine others never feel this way and are able to handle things much better. Yet the truth of the matter is that meeting the needs of small children whilst running a household and preparing meals – with as much love, gentleness and connection as we would like – is incredibly hard work. And especially without the support of an extended family, tribe or community.

Of course there are times of joy and delight as we share moments of love, play and tenderness, yet this is against a backdrop of many months, or years, of constant caring. Slowly, we begin to see just how much of ourselves, our very essence, we pour into mothering each and every day and night, year after year.

At length, we come to realise that to continue doing this work we must care for ourselves, although this can be difficult and feel hilariously impossible, especially if we do not have practical support. As Angela illustrated earlier, caring for ourselves can be a milestone we arrive at after many years of giving everything we have. Yet as mothers we *want* to do this work, even when we are exhausted and really do not feel like getting up to feed or comfort them. We do not want them to be sick, crying, upset or alone. We want to hold them, love them and nurture them, yet at the same time this is hard, constant, skilled and demanding work, taking much of our energy. We have to remind ourselves of its worth and value.

"My first was a delight. She was bright, sunny and full of joy. Rosy and calm, slept through the night; she made it easy for me to decide to have another baby right away.

My second had colic, she cried all the time. My husband and I used to take 2 hour naps at night so we could sleep. My twins put me to work. They were unplanned and a surprise. Double the fun, double the load, quadruple the babies. When they were born my eldest were 2 and 3. I was just getting a feel for motherhood, and all the tasks involved, before I was hit hard. I had to learn to do everything alone and exhausted. Baby number five is pleasant and independent. He is a smart cookie and speaks clearly at only 2 years of age. He is learning from his siblings at a remarkable pace, while teaching them about patience and family love.

The most difficult times were when my four oldest were all under 4. I was alone with four little ones with very little help. I made the conscious decision to change the way I was going to raise my children and without my family tribe. My husband worked many hours to keep food on our table and a roof over our heads. I learned to care for my kids, keep home, make meals and homeschool. I taught myself to be a different kind of mother. I learned to be connected with my children through rough times and began understanding the relation between my actions and their reactions.

One of the greatest lessons I lived, over and over, is to take care of myself. I learned that if I'm going to take care of them, then I have to take care of myself, physically, emotionally and spiritually. I've realised many things over the years; that rough patches some of us dread are actually great periods of growth. When I removed myself from the feelings that unpleasant things were happening to me and that I was the victim of my life, I began to understand the magnitude of the rough patches and their ability to transform my life for the better.

I remember being up all night, not sleeping at all for months; breastfeeding them, when one finished the other one was starting. I was on call. All Day and Night Long.

I remember not having help because I pushed family away as I didn't want to receive criticism for doing things differently. This led to severe exhaustion, moodiness and depression. I remember having to face the reality that I had to change old patterns of criticism, guilt, shame, yelling and hitting from my children's lives, and learning to change, alone, with no help or support other than from my husband who worked all of the time to cover the cost of such a quick growing family.

I remember trouble after stopping breastfeeding my twins because one cried non-stop because all he wanted was to breastfeed, but was unable to because he had nipple confusion due to supplementing. I remember crying in my bathroom into towels, because I didn't know what I was going to do with myself, and how I was going to give my children the best of me when I was bone dry. I remember crying into the pillow due to intense moments in the afternoon, in which I was beating myself up for snapping at one of my kids, crying because we didn't know what we were going to feed them, or how we were going to survive with a loaf of bread, hot dogs and a few cabinet items when pay day was eight days away...

I understood everything through these rough times – even though it took a while to sink in. I understood my twin who was crying due to nipple confusion is the type of person who thrives on consistency and on routine – any change in schedule makes him nuts. I understood that my daughters, who are older, are my emotional teachers. They taught me to balance myself and my emotions so they don't overtake me, meaning I don't lash out or diffuse them onto others.

I learned we are always provided for when we have faith and ask, when my oldest friend showed up at my door, unannounced, with a box of food for my children, and when our wonderful neighbours brought our children Christmas presents one year out of the kindness of their hearts (all four of them, for they knew in their hearts that at this time we could not). This is something that still fills me with joy. I learned that shutting out the bad shuts out the good also and allowing others to care and help is part of life, as is learning to do it alone.

But mostly, I learned we have the power to do, to understand and to get through anything – as long as we are open and willing."

Violet, Mother to Sasha, 10, April, 9, Sam and Josh, 7, Isaac, 2

Without such introspection and motivation for change, Violet could have continued fighting her way through motherhood, finding it difficult, trying and unpleasant much of the time. Inspired by her love for her children, she knew she wanted things to be different. Rather than blaming herself or her children and becoming lost in her emotions, instead she found awareness. She discovered that as their mother, *she* was the emotional and physical landscape upon which her children grew. So rather than trying to change them, she changed herself, which paved the way for her to create herself anew and to become the kind of mother she so wanted her children to receive.

Through losing ourselves to the constant physical and emotional overwhelm of mothering, with reflection, love and determination, we *can* find ourselves anew. We can create new ways forward, making new paths of connection, understanding and authenticity.

Journeys through children's illness

Mothering a snuffly baby who has a temperature and cannot feed or sleep is an immensely challenging task. Yet when illness is prolonged, our baby has multiple conditions, or medical help seems unable to provide answers, mothering becomes incredibly stressful. We are left caring for our baby, day and night, knowing that something is wrong, yet struggling to find answers. Through such times we develop immense knowledge, strength and determination, yet these are hard-won qualities; we only learn just how strong and determined we can be because this is the way we have *had* to be, because we had no other choice.

"There were many wonderful and rewarding moments with our first baby as we experienced his 'firsts', but it was also a time of great worry knowing instinctively something was wrong. We were constantly dismissed by health professionals, despite doing everything we could to seek medical attention throughout the first year. We were often given opposite advice to what should have been given for a baby displaying signs of severe food intolerances, struggling to maintain weight and constantly fighting viruses. We were told: 'feed him up with high fat dairy', 'wean at 4 months to dry up the vomit' (he got a lot worse on solids, choking until he was blue in the face regularly), 'he doesn't need milk in the night from 6 months', 'let him cry', 'maybe you're giving him too much attention'.

We were constantly asked by medical staff, 'Is this your first baby?' as if we were simply overanxious parents. We felt low and alone, trying to put on a brave face whilst other parents were seemingly having a great time, knowing in our hearts that he wasn't right and feeling helpless in being able to resolve it for him.

It wasn't until he was 13 months, very run down with yet another virus, rapidly losing weight, breastfeeding constantly, having refused to eat almost all solids for months, crying and unhappy a lot of the time that we finally got some attention from the medical profession further afield. Breast milk alone was simply not enough to sustain him any longer. Following many unpleasant and invasive tests, he was suspected to have multiple, severe food intolerances and ended up having to be tube-fed for 12 hours per day for months to get his strength back as we started from a strict diet of chicken, pear and rice only.

It was a horrendous few months, getting 2–3 hours of broken sleep most nights whilst we monitored the machine, with a lot of setbacks, not knowing where it was going to end, whether we were going to have to do this for years whilst he refused to eat the minimal diet he was allowed. We had no day-to-day help, administering nursing ourselves, clearing up vomit continually as he struggled to cope with the prescription milk being pumped in.

We felt awful to the core having to do this to our own child in the hope of making him better, cried most days and just hoped it wouldn't damage our relationship with him for the future. Fortunately, his weight and condition gradually improved and we were able to try removing the tube. It was then a constant and painstaking struggle for a further 12 months until he regained his confidence with food and we got to the point where we had a range of foods he could eat and no longer went through long cycles of not eating and losing weight rapidly again.

During this time I had to return to work, exhausted from breastfeeding many times per night and I felt like nobody understood what we were going through. People assume they know about this issue as babies often have a straightforward milk intolerance to some degree, so they assume this is the degree of issue you're experiencing also.

We are now very fortunate to have a happy and healthy 3-year-old who appears to have outgrown most of his food issues, loves to eat, and can only hope our experiences have no lasting effect.

This taught us just how deeply we love our children, how lucky we are to have them, how maternal instincts should be trusted at all cost and how persistent, dedicated and resourceful we can be as parents in the quest to look after our children the best we can. For a long time afterwards, we continued to be emotional about what happened, feeling a sense of loss as we missed out on so many of the pleasures of having a new baby as every day was a struggle. Then, we also felt guilty about feeling this loss, as we knew how lucky we were to not have gone through much worse as so many parents sadly do."

Louise, Mother to Flynn, 3.5 and Rowan, 10 months

As poorly and desperate as her little son must have felt, we can imagine the comfort and reassurance he received at being cared for so responsively, and the lifeline which breastmilk and the process of breastfeeding provided through this difficult time. Louise speaks of trusting her instincts and awakening to the vast depth of love we awaken to as parents, and how such love becomes a source of motivation, strength and determination to persevere through prolonged difficulties.

Angela reflects upon the early years of mothering her son who had severe food allergies and eczema;

"He had a long, stressful birth, my baby was stressed and his collar bone broken. Looking back, I think this is why he developed such severe eczema; I've since learned that stressful birth can lead to this.

I struggled to breastfeed and we stayed in hospital for 10 days and had help until we made progress. Looking back, breastfeeding was something I was passionate about before becoming a mother; I did a dissertation on it and was an advocate before I came to it myself, so this prior commitment helped me persevere.

Between 3–6 months my son developed severe eczema, covering his whole body. Up until age 7 he woke every night continually, scratching himself until he bled, this was the hardest time of my life and I say that in all honesty, after having gone on to have four more children. The first time he slept through, when he was 7, I woke up and honestly thought he'd died as this had never happened before.

The nights were the worst; seeing your child half-awake, half-asleep in a distressed state, crying and scratching until he bleeds all over, knowing there is nothing you can do, is utterly horrific. He had sores all over, his whole body was an open wound and he got repeated infections.

The nights were hardest for him, it itched and itched, he could only stop the itching by scratching and scratching until he bled, then it started to hurt and feel sore. Every night we would be up, for hours and hours on end. I would run him baths, read endless stories, watch videos over and over and over again. I can still remember all the words and the tunes of the Thomas the Tank Engine videos we watched. This seemed to help take his mind off it, but for me, was utterly exhausting. I was doing this on my own every night, and seeing your child like this is utterly heart-breaking.

You know the ultimate physical, emotional and mental exhaustion you have after having a baby, you are so spent down to your bones; well, I was like that for 7 years. When he was 18 months me and his dad separated and I lived with my mum. My dad was ill at this point and I knew he needed space, so we moved again. It was poor housing and it was difficult; looking back I don't know how we got through it, but it shows you, you don't know how strong you can be until you have to be, and I think of it sometimes now and remind myself what I've come through.

My Health Visitor was supportive, she referred me to a dietitian who diagnosed him with severe food allergies to all food additives and salicylates, naturally occurring trace elements found in nearly all naturally occurring foods as well as medicines and toiletries. It was a huge thing to learn about, these elements are found in most fruit and vegetables, the only fruit he could tolerate were pears, he couldn't have dairy or eggs either, they also occur in most shampoos and body products, plus he couldn't have anything with artificial additives, so his diet was really limited. He lived off chicken, rice, pasta, sweetcorn and pears.

I had a lot of difficulties with his grandparents who wouldn't believe he couldn't have things, so would give him foods he was allergic to and say he was fine, but once the food began to be digested, he would be in terrible pain for days. I found it hard when we went to parties and he couldn't eat anything, we used to take his own food, it didn't seem to bother him, but it upset me.

I talked to him about it a lot, and by age 2 he could say what he could and couldn't eat, he was a bright little thing. But it was hard, they tried a lot of different treatments, he had mud bandages where I had to wrap him in mud covered bandages for hours at night, his whole body, it was so messy and he looked like a little mummy, it was uncomfortable for him.

I remember one doctor saying it was the worst case of eczema he had seen in his entire career, in all honesty he looked like a little leper, he had scabs all over his body, his skin was literally falling off, but he was such a pretty little thing...

In that time, I also had another baby, and my mum died when my son was 5 and my new daughter was 3 months. It was an incredibly hard time. For the first few years I was a wreck, an absolute physical and emotional wreck. I was completely drained, yet in time as I recovered I realised how strong I truly was.

After what we went through for those first seven years, having my other children was a walk in the park. I've learned so much, I know so much more about my own strength and know I can cope with things. I look back now, as he is 23, and think what a great person he is, how close we are, how proud I am of him, and know we are great friends and always will be. I think going through hard times with your kids, although it's awful, makes you closer."

Angela, Mother to Ozzy, 23, Amelia, 18, Marianne, 17, Aeryn, 10 and Willow, 8

The strength, experience and depth of love Angela forged through these difficult years became the bedrock for her family relationships. She now enjoys rewarding relationships with her adult children alongside mothering her younger daughters. She developed a wealth of knowledge, experience, empathy and compassion which she shares with other children, parents and professionals through her work.

The mothering path, particularly when beset with challenges, forces us to bore to the very depths of ourselves. We discover our true strength and wisdom. Through doing so we develop deep trust, confidence and connection with our inner wisdom; something which cannot be lost and which never leaves us, even if we lose sight of it for a while. Such learning continues to guide us in our mothering, as Louise and Angela illustrate, as well as providing valuable insights into other aspects of life, work and relationships.

Relationship difficulties and separation

Becoming parents places great pressure on relationships; our lives, roles and responsibilities change irrevocably, sometimes in different directions. Our own expectations of, and approaches to, parenting may differ, bringing to light differences previously undiscovered. For these reasons and many more, relationships can become sources of anxiety and emotional stress. Certainly, couples may grow together, through communication, humour and shared love and commitment to our babies. Yet sometimes growth becomes divergent, as though we are growing in different directions, with our priorities and sources of joy and fulfilment seeming to correlate less and less.

Many of us grow through these changes, evolving together and becoming closer, yet for others, we realise things are not developing as we hoped. As mothers striving to provide a nurturing environment for our children, such difficulties can become a source of incredible stress. We must negotiate harsh terrain and make difficult decisions regarding perseverance, communication and separation.

"Things were not always smooth with my husband. When the kids were little it often felt like it was me doing things with the kids and he would undermine me. He didn't understand where I was coming from, or even try to.

I remember telling him I felt he didn't support me emotionally or spiritually, he replied he pays the bills, as if that was his only responsibility. He had very old-fashioned attitudes about women looking after children and men working; I wanted more than this, I wanted his emotional and spiritual support, for him to share the joyful bits. I think he missed a lot of them growing up.

His attitudes come from his own upbringing. His dad wouldn't hold our kids when they were babies. These differences in upbringings and our attitudes and expectations made it hard; I think we both felt isolated and resentful at times.

At age 9, my eldest, Simon, hit puberty and developed the classic 'Kevin' attitude almost overnight. Simon and my partner clashed and it was very much hard work. I kept the closeness and channels of communication open with him, but it was hard and there were times when my relationship with him was on a knife edge. My partner and his family didn't help at all, I worked my socks off to maintain a relationship with Simon.

With Edward, my younger son, it never felt like this, it was just an easier relationship. But with Simon I really had to work at it. I tried very hard to talk to him and not talk down to him, I tried to understand where he was coming from, even if we didn't agree. I worked really hard to maintain communication and took a lot of time to explain to him that communication is the only way you can maintain relationships.

Simon loved music from an early age and I always looked for opportunities for him to experience it. One year we were on holiday and there was an outdoor evening performance, I knew he'd love to go but his father wouldn't, Simon picked up on this, so instead of being enthusiastic, acted dismissive, although I knew he wanted to go. What followed was my husband storming off in anger and my son crying; he'd really twisted himself into a knot inside, he wanted to go but knew his dad didn't. I took the time to understand him and talk him down.

We've had similar situations over the years, Simon getting into a situation at work or having issues at school and his dad reacting angrily. I would take the time to build bridges to him, and for him. He would get really depressed, and think himself into dark situations. It used to feel like I was building a ladder down into the hole with him, listening to him then lifting him out, back into the world. It was bloody hard work, but the alternative was letting him fall into a deep hole of depression and doing nothing about it.

It's been hard over the years, practically and emotionally, but we have a good relationship now and he is happy in his own life. I know I've changed the cycle and definitely done my best for him, although his dad doesn't recognise this. We've since separated and looking back I wonder if I should have done it years ago, when the children were younger. I do worry how his angry and dismissive attitude could have affected them. As a mother your responsibilities are primarily towards yourself and your children, and now my sons are grown up, I'm taking the time to nurture and focus on myself."

Amy, Mother to Simon, 25 and Edward, 19

Parenting and relationships can become incredibly charged, complex and difficult when partners are not seeing things from a similar perspective. Amy's commitment to recognising and validating her son's emotions, as well as nurturing his interests, clashed with her husband's childhood experiences and approaches to discipline.

Coping with her husband's expressions of anger and her son's intense emotions, Amy found herself journeying through a difficult and conflicting emotional terrain. It left her little time to take account of her own needs. Yet connecting within, Amy became clearer about her personal priorities as a mother; she chose to follow her instinct to nurture and maintain communication with her son and continue to support him through his emotional development. Amy questions whether she should have made changes sooner, yet there are no right or wrong decisions in such situations. All we can do is listen within, do our best for our children and do what feels possible with the energy and resources we hold at the time.

"I spent a lot of time worrying about how my relationship with my husband was affecting our children. I was exhausted from worrying constantly and trying to shield the kids from the situation. I felt leaving would give them a better chance at being happy, yet I also felt so guilty and responsible. I had to be strong for my children. They are my number one responsibility, I worry how things affect them growing up in this way.

I had to let go of all the emotions, guilt and worrying and just hone into my children and myself and be strong and think very clearly about what was best for us. I became aware with the passing years how my children were becoming more aware of the situation.

I had to be strong and believe in myself, trust myself that I can do it, to reach out, make new friends, create a new home and somehow hold it all together emotionally, mentally, physically and financially. I did it because I knew the strength of love I felt for my children, and saw how the difficult emotional situation was affecting them, they were starting to blame themselves, I didn't want them to carry this over into their own adult relationships.

It was with this realisation that we moved forward, found strength, a new home and a new way of life. In the hard times I found myself taking myself backwards to intense moments during their births when contractions were so powerful I believed I couldn't take it anymore. I remembered moments which feel like forever, when the baby is moving downwards, large skull passing through bony pelvis; intense, terrifying. The knowing that although you do not want to, you must go through this, there is no getting around it, or giving up. Then, somehow, accessing deep power and strength, and roaring the baby down, and out; breath, power, focus and strength combine to make you feel as though you are capable of anything. It is this memory of deep strength from birth that guided me through an immensely difficult situation, a separation and the building of a new way of life."

Rebecca, Mother to Robbie, 14 and Sylvie, 11

Rebecca's recollections of facing intense situations, and the parallels with birth, reminds us that realisations at one stage of our journey remain within, constantly available to inspire, motivate and remind us of our true depths of love, strength and capability. Such milestones never leave us, and as we glimpse the depth of our strength, we are able to trust our instincts and make the very difficult decisions which we know, within, are for the best. Yet this is never an easy element of our journey, as Vanessa illustrates;

"Regardless of our differences and distance, I couldn't think of having a family with another person; our problems weren't really problems, it was just miscommunication. I couldn't think of my children being, like myself, children of divorce. So I shared my feelings of being ready for another baby.

I was tired, true, but I was happy and sure I wanted a big family. But he didn't. We came to a rock, not a tiny one, like previously, where we just went around it. No, this was one of those rocks that somehow create a gap that turns into Big Canyon. That sort of rock.

Going back and forth in my insecurity, I thought it was not really okay for me to force him to have more children, we already had two, he told me, and I could not make words to express the feelings inside.

Every so often my heart would lean towards babies.

Years later, there I was in the bathroom, stick in hand, staring at the clear sign that I was expecting. I will not, cannot, share the words my partner told me that night; those words were muffled by the sound of my heart breaking.

Over the next week, there were three conversations, all in which I stated why I wanted another baby and where he stated why we could not.

'Selfish' might have been the word that hurt the most.

I checked in Thursday and said goodbye to my baby. I closed my eyes and asked to wake up without this burden in my heart.

My heart would take a long time to recover. I would go to great lengths to find us a new home, one not filled with memories of heartbreak. It took two years of trying. And after all that time I decided I was a better mother when it was just the three of us.

So I came to grow wiser, I let my children depend on me as much as they needed, gave them freedom and pulled them back, only to let them go again. I became their advocate and stood by them and threw away the notion that divorce would shatter them.

It would not, you know why? Because I would not leave their side. I would be away, but I would be there.

Life changed, I found a new city, new apartment and started a new, unfamiliar life. Learned to accept help, made decisions, went through with them.

After separation we both wanted as much time as possible with the kids, and being home schooled, it became possible to share custody, equal parts, both ways.

I will not lie; the first two weeks the children were away I didn't know what to do with myself. I was sad and felt like I'd shot myself in the foot. I knew I could not go back to what was before because I was a different woman now.

But things were different now and I was going to have to make the best of it. Might as well heal my little heart and read. Learning to let go was a huge step. Sometimes we need to let go, especially when it hurts.

It took months to allow people into my circle, months to allow one special person to come closer.

I believe this was very important. I wasn't looking for someone because I had a happy life with my children and myself. I was running, living next to a park, reading, educating myself, educating my children like I believed it should be done.

But time heals all things.

And I write this journey with a baby growing inside me, fruit of a love so kind that it had to reach me only after I had grown. A love so kind that it was up to me to accept it.

I said 'I think we're having a baby' and he smiled and hugged me while a romantic song played in my heart and he voiced his love for us: 'A Baby!'

A baby growing from a mother that will no longer fight to breastfeed or co-sleep, because there is no battle to be fought. This is how I nurture my children. This is how I mother them."

Vanessa, Mother to Lilo, 10, Boo, 8 and Sammy, 1

Amy, Rebecca and Vanessa illustrate what it means to not only *go* through difficult times, but to *grow* through them. Reflection through difficulties enables us to become clearer in our own minds about what is important to us and how we would like to mother our children. Such clarity then enables us to begin to bring these changes into being across our physical landscapes.

Leaving a partnership with a person you love, or have loved, and have children with, even if you know the relationship is no longer healthy or nurturing, is a long and emotionally exhausting journey. We become aware of our deepest fears and vulnerabilities, and experience the grief that comes with loss of our past hopes and security. We may worry, extensively, about the outcome for all, uncertain whether to leave or stay, fearful of either and the consequences of both. These are some of the hardest decisions we may make. Yet such situations awaken us to new aspects of ourselves – to our resilience, tenacity and strength of mind – alongside bringing to our attention parts of ourselves in need of being listened to and tended to, as we model to our children ways forward and meeting milestones of growing through conflict and change.

Mothering ourselves

When we are exhausted, depleted, facing multiple challenges, it can be hard to know which way to turn and how to carry on. Yet carry on we must, for we have our children to care for. And rather than depleting ourselves further as we continue through challenges, instead we can mother ourselves. Just as we would scoop up our crying, frightened child into our arms, hold them, listen to them, then soothe and reassure them; we can do this for ourselves also. We can cultivate an attitude of love, acceptance, gentleness and compassion to ourselves and repeatedly banish from our inner landscapes critical, judgemental thoughts.

We can honour our own emotions as we would our children's and give ourselves the space and time to explore our own feelings and unmet needs. We can value ourselves on a level equal to our children, partner, family, colleagues and friends and know that we, too, deserve to have our own needs met, be listened to, heard and loved. We can remind ourselves that if we do not give ourselves this attention, we run the risk of becoming depleted, being unable to love and give as we would like.

Far from being selfish, we are modelling to our children how to care and value ourselves, and that Motherhood is not about endless self-sacrifice, martyrdom or servitude, but rather a deep respect and recognition of the great value held in loving and nurturing others as well as ourselves.

In the difficult times, when we feel we do not know what to do, we have the opportunity to turn *within*. Hard times bring us the space and impetus to discover *more of who we are*. We can uncover what is real *for us*, and what is not; what is authentic, genuine and important for our lives and our families now and in the future, and what is not. We become clearer about what we would like to cultivate and develop further, and that which we are ready to surrender.

Coming to such a place is liberating; from here we can create ways of living and mothering which embody our truth as best we can each day;

"I listen to diverging opinions and let them go. Every day I learn. I do not have room for petty, mean, negative or rude. I have time for growth, compassion, dancing, love, hugs, saying sorry, holding hands, combing hair, healing cuts, kissing, educating, reaching our potential, receiving, being happy.

And mothering babies."

Vanessa, Mother to Lilo, 10, Boo, 8 and Sammy, 1

Let us not underestimate the power of turning our attention within; as Angela illustrated through her journey through postnatal anxiety, alongside seeking help, she spent a lot of time thinking and talking with herself, training herself to perceive things differently, to grow new ways of thinking, beyond her fears. Such self-knowledge is precious, hard-won and lifelong. If we experience such difficulties again in the future, we are much more able to recognise the warning signs, know we are strong enough to cope and now possess the knowledge, skills and ability to nurture ourselves through these times of vulnerability;

"Coming through this terrible depression, when I was in a very low place with two little ones depending on me, made me realise I can get through things, I am strong, and if anything like this happens again, I would be able to cope."

Harriet, Mother to Riley, 4 and Leon, 1

Milestones of transformation through difficulties lie in accepting all parts of ourselves and holding ourselves in fierce, unconditional love. Here we become more whole, reducing inner conflict as we reclaim those elements of ourselves previously lost to feelings of failure, anger, guilt and shame.

Often, we perceive mothering as things we do for and with children; certainly much of our time is taken up in this way, yet our journeys of transformation happen within, upon our inner landscapes – our places of emotion, memory, awareness and feeling. Yet, truly, the landscapes are one, for transformation upon our inner landscapes creates shifts in our perception, experience and interactions in the outer world.

Yet to make space for such transformation, as Michelle illustrates below, often we have to let something go; it is difficult to deepen into loving ourselves and our children if we are holding on to anger, resentment, self-criticism and harsh inner judgement. Yet if we give ourselves permission to move into milestones of acceptance, we begin a process of letting go, surrendering those inner dialogues which no longer serve us or nurture us. We create the space to become more kind, loving and nurturing to ourselves, enabling us to welcome the waves of transformation such shifts create;

"Could I have tried harder to turn my baby from breech? Cleaned the floor more, drunk more raspberry tea? Could I have said 'no' to induction and the C-section and waited for more days for my little boy to arrive, and persevered more with breastfeeding?

I've asked myself these questions and many more, yet now is the time for me to heal and move on. It's happened, perhaps my role now is to share my story, to help friends with expressing tips.

Be kind to yourself. It's a noble thing to be human and to have a baby. Above all, enjoy your baby. Love them, love yourself and love our world. I am giving myself a moment now to reflect upon who I am and what has happened. I will give myself a hug and say well done. I love and accept the person I am today."

Michelle, Mother to Skye, 3 and Oakley, 1

Mothering, and especially mothering through challenging times, brings opportunities to deepen into self-love, self-care and self-acceptance, as well as igniting great learning, discovery and transformation. As Lucy illustrates, mothering through difficulties can bring to the surface strengths and aspects of ourselves which may not find expression through the smoother times. We realise how truly strong and sturdy we can be, how fierce, powerful and committed, even within our feelings of doubt and vulnerability.

"Mothering through the hard times as well as the smooth awakened me to a force so deeply powerful and strong inside me – the power of love and tenderness, and trust and of being able to get through anything due to this force. I was pretty shocked for a long time that I even had this inside me! It didn't feel like I was ever 'sacrificing' myself; you just do what you feel moved to do for your children from a much deeper place where you know you are powerful and invulnerable.

Little me can be a powerful, strong Mamma bear who can stand up for my children and do what she feels is right for them no matter what and against opposition, because of the knowing in my heart and a feeling in my gut that there is no doubt about my convictions (despite getting a little rattled at times), and no one can take that away from me.

These feelings induced a pivotal change in my awareness of myself, of my innate power and of my faith in the deep knowing of the power of the love and connection between a mother and her children. And I believe that this being nurtured and allowed in its most natural state could literally change the world for the better family by family."

Lucy, Mother to Abbie, 18 and Millie, 14

Let us not attempt to change the past, or lose ourselves in guilt, anger, sadness or regret. Rather we must *find ourselves*, more of our true selves as Lucy so discovered, through loving ourselves and our children and continuing forth upon our mothering path. Let us come to a peaceful acceptance of past events, recognising accrued strengths and learning and acknowledging and celebrating all that we do in raising our children with love, gentleness and connection. Let us be kind to ourselves through the difficult times and give ourselves full permission to celebrate and enjoy the happier, smoother, simpler moments, reminding ourselves once again of the milestones of change as we continue to progress along the ever-unfolding path.

Chapter Eight
Changing the Legacy

For those of us whose childhood memories evoke warm feelings of family togetherness, embarking upon our own mothering journey, whilst daunting, often feels part of the natural progression of life. We know what it means to live in a loving family and look forward to replicating this with our own children. Yet if we do not perceive our childhood as having been consistently positive and nurturing, we may approach motherhood more tentatively, and from a very different perspective, if that is, we choose to become mothers at all.

Approaching motherhood after a childhood which lacked positive, gentle and consistent nurturing, women spoke of experiencing flashes of anxiety and concern about their potential skills and abilities to love and mother their own children. These are landscapes of hidden, ambiguous feelings, hurt, fear and uncertainty; yet they hold much potential for awakening and transformation as each woman begins the uncertain journey of creating her family life anew and in her own vision.

Women shared how embarking upon mothering caused memories and fears to surface within their otherwise happy and well-structured lives. If our childhood was not consistently nurturing we may find ourselves fearing we are incapable of loving and mothering our baby, fighting insidious fears that, despite our best efforts, we will go on to replicate the difficulties that we experienced with our parents with our own children.

Such feelings are unwelcome, seeping into what we expect to be times of great happiness and excitement. We can find ourselves revisiting feelings and memories we thought we had left far behind. Yet as we bring awareness to such parts of ourselves, learning to love and mother our children can become a process of profound healing, change and transformation.

Our childhood legacy

Some of us may reflect upon our childhoods and feel that whilst our immediate physical needs were met, due to issues within our family or wider cultural norms of the time, some hurt or trauma, due to limited recognition and nurturing of our emotional needs, still resides within us. Some of us may recall difficult experiences and relationships with our own parents and understand how this has impacted our sense of self-image and self-esteem through young adulthood and beyond.

"One of the biggest challenges I've faced is that I was not loved unconditionally by my own mum, because of her personality disorder (Narcissism). I've had counselling to get my own feelings together. Because of my childhood, I doubt myself constantly and have found it difficult trusting myself and having confidence in my abilities."

Ashley, Mother to Lisa, 3 and Anna, 1

If we did not perceive ourselves as being loved, nurtured or trusted by our parents, our mothers especially, we may have struggled to love, trust and accept ourselves. This would've meant that we set out on life with fragile foundations. Yet, in retrospect, we can see how we developed strength, courage and insight through our early life journeys and developed many qualities and skills which serve us well in adulthood.

Yet as we embark on motherhood ourselves, uncertainty surfaces as we realise that *we* are now the parent; *we* are a mother with all of the power and responsibility to love, care for (and potentially hurt) a child. Our experiences meet us twofold; at the forefront is our resolve to do things differently; we know what it is like to be hurt, to feel alone and grow up without a strong, safe and reliable connection to our own mother. Women explained how they wanted to do things differently and better, creating for our children a childhood of safety, love and belonging; a childhood from which they do not have to recover. Mothers explained they wanted their own children to look back and feel they were always loved and cared for, that their family was, and continues to be, a safe and welcoming place to return to, a place they will always belong.

Yet alongside our hopes of doing a better job deeper fears emerge; we may fear that, however hard we try, we may end up replicating negative, destructive relationships with our own children. We may wonder, once again, why our own mothers were unable to respond to us with presence and tenderness, wondering if there was something within ourselves which precipitated such response, fearing, once again, we will, somehow unconsciously, replicate such patterns.

Writer and family therapist Dr Karyl McBride works with women striving to recover from difficult relationships with their own mothers. Through her book, *Will I Ever Be Good Enough? Healing the daughters of narcissistic mothers*, Dr McBride offers a message of hope, explaining that a wounded childhood does not have to mean that a woman will go on to wound her own children, and with support, she can go on to heal and be a loving, consistent and caring mother. Dr McBride states;

"Many of my clients are in a state of hopelessness and depression when they begin therapy, but I am always happy to inform them that there is good news and hope. When a daughter chooses to invest in herself, face the wounded childhood and history, and complete the recovery process... things begin to change. Learning to stop the repetition compulsion, to separate from your mother, build your own sense of self, and free yourself from the damaging internalised messages, you set out on a whole new healthy, optimistic journey...

...To have worries and fears about your parenting is normal, but the women [who are daughters of narcissistic mothers] have concerns that are a few steps beyond those of most mothers-to-be. Of course, we strive to do the right things for our children, and none of us wants to pass along our own undesirable legacy. Breaking the cycle is a challenge when you have no positive role model as a mother. Daughters of narcissistic mothers often feel as if we are blazing our own trail of love in raising *our* babies."

It *can* feel frightening at the beginning of this journey, as if you are somehow damaged inside in an unmendable way, and that this is difficult to explain to others; that somehow, despite, your best efforts, you may end up treating your child in the same negative way as you yourself were treated, despite immense effort not to. No matter how outwardly successful and happy women may seem, and truly be, this is a real and terrifying fear which can be hard to shake off and difficult to speak of.

"I wanted my baby to be a boy, because I had had a pretty appalling relationship with my mother and feared replicating it with a daughter."

Marty, Mother to Jessie, 21 and Lizzie, 16

In pregnancy our fears hold the greatest sway upon our inner landscapes, yet once we become mothers, we begin to build a catalogue of mothering experience; we love and hold our babies, feed them, comfort and care for them. Each and every one of these experiences becomes currency in our inner reserves; yes, we have the negative investments of a challenging childhood legacy, but now, so too do we have regular instalments of positive, loving parenting interactions which, over time, begin to counteract our fears of replicating past negative experiences, showing us we *are* indeed doing things differently.

Understanding why brings freedom from fear

In the beginning, when our mothering experience is little and our fears are many, mothering landscapes feel daunting and uncertain. One of the greatest reasons for such depth of fear lies in the trouble we have in understanding *why* our own mothers behaved as they did. Many children who have experienced abuse, neglect or lack of adequate love and nurturing grow to blame themselves for the behaviour of the adults around them. Sadly, they perceive their experiences as being normal; the result of their own behaviour or existence.

Such beliefs are deeply damaging and erode a child's developing sense of self, worth and self-esteem. Such beliefs and feelings can become deeply held, continuing to adversely and unconsciously influence and undermine individuals long into adulthood. Yet when we give ourselves time and space to look back and reflect (seeking support where necessary), we can begin to gain fresh and liberating adult perspectives. We can learn to build our self-esteem and recognise and release beliefs which are damaging, negative and limiting. We can grow to realise that things were not our fault and that we did not cause or deserve such experiences.

We can come to see some of the reasons which may account for our parents' behaviour, rendering them incapable of authentic empathy and unconditional love; perhaps they were ill or in a difficult or abusive relationship and were doing their best with the limited capacity and resources they had at the time. Could it be that they themselves experienced trauma, abuse or neglect, failing to receive authentic, sustained and unconditional love? If this was the case, perhaps, also, they did not have the support they needed to undo the damage done and grow beyond this.

Collective perspectives are shifting, developing a greater understanding of the value of nurturing children's emotional development, yet it has not always been this way. Learning more about the trauma in our parents' lives can increase our understanding as to why they may have lacked the emotional or practical capacity necessary to consistently love, nurture and connect with us, their own children.

Whilst such understanding does not excuse or justify cruel, abusive, neglectful or dismissive behaviour, it can be crucial in helping us to see more of the story of our parents, as then, we come to realise that things were not our fault. This frees us from thinking there was something so wrong with us that we deserved to be treated in such a way, or that our presence precipitated such actions. We realise that this ill neglect was caused by our parent's psychological issues due to their own circumstances; therefore we can see that with a commitment to doing things differently ourselves, we *are* able to create different childhood experiences for our own children;

"Through reading, I came to understand my mother's personality type and issues, I realised how and why she acted as she had. The relief and liberation was overwhelming, and freed me immensely to be my own person, and so, importantly, to mother my children as I would like to. I simply felt *that was her and this is me*. Once I gained understanding from a psychological perspective, (a narcissistic personality and lack of empathy which permeated all her relationships and probably stemmed from her own childhood) I could let go of the idea that I was to blame for her behaviour as she led me to believe.

Such feelings had subtly eroded me in many ways over the years, as I genuinely believed I had caused, and deserved the emotional abuse and neglect I had received, yet once I gained understanding of her personality, this self-blame dissolved as I understood more; it was there on the page in black and white describing the complexities of my childhood exactly; it was all she could offer as she has limited emotional capacities.

I felt free to move forward and be my own person, to discover more about myself and create the kind of family life I wanted my children to receive. I knew I would not pass on a negative or hurtful legacy, and that I was, eventually, free from the pain and shadow of the past; I could step forward and live life free and happy with my children. It is not always easy, and there are many ups and downs and times I worry I'm not being good enough, yet the freedom I feel to try my best, make mistakes and create our own family is liberating."

Chloe, Mother to Richard, 14, Bella, 10, Abigail, 7 and Geoffrey, 4

Like Chloe, once we realise we are responsible for our own actions, motherhood can feel so liberating; we realise we *are* free to create for our children the kind of childhood we want them to receive. Whilst we may fear we are not good enough, and at times worry we will somehow replicate past patterns, with conscious awareness of ourselves we *can* change the legacy, creating a different, more loving, nurturing and kind childhood for our children, and in doing so, we deepen into and heal ourselves.

Sensitised and aware

Rather than perceiving ourselves as damaged, we can instead look at things differently. Rather than seeing ourselves as lacking, we can re-envision ourselves as being *sensitised to the importance of expressing unconditional love and empathy for our children.* Through our personal experiences we are tuned in to the real need of raising children in a way that they receive and experience gentleness, acceptance and unconditional love.

Rather than letting difficult past experiences define and debilitate us, we can see them as the grit from which we learn the incredible importance of kind and conscious parenting. Such experiences remind us just how valuable it *is* to spend our time with our children, freely giving our love, care and attention and checking in to ensure they are receiving it.

As Margaret illustrates, difficult childhood experiences can become an inner compass, helping guide our way as we navigate the mothering path. Feelings of guilt and discomfort can be catalysts for transformation, guiding us within to discover more of our own truths, helping us to become more aware of how we want to interact with our children and how we do not;

"As a child my parents were emotionally and physically abusive, my father was an alcoholic; they weren't good parents. I remember vividly something that happened when my eldest, Leon, was a toddler. He was 3 or so, and he was very trying. He would push the boundaries a lot, he was into everything and I found it hard. He was hard work, but he was normal, it's just what they're like at that age. I remember smacking him on the legs out of frustration and annoyance on one occasion. This brought up such deep feelings which I just had to stop and be with completely. I could see myself, in this moment, replicating how my parents treated us.

We were bashed about a lot. It was very much: 'Do as we say not as we do, and if you don't you'll be thrashed.' I remember stopping and reflecting in that moment, realising this was certainly not the way I wanted to go.

I apologised to him and said I shouldn't have done it. I explained to him how I'd been feeling, but that it wasn't right for me to have done that. I told him how sorry I felt and that I'd never do it again, that I loved him very much and it wasn't his fault. And he seemed to understand. He was only young, but we had this dialogue and it was really meaningful. I feel he understood.

I've never hit them again. I saw what was brought up in that moment, all the memories and what it had been like for me, and knew I never wanted to go there. I realised I had the choice.

I'm authentic and they trust me. They know me, and I feel it comes from deep within. With my own parents there was no congruence, it could shift and change, we never knew what they were thinking, and things that had been the right thing could suddenly change.

Hopefully mine know for themselves what feels right or wrong. I try to make sure I come over honestly. I would explain why I did things, and we'd talk through decisions. I've taken care over discipline.

My own parents told me and my siblings that they owned us and we did what they said. I didn't want this for my kids. I wanted them to have their own identities. I chose not to take an authoritative approach, but instead wanted to learn about my children; I took an attitude of learning and curiosity about who they are. Now they both have strong feelings of who they are and they have their own voice. Neither are afraid to challenge authority if they feel it necessary; I still have some hang-ups around this. But I can see all of this clearly now, and see how my approach to parenting has helped my kids feel confident in knowing who they are."

Margaret, Mother to Leon, 22 and Rebecca, 17

Margaret's journey is tender and humbling; her story illustrates the very essence of the transformative potential within motherhood. From a childhood of physical and emotional abuse, Margaret realised in that moment she had a choice; she consciously chose to act differently. By bringing consciousness and awareness to our situations, and by taking the time and space to look at arising feelings and memories, we realise what a powerful position we hold as mothers, and the power we have to be different. Like Margaret, we can choose to take a different path, to get to know our children for who they are and create a new family blueprint based on connection, communication, trust, respect and honesty.

Our transformation through this element of mothering is twofold; we resolve to be different upon our inner landscapes, and this creates changes across our outer experiences with our children. And our outer experiences of loving, being with and caring for our children create ripples of change, awakening and raising consciousness upon our inner landscapes. Our growth and transformation continues, spiralling through and between both landscapes; enabling us to become the mother we want to be.

Mothering ourselves

If we have not received gentle, consistent care and nurturing as children, it is likely that we have had to take care of ourselves, and often others, as a matter of course, throughout our lives. We may not have recognised this caretaking, or guardianship, as being similar to mothering, instead, we might have feared we have no mothering aptitude or instinct at all, even prickling at the word. Yet as we reflect through a different lens, we begin to see things differently.

Through *not* having grown with consistent, gentle, or responsive nurturing of our physical, mental and emotional needs, we become accustomed to looking after ourselves.

By not having an active mother or mother figure, our own mothering instincts awaken *before* we have children to enable us to care for *ourselves*. So although we may not have previously recognised it in such a way, we are *already* able to be strong, nurturing and caring towards ourselves and others, because we have had to be. Rather than perceiving ourselves as lacking, damaged and inexperienced, instead we can see how we have honed and developed many of the skills, qualities and approaches which will serve us well in loving and mothering our children.

Becoming conscious and compassionate creators

Through our awareness and desire to do things differently we become creators. We do not have to unconsciously repeat the same patterns, (although we may fear we will). We can choose to break the cycle and change the legacy; we can transform our experiences into the positive energy and creativity with which we come to love our own children and create new family blueprints which pave the way for future generations of our family. We can choose to *become* the loving, caring, kind, patient mothers we never had, and in choosing to parent our children differently, so too do we heal ourselves and grow immensely.

With conscious awareness we can become aware of how our own childhood still influences us across our inner landscapes and we can choose to change things. We can begin to catch ourselves thinking negative, critical or judgemental thoughts towards ourselves. We can recognise this as the legacy of our childhood, instead choosing to talk to ourselves more kindly. We can talk to ourselves in the same way we would hope to talk to our children; with kindness, respect and recognition of our strengths and successes and respect and tenderness for our weaknesses and vulnerabilities. If we hope to create families filled with love, connection and compassion, we must begin to talk to ourselves in such a way, and hold ourselves in the same unconditional love and acceptance with which we hope to hold our children.

Perfection and acceptance

If we were not mothered well, we may perceive any slight mistake, deviation from ideals or difficulty with our children as evidence that our worst fears have been confirmed; that we are replicating the negative relationships within which we grew up. We can put an awful lot of pressure on ourselves to be the *perfect mother*, fearing if we are not, we are just the same as our parents.

Yet as we journey to love ourselves unconditionally, accepting ourselves as we are, as women healing, learning and doing our best, we slowly release this need for perfection, and can instead, find milestones of happiness in accepting and loving what *is*. We love ourselves for our strengths and all we are good at, and just as we love our children for all their weaknesses and vulnerabilities, so too can we learn to embrace ourselves in all our fragility and imperfection, recognising our intentions are always to do the best for our children, even if we do not always manage this.

This valuable milestone helps us see life from a more balanced perspective; the usual ups and downs of normal, loving family life. There *are* arguments, tantrums and tears alongside joy, fun and laughter, and there are apologies, cuddles and communication. No one is perfect all of the time; people love one another and support each other to move through, and learn from, difficulties.

A bad day or difficult situation can leave us feeling shattered, yet as we get some rest and the necessities of family life continue, we can regain perspective. Rather than attaching all our focus upon the negatives, we can widen our perceptions, arriving at a more balanced way of seeing. We all have trying days, and rather than seizing these events as evidence of our failure, instead we can see how we continue to love and hold one another through such times.

Recently, after some hours of sibling bickering and tantrums, I got us out of the house for a walk, which escalated the moaning and shouting. I felt upset that my daughters were upset; I believed I was failing them, making mistakes and reacting to their emotions rather than holding a loving, supportive place for them to come together, express themselves and move on. I was hard on myself. This day passed, as they all do, and with a bath and bedtime it slipped away and the week continued.

Another bedtime later that week I asked my daughters the simple question, 'How would you describe yourselves in five words?' One replied, 'I'm beautiful, kind, patient, caring and loving,' then settled down to sleep, cuddling her brother. In that moment something changed for me; I realised there will be bad days, there will be tears, tantrums and arguments, yet it is the way we treat each other through these, and through all of the other everyday moments, which make up our family. My eyes filled with tears of joy and my heart felt warm and balmy as I thought, *Yes, we are creating a loving family. We are not perfect and there is no need to try to be; we are happy, we communicate, and my children feel happy about who they are.* This was a deep treasure. It was so meaningful to me to see how, when loved unconditionally, children develop a strong and positive sense of who they are.

Creating new images of family life
When we do not have positive experiences of nurturing mother-child relationships to draw upon, it feels as though we are beginning without a familiar blueprint of healthy family life. Instead, we are creating new images of family life according to our own values. And whilst this is a path of positivity and hope, so too is it a path of uncertainty. Keen to create mothering relationships which were positive and nurturing, women identified three areas as most important to approach differently: validating and respecting children's emotions, compassionate communication and positive messages around food and body image. Interestingly, these three elements – emotions, communication and food – underpin the very fabric of family life.

Women highlighted the very essence of mothering, recognising a deep desire to nourish their children's minds, bodies and hearts with love, respect, connection and understanding. Whilst it is sad we may have come to such understandings through *not* having received such nurturing ourselves, through our experiences we gain profound insight into the value of connected, responsive and gentle mothering, which can become the foundation and guiding light for our own parenting journey;

"Because I had anxiety myself, I panicked during pregnancy as I

272

didn't want my kids to get it too. I began reading about how to raise a happy child and discovered attachment parenting.

I read lots about natural parenting, birth and attachment parenting. I began to think there was a link between my parenting and my anxiety problems, and part of this was that my mum had to leave for a while when I was a toddler.

This set me out on a journey of looking at my own childhood, and working through a lot of issues, memories and anger, this was hard, but very healing, it led to things shifting a lot and me and my mum are in a really good place now."

Charlotte, Mother to Rachel, 4 and Daniel, 2, and Isobel, 6 months

Valuing relationships and communication

Recollecting difficulties with their own parents, women recalled not feeling listened to, being dismissed, alone and invalidated. We may remember oppressive, controlling or manipulative family relationships and hope to develop and maintain more respectful, mutual and loving communication with our own children.

An aspect of family life I have come to value over the years is the time my children talk at bedtime. During the early years, there were many nights I was so worn out with exhaustion and frequent breastfeeding I felt exasperated by their seemingly constant need to chatter on and on about their ideas, feelings and experiences. *Why would they not just go to sleep!* I screeched to myself.

As the years have passed and their need for such physical intensity has lessened, the bedtime chatting has remained. Yet now it is an element of our day I have really come to value, feeling truly glad we stuck with it, despite my many frustrations. Now as they leave their years of childhood behind, I feel blessed to still get to listen to my girls tell me about their feelings, experiences and perspectives and feel happy they *want* to talk to me about such things.

We still have the silly stories and emotional woes, yet now I listen to their feelings about friendships, worries and hopes for the future, as well as many questions about the adult world. I do not recall such a sense of support and connection with my own mother and feel grateful for our continuing close relationships as they grow.

Margaret reflects upon how she has created a different way of communicating with her own daughter, compared to her own upbringing, and how this has been a source of support, trust and sharing through her daughter's adolescence;

"Another aspect of how I've done things differently is the relationship and openness I have with my teenage daughter. As a teenager myself, my parents didn't talk to me about sex, apart from saying if I came home pregnant I'd be thrown out. I've done things differently with Rebecca.

My daughter and I discuss it, she's shared some of her friend's experiences with me, of things that happened to them, and she's told me she feels sad they've had these experiences. I'm happy that we can chat about these things. I make a point of emphasising the love aspect and how this goes with the relationship, that it isn't just about the physical sex. I hope she'll continue to talk to me if she wants to.

Being able to chat it through with her makes me reflect on how it was for me... growing up without this kind of support and communication."

Margaret, Mother to Leon, 20, and Rebecca, 17

Margaret illustrates the great value in taking time to cultivate open, nurturing relationships, trust and communication with our children. When listening, sharing, and respectful communication is a part of the fabric of our family life, our children are much more able to come to us with their issues and worries, knowing we will listen, rather than shout, criticise or punish. Such communication provides much needed support and a safe space to explore feelings and experiences for our teens as they navigate the fast-paced and rapidly changing world of adolescent relationships.

Margaret illustrates that we certainly can change the legacy of our childhood relationships; we do not need to perpetuate patterns of oppression, punishment and harsh communication. Rather we can work on ourselves, nurture the parts of us which did not receive as much love and listening as they needed and go on to consciously create nurturing, genuine, respectful relationships with our own children.

Validating children's emotions

Past parenting paradigms held adults as authoritative power figures, placing little value on listening to and validating children's emotions. Women recalled being told off for crying and expressing feelings; being ignored, overruled or dismissed. Such authoritarian approaches have left many adults with discomfort, confusion and inhibition around expressing emotions, resulting in them having issues with forming meaningful, intimate connections with others.

In parenting paradigms past, and still, occasionally, present, children's expressions of anger and frustration were deemed "naughty" and unacceptable, as was crying and expressing hurt and difficult feelings of jealousy, overwhelm or sensitivity. We were rewarded for being "good" which generally meant being quiet, obedient, and successful, and punished, sometimes physically, for being "naughty" when expressing feelings, opinions or aspects of ourselves which went against parental or social expectation.

It is likely that our parents were also parented with such authoritative discipline and little regard for emotional expression and validation; yet society is changing, and thankfully we can now access information about the benefits of nurturing our children's emotional expression and parent them in ways which cultivate a greater sense of empathy, compassion and connection.

As parents sensitised by our own experiences, we often feel strongly about the importance of recognising, respecting and validating our child's feelings. Whilst sometimes more time consuming than simply telling them to 'stop crying', such approaches are investments in our children's mental health, emotional intelligence and wellbeing. I try to recognise and validate my children's emotions using simple phrases such as, 'I can see you are really sad that you've lost your ring, it was so special to you,' or 'I can hear how much you wanted to stay at the park, you were having fun.'

Whilst such responses do not change the physical situation, they do allow children's feelings to be recognised and validated rather than being dismissed. In my experience, such approaches help children to verbalise and understand their feelings, enabling them to move through those feelings rather than bury them inside. Unprompted, I have seen my children recognising the feelings of others in the same way, and developing a greater capacity for empathy than I believe they would have if they had repeatedly been told to 'stop crying and be good.'

"One aspect which is really different in comparison to how I was brought up is validating their emotions. I'm allowing them to have their feelings and supporting them to understand why they feel how they do. I think it's so important.

I remember when I was little I'd made a zoo out of toy animals for my little brother to visit. I'd spent a long time arranging the animals and used the clothes drying rack as an enclosure. In my mind I knew what I wanted my brother to do, I wanted him to come to the zoo as a visitor and for me to point out all the animals using a stick.

But you know what it's like when two little kids have their own ideas about a game; he came along and started picking the animals up and playing with them, he wasn't playing the game like I wanted and I'd spent so long trying to make it all nice for him. I felt frustrated and hit him with the stick.

I remember my parents coming over and hitting me with the stick. They didn't take the time to see it from my point of view or ask about my feelings and what happened. With my kids now I empathise with their feelings.

By my not having had the empathy myself, I realise how important it is, so I give it to them, I feel it's a contributing factor to self-esteem. I had my basic needs met, but there are more subtle needs, emotional needs, and if these are not met it feeds into self-worth, of always wanting to please people and not think about your own needs and feelings.

I don't want it to be like this for my daughters. I don't try to persuade them to talk to people if they don't want to, or to do things that don't feel right for them, I'd like to bring them up to know it is okay to trust their own judgement."

Faith, Mother to Dominic, 16, Stella, 4 and Emily, 2

If we have not been met with empathy and validation of our own emotions as children, it can be hard to offer this to our children. Similarly, our children expressing their strong emotions can bring to our awareness our own unhealed memories, trauma and sadness. We may want to meet our children with tenderness and empathy, yet find ourselves reacting with frustration and anger. Rather than criticising and judging ourselves harshly, instead we can hold ourselves in the same fierce, unconditional love we hope to hold our children; giving our empathy and understanding to our inner child and the parts of ourselves that are hurting and being triggered by our children's behaviour and expression.

We can remind ourselves that we are learning, we are doing our best, and, in our awareness, hold onto our hope to change and be more loving, gentle and connected with our children. We can simply do our best, be gentle upon ourselves and try to respond with more consciousness and less reactivity next time. We can reflect on our actions, apologise and talk to our children honestly. We can commit to taking better care of ourselves and our needs for rest, time and connection; we can take time to exercise, write, reflect and meditate.

We can work upon our inner, emotional landscapes, sending love back to our inner child as past memories surface. Talking with a therapist or friends on a similar journey can be of help.

When we embrace motherhood as a journey of transformation, we begin to see how each and every challenge and experience can become an opportunity for further learning, awareness, healing and conscious change. Naomi Aldort's *Raising Our Children, Raising Ourselves* is a valuable resource for further understanding and validating our children's emotions.

Mealtimes and body image

Mothers spoke of their parents' attitudes to food and body image, as well as negative memories of childhood mealtimes, and how they felt these cast a negative legacy upon their young adulthood. These mothers were clear that they were going to do things very differently with their own children. They were keen to pass on positive messages around body image, mealtimes and food and this seemed especially important for their daughters.

Eating is fundamental to our survival. The preparation, eating and clearing away surrounding mealtimes necessitates regular activity and family togetherness many times each day. We know from our own experience that keeping our babies and children fed is a near constant activity taking up much of each day.

Mealtimes and food preparation are synonymous with mothering; it is the way we nurture and sustain our children's bodies. Therefore, if there are difficulties in our relationships we can see how these can be played out around the dinner table, with issues around food quickly becoming emotional, confusing and entrenched. Many women shared the memory of being told, or forced, to eat everything on their plate at every meal, regardless of whether or not they liked the food or how full they were.

Such approaches are indicative of older cultural attitudes, yet at the same time they have an emotional impact on growing minds. Women shared how they had internalised unhealthy messages around food and control alongside difficulties in relationships. This led to negative emotions and perceptions becoming infused and entwined with food and body image. Through such reflections we gain awareness, and from awareness we grow in understanding and open the door for transformation to occur; we are empowered to create different experiences with our own children and this is how social change and transformation takes place.

"I was brought up with a mother who wasn't happy with her body image or weight. She dieted a lot, I remember her eating diet foods she didn't like, then eating chocolate in secret. I was forced to eat all the food on my plate, whether I liked it or not, and whether or not I was full.

I remember my mum reading dieting magazines, and weighing herself a lot, this is what I grew up in; watching my mum deprive herself then eating foods she liked in secret. I remember it being my mum's birthday, I remember thinking she wanted to lose weight, so I went to the health food shop and bought her healthy foods to help her lose weight. I thought this would make her happy, but I remember her not being happy about the presents.

As a result of what I grew up with I developed eating disorders, but I made a conscious effort to overcome these and develop a positive image of myself. Now I love my body and see it as healthy and strong and choose health giving, nourishing and delicious foods.

I've been conscious not to replicate these patterns with my children. It takes strength and effort to go against the common way of doing things, the culture of diets, of women having to be thin.

I set out to give my daughters a positive attitude towards food, to see it as a wonderful and nourishing thing. I want them to see lovely, healthy food as the thing that gives them energy to get strong and play. I put a lot of effort into our meals, and make healthy, organic and nourishing food that is nice and is good for them. I'm positive about food as nourishing, and not perpetuating the message of good food as boring and nice food as bad. You can make delicious wholefoods and sweet things that are lovely to eat as well as being full of nutrients.

I don't expect them to eat everything on their plate, and would never force them to, I want them to be able to decide for themselves; to be able to listen to themselves and know when their body has had enough. I want them to be able to trust themselves, and their own judgement."

Faith, Mother to Dominic, 16, Stella, 4 and Emily, 2

Many of our unconscious attitudes and values towards food and body image are entwined in our relationships, perceptions and childhood experiences of food and mealtimes. We can see how difficulties in self-image and feelings around weight and appearance can easily translate to a lifetime of dieting and disordered eating. Our emotions are closely linked to our eating habits; low self-image, self-esteem and confidence, as well as feelings of lack of control, can translate to complex and not always nourishing relationships with food.

Margaret speaks about food and body image in response to the question, 'How has mothering helped you to grow, change and transform within yourself?'

"I had a lot of hang-ups around body image due to bad parenting. I was made to eat everything off my plate, whether I liked it or not, or was full or not.

When I got a bit tubby, which was inevitable, as I was eating more than I needed, I was chastised by my parents; my father called me some really nasty names.

I developed anorexia and bulimia, I was struggling with myself and had real issues with food, diet and body image.

When my son was a toddler we used to take a long walk with the pram most days, it was a good walk uphill into town. I remember feeling one day how wonderful my body was for giving birth to this person and how wonderful he was.

From here, I experienced a total transformation of how I viewed myself; I began to feel very proud and thankful of my body for what it had done, and how it continued to be strong as I walked that day, and looked after my son.

It was very healing.

It's complete nonsense to force a child to eat something they don't like or to carry on eating when they're full. Of course I've been very different with my own children and they both seem to have a good, positive image of themselves, with no apparent issues around food and body image."

Margaret, Mother to Leon, 20 and Rebecca, 17

Margaret's story is a beautiful example of how the interweaving terrains of our mothering landscapes can be healing and transformational for our children and ourselves also. From her childhood experiences she resolved to do things differently; to not perpetuate negative attitudes surrounding food and body image. Through birthing, mothering and caring for her children, she began to see herself and her body in a new, positive light, liberating herself from previous limiting and negative self-perceptions. She became able to love herself more fully and recognise her own strength, worth and beauty through the process of mothering her children. Our growth, healing and transformation truly pays forward; creating sustained change and new ways of being for both ourselves and our children.

Milestones of transformation, reflection and acceptance not only invite us to do things differently with our own children, but to make significant, sustained change in our own lives. Making real and lasting change enables us to live our lives in accordance with our own truths and values, truths and values which may be very different to the beliefs we grew up with. Taking the time to look within ourselves, and allowing healing to occur, means we can let go of past limitations and love ourselves more fully and with greater authenticity. From here we create more grounded, balanced foundations from which to love, nurture and mother our children.

The journey of unconditional love

Mothering is a journey of love. We learn to feel unconditional love upon our inner landscapes, and how to put this into practice upon our outer landscapes. Yet such love is rich with potential for wider healing, awakening and transformation. By having such love in our system, it gets to work on ourselves also. Just as our children flourish in receipt of being loved unconditionally, parts of ourselves which may not have received such love rise to the surface to be released and receive love.

The powerful love we experience as mothers can rock our world, and at times feel overwhelming. Certainly, this love can feel euphoric and joyful, especially if we have the help of high and prolonged levels of birthing and breastfeeding hormones. Yet so too can it feel intense, shaking our once steady minds and lives, bringing to the surface memories and emotions of when we did not receive such love.

Such love is transformational, and if we trust the process, not putting any limits on its flow and power, difficult memories and emotions may arise, and have the potential to be met, heard and released. This is not solely an intellectual process, but an alchemical, spiritual one linked to resonance. Less something we do, and more something which unfolds as we surrender to the process of loving our babies and letting this powerful love overflow and awaken consciousness across our inner landscapes.

When my first daughter was a baby, around eight months or so, she had woken from her nap and I was chatting to her on the bed. As I looked at her trusting wide eyes and felt her open, loving innocence, the love I felt was immense and overwhelming. Huge waves of emotion cascaded from my heart and tears were running down my cheeks. I felt so deeply happy to be a mother and to have this beautiful baby to care for, yet at the same time memories arose of feelings and times I struggled and felt alone.

Through opening up to mothering my daughter and allowing myself to love her as fully as I could, my heart opened and brought out memories of pain and sadness; those aspects of myself which did not resonate with the vibration of love. I let my tears fall, and as she smiled and kicked beside me, I simply breathed. I used my yoga practice and breathed deeper than the feelings, letting myself feel, and letting myself cry. As the intensity of a thunderstorm is followed by freshness and serenity, so too did I feel very calm and peaceful when these feelings had ebbed away. Something profound and healing had taken place, and this experience of great love creating transformation became the inspiration for *Milestones of Motherhood*.

Ronne illustrates this alchemic process as she shares how loving her baby son awoke parts of herself requiring deep healing, a type of healing which occurs as we find we are capable of *giving to ourselves* the powerful unconditional love we did not receive as children. Her words are captivating and beautiful; I hope they bring wisdom, courage and inspiration to those of you who are on your own healing journeys;

"As I held Dan and soothed him when he cried and sang to him, I could feel wounded places inside me beginning to heal.

I had not had good mothering. My mother had many, many emotional problems and mental health issues, complicated by the loss of much of her family in the Holocaust while she was safe in the United States. When she was pregnant with me, her surviving brother and sister, along with many other Holocaust refugees, began arriving in the U.S., and many of them stayed in our house temporarily. One of my older brothers, who was five at the time, says he remembers 'Months of crying – people sitting in the kitchen and crying...' as they related to my parents what had happened to the friends and loved ones they'd left behind in Poland.

As the youngest of three children, and the only girl, I was treated differently – my father was protective and affectionate with me in a way he hadn't been with my brothers, which aroused jealousy and resentment in my mother. She was never physically affectionate with me, and was often deliberately withholding because she said, 'Your daddy spoils you!' (The 'spoiling' consisted of telling me bedtime stories, taking me for walks and to the playground, and occasionally buying me treats like a box of crayons.)

When I was six she had a major breakdown, and though she recovered somewhat, her mental health was precarious after that. All of my father's attention was now directed towards her, and I was pretty much left on my own. She was hospitalised several times as I was growing up – times I felt were a respite from her scary, erratic behaviour and her constant lashing out at me.

After that kind of childhood, I wasn't sure I would be a loving mother. So it was reassuring when I found that I was able to love my child so deeply and completely.

So perhaps that is one of the biggest ways motherhood has changed me – it helped me heal the wounds of my own childhood through creating a happy childhood for my son."

Ronne, Mother to Dan, 28

Through loving her son, Ronne realised she was *capable of loving unconditionally*. For those of us who did not receive this as a child, *knowing* we are capable of giving such love to our child is life-changing. For if we grew up without such nurturing, a part of us may still fear that we are undeserving of such love, that we are unlovable and unworthy; and not capable of giving love to our own child, let alone receiving love from them.

Simply knowing we can laugh with our children, play and have fun together and hold them gently to our hearts when they cry is a priceless joy to those of us who did not share such close affection with our own mothers.

Alongside rejoicing in our capacity to love, so too can the experience of loving our children unconditionally create a renaissance in our perceptions of ourselves. As Margaret illustrates, we can rediscover and welcome home parts of ourselves previously lost to fear, pain, shame or trauma;

"My childhood experiences left me with little self-confidence, I was very self-critical, my parents had been neither kind nor loving, this left me lacking and needing to give myself this love.

I doubted my ability to be a good mother, yet once they come, something takes over. I felt a heartful connection with this little thing growing inside me, there is something immensely comforting about that. I was anxious, but in time something else emerged; a feeling which came from the heart, and this took over. I felt connected to my baby and feelings of powerful, unconditional love overtook anxiety.

I feel blessed by the two wise beings forged in my womb for they truly taught me how it is to Love another Unconditionally. The journey of Motherhood has been a blossoming of my heart to Open, wide enough to also love myself unconditionally, just as I am.

Able to accept and Love all the parts of myself, many of those lost previously to denial, suppression, unworthiness and shame, it is like a coming home to who I really am. As I come home to my treasures, I see the gifts of life I have been given and there is such Gratitude, Joy and Love that flows from my heart."

Margaret, Mother to Leon, 22 and Rebecca, 17

With courage and bravery, we can choose to face our feelings, to go within and look at the parts of ourselves feeling hurt, trapped, shamed or angry. We can write about our feelings, talk about them with a trusted friend or therapist, we can look at them in quiet moments, we can let our tears fall and seek counselling or therapy. We can explore ourselves through meditation, visualisations, art, drawing, writing, yoga, inner child work, giving our feelings expression and outlet. Those parts of ourselves which have not been loved are drawn to the surface, called to be seen, heard, loved and let go. And by so doing, we come to know ourselves more deeply and create more space within our inner landscapes within which to deepen into love, empathy and compassion.

Love brings change, compassion and forgiveness

Alongside inner healing, such love can bring waves of change and compassion to our perspectives and relationships. This is a journey of personal maturation, yet as we gain greater empathy and compassion for ourselves, we increase our capacity to feel these things for others. Being able to see from a broader perspective, with greater empathy and compassion, can be tremendously transformative in our relationships with our own children and parents. It can also help us to relate better to other members of society. As we deepen in such awareness, our own fierce hurt and emotions find expression and do not cloud our perspectives as much as they may have done previously. We find freedom to look from new perspectives and create new ways of relating which have their roots in greater understanding and authenticity, rather than originating from places of emotional pain;

"There's been hard times between my mum and me; there were

still unresolved issues and feelings when I became a mother myself. I remember her being angry, controlling and losing her temper with me a lot as a child. I had anxiety and blamed her for that.

When I became a mum myself, I had a long stop-start labour ending with a Caesarean, which was not what I had hoped for. I had postnatal depression and anxiety, and this happened with my next babies also. Each time, amidst the depression, fears and anxiety and uncomfortable thoughts and feelings towards myself and my baby, strong feelings and memories from my childhood came flooding back. I felt like I was drowning, swamped by these memories at a time when I was feeling vulnerable with a new baby and toddlers to look after. These were not good times, and I did question myself and my life at times.

I realised this was something I had to get through, so I read a lot, I learned to accept myself, to accept help and to let go of the idea of being perfect. I used natural remedies and placenta essence to support myself and focussed on loving my babies, looking into their little faces and starting to get to know who they are. I think this helped a lot. I realised each time that I could get through it. On reflection, I've come to see this process and the depression and intensity of feelings as a kind of initiation. I've faced it and feel I've come through it much stronger, so much more able to trust myself. I know I'm strong and can cope with things.

Also I decided to really face things with my mum. I faced my feelings instead of trying to push them away, stay angry and blaming my mum for what she was like. When I was in a particularly low way I realised she may have felt this way too, that life is hard, that you can't always be perfect and we just have to do the best we can. I guess I started to realise that it was quite likely that it would have been hard for her too and I began to reflect on her life, not just my anger and resentment towards her.

Her own father was violent, she was just trying to be better than he was, and she was. I used to think she was controlling and had a bad temper and I blamed her, but now I can see it more from her perspective and how tough it was for her. Even now I'm quite defensive and still have anger towards her, but I'm working on this. I used to think this was just what she was like, but with reflection I realise her dad was even worse, more angry and physically violent to her and she was just trying to be better to me than her dad was to her.

And I'm trying to be a bit better to my own kids, I'm learning more, and when I have hard times with my kids now, I'm able to be more gentle on myself, to remind myself that I'm learning too. I try to be less angry and controlling than she was.

Through this process of reflection I've come to realise there were actually lots of things I liked about my childhood and I want to do these things with my kids. I liked how my parents were open-minded and open to different cultures, had friends from around the world and took me to many places. I like how they valued us spending time outdoors and how my mum and dad always encouraged my creativity and individuality. They encouraged me to do what I liked doing and let me make my own choices.

I came to realise that she was not out to hurt me, and because I sometimes feel angry towards my own kids, I can see how she was like that too, but I know that at the same time just how much I love them and imagine she felt that way about me too."

Charlotte, Mother to Rachel, 6, Daniel, 4 and Isobel, 6 months

Charlotte's story is powerful; a detailed insight into the profound power of transformation through mothering across our landscapes. Time spent feeling our emotions rather than pushing them away, taking time to be with our children, reflecting upon our perceived shortcomings and developing compassion for ourselves brings new perspectives and waves of freedom. Such fresh perspectives bring new opportunities to perceive ourselves and our own parents as people as well as parents. Like Charlotte we can see how they may have struggled with similar issues as they figured out how to be mothers themselves. Whilst we may still feel hurt, through reflection and our own mothering experiences, we grow in understanding of the complexities of parenting.

The essence of these milestones of growing empathy and compassion lie in giving *ourselves* the love, empathy and compassion we did not receive as children. The more we are able to love and accept ourselves, the more we are able to love and care for our children. Hence, the cycle of forgiveness, freedom, love and acceptance begins, providing a real alternative to the negative spirals of replicating hate, anger, resentment, blame and bitterness. As the cycle gathers momentum we can genuinely change our legacy and create new, more nurturing and connected ways of mothering and living.

"My own childhood left me lacking and hurting in many ways. I realised it was up to me to give myself the love and acceptance I needed. I began some simple practices of Buddhist compassion. I took a little time to practice the loving kindness practices every day. I started with myself first. I needed so much care in this way; it was what I was crying out for. And I attribute this ability to be able to deeply and truly love myself to being a parent and knowing the depth of love I feel for my own children.

The practice involves imagining the person sitting in front of you, either as an adult or a child, and offering them loving kindness. I did this for myself for a while and truly grew to love myself. Next I saw my dad sitting in front of me and my heart cracked open. I could see his own profound suffering, I could see the man he was, and the pain he had endured. I saw the little boy who was blamed for his own father losing his life at sea. I saw how this affected his whole life. I felt myself saying, 'I don't condone what you did to me as a child, but I do forgive you.' I felt deep acceptance and forgiveness.

Offering this type of loving kindness to yourself and others moves you away from a place of cruelty and towards unconditional self-love and acceptance. Without doubt this greatly helps me on my journey as a mother and through my entire life."

Margaret, Mother to Leon, 22 and Rebecca, 17

Through opening her heart to unconditional love Margaret gave herself the valuable milestones of acceptance, inner peace and contentment. Her spiritual practices of compassion enabled her to come to a place in her life where she no longer carries anger and resentment towards her parents. She has learnt to love and care for herself and is able to choose to mother her children with compassion, acceptance and empathy rather than reacting from, and replicating, past harm. She is free.

We do not have to unconsciously recreate patterns of harm, abuse and trauma for our own children. How we mother lies within our own control, we *can* change the legacy, and unconditional love *for ourselves* is the essence and guiding light of this journey;

"Recently, on a visit home, our son Dan told me, 'There isn't one thing I'd change about my childhood.' I thought, 'Wow. We did it, we created a happy home for our son and gave him the confidence to grow up and leave it. That's more than my parents did for me.' Despite feelings of failure I still struggle with at times, I feel that's a big success.

Through being a mother I learned I have a capacity to love that I never imagined possible. I learned beyond a doubt what the term 'unconditional love' means, and that is a priceless gift."

Ronne, Mother to Dan, 28

Chapter Nine
Journeys of Identity

Identity encompasses the way we make sense of who we are, how we structure our lives, and the values we hold. Prior to motherhood our identities are formed through many aspects of our lives, including, but not limited to such things as: employment, hobbies, sports, qualifications, interests; the culture we are part of; our family, friendships and relationships; our personality, beliefs and values; our appearance; our tastes in music, food and fashion; our past experiences; our lifestyles; our passions, dreams and hopes for the future.

Certainly, our identities are multifaceted, yet they become entwined with what we do most often and what we feel valued for, and for many of us, our careers constitute a significant part of our identities. Therefore, when we become mothers, our core sense of self can feel shaken, for the way we spend our time and receive recognition and value changes profoundly. Many of us quietly face feelings of loss and uncertainty alongside the excitement of new motherhood as we let go and refocus our attention.

We become busy with baby care, finding our feet, finding new friends and adjusting to new lifestyles. Yet in the quiet moments we may reflect and realise just how different our lives have become; we can experience uncomfortable, panicky feelings around our sense of identity, or more specifically, our sense of *lost* identity. Immersed in early motherhood we are new and fragile; we perceive elements of ourselves we have *lost*, yet we are not so far into motherhood to understand the full potential of the emergent aspects of ourselves that are still developing. As much as we love our babies, many of us fear we have lost ourselves and become "just a mum"; as though our personhood has been misplaced amidst the nappies and laundry, our identity existing only by proxy as we become known as *Josie's mum*.

Yet as much as this journey brings a sense of loss, something greater unfolds as we discover new meaning and elements of ourselves brought to life through loving and mothering our children. At the very heart of this journey is the discovery and embodiment of the deep *meaning and value* we receive through mothering. It is the ownership of such value that becomes the fire which burns through doubts, and blazes the trail for the awakening of a new, deeply rooted identity.

In the beginning

The changes brought about by pregnancy are vast, yet women explained that pregnancy itself, whilst feeling new and exciting, did not bring significant changes to identity. Rather, our growing bump and sense of excitement and apprehension are incorporated into our overall identity. We are still ourselves, but pregnant. Simple as this sounds, this perception of ourselves is significant, for as we come to birth and mother our babies, for many of us, this perception wholly changes;

"I think my priorities have changed – I've found mothering all-consuming; even though I'm back at work now, I haven't returned to other activities I used to do in my leisure time. I plan to, but at the moment I want to save my time and energy for my son. I define myself as a mother first now – even when I'm at work, I'm still a mother."

Hazel, Mother to Barnaby, 15 months

Our birth experiences initiate us into motherhood, stripping us bare, shattering our sense of self-image, control and identity. For to bring forth our babies, however they are born, we must surrender all sense of control and allow powers stronger than ourselves to course through our being, fracturing, and in time, wholly rearranging, our inner landscapes;

"I'd read that your birthing experience brings you whatever you don't expect. And as an anthropologist I think of a woman's first delivery as a rite of passage; the physical trial that takes you from maidenhood to motherhood.

Some say it gives you the medicine that you need.

So what did mine give me? It felt like a lesson in patience and expecting the unexpected as well as a reminder I can have utter faith in my body and amazing support team."

Mary Ann, Mother to Edward, 7 months

Birth is a metaphor for our transformation through mothering. The intensity of birth, and our subsequent surrendering of control, introduces us to something greater than ourselves. It shows us our power, strength and depth as a woman – not just as an individual defined by their job description, but as a primal birthing mother. *This* is why birth has the potential to be so transformational. And however it unfolds, it strips away our veneer of control and individuality and initiates us into the *collective* experience of mothering and the potential power of the Feminine.

Our identities as mothers run far deeper than the details of how our births unfolded. We find such strength and power in breathing through contractions, receiving our baby with tearful tenderness after a 58-hour labour and assisted delivery, holding and feeding our baby despite our limited movement and pain of our Caesarean wound. We find new stores of tenacity and determination to love and mother, and it is our *continuation* through vulnerability, trauma, elation, joy, pain and power that blasts apart our previous identities and becomes the bedrock for our newly emerging, wiser, stronger, *Mother Selves*.

Perceptions of motherhood – *just* a mum

Before we become mothers we rely on what we see around us, as well as portrayals of motherhood, to form our ideas and expectations of what motherhood is like. Yet beyond glossy, mess-free images of women and children in the media, there are few positive, mainstream narratives which celebrate and value the substance and ethos of mothering. Certainly, these can be found, but we need to actively seek them out. Women explained that they felt current society, whilst seeming to promote "family values", places little value on the actual work of mothering, and especially on women choosing to stay at home and mother their children themselves in the early years.

To the wider world, mothering work is largely invisible. Mothering is seen as something insignificant; something women just get on with around their careers. Louise reflects upon her initial perceptions of motherhood before having children and puts into words how both the practical and emotional landscapes are wholly underestimated, misunderstood and misrepresented;

"I think the role of mother (and father) is vastly underestimated. I underestimated it before having children, simply thinking of the practical side and not realising the importance of bonding, trusting, guiding, nurturing and the impact a parent's own actions as role model have on developing a child's emotions, approach to life, preferences, behaviour, empathy and future self. I used to see mums playing with their little ones when I had a rare day off work and think what a 'cushy' life they were leading! How wrong!"

Louise, Mother to Flynn, 3.5 and Rowan, 10 months

Dominant cultural messages place little value on parents being with their babies and children full time. Instead, mothers are persuaded back to the workplace with the offer of free childcare, and encouraged to return back to "normal" as soon as possible. As Vanessa illustrates, there remains the all-pervading message that if we are meeting our children's needs ourselves beyond early infancy we are deemed to be contributing less, and our activities, daily work and investments are somehow less valuable;

"I kept studying and finished my course, up until my last day of pregnancy, due to family pressure, because a mother could not be 'just' a mother, as if being a mother was just something you do on the side, your career having to come first."

Vanessa, Mother to Lilo, 10, Boo, 8 and Sammy, 1

Mothering is so undervalued socially that there is rarely a description for it on many official forms. Filling in applications for bank accounts, mortgages, surveys and the like, there are many boxes to tick which describe career and work patterns, yet if we opt to fulfil our children's needs ourselves (which is a recognised, valued and paid occupation when we look after or educate other people's children) we find ourselves somewhere in the no-woman's land of 'unemployed' or 'homemaker', neither of which truly provide an accurate description of the valuable work we do. We can see how our identities can feel shaky, at least in the beginning, when we spend all or most of our time caring for our children, especially as we suddenly become invisible in the wider world;

"I don't think stay-at-home mums are recognised or valued by today's society. There's been a huge shift away from women choosing to stay at home with their children since my childhood. This saddens and angers me. The government talks about family values while supporting working mums and funding nursery places. I'm not saying there should be no support for working mums, but the fact of the matter is there is NO support for stay-at-home mums.

It's the norm now to go back to work and I suspect that if the same benefits were given to stay-at-home mums then working mums would be less of the norm. Many friends that had their children when they were younger regret going back to work and have said if they could have their time again there is no way they would return to work."

Deborah, Mother to James, 4

Marty reflects on her years of mothering her now older children full time and explains how, in the eyes of society, these years she knows as being so inherently valuable, account to nothing more than "time wasted";

"You ask to what extent I feel society values and recognises mothering.

I reply, not at all.

I am acutely aware that as far as society is concerned, and in accordance with all prevailing mainstream political narratives, I have 'wasted' my life and education doing 'nothing'. It is hard to have to justify oneself repeatedly, and I have worked through a very large number of 'spins'.

What helps me most in keeping my resolve strong is the undeniable quality of the finished product. Twenty-one years old and approaching her graduation, Jessie is a lovely young woman capable of rising to any challenge she may decide to take on in life. She is also now able to give me emotional sustenance instead of the flow being all one way. I really enjoy her company and am so incredibly proud of her."

Marty, Mother to Jessie, 21 and Lizzie, 16

Whilst many may perceive our time spent at home caring for our children – breastfeeding them, listening to them, reading them stories, taking them to playgroups, preparing meals and eating with them – as "doing nothing", a shift in our thinking takes place as we, ourselves, begin to recognise and value the great meaning and worth inherent in our mothering work. And as we come to recognise everything we do as being valuable in laying the foundations for our children's physical, mental and emotional health and wellbeing, so we deepen into our new identity, feel our strength, and become more comfortable stepping outside of the dominant discourse;

"Another challenge women go through is to do with their identity. I still feel that society doesn't fully respect the enormous value of the role of parents – mums' particularly, as when the dads do it, don't they get admired!

Much of the work women do as mums, apart from the delightful and lovely bits engaging with the kids brings, is utterly inane, downright boring, tedious and repetitive and in no way valued – such is the nature of much of the domestic requirements of being a mum.

My husband would admit it was easier to walk out of the house and go to work than be on duty at home. So not only do women do invisible and disrespected labour, they are also not credited with any of the identity and kudos a working status brings.

It took me a long time to come to terms with this – even longer as I continued to stay at home and home educate. But as my children grew – as they became educated – I began to realise that it was the role that parents took and their involvement with their children that decided whether education was a success or not, whether they were in school or not. This role of parents – mums particularly as it's mostly mums doing it – is to my mind one of the most important that a person can undertake. And as I understood this I began to feel better valued as a person with an important identity. It's hard though to express that in a society and culture which I feel does not uphold it."

Ross, Mother to Charley and Chelsea, in their 20's

At first, we may feel overwhelmed by constant, repetitive work, much of which is invisible, tedious and totally unrecognised by the wider world. We may, at times, feel we are failing, losing ourselves, becoming trapped by domesticity and are no longer strong, empowered or independent women. Yet as we continue onwards, we begin to understand the worth of our work, and the true value of mothering.

Discovering greater meaning and fulfilment

Society teaches us to seek fulfilment, recognition and belonging in the opportunities and achievements of the outer world. Yet as we hold our babies in our arms, feed them through the night, feel their warmth as they sleep against our bodies, hold little hands and listen as wide-eyed children share feelings and stories, we uncover an inner world rich with meaning and fulfilment.

As we begin to understand the inherent value of really being there to nurture our children physically and emotionally, transformation in our landscapes of identity begins to awaken. As Melanie illustrates, such recognition of the value of what we do brings greater strength and confidence in who we are;

"After the first few all-consuming months, as my son grew and I started to get more like myself again, I began to feel guilty. Yes, guilty for not doing something other than being a Mum. Stay-at-home mums get remarkably bad press and if you choose to be a stay-at-home mum, like I have thankfully been able to be, it is amazing how society makes you feel: 'Yes well, being a stay-at-home mum is all very well, but you really should be doing something.' As if looking after your child makes you less of a person.

Of course, you don't do anything because you're 'just a mum'.

It took me a long while to realise that being a Mum, being there for my son, is actually okay and a tremendously good job to have. Anyone who doesn't like my decision can just sod off. I will live my life the way I choose to, the way that is best for me, my son and my family.

That doesn't mean that I don't crave adult conversation sometimes, hence my volunteering for the Breastfeeding Network. It has been fantastic – it gives me the chance to give something back to new mums who need help, gives me the mental stimulation I need and as I only need to give a few hours a month it doesn't interfere with the time I have with my son."

Melanie, Mother to James, 1

As we discover more of the value inherent in mothering and deepen into our new identity, the perceptions of others begin to hold less sway. We become stronger and more confident, knowing that the work we do is significant and worthwhile. We become authentic; what we feel on the inside is how we act on the outside; we express our values through how we live our lives; we have less to prove; we know within who we are, and live our lives accordingly, with less need for external validation.

Mothering as metamorphosis

Just as a caterpillar passes through a number of formative stages before it transforms into a butterfly and is able to spread its wings and fly, so too do we experience a number of stages in our own journey through motherhood. Initially, we may feel lost and overwhelmed, yet with time, and as we begin to recognise the intrinsic worth of what we do, our confidence increases. We differ from butterflies in that the caterpillar will only complete this journey of metamorphosis once during its lifetime, whereas as mothers our identity continues to shift alongside our children's development.

Embryonic – pregnancy and early formation

Pregnancy is a time of inner formation; the conception and embryonic formation of our *Mother Selves*. As our baby grows our identity begins to shift physically, mentally, emotionally and socially as we expand upon all levels to accommodate our baby. Just as we furnish our homes in preparation for baby's arrival, so too do we furnish our inner landscapes.

As we approach labour and birth our advent into our mothering identity takes on a more concrete form. Through the strength of labour contractions, possible interventions, colossal hormonal peaks and the euphoria of meeting our baby face to face, it is with much intensity that we are initiated into our new, fledgling identity as a mother.

Caterpillar – hard work with a sole focus

Just as the caterpillar hatches from the egg and awakens to a new world, so too do we find ourselves awakening to the new postnatal world of learning to love and mother our baby. The caterpillar's new life is busy; its sole focus feeding and growing, for without such an intense urge to feed and grow it will be unable to begin the next stage of metamorphosis. We, like the caterpillar, are busy awakening to the constant intensity of meeting our baby's needs. All our time is taken up by feeding, changing, settling, soothing, and learning to love.

We are beginners; we need to listen in a different way in order to decipher this new language of non-verbal communication. As Melanie recalls, at this time so little of our attention is focussed upon ourselves; we know we are changing yet there is little time to process this or gain a wider perspective as we are consumed with caring for our newborns;

"The first few months were the hardest. I felt like a shadow of my former self. Being with my son and looking after his every need was all-consuming and so (dare I say it) uneventful in the first few months – I was a milking, nappy-changing automaton. I really didn't feel like 'me', a 'person', for quite a while."

Melanie, Mother to James, 1

The caterpillar eats constantly and grows immensely; his sole intent is the discovery and consumption of food and this is where his eyes allow him to focus. Similarly, in the early stages of motherhood, we do not have the necessary objectivity to see just how much we ourselves are learning since we are entirely consumed by the tasks of baby care. Yet, like the caterpillar, tremendous inner growth is occurring even if we are only slightly aware of it. It is only as we progress further on our journey that our perspectives widen and we become aware of our great learning and the transformation unfolding within.

Cocoon – letting go, dissolving and reforming

The magical metamorphosis of the caterpillar is fascinating; how, we wonder, does the caterpillar become the butterfly? What happens within the cocoon? Once the caterpillar has shed its skin many times and reached a certain size, it spins a cocoon around itself then releases enzymes which dissolve its entire body. What is less well known about this captivating process is the role of the near-magical *imaginal discs*, which are a group of very specifically organized cells. Imaginal discs contain the blueprint for the formation of the butterfly, and they've been within the caterpillar since its formation in the egg. Fuelled by nutrients in the enzyme soup, the imaginal discs awaken and programme the formation of the butterfly, holding the image of what the cells are to become.

This is a breathtaking process and inspires awe and wonder at the power and intelligence of Nature. We can liken our own transformation, growth and re-emergence to that of the butterfly. As caterpillars we focussed on meeting the constant needs of our babies, shedding our skins a number of times as we reached new milestones of understanding, love, confidence and trust. Yet our emerging identity remains in flux; fledgling and fragile in form.

Like caterpillars, we become dissolved within the new environment of our cocoons; we've had to let go of our previous ways and identities and are consumed by the new world and work of mothering, but as yet, our imaginal discs have not fully created the new self; growth is occurring, but our wings are not yet formed.

Just as the caterpillar must surrender to its dissolution, motherhood calls us to completely let go of our previous versions of ourselves. And we do not embrace the new immediately; our metamorphosis requires us to spend some time in the coocoon, suspended and incomplete, whilst *our* imaginal discs hold the vision of us as the mother we wish to become.

This time in the soup can be disconcerting; a new identity takes time to emerge. We can feel busy, uncertain and a little lost; our bodies feeling strangely unfamiliar, our minds intense with new thoughts, our emotions overwhelming. Catherine brings this process to life as she shares her own inner journey of dissolution and reformation through motherhood;

297

"At the stage I'm in right now, I find it difficult to assess my sense of identity. This is one of the biggest challenges. My children are still only one and three so I can see things will change a lot over the next few years, but right now I often feel quite at sea in terms of who I am and where I'm going.

Before I had children I lived a fast-paced lifestyle as a lawyer in central London. I was very well paid, had a job I found mentally challenging, enjoyed the interaction with lots of close work colleagues, and had a busy social life. I was also physically very fit; I cycled with a club every week, was a regular runner and went to yoga classes. I felt relatively confident in my physical appearance, and had many interests I could pursue as and when I wanted.

I wasn't prepared for how dramatically my life would change when I became a stay-at-home mum. I didn't know what sort of mother I would be, and in particular, I didn't realise I would find it almost impossible to leave my daughter for almost any time at all during at least her first year. I breastfed her and partially co-slept too. I just wanted to be with her all the time; I felt that that was what she needed. I didn't find it at all easy to leave her with anyone, even her father, for anything other than very short periods. This meant I just stopped doing almost everything I'd done previously.

It took me months before I even felt able to go out for a half hour run to get some exercise. I stopped yoga and cycling completely, which I now regret as I have all sorts of back problems arising from two consecutive pregnancies with very little exercise in between.

By the time my second daughter was about a year old I started to feel very run down physically. As well as being constantly tired from lack of sleep and the very physical nature of caring for two little ones, I realised I'd also neglected my own body by essentially giving myself to my children 24/7. I loved breastfeeding and co-sleeping but I felt I desperately needed my own body back; I was in constant discomfort from my back. I also felt I'd lost an awful lot of confidence in myself in terms of my appearance, mainly because of the lack of fitness. I hadn't realised before how much my body was a big part of my identity and how important it was for me to feel comfortable in it.

It took me months to actually work up to making any changes, but I finally joined a gym and started doing yoga again several times a week. It just felt absolutely wonderful to take that step. It was definitely a huge milestone for me, claiming some time for myself and reclaiming my own body."

Catherine, Mother to Lucy, 3 and Tess, 20 months

Catherine's insights illustrate how we need to let go of all that went before, and allow ourselves to be dissolved in the meeting of our baby's needs to *learn* mothering. As we meet our baby's needs we become the vision of the mother we want to be; then, once we have fully assimilated the mothering way of being into our core selves and understand the great value of meeting our children's needs, we begin to feel the whisperings of other strands of our being and are able to eke out a little time to weave these into our lives once again. Catherine also speaks of the important milestone of caring for ourselves alongside meeting the needs of our little ones.

Mary Ann illustrates how maintaining the threads of her writing helped her to fully enjoy time spent mothering her son;

"In the early days I got very tired and emotional at times, but I was surprised how much I enjoyed motherhood. I'd been worried I wouldn't be able to cope, and so as the days went by and I began to find I could cope and got used to being a Mum my confidence, and relief, grew.

I actually found I love being a Mum. Perhaps the fact I've continued writing helps give me a sense of balance in my day (I didn't write every day, but I do write most days when he sleeps, even if only for a few minutes!).

Most of it is 'being mummy', but a bit of it, since quite early on, has also been 'being a writer' – I think that helped enormously, having moments of that amongst the rest of my day."

Mary Ann, Mother to Edward, 7 months

Flying – I'm me but enhanced!
Just as the butterfly emerges from a long process of growth and transformation, unfolding its magnificent wings in the sunlight before beginning to explore the wonders of its new world, so it is for us as mothers. After an extensive time of growth through the journeys of conception, pregnancy, birth and the early days and months of our child's life, so too do we begin to reflect, emerge and recognise the depths of our own growth, formation and learning. We've let go of activities and aspects of our identity from our previous life, have perhaps felt loss as we explored our intense and apparently chaotic new environment, yet we've continued along our path each day, coming to realise the value of mothering. And alongside this process we have nurtured latent aspects of ourselves, so that we've emerged reformed; strengthened and brilliant in our identities as mothers and as women.

"I can honestly say that now I'm probably the most comfortable with 'me' I've ever been."

Melanie, Mother to James, 1

"I'm a new me, it's not so much that I've developed new qualities, as that the hopes I had are intensified. I was capable of patience before, but it's been tested a lot more now. I could be kind, gentle and creative, but now I have to be, so I pull it out of the bag better, and more often."

Eleanor, Mother to Thomas, 3 and David, 10 months

"I don't feel I've changed my identity, as such, but become more of who I am, and stronger in my views. In some ways, I became more serious because parenting was (and still is) such an important issue to me."

Veronika, Mother to Bethany, 19 and Eliza, 17

Women said that motherhood, instead of being a time in which they sought to change themselves, was rather a time of finding themselves. For it is through our continuing commitment to the mothering path that we discover *more of who we truly are.*

Mother of five, Angela, reflects on her personal journey of identity and how she felt she got *more* out of life as a mother, and continues to do so as her children reach adulthood;

"So many people want to 'get back' to the way things were before they had kids, but it wasn't like that for me. I'm still the same person, so don't feel I have to 'get back' to anything, I'm the same person just going down a different path.

I don't think you lose your identity as you become a mother, for me I'm me, but I'm an enhanced version of myself! I'm better than I was before! I think you get more out of life with kids.

When my kids were little I took them to festivals. I'd been before myself and had all the time to do what I liked, but the times I took my kids I saw a different side of it, I saw it through their eyes and we did different things, more child-focussed things, so I was still doing what I liked to do, but I was sharing it with my kids. I was still who I am, but with children, it didn't feel like a compromise at all.

I feel people strive to go back to work quickly, then end up feeling torn; someone suffers, either the kids as they're not getting what they need from you, or you suffer, as you're trying to do too much and not becoming who you're supposed to be.

For me identity has never been about going back, but about moving forward, with a child, in a different way.

I got to know different sides of myself I didn't know were there through having my children. I didn't realise what I was capable of doing. When I look back to when I was 20 I wouldn't have thought I could have got this far and done what I have. My goals are totally different now to what they were when I was younger. I wouldn't want to go back to how I was before and my focusses then. Now my life revolves around kids, my own, the ones I work with and those in my community; this is who I am and it's what makes me happy. I feel like I've got lots to give and share with others from what I've learned over the years."

Angela, Mother to Ozzy, 23, Amelia, 18, Marianne, 17, Aeryn, 10 and Willow, 8

For many of us, motherhood awakens us to the discovery and creation of new passions, interests, ways of being and careers which resonate beautifully with our mothering identity and which bring feelings of fulfilment, purpose and authenticity as the way we now spend our time resonates more fully with who we truly are;

"Through being a breastfeeding mother, I've discovered a whole new life, and now support other mums to breastfeed. This is all done on a voluntary basis at the moment, but has become central to who I am. I definitely feel more motivated by what I do and what difference I make than by what I earn. It's a shame you cannot pay your Council Tax through goodwill alone."

Ann, Mother to Ella, 4

Through having my children I awoke to a deep passion to nurture other mothers through pregnancy and birth, and to work with children and families, holding a space for free play, learning and creativity in nature. Over the years I brought these stirrings of purpose and fulfilment into being through setting up a natural parenting playgroup, writing, becoming a doula and pregnancy yoga teacher, training to become a Forest School Leader and setting up a small Family Forest School in an area of woodland near our home.

For others, their experiences inspire them to become breastfeeding Peer Supporters or Counsellors; Hypnobirthing instructors; to run play groups or set up a sling library. Some mothers, passionate about various issues surrounding mothering, share their views through the process of writing and publishing; whereas others feel drawn to bring mothers together, so found groups and workshops in the community and online. We may create businesses inspired by elements of our children's experiences, and environmental issues can hold greater meaning.

Discovering new passions and elements of ourselves is one thing, yet finding the time and space to bring them into being amidst mothering is quite another and can bring with it new challenges and frustration. Yet if we embrace the changes, slow pace and initial chaos, rather than quickly striving to return to our previous normal, mothering can become a path of increasing self-knowledge. In all of its constancy, intensity, pressure, challenge and beauty, opening ourselves up to nurturing our children wholeheartedly can awaken us to more of who we truly are; it is a path of self-awareness and self-realisation.

Shifting identity

Only in rare circumstances is a person's identity formed in isolation. Rather, it is formed through our interactions with those around us, traditional media and social media, and in how we believe we are perceived by others. Development of our identity is organic and complex, and at times our identity may seem vulnerable and shaky. It often shifts – linked as it is to our deep feelings and perceptions of ourselves and how we feel we are seen by others. Yet, fundamentally, it is continually tethered to our self-image and self-esteem, our experiences of mothering, our relationships and interactions with others, and the extent to which we feel what we do holds value.

Certainly, our journeys of self-esteem are rich in complexities and pitfalls – after all, which mother hasn't scrolled through social media with the sense that other mothers are more tidy/capable/happy than she is? – yet within these journeys lie milestones of *valuing ourselves*.

Tess brings this journey to life as she speaks of her, at times turbulent, journey of changing identity as she mothered her three adopted sons;

"In the first six months or so of having the boys (when the twins had just turned six and the younger one was four), I had quite a bad experience with my identity as a woman.

I'd worked, running my own business and then as a psychotherapist, right up until a week before we got the boys, and I hadn't appreciated just how much my personal identity and perceived

302

'status' was linked to working and being successful in my career.

When the boys arrived, I suddenly found myself doing household chores that I'd never actually done before (we'd always had a cleaner, whereas now I was taking a year off work I'd decided to do everything myself). In particular, the amount of laundry from three very active, outdoorsy little boys was overwhelming. This became a lot worse when, two months into the adoption, our youngest son became doubly incontinent for a few months, probably due to the changes and stress of adoption plus starting school.

Aside from the worry I started to feel I smelt of detergent, or worse, of urine or excrement wherever I went, this went alongside what are probably typical 'new mother' things such as not having time to wash your hair, forgetting to clean your teeth and so on. As a result, I felt constantly that I looked, sounded and probably smelt like a drudge. I now imagine I probably didn't – I might have looked very tired though!

But it was made worse by people's reactions when I was out and about with the boys. I'd never experienced strangers addressing me a lot in supermarkets and so on, but with three cute little boys who looked like triplets (I dressed them the same at this point for easy visibility when out and about) I was getting comments all the time, positive things ('How cute they are!' / 'You've got your hands full!' / 'I bet there's never a dull moment!' etc.) but I could feel my identity slipping away from my old 'successful', 'working' self and into an identity 'by proxy', as a mother, and as a run-down mother at that!

Looking back, I think I was exhausted and experiencing a kind of shock at the huge transition in my identity. Everyone meant well, and in fact I was managing to run the home and the family okay on my own. The truth is, now the boys are a couple of years older I actually miss having those comments – we still get them but less often."

Tess, Mother to Adam and Aidan, 8 and Shaun, 6

The *Collective of Mothers*

Through pregnancy, a woman's identity begins to change; she becomes part of a collective: the *Collective of Mothers*. Like Tess, no doubt, we can all recall experiences of being out and about during pregnancy and with babies and children, and the comments, advice and sharing of memories showered upon us. Our identity and place in society changes; we are no longer simply women or girls – individuals, solely defined by our careers – we now take on the collective and archetypal identity of *The Mother*.

Hanneke puts this into words beautifully as she reflects upon how having a baby of her own led her to feel part of "the mothers" ; a collective which she had always seen but remained on the outside of, never before understanding the depths and intricacies contained within;

"As a wife and mother I feel this constant bunch of happiness in my heart. It is so full and comfortable that, if you just forget about the discomfort and challenges, I feel entirely content. Yet as I look a little more inside, there is so much I learned and things which give me strife. I think mothers are so unheard. In becoming a mother I learned a lot about myself and how to stand with a baby in society. Motherhood is a much bigger part of life than I thought beforehand. I feel part of 'the mothers' now. There is something you all of a sudden know and have in common. Like when you lose your virginity. You are exposed to a mystery of life.

Being out in town with my baby displayed a whole new world. I remember how it was funny that I only met happy people. Almost always when turning my head while carrying my daughter there was somebody trying to make her smile."

Hanneke, Mother to Vita, 2

Once our babies are here, our place in society shifts and an element of our individuality and anonymity is lost; we become part of a wider social collective which other women, some whose children have long since grown, know themselves to be a part of. Often, they are keen to connect with us. We are approached by mothers we have never before met, who comment, share experiences and show interest in our children's character and wellbeing.

Sometimes wearing, sometimes welcome, such interactions can take us by surprise; at times we may appreciate the positive attention and interest in our baby, and when we are run down, exhausted and feeling wobbly in our parenting approaches we may find such comments unwelcome and intrusive.

Yet when we take time to view these comments through a lens of compassion and reverence for motherhood we can develop greater empathy and understanding for these well-wishers. With reflection, we see that the majority of people who speak to us are older women. They smile at our children, share experiences and enquire as to their wellbeing. Yes, sometimes specific comments may jar, but looking beyond the words, we can see the good intentions inspiring their interactions.

For a woman whose children are fully grown, seeing a mother out with her little ones evokes memories of her own experiences of early motherhood. Moments of joy, tenderness and loss may be recalled; a small hand held in our own, small shoes climbing steps, rosy cheeks of teething toddlers. When we have children we do become part of the *Collective of Mothers* and it is certainly a milestone to recognise this, and to recognise how our children may ignite a reawakening of this collective identity in others.

Rather than being cross or irritated by such encounters, let it become one of our milestones to recognise that, whatever our parenting style, and whatever our age or era, as women and mothers we have so much more in common than that which separates us. As mothers we are part of a collective identity, and we *do* share many interests, despite our individual approaches. What do we have to lose by smiling back and sharing memories and a little time with other women who once walked the mothering path as we do? Let us recognise and reclaim our shared Feminine identity across our generations and communities and deepen further into the value of investing time, love and energy in nurturing children.

Identity, employment and fulfilment
Our identities are, for many of us, largely defined through our careers; such a definition is not restricted to us as women, but pervades the entire culture. From the earliest age, children are asked the adult-centred question, 'What do you want to be when you grow up?' – a question which has little relevance or meaning in their lives at that moment. Throughout life we are taught to "be successful" which generally equates to the accumulation of money and material possessions; we are taught from an early age that our sense of identity and worth is based upon what we do and what we are paid for.

Yet, as a society, we are beginning to realise that successful careers and the generation of wealth and material goods do not necessarily equate to mental and physical health, emotional wellbeing, connected relationships and feelings of happiness, belonging, fulfilment and contentment. Certainly, we can find our work fulfilling, yet despite our material comforts many of us feel a sense of something missing, some lack of intrinsic meaning and fulfilment of purpose.

Interestingly, as our bank of mothering experience increases and we come to discover firsthand the deep sense of value and meaning inherent in being with our children, many of us come to feel a growing sense of fulfilment, purpose and intrinsic meaning which may not have been present in our lives previously. Certainly, elements of mothering and keeping our homes running can feel dull and monotonous – it is the endless piles of dishes to wash which I find ever so wearing – yet there are so many moments of interaction and connection with our children which are rewarding in and of themselves which provide the sense of purpose and intrinsic meaning many of us have been yearning for;

"Being a mother is the first 'job' I feel I'm naturally good at and truly find rewarding, despite being reasonably 'successful' in most people's eyes in my career. Being a mother of two small children is hard work and requires extensive multi-tasking skills, but there is an extra level of energy that I can find to keep me going despite no 'lunch breaks' or 'clocking off'. It can sometimes seem relentless and is 24/7 (unless you get a lot of help) but I find it is tiring in a good way, compared to working in an office."

Louise, Mother to Flynn, 3.5 and Rowan 10 months

Yet in the period prior to understanding the true value of our mothering work, and as we step away from the recognition and validation our working status brought, we can feel at sea, as if our previous lives have been swept away. Alongside losing the status and recognition employment brings, so too do we step away from financial independence, especially so if we choose to reduce our working hours, take extended maternity leave or become stay-at-home mums. For many of us, making our own money has been a significant element of independence in our adult lives, so as we make the choice to step away from the workplace, even for a little while, so too are we creating changes, and perhaps challenges, to our family finances and sense of identity.

Yet women repeatedly make this choice because we place *greater* value on time spent with our children, although as Deborah illustrates, such shifts in our financial identities can, at times, bring up insecurities and issues in our relationships, perceptions and feelings;

"We are lucky that we have a low mortgage and have been able to survive financially on my husband's wage. Although not materialistic, I have found it difficult at times not having my 'own' money probably due to the fact I've always been in charge of my own finances.

Even now this issue comes to the surface from time to time. However, I remain adamant I'd rather have this feeling occasionally than sacrifice precious time with my son in order to earn money for materialistic things. If we were struggling to put food on the table however, then that would be a different matter."

Deborah, Mother to James, 4

It *can* be a tough transition from the familiarity of employment where we felt confident and respected for our professional, academic or practical contributions, to full time mothering where, at least at first, and in times of stress, we find ourselves exhausted, confused and overwhelmed. We are in a time of flux; stepping away from the professional, intellectual and practical elements of ourselves honed through our careers, and awakening to new elements of ourselves that are required to meet the physical and emotional needs of our baby.

"It's been hard to move away from the validation of a proper grown-up professional job to the very different, less tangible rewards of mothering small children. I actually do still work and earn money, albeit it only in the evenings, but I seem to feel this intense need to make sure that people know that – that they appreciate I may be a mother but I am also 'still someone'.

I find this an odd attitude in myself because I don't see mothers without jobs as being 'not someone' and yet I have to defend and justify my own position.

It's a struggle to keep my intellectual muscles exercised – I'm used to being sharp and witty and clever and incisive and fast-acting, and these are all qualities that are less important for mothering small ones. Three-year-olds seem to prefer a more base kind of humour.

On bad days, I wonder where my personhood went, and try to recall when someone actually addressed me by my own name."

Eleanor, Mother to Thomas, 3 and David, 10 months

Eleanor speaks of another aspect of nourishing ourselves – alongside attempting to meet our needs for rest, there may be elements of ourselves which are craving avenues of expression and fulfilment, which are not so immediately expressed through motherhood. Through recognising these elements of ourselves – our mind, wit, sense of humour, practical skills, interests and creativity, in short, the things which make us who we are – we honour our whole selves. We can let these parts know we are listening, that we have not forgotten them, just that we have put them on hold for a time as we focus so entirely upon our babies. And as our children grow, there will be more time to revisit these aspects of ourselves.

Some women explained how they share their passions with their children, albeit it in slightly different ways to how things were before. Women spoke of hiking with their toddlers in carriers, walking and cycling together, playing football, baking, travelling, swimming, skiing, painting and crafting together. Sharing such activities with young children brings its own frustrations, and certainly the pace is different, yet also there is joy in being able to introduce our little ones to the elements of life we find fulfilling.

Milestones of value and recognition

We grow to value mothering as we come to recognise the benefits our constant care, attention and presence brings to our babies, children and teens. We feel the intrinsic joy and purpose mothering ignites upon our inner landscapes, despite our tiredness and day-to-day frustrations. We see the joy and security our children receive from our presence and recognise that everything we do, however apparently simple, benefits their growth and development.

Indeed it is *because* many aspects of mothering – swaying and soothing babies to sleep, reading stories, breastfeeding through the quiet hours of the night, slowly walking, picking up leaves and feathers, watching the diggers on a building site, baking together, listening to emotions and fears, and sharing a home-cooked dinner – are so simple, they are at risk of becoming invisible and of being replaced with something seemingly more interesting, complicated and marketed as having greater external value.

Mothering work requires a constant input of our physical, emotional and mental energy, yet so much of this work is unseen by others; happening within our homes, or in places where we are only seen by others doing the same work. Rarely are our constant efforts recognised and given the value they deserve through research and by wider society.

Certainly, there are hard times – days which are marked by tiredness, tears and tantrums – when we feel shaky in our mother-identity, but they pass. We can remind ourselves of the milestones of acceptance, self-care and the constancy of change. We can take a step back, deepen into our self, listen to our own needs, and then see our children for what they are: young, immature, not yet fully formed and not yet capable of emotional regulation. We can try to see things from their perspective, feel their frustrations and remind ourselves to give them and ourselves a little time and space.

Sometimes, and despite knowing the value of mothering, it can feel impossibly hard to keep at this work. Yet such feelings of frustration and fulfilment can co-exist, oddly comfortable side by side. Time and again, mothers put the complex and contradictory nature of mothering into simple words, saying:

'It is hard work, but I love it and wouldn't want it any other way.'

Love *is* our work

We do this work *with love*; our efforts are not driven by external targets, funding criteria or learning outcomes, but our intrinsic love and desire for our children to be happy and healthy.

Each and every day we are engaged in important work, and as we see this more clearly, we become stronger and more grounded in our mother-identity. It is important to remind ourselves of the awesome, valuable work we do each day. Let us bring this to mind on the bad days when we are struggling, overwhelmed and feeling alone, unsure how we can carry on, but knowing we must.

Each time we listen, empathise and validate our child's emotions, we are teaching compassion and respect for the feelings of others. Each time we enforce boundaries, with gentleness and perseverance, we teach respect for each other; the value of communication and compromise. Each time we prepare and share food we are nurturing and sustaining them physically and emotionally, nourishing minds and bodies, contributing to health in the moment and throughout life. Each time we talk, read, share, play and laugh together we reflect their worth, building the foundation for their growing sense of self-esteem. Each time we meet our child with love, and hold them with gentleness, we teach them about the capacity to give and receive love, and knowing they are worthy of this love we lay the foundations for positive and healthy future relationships.

Through making mistakes, losing our temper, reflecting, explaining and apologising we share ways of developing and maintaining relationships: understanding feelings, finding kindness, saying sorry and moving through conflict with love.

Such mothering is constant and often thankless, unseen hard work. Yet it *is* worthy and valuable; let us recognise the value of our work and the contribution it makes to humanity.

A meaningful contribution

Once we come to know the worth and meaning inherent in mothering with dedication, gentleness, love and respect, we can take great pride in our work. Far from "not contributing" (economically) and "doing nothing", raising our children with commitment, dedication and respect contributes *significantly* to the continuation and advancement of humanity;

"Society as a whole doesn't value mothering as a career. Personally I think stay-at-home mums are a valuable piece of the community, I believe there should be more stay-at-home mums, lots more! There's so much pressure to pick up your career too soon; this is the direction we're funnelled into by the powers-that-be who value the economy over our children's wellbeing.

I value stay-at-home mums so much because we're building the next generation. If we want the next generation to be compassionate, respectful and value their lives, others and the environment, then we need to be there bringing them up with compassion, respect, connection and love, and stay-at-home mums do this by caring for them, but loving them too.

At the moment, looking at society, it doesn't seem like this is happening, but the more people who value respect, kindness and compassion, the more it spreads. We can help each other, and hopefully, parenting this way it'll get passed around. When my kids have kids hopefully they'll bring them up in the same way, and we are building a generation of caring people by loving them, and getting them to love what's around them, the planet and fellow man."

Angela, Mother to Ozzy, 23, Amelia, 18, Marianne, 17, Aeryn, 10 and Willow, 8

As mothers we embody qualities sorely needed in the wider world; we know, through our heightened capacity for empathy and connection, the results of violence, greed and injustice. Each day we work to steer away from violence and inequality and promote understanding, equality, creativity and love. We grow to understand needs and personalities, emotions and relationships. Meeting our milestones brings us the realisation of the great things we have to offer the wider world and how the world could be so very different if the qualities we embody, *The Qualities of The Mother* were employed through governance, business, education and politics. We know there are things which matter far greater than increasing profit, vested interests and fulfilling learning outcomes. We are schooled in the intrinsic value of connection, nurturing and sustaining humanity, and have much to offer the wider world.

"There is no price you can put on good mothering and the impact that has on a personal and global scale."

Veronika, Mother to Bethany, 19 and Eliza, 17

Awakening spirituality and Femininity

Mothering can herald a renaissance in our relationship with our Self. If we did not have good self-esteem before having children, and if we did not know and love ourselves, mothering can give us the chance to deepen and nurture our inner relationships. In the eyes of our children we are not defined by our job or salary, appearance or qualifications. Our children see us, and need us, simply for who we are: their mother; their world. We can begin to value ourselves for the mothering work we do and find ways of feeling good about who we are and what we do. We can recognise that loving our children *is* a valuable, meaningful and useful thing to do, and that our work makes a lasting, positive contribution.

Parenting, also, has the potential to deepen our sense of spirituality. Spirituality and religion offer avenues of meaning, connection, faith and understanding in daily life. As many of us spontaneously experience such feelings through loving our kids, it is easy to see how mothering can inspire spiritual awakening and deepen our existing path;

"Through mothering I've become aware of deeper truths of life, of a deeper natural process at work, an unfolding of life, of which we are just a part. It feels like I'm developing spiritually, maybe I would have grown this way anyway, through learning yoga, but through mothering the boys I've come to recognise a deeper connection and recognition with animals, seeing them mother and feed their young, and seeing them and us as parts of this wider process of life. I have come to a place of trust, acceptance and letting go, we can't control life and the processes at work; we can only nurture it."

Natalie, Mother to Sam and Oliver, 2

When infused with belief and meaning, be that of religion or spirituality, the joys and challenges of mothering become rich terrain to explore and live our beliefs, for we are certainly challenged each

311

day to develop patience, acceptance and unconditional love.

"I try (!) to live each day with love, joy, peace, patience, kindness, goodness, faithfulness and gentleness. My identity is who I am as a child of God, not what I do, but I am thankful for the little lives He's put in my care for this season. I try to rest in His strength and grace to meet this calling."

Lizzie, Mother to Izzy, 6, James, 4 and Lloyd, 1

"I see mothering as an expression of karma; I've worked through many lessons from my childhood and this influences how I bring up my own children. I see just how much they teach me, that we are souls on a shared journey, learning and evolving together. I believe we chose these lifetimes to come here together, to work through issues and teach one another about love and forgiveness. My Yoga practice brings faith and spirituality which helps keep me focussed in love and reminds me of the spiritual work inherent in parenting alongside the physical."

Faith, Mother to Dominic, 16, Stella, 4 and Emily, 2

Alongside spirituality, women spoke of feelings of fulfilment and purpose through pregnancy, birth, breastfeeding and mothering which awoke, or strengthened, their sense of Femininity and Feminine identity;

"Having been a tomboy whilst growing up, and seeming to prefer mostly male company as an adult, having kids brought out the female side of me. I came to really value and appreciate more female company when my children were growing up. Not in the way that I was concerned about my appearance and those kind of issues, but of the connection with other women in similar situations. Now my boys are older, I feel I'm changing again and feeling I'm wanting more male company again. Yet those intense years of mothering really brought me in touch with my femininity and I definitely grew into being a woman more than I had previously."

Amy, Mother to Simon, 25 and Edward, 19

"I feel far more confident in my identity as a woman since becoming a mother, it makes sense to me. I know it's not politically correct but so much of it feels like exactly what I'm designed to do."

Lizzie, Mother to Izzy, 6, James, 4 and Lloyd, 1

The mothering path can awaken a woman to new perceptions about her body; each one of us can experience more fully our Femininity as we use our bodies for holding, nurturing and feeding our babies. Pregnancy is often the first time in our lives we welcome the rounding and softening of our belly; and so our milestones see us embracing our changing shape, feeling pride in the strength and wisdom of our bodies, and sloughing off the shallow, insidious, profit-driven messages of the fashion and beauty industry. Decades later we can smile at the memories the faded silvery lines on our skin still hold; the times, so long ago, when we were so young, so new to mothering, and at the very beginning of our shared journey.

We can deepen in recognition of our Feminine strength; we may not have previously considered ourselves "strong" (in the patriarchal sense of the word), yet through mothering we realise the depth of capacity we have for love, empathy, inner knowing and endurance. We can recognise the greater meaning within the cycles of Femininity, how our bodies are immensely wise, strong and powerful, and able to bring forth life *and* to love and nurture that life. When we embrace the true value of this worthwhile work, we realise the futility of defining ourselves merely through career or appearance. Instead, we embark upon milestones of much greater meaning – intrinsic purpose, love, fulfilment, inner wellbeing, deepening Femininity, loving self-discovery and true acceptance.

Chapter Ten
Independence and Letting Go

Motherhood is a journey of change; just as we feel we are making progress, have overcome a certain stage or challenge or found a new rhythm, it is not long before we hear the whispers of change once again. As much as we may long for our babies to sleep through the night, their need to breastfeed to become less frequent, or the constant work of changing nappies to be behind us, as these stages do pass by, and perhaps we welcome new babies into our family, we come to realise just how quickly our children grow. Bittersweet emotions churn inside us as we realise that as much as parenting is a journey of love and great endurance, so too is it a journey of letting go.

We discover the inner conundrum of mothering: that we are *loving them to let them go*; that their growth is growth outwards, onwards and away. As much as we know this is exactly the way it should be, and as much as we hope to create a stable, loving foundation from which they can extend their lives beyond our arms and homes, these are bittersweet milestones; entwinements of love and sorrow, joy and anguish, as we come to realise that mothering is a complex landscape of uncomfortable opposites: holding close yet letting go, protection yet freedom, security and surrender.

Whispers of independence
Mothers of young babies spoke of the gentle caresses of these winds of independence, of their baby's expansion into the world;

"He slept for an extra two hours and I just didn't know what to do with myself!"

Victoria, Mother to Lucas, 6 months

Women spoke of feelings which arose as others held their babies and baby was happy, or, after months of close, drawn-out bedtimes where babies slept only in our arms or latched onto our breast, baby happens to fall asleep herself. Even if this only happens occasionally, such times are significant; they bring up feelings of not being needed so acutely after such a prolonged period of intense mothering.

In these moments we experience the quickening of the complexities of love, dependence and letting go, themes which become more pronounced over the coming years. We feel the space and freedom of not being needed so intensely, happiness at witnessing onward development and pangs of sorrowful tenderness as we realise a special time of closeness is passing by. We feel the complexities and ambiguity within our emotional landscapes and how love for our children permeates everything we do.

"Looking back on the first six months it's been such a precious time and I'm now beginning to see him change into a more mobile person and beginning to try and physically travel away from me – it feels quite momentous. I see him ever so slowly growing up and away in tiny steps; I feel joy, pride and a tiny bit of sadness. He's ever so slowly becoming his own person."

Mary Ann, Mother to Edward, 7 months

"When Tom just turned 4 I had my first overnight stay away for work. I phoned home in the evening and Tom had a proper conversation with me, telling me what he'd done that day. I hadn't known him speak like that on the phone before and felt quite emotional. It seemed like a big step that he was comfortable with me being so far away – a new freedom for us both. The following day, when I was back at home, Tom said it was okay for Mum or Dad to go away, so long as he had one of us. I felt this was a milestone in our development as a family."

Lona, Mother to Tom, 4

Through our continued presence and gentle guidance we hold the space for our children to explore and expand the boundaries of their comfort zones. From the foundations of trust we have built, they begin to find comfort and safety with others as well as ourselves. We nurture their independence, too, by giving them the space to explore as we wait and watch their efforts, stepping in when they are tired, have had enough of the stimulation of the outer world and need to find peace, sanctuary and relief. This process, which begins in toddlerhood continues to unfold in ever intensifying waves throughout childhood, adolescence and their young adult lives.

Perception, trust and unfolding development

As our babies become more verbal we soon get the message, loud and clear, of their needs, wants and preferences. Our mothering shifts from nurturing an infant to negotiating with a headstrong toddler. As this shift in development sweeps changes across our outer landscapes, we face opportunities for growth, learning and meeting new milestones within. These are largely milestones of perception and trust: how do we interpret our child's shift in behaviour, and how should we respond? Society is quick to label and quash our children's newfound sense of assertiveness, and our milestones require personal, inner perception to inform our ways forward.

Do we choose to "put our foot down" and ensure we are "not being manipulated" by their "demands", or do we recognise this change in communication as a newfound sense of expression, a significant milestone in their unfolding development? Certainly it *is* challenging, frustrating and exhausting at times to be met with a vocal, strong-willed toddler asserting his preferences for the green cup and sparkly spoon once again when all we want to do is get dinner over with, tidy up and get them up to bed, yet reflections upon our inner landscapes can bring us new perspectives alongside the frustrations at this shift in our child.

Of course, we want our children to become independent and fully expect them to do so, yet it can be quite a shock when they first start discovering, and asserting, their newfound sense of voice and power. As toddlers become aware of their own agency and separateness from us they begin to explore this when they discover they have the power to use the word 'no'. They love it, and use it liberally and gleefully. When my son was three he coined his phrase 'NO and NO' which he repeated frequently just to be sure I clearly understood.

Milestones of understanding, trust and perception can help us mothers view such behaviour as the budding beginnings of strength and future independence; they enable us to see an element of value and purpose in such behaviour, rather than simply seeing them as being oppositional and aggravating.

If we only ever see our toddler's behaviour as "naughty" or "demanding" we can quickly become frustrated and lose sight of the little person expressing their needs and emotions and exploring their ability to create change in their world. We can find ourselves trapped in a negative spiral of battling wills, clutching at pieces of advice to manage our "difficult child".

It is a valuable part of our mothering journey to reflect upon what we genuinely want for our children, both through childhood and their adult lives. Collectively, there still persists the idea of children being polite, well-behaved and obedient, happy to do as they are told, dress, eat and learn as directed and happily accept that many of their choices and opportunities for learning and expression are prescribed by people other than themselves. When our children respond well to these value structures, we receive positive feedback and are told to feel proud, that we are doing a "good job" as parents; that we are raising "good" children.

Yet when we cast our minds forward and consider what we truly want for our children as teens and young adults, the idea of the "good child" becomes more questionable. Many of us want our children to feel confident and be aware of their own needs and feelings, as well as those of others, and be able to make their own decisions; to be confident saying 'no' as well as 'yes'. We want them to know themselves and feel able to create their own direction in the world in a way which feels valuable and authentic. With reflection we can see how paradoxical and largely unworkable these opposing sets of expectations are.

As we come to see our children's strong-willed behaviours as attributes that will serve them well in adult life, we can learn to work with them rather than against them, fostering independence whilst at the same time encouraging safety, empathy and consideration of others. Like many mothers, I hope for my children to grow to be assertive and confident, to know and do what feels right for them and to be able to turn away from that which does not, rather than go along with what others are doing, or telling them to do.

When my daughters say 'no' to me, and tell me that they will no longer be attending their gymnastics classes as they do not enjoy them anymore, and have ideas and make decisions that are different to what I had in mind, I am reminded to look within. I am teaching myself to look at my own reactions, to recognise what *I* would like for them, but also to remind myself that they have their own ideas and preferences and require space to explore who they are becoming.

These are tough milestones for mothers, for as our children explore and grow more deeply into who they are becoming, we must let go of the images *we* held for them, of who *we* hoped they would be. Instead, we must deepen into recognition and acceptance of *who they are*. For these were *our* visions and projections, based on our own hopes and dreams, and our milestones remind us to look at *what is*. When our children are reaching for greater exploration, independence and self-expression, even if this is in a direction which differs from what we imagined for them, we are given opportunities to reflect: do we try to keep them adhering to our hopes and visions, or do we support them to become more of who they truly are? Do we deepen into the truth of what it means to love unconditionally?

Milestones of protection and surrender

As mothers we deal with paradox and contradiction on a daily basis; we want our children to be independent and to explore the world, yet to know where they are and be safe; we want them to climb trees but not fall; to develop relationships and be happy, but never sad, hurt or lonely. We are grappling with the nature of life and the risk inherent within it; we know that climbing, flying and exploring, both physically and metaphorically, carries the chance of falling, being hurt and becoming lost, yet if we never dare to climb or venture further, how will we grow?

"As time goes on the children's milestones are more defined; starting playschool then infant school – the first time I left one of mine at school felt like a big shift in my mothering role. A lot of milestones follow; the first school play, the first outing without me, them reading me a book instead of me reading them one, losing the first tooth, the first party.

Letting go is not easy and the first time they go off with their friends is much harder for a mother than for them. Seeing them upset over something and knowing it is out of your control to keep them happy is not easy either. I wanted to take on all their pain and upset, but they had to find out how to deal with things without me always there."

Anna, Mother to four daughters and two sons, all now adults, and grandmother of four

Our children's expansion into the world is a bittersweet paradox; we know, intellectually, that it is positive for them to step out beyond their immediate family, yet instinctively we are primed to keep them safe and close, by our side and away from danger. Deborah puts into words these contradictory feelings;

"I have put pressure on myself to be 100% perfect for him – unrealistic. I want him never to be hurt – unrealistic. I want him to be happy all of the time – unrealistic. I wish I could keep him a small child and always with me – unrealistic. I will always try to do my best and help him in any way I can. I love him beyond words can say."

Deborah, Mother to James, 4

Here we discover milestones of trust; we know we must let our children go, giving them the space and leeway to explore, yet we may feel as though we are letting go into a void. Once again, with reflection, we discover we are meeting milestones of deepening trust. For we are not letting go into nothingness, but rather into trust; trust in our child and their own abilities and decision making, trust in our mother-child relationship and the foundations of love and communication we have nurtured, trust in the goodness of other children, parents and people, and trust in the wider process of unfolding development and the process of life.

Ultimately, we are deepening into trusting ourselves and our inner knowing. We trust that we will recognise how much freedom to give, how much space and independence, when to let go further and when to stop and reel them back. Often, with our first child especially, this is not a terrain with which we are familiar, but a journey we must feel our way into, swinging too far in one direction, and then perhaps the other, observing, reflecting, communicating, making mistakes and rectifying them as best we can. It is as much a time of anxious growth, unfolding and apprehension for us as it is for our children;

"I cried when the lady at the school reception assured me my boy will be fine when he starts there. Mostly, though, I'm thrilled when he walks away from me – at two and a half, he'd never been away from me, and when he started going to playgroup, the first couple of times, he was distraught (as, of course, was I). Now, seeing him confident enough to be apart from me is a joy, and we are both always so delighted to be reunited. I enjoy finding out things about his day that are closed off from me, and hearing him tell me what he's learned from those who aren't me. Perhaps when he was younger I'd have been slightly jealous – now I feel sure he loves and needs me and has an entirely stable trust in me, and he feels sure I'll always go and get him and bring him home."

Eleanor, Mother to Thomas, 3 and David, 10 months

As our children show us that they are able to depend on people other than ourselves for their safety, security and wellbeing, it can feel quite emotional; we are happy they are growing up, growing onwards and developing loving, trusting relationships with others, yet there is also a pang in our hearts, a part of us which feels time spent with others is time away from ourselves. Yet this is the journey of mothering; to love and protect and simultaneously hold a space for freedom and growth outwards, away from the closeness and protection of our homes and hearts.

320

Journeys of change and surrender

I have, once again, been trying to tackle our home and sort through items to clear out and pass on. Our house, like the homes of many families, is stuffed with stuff. Babies and children seem to amass things. Yet it is not always easy for us to clear the clutter. Because to mothers, whilst the object itself may be outgrown, of little use, value or significance to others, such objects can hold memories and tender emotions.

I have been looking through our shoe basket sorting shoes which are outgrown and ready to be stored away for the next little foot to fill. I came across a tiny silver tap shoe. We really have no need to keep this shoe as it does not fit anyone in our family anymore, and I cannot even find the other one. Yet looking at this tiny shoe, I am transported back to the autumn when my tiny middle daughter decided she would like to start dancing like her older sister. She looked so adorable in her costume and shoes and she happily tapped her way around the room, mostly in time to the music. The girls would practice at home together and make up little shows in the living room.

There is nothing remarkable about this, it happens in families each and every day, yet to me the memories awakened are special; they remind me of times gone by, never to be had again. We have less dancing shows now as their interests have changed and our home is instead being filled with clay, lego, mermaids and horses.

Next, I found a tiny pair of swimming shoes, the ones with rubber soles to protect tiny feet when paddling in stony waters. My mind drifted back to the summers when both of my daughters' feet had inhabited these shoes. Of times spent paddling in streams and rivers, camping trips, and the day at the lake when the girls learnt to swim underwater with snorkels. I recalled the days of sunny picnics, breastfeeding in the shade, making tiny stick rafts for fairies; the time we saw a dragonfly and an eel.

Would I have remembered these days if I had not found the shoes? Perhaps we find it hard to part with our children's things as we somehow fear we will lose the memories too. Maybe in doing so, we realise that those special days of childhood really are behind us and we feel sad and wistful. Of course we know our children grow, yet there is something special about the times they were young. Somehow, we forget the struggles; the times they were sick all over us, the long nights feeding and soothing. We forget the hard, grumpy, messy, frustrating, exhausting times, and we hold onto the soft, chubby, milky tenderness of the baby memories. These are our milestones of change and surrender.

When we are struggling and daily life seems a long way from a lakeside picnic, it is these times of simple shared happiness which we can draw upon to remind us of the constancy of change. Such memories sustain us, reminding us to carry on, to get through, and inspire us to know we will create and enjoy more times like this once again. We remind ourselves that time passes, and that challenging times too will pass. Becoming more conscious of the cyclic, ever-flowing nature of mothering helps us to more fully enjoy the good times, and to cope through the challenges, knowing, as difficult as it is at the time, that this will pass.

This knowledge is sustaining me now; I am struggling to mother with a broken leg, and although the help of friends is wonderful, I am finding it challenging and traumatic. But I just do my best, do what I can and let go of what I cannot, and find comfort and reassurance in the milestones of surrender and change.

So as I let go of the tiny shoes, I create space in our home for the new, for the bigger sized wellies, sandals and walking boots, the new wave of wetsuits, swimming stuff and school shoes. As I reflect I realise the importance of embracing the times we have; of living them and being fully present, and then, once these times have past, to let them and their paraphernalia go so we can create, within ourselves and our homes, the space to welcome in the new.

For how can we progress, evolve, change and grow if we hold too tightly to what has gone before? For change to flow through our landscapes, we must let go of what has been, making space for the new, retaining the memories and learning to enrich, inform and enwisen our onward journey.

This preparing, nurturing, then clearing of space in anticipation for the next wave of needs and stages of development is an essential element of our mothering, and its pattern is mirrored in our menstrual cycle. Rather than holding on to everything and being constantly productive, our female energy is cyclical; in the spring of our cycle, our womb lays down the nutrient-rich lining in preparation for the summer heights of ovulation and potential conception where our energies are outward, strong and creative. Then in our cyclic autumn our womb prepares to clear and let go of this month's work, our energies are of shift, change, speaking up and letting go; we are preparing for winter, to bleed, to let go of what has gone before, to have some quiet space to rest, to clear and to be, before the whispers of the new potential begin.

Such approach to menstruation is known as *Conscious Menstruality* and provides a source of insight into how to flow with ourselves, our energies, our bodies and our minds. It is an invaluable way of knowing and nurturing ourselves as women especially as we feel the winds of change, transformation and independence across our mothering landscapes. *Wild Power* by Alexandra Pope and Sjanie Hugo Wurlitzer is a fabulous resource for learning more.

Milestones of trust and surrender

Our letting go is amplified as our children grow through adolescence and reach for independence in ever-widening circles. Yet milestones of change and surrender are not the only elements sculpting our landscapes at this time. Alongside the extra space our children crave, so too are we challenged to develop and change our relationships to enable connection, communication and support to be maintained. A journey of deepening, and at times tentative, trust lies at the heart of our path.

As Anna, a mother to six now adult children, illustrates, much of her own growth at this time was found in the process of letting go and deepening into trust of herself;

"One major milestone was when my first child turned ten. I remember being filled with awe that I had a child 'in double figures' – particularly when I was still under 30 myself. That feeling was magnified three years later when she became my first teenager! My eldest was 19 when my youngest was born so I had around 26 years of teenagers in the home, and felt that the 'terrible twos' were a walk in the park compared to some of the teenage challenges.

There are a lot of milestones in the teenage years as they do a lot of growing up, changing and working out who they are or want to be. During this time friendships change and they may bring home boy or girlfriends; that can be quite a milestone. Dealing with my feelings when they went off on their first holiday away from home at the end of primary school is nothing compared to the anxiety as they go off on their first teenage holiday with friends – especially when it's often to some wild, party destination abroad.

What I came to learn was that I had to try to trust them. If I had given them information and felt they had the knowledge to make decisions for themselves then I had to stand back and hope for the best. I learnt my lesson with my eldest when I was far too protective and didn't let her have the freedom she needed. Inevitably she took it anyway. After that I always tried to be open to my teenagers' desires for independence."

Anna, Mother to four daughters and two sons, all now adults, and grandmother of four

Furthermore, Angela puts into words the complex, ever-evolving balance of communication and deepening trust which characterises the mother-teen relationship;

"When parenting teens and pre-teens, in my experience, there's a fine line between caring and mollycoddling and giving them independence and them having too much leeway. It's a balance and it takes time to find. I think a lot of my mothering comes from how I was brought up; my mum and dad gave me independence and were not overly strict, but they had rules. And the more responsible I was, the more leeway I got. This is how I've been with my own kids, and importantly it's about keeping openness, trust and communication.

Take alcohol for example; I remember being on holiday with my family in France when I was a teenager and we had wine with a meal, it was not a massive thing and I didn't feel I had to do it behind my parents' backs. With my own kids, I've always been honest with them, I listen to them, and we trust each other. I've not been overly strict with them, and I will talk to them a lot about things, about alcohol and experiences associated with it, and how to experiment with it safely.

Now my older teens are having experiences of their own with alcohol; they know how to do it safely, where to go to be safe, and that if something goes wrong, they will phone me straight away. Whereas if you are overly strict, and don't have that trust and openness, if something goes wrong and they're in trouble, they'd hide it if they felt they couldn't come to you. This does mean I get some phone calls late in the night, and I talk to them as they're walking home, but this is exactly the way I want it; I know where they are and that they're safe, and they will always talk if they need or want to.

This is the case with everything; if they can't tell me about something because I'm too strict, that's when you lose that closeness and trust and they can't come to you and tell you. It's the same with sex and contraception, so many young teens don't have the information, and don't feel they can talk to their parents, so they have sex and become pregnant. With mine I've not wanted to hide things from them, and in turn, they haven't felt they needed to hide things from me. I'd rather they knew too much than too little, and beneath all of this is trust; we talk openly about everything, I trust them to do what is right for them, and they trust me and they know they can come to me about anything and I won't judge them or tell them off, but I'll help them.

Their friends talk to me too as they can't talk to their own parents as they are too strict. Often their parents will say they are not allowed to drink alcohol or have sex, but they may still want to do this anyway; for me, it is so important they can come to me and I can help them to do this safely, rather than them take risks and keep it hidden. Most of the time they want to do these things safely, but they need some help to know how, like knowing where to get contraception, rather than not being able to ask and having to take risks.

We have a huge amount of trust that we've built up over the years, for example if they broke something, or made a mistake it's better to feel they can tell me and I can help them sort it out, and we've continued in this way as they've grown up. They know they can come to me with any issue and they trust me, and this trust goes the other way too, for I can put more trust in them too.

It definitely is a fine balance, but I think I managed to find it by remembering what it was like to be a child and a teenager. I put myself in their shoes, rather than just seeing it from my perspective as an adult. I remember what it is like to feel hormonal, and wanting to be grown up. I feel it's so important for parents to put ourselves in their shoes, to get down to their level and know what it feels like from their perspective. If a child is scared of a dog, we can tell them not to be, that it's only a dog, yet if we get down on our hands and knees and see the dog running towards us, it seems very different and we can see how they feel, and remember. This goes for all ages, it's about seeing things from their point of view, rather than just telling them what we want them to do from an adult perspective."

Angela, Mother to Ozzy, 23, Amelia, 18, Marianne, 17, Aeryn, 10 and Willow, 8

Angela's reflections contain much wisdom and illustrate how deepening trust remains essential to our mothering landscapes. Such milestones are mutual; through trusting our children, they in return place trust and respect in us, which becomes a source of support and reassurance as they navigate adolescence.

Angela brings to life milestones of authenticity; for her, honesty, trust and respect are not "strategies" for "managing teenagers", but are the core of her relationships;

"Over the years I've realised you need to believe in your own style of parenting, to trust yourself, not follow the steps in a book that tell you how to get your child to sleep for example; every child is different and they all need different things from you at different times, and it is our job as mothers to work out what they need and give this to them. It is about being confident in yourself to work out what they need, and that you are able to give it to them.

When my first son was little, I parented him how I thought was best, I breastfed and slept with him, these things have all got names now, like 'attachment parenting' and 'natural parenting' but for me, this was just what I believed to be best for my son, I hadn't read about it in a book, it's what felt right.

I have five children and they're five different characters. There are similarities in the ways that I've parented them, but there are differences too, as you get to know the character of each child, you get to know what works for them and react accordingly.

Trusting yourself is really important; I had to learn quickly especially with the health issues my son had, but these days there is so much advice, people are bombarded from every direction, and I feel mams need to step back and trust their own instincts. In the beginning we flounder, we look at our baby and think, *What do they need?* We may feel we don't know and go to a book, but it comes in time; we do know as mams, inside, what our children need. For me it's simple, and is the same at every age; we look at our child and ask, 'What do they need from me?'"

Angela, Mother to Ozzy, 23, Amelia, 18, Marianne, 17, Aeryn, 10 and Willow, 8

Alongside Angela's milestones of deepening love and trust are milestones of empathy. Empathy is the ability, and willingness, to understand, and care for, others. Angela speaks of remembering how it feels to be a child or teenager herself; these milestones are significant, for as busy adults it is surprisingly easy to forget how different things look and feel through our children's eyes.

Our milestones are interconnected; to empathise with our children's feelings and to respond to their individual needs we are required to trust ourselves, to trust in our commitment to being there for them while maintaining open lines of compassionate communication. Mothering is a long game; our foundational work through the years of childhood allows us to truly know and see our children for who they are and want to be. Through such insight we can remind ourselves to see the needs behind their behaviour and keep working hard to nurture trust and communication through the second decade of parenting.

Leaving home

Our children leaving home is perhaps the most monumental milestone of our whole mothering journey, second only to their birth. Through pregnancy we nurtured them safe within our bodies, then once they expanded to the very edges of our wombspace, so they were born. We do our best to love and care for each child through their years of dependency, preparing them for the eventual – a life beyond our homes. We know this is the way of things – loving and letting go – yet we must revisit this emotional intensity as our children expand to the very edges of our homespace and then step out and beyond into greater independence;

"Letting them go and leave home is the hardest thing, but you don't ever really let them go, we still have a close relationship and are in touch regularly. I let my eldest son move out, but it was so hard and it broke my heart! But I pretended it was alright as I knew it was right for him to move forwards in his own life. I didn't want him to stay for me. I knew I'd given him tools to live independently; he still lives in the same town and knows we are here if he needs anything. He visits lots too.

It's so important they know they can always come back, it gives them their independence as they know there's a safety net if they need it. Knowing that gives them confidence as they're more likely to fly if they know they have a fall back, someone to catch them if needs be.

It's like climbing a mountain; if you don't have a rope, you might cling to the mountain, frightened to move higher in case you fall, and limit yourself and not explore your full potential, yet if you have a rope, you're putting your trust and confidence into something else as well as yourself. You feel safer and you're more likely to push yourself and explore what you're capable of, knowing there's something there to hold you and catch you if you fall.

That's how I see it with my son, although he's left home now, he knows I'm always here for him, and it gives him confidence to explore his own life."

Angela, Mother to Ozzy, 23, Amelia, 18, Marianne, 17, Aeryn, 10 and
Willow, 8

Just as we support our toddlers as they climb and stumble into early independence, and their curiosity and confidence is strengthened by the space we give them alongside our continued presence, so too is this the case as our children step forwards as young adults. We acknowledge their need for greater space for self-expression, yet strive to maintain the threads of love, trust, connection and understanding for them to fall back upon when needed.

Angela's words resonate with my own young children's unfolding milestones of independence; I continued to breastfeed them, letting the milk and comfort of the breast be available for them until they no longer needed comfort and connection in this way. Similarly, my daughters made their own decisions regarding sleep; sometimes they sleep with me, and other times they sleep in their own beds. At nearly eleven, my eldest daughter will sleep in her own room, but return to me at times of family stress or crisis, or if she feels frightened. Leaving this option open to them is another example of the metaphorical safety net Angela speaks of; they can step into and explore their independence at their own pace, listening to how things feel, learning to rely on themselves and knowing they can return for my support should they need it. I envisage that this will continue to be the essence of our landscapes of independence over the coming years as they grow.

Letting go across our inner landscapes

As children leave home our inner journey becomes unfamiliar; intense emotions create wrenching surges which reform our inner topography. Relationships with our now adult children evolve quickly and in new directions. The magnitude of anxiety and grief as we let our children go from the everyday closeness of our hearts and homes cannot be underestimated; as with our children's births, this is a time of great change and emotional overhaul;

"It all builds up to one of the final milestones, leaving home, whether to travel, to live with a friend or University. One of the saddest moments of mothering for me is going into their empty room after they've left. One day it is full of life and the next it's a cold shell. I've spent a fair bit of time having a few tears in newly vacated bedrooms. Of course they return, they have changed and grown and got used to a different way of doing things. The house fills with life again, until the next time they venture into the world.

While I used to cry when the children left, my husband took a different view. He would say this is what we've been aiming for as they grew: to produce an adult who's ready and able to go into the world and make the most of their own life. Of course he's right and it helped to know it was a job well done, but it doesn't stop me feeling the loss."

Anna, Mother to four daughters and two sons, all now adults, and grandmother of four

"When my daughter left home at 19 it was a gradual process. She moved into a flat in the same town whilst we continued to work together. After a few years she moved half an hour away and got a new job. By that point everything between us had changed.

She was doing all the things I wanted her to do: making sensible life choices, making plans for the future with her partner, taking her time and not trying to rush into life with babies and responsibilities. Our relationship as mother and daughter had, little by little, begun to transform. We were beginning to get to know each other as adult women, sharing experiences, dreams, and hopes for the future. And now, although I'm her mother, we have an awe-inspiring friendship. I'm so proud of her and her achievements and decisions; she's become one of my closest friends.

When Richard, my eldest son, started sixth form it was taken for granted he'd go to university, but nothing could prepare me for the emotional rollercoaster to come. Thankfully, his final year was helped by trial separation periods. He went on a trip to New York, a boys' holiday, and we left him at home as we went on a family holiday. I prepared myself as much as I could by trying to prepare him for living alone.

When the time came to say goodbye, nothing could prepare me for the trepidation, happiness, elation, sense of pride, and terror as I hugged him goodbye. Those feelings were so intense; I physically struggled to let go of him.

Naturally, I cried solid for eight hours, the worst weekend of my life, with so many feelings consuming my thoughts. My body physically ached for days and six weeks later I'd had every illness under the sun which I believe is down to my body grieving his departure.

The sense of missing him sometimes hits me out of the blue and I have to take a step back, have a giggle to myself, reminding myself he is only 2.5 hours away, and we do Skype every week, but you can't help asking yourself: have I done enough to prepare him? Will he make friends? Can he really cook for himself? Does he really know he can come to me regardless of what is going on in his life? Does he miss me as much as I miss him?

As each day goes by, I'm slowly learning to let go of the need to control what goes on in his life in order to protect him. I have to trust that I've brought him up to make the best decisions for himself, that he is able to care for himself and able to accept and ask for help and I have to believe that he has the desire to be the best he can be. I am so proud of him and am honoured to see him turning into a wonderful man."

Jane, Mother to Aleisha, 24, Richard, 18, Sam, 15 and George, 9

Such inner shifts are intense, multilayered and complex; we have nurtured our children in our hearts and homes for decades and although we *know* it is right for them to move forwards, the intensity of the change can still shake us to the core.

As with their birth, we must let go into a process larger than ourselves, placing trust in ourselves, in our children's unfolding development, and the inherent goodness of others and the natural process of life;

"It was a very memorable occasion when we took my son to university a long way from home. We helped him to his room with his belongings, I remember how he picked me up and gave me a great big bear hug. He reassured me all was well and let us know it was time to leave. I experienced a deep sense of knowing in my heart and soul that it was time to let go and give him back to the Universe. A feeling that I'd been the best mother I could possibly be to help him prepare for this day."

Margaret, Mother to Leon, 20 and Rebecca, 17

"In some respects, letting go for me was easy; I loved mothering them whilst they were little and were proud of who they were as young adults. I'd done my best, enjoyed it and was ready, I wasn't pining for another baby, or for them to be young again. We all felt ready for the next stage, so in this respect it felt right and was easy.

But in other respects it was really hard. I've always found the practical side of things harder; I'm a worrier about detail, I worried a lot about how they'd manage, were they going to manage financially? But I knew that at the end of the day it was up to them to make their own decisions and live how they chose. Each kid is different and you have to let them make their own choices and learn by their mistakes.

My youngest is keen to move to Australia; this isn't something I particularly want – for him to be that far away from me – but I have to accept that that's what he wants to do.

In the end I have to trust I've done my best and I have to trust in them. But as a mother I don't think you ever let go completely."

Amy, Mother to Simon, 25 and Edward, 19

And Veronika, too, acknowledges the mix of deep emotions she experienced when her daughter left for university;

"I cried my heart out when my elder daughter left for university. Oh, the grief! But what was more shocking was how quickly I adjusted to the change. Every part of parenting prepares you for when they leave home, so I'd really had eighteen years of preparation.

It is incredibly exciting to witness my daughters as young women making adult choices, like what foods to buy and making sure the rent is paid. My younger daughter is balancing A levels with a part-time job. It thrills me to witness this independence, especially when many people are so negative about attachment parenting and full-term breastfeeding and that such children will 'never grow up'.

My daughter is flying, she is so happy. Yes, of course she misses my cooking and the love of family life, but she had 18 years of an abundance of nurturing so that she could fly when she did leave the nest. And that's what she's doing. Flying."

Veronika, Mother to Bethany, 19 and Eliza, 17

Veronika also brings to light the milestone of recognition. This milestone reminds us to be proud and comfortable with ourselves; to see that we nurtured and maintained an environment which supported our children to grow, unfold and explore their potential. They did not simply get through (or survive) childhood, they thrived, taking with them embodied knowledge of what it means to be mothered with acceptance, trust, understanding and unconditional love.

Yet as Ronne illustrates, children leaving home can also be a catalyst for reflection on the enormity of our past journey;

"One of the hardest things for me was the sense of loss I felt when my son left home, first for a gap year and then university. It's a complex, difficult cluster of feelings – part of me felt such pride at his achievements and independence, while another part mourned (and sometimes still does, even after ten years) the loss of the child and joys of childhood.

Two moments in particular stand out: one was seeing Dan leave for school on his last day of class before he took his A levels. I watched from the window as he left, hoisting his backpack onto his shoulders, adjusting his earphones as he did every morning, and realised this was the very last time I'd see him do that – this was his last day as a 'school boy'. I had a vivid memory of picking him up from nursery one afternoon, 14 years earlier – the nursery was adjacent to the infants' school, and as we went Dan walked over to the infants' side and said, 'I'm going to walk here and pretend I'm a school boy!' He'd been so eager to grow up – and now here he was, leaving his school days behind. How had time gone so fast? I turned away from the window and wept.

Some months later, when Dan was working in London I had the radio on and heard a song by Gabrielle, it was 'Sunshine', and I remembered the first time I'd heard it, years earlier. Dan had been watching Blue Peter after school, he'd called me into the living room to listen to the song. 'She wrote this for her son,' he told me; as I listened to the beautiful lyrics they really resonated with my own experiences of loving my dear son, my own wonderful star. Hearing that song made me yearn for those days of closeness and cosiness – me in the kitchen making Dan's tea, Dan in the living room watching Blue Peter, school the next day... our safe, happy world; I burst into tears and howled. I am filling up with tears even as I write.

Of course I don't want my son to come home and be a little boy again, I rejoice in his having grown into a fine, responsible adult, but I miss the days of his childhood – maybe because they were so much happier than my own childhood had been. Maybe it's my own childhood I'm mourning for."

Ronne, Mother to Dan, 28

Ronne's tender words remind us what a true joy and privilege mothering can be. We have these short years to create a space of unconditional loving care to nurture our precious children's foundational experiences of life. For those of us with children still young, let us receive the wisdom of Ronne's words and remind ourselves to enjoy the tenderness and love alongside the exhaustion and frustrations.

Retirement and recognition

Yet where is the recognition for the long, meaningful and transformative journeys we have walked, journeys which have taught us so much about love, emotion and what it means to live a human life? Where is the recognition for the valuable, constant, practical and emotional work we have invested into our children's foundational decades?

Loving and nurturing a child or children, unconditionally, through their infancy, childhood and transition to the adult world is vital, important work.

Conscious mothering makes an invaluable contribution to humanity, yet recognition of such vital work is sorely lacking. Much of the work across our physical and emotional landscapes is rarely perceived by society, which seems to be largely unaware of the myriad benefits the mothering investment makes;

"Then you get to the other end. When men retire much fuss and feeling is expended on acknowledging the enormity of their life change. When mums have to let go of their children – when they have to 'retire' from their hands-on parenting – we are disrespected by the abominable term 'empty nest syndrome' and are expected to just 'get over it', yet the enormity of this transition is just as painful as retirement from a lifetime job! I think this is another understated milestone that is part of the cultural disrespect of women and mums and the contribution they make to society."

Ross Mother to Charley and Chelsea, in their 20's

Ross's words are powerful; they speak of the grave lack of respect for and recognition of the value of mothering and parenting. As mothers we can honour her words and begin to create milestones of change by recognising within ourselves and others the vital, inherently valuable work we do.

Independence sparks reflection and change

Once we have held the space to feel and process our emotions, our children leaving home can be the catalyst for new projects and inner growth. We are able to focus upon ourselves in ways we have not been able to for decades, be this self-care or new work or study. We can feel the family dynamics shifting, creating space for greater focus upon partners and younger siblings. Our transformation does not cease once our children leave, rather it propels us in different directions, in both our inner and outer worlds, bringing to our awareness areas for growth, healing, grieving and exploration. Indeed, our children's independence can ignite elements of ourselves which have previously been hidden away;

"I'd like to talk a little more about Leon going to University... I felt this was definitely right for him and was so happy for him to soar. Yet this brought things up for me too, around my feelings and transformation.

I've struggled with issues of self-worth from my own childhood, and didn't feel I was good enough to go to uni. Yet conversations with him and seeing him enjoying this new part of his life felt inspiring to me, and pushed me to go to uni myself. I see how I've been learning from him and what he's doing, and his growing and thriving has allowed me to reclaim parts of myself.

As I began to see my children as adults with their own lives and independence this allowed space for me to follow a path of my own. There is now space for me to explore more of my own interests and I'm studying an MSc.

For the last 22 years I've been parenting, and although I have always worked part-time around this, parenting has been a very valuable job and that is where my focus has been. There was something around his graduation, and some of the lovely things he said which made me feel it has all been very worthwhile and every ounce of effort I've put into his journey was worthwhile and meant something. My heart grew bigger and bigger; I realised that parenting has been the best and most important job and everything else was secondary."

Margaret, Mother to Leon, 22 and Rebecca, 17

Margaret's experience beautifully illustrates how our children's independence can invite us to reflect on our lives, as well as sending us forward into new directions. And as Margaret has done, we can come to see the mothering journey as a whole, and truly understand the inherent worth in *all* that we have given to our children.

Angela, too, expresses such milestones of recognition as she reflected on how much knowledge and experience she gained through decades of mothering and how such skills contribute to her professional training;

"My eldest is 23 now and my youngest is 8; after working and volunteering in school for a few years I'm training to be a Teaching Assistant. Studying has been enlightening for me as I didn't realise how much I knew. The things we're studying on the course are things I've been doing for years with my own children.

The course requires me to look into my communication more deeply; it forces you to look at what you do and why you do it. Now I can reflect and see what I do and say why I'm doing it, now I really have come to value myself and see how much I've learned through mothering and value the contribution I can bring to others. The course has really brought me validation of my own knowledge and I feel more confident and appreciate receiving good feedback.

With mothering there isn't really this validation unless it comes from yourself saying, 'I've done a good job,' or occasionally from others who say little things and compliments about your kids or parenting, but mostly it's from within and I think this is what people can struggle with sometimes, it's all too easy to feel like you're not doing a good job.

Now, as my three eldest are growing up and my youngest are becoming more independent, I feel like I've got a new life ahead of me and I can do some good. It's just the opposite of 'empty nest syndrome'! My life feels good and full, even fuller, as because of our relationship, we'll always be connected and close, but now there is more space opening up ahead for myself too. I have new kids in my class and I'm doing something for them, I feel confident and looking forward to new things ahead."

Angela, Mother to Ozzy, 23, Amelia, 18, Marianne, 17, Aeryn, 10 and Willow, 8

As we gain a little breathing space, time to reflect can help us to understand just how much we have learned. For to mother with connection and empathy, we must open ourselves up to seeing things from the perspectives of our children and others. We see, feel and understand the world in myriad new ways. We deepen in our capacity to listen, to understand, communicate, mediate, organise, educate and hold together, and with reflection we can see we possess valuable skills which can be transferred in many directions. Yet alongside new careers or projects, we can slow down and rest, and pour some of our nurturing energy into ourselves;

"Mothering has made me more resilient. I've taken my job seriously but hope to be lighter in myself now they're both young adults. I'm aware I'll never stop being a mother, and my heart will continue to explode with joy or contract with pain as I witness the stories of their lives unfold.

But now it's time to really mother myself.

I'm coming to a place in my life where I'm celebrating the woman in me and enjoying the time I get to invest in myself. Being a conscious and dedicated mother means I have the skills to nurture myself into full being so I can live the rest of my precious life with fun, grace, integrity and joy."

Veronika, Mother to Bethany, 19 and Eliza, 17

Ross also highlights the importance of our continued growth, reflection and transformation, as well as the milestone of taking full responsibility for our own lives and identities. Letting go of aspects of our mothering identity and close connection with our children can be challenging, but it gives both of us the space to move forwards;

"My two babies are now my best friends at 21 and 24! I'm confronting building a life without them in the house, although not without them in my life. I can't ever see that happening. But it is of course another milestone that all parents have to go through, similar to all relationships we experience; the knowledge that they can never stay the same.

At this milestone I believe we have to look to ourselves, be responsible for ourselves and not depend on our children. We have to manage our own lives with both independence and connection with them. And ride out with dignity all the different hurdles being a parent brings so that we teach our children through our demonstration to be good parents too."

Ross, Mother to Charley and Chelsea, in their 20's

Holding on too tight to our children can become stifling; we must acknowledge the milestones of change and let our relationships take on new forms, once again trusting, letting go into the void and the process of relational metamorphosis, giving our relationships time to dissolve, and be refound and re-formed as we connect once again as adults. We must let go of what has been before, just as we have many times previously, and allow the space for relationships to evolve from close dependency to friendship;

"The friendship aspect between my daughters and I is stronger than ever. We can share anything and have a lot of fun."

Veronika, Mother to Bethany, 19 and Eliza, 17

"As they grow, things change and you develop new relationships with the people they are now. As mine got more independent and I've had space away from always needing to care for babies and small children I've made a point of spending time with them individually, it's not easy to do when they're smaller if you have more than one child.

In my work I specialise in autism and one of my older daughters is interested in this too, I saw an autism conference in London so we're going together and will spend time in London too. We're able to do more adult things together now as the younger ones are growing up. I've booked a concert with one of my younger daughters, and an overnight shopping trip with the other. It's awesome to be able to do these things together, and the fact that my kids want to spend time with me as adults.

My son is proud to see me when we are out in town, as are his friends, and we will happily go round some pubs together. As they grow, this time of mothering is about finding the balance, for now you can be their friend as well as their parent. You need to recognise when you can be their friend and that you can be their parent when needed."

Angela, Mother to Ozzy, 23, Amelia, 18, Marianne, 17, Aeryn, 10 and
Willow, 8

This new phase requires us to seek balance as we begin to differentiate the times our children choose to relate to us as friends and as equals, and the times they still need us as parents. Again, there is no roadmap, rather we feel our way with our knowledge of our child, our intuition, empathy and understanding of the situation. As the culmination of a long journey of mothering, coming to a place of equality, where we can relate to our children as friends yet still offer support when needed, is something to be cherished and celebrated.

Yet the cycle of life continues and the mothering path flows ever onwards. Our milestones continue parallel to, and independently of, our children's adult lives. Our children may become parents and as our sons and daughters begin to walk their own paths of motherhood and fatherhood we begin a process of reflection, and at the same time creation, as we walk alongside them as both mother and grandmother;

"Leaving home is not the final milestone; that starts when they bring home 'the one' – whether they intend to set up home together or get married. The wedding day is probably one of the biggest milestones; it is certainly one of the most joyous to see them so happy.

After that, the big milestone for me was finally becoming a grandmother. To see my own child hold his son in his arms, to see him being called daddy, and to hold in my arms a tiny person who descended from me, is one of the best moments of my life."

Anna, Mother to four daughters and two sons, all now adults, and grandmother of four

The very essence of mothering is love and surrender; letting go of what has been, creating space for what will come, and nurturing what arises. This cyclic flow of mothering is the cycle of Femininity and our menstruality; surrender, creation, nurture and surrender once again. Certainly, we must love, but we must learn not to hold too tightly nor be too controlling in our ways of doing things and the direction of our children's paths, for otherwise we risk smothering the beautiful unfolding of the beings we are nurturing, or cause them to use their energy to kick against us.

Such patterns are the rhythm of our menstrual cycle and the natural world, and developing awareness of them is key to our continued growth and transformation. We must love and nurture *what is* to the fullest of our ability, then once that stage is passed, let go, become still within ourselves, and make ready a space for the new to emerge and be cultivated;

"Being a mum is a series of 'letting go's on our part – letting them go from our bodies and letting them go emotionally as they grow. It's a whole series of 'letting go's and these are the milestones we have to face. And perhaps we have to let go of ourselves too, not fight on to be the same. Recognise that mothering changes us – will go on changing us as we face the different milestones it brings, and as with all aspects of life, manage the transitions as best we can at the time. Whatever we go through – it'll change anyway!"

Ross, Mother to Charley and Chelsea, in their 20's

Chapter Eleven
The Qualities of the Mother

Mothering is a lifelong journey of awakening through body, mind, emotion and intuition. From the very beginning we are investing ourselves deeply; giving from our very bones our love, time and thought. Our very essence is given, for decades, in the creation and nurturing of our children. We are their power station, their universe, their fundamental experiences of the world. Through mothering we journey deeper into ourselves, discovering our capacity, capability, inclination and motivation to carry on loving, caring and being there.

In our endeavours, like miners of past excavating ever deeper into the Earth in search of mineral riches, so we journey deeper into the core of our being in search of treasures to inspire and uphold our journey. We uncover reserves of love, gentleness, strength and understanding which will sustain, inspire and reinforce our passage. Through our excavations we come across areas once lost or damaged by pain, loss, trauma, sadness, neglect or shame. And as we find our way through these difficult, exiled areas, we find potential to heal and grow.

When we look at the word 'transform', it refers to our *changing form*, a shifting or expansion in our way of being. Parts of ourselves evolve, change and grow, and as elements of our selves change, our whole being alters in the reconfiguration. Transformation is not necessarily about becoming a new person, or losing our old selves, rather we are awakening more deeply to who we are, and who we have the potential to become. The day-to-day, decade-by-decade processes of learning to love and care for our children – the tiredness, the challenges, and the overpowering feelings of love, angst and wonder – transform our previous ways of thinking and feeling, shifting our priorities and values in mothering and beyond;

"Becoming a mother changed me more than anything else in my life. I've always had a tendency, as a younger sister, to surround myself with confident types and see myself as inferior; others seem more confident, popular, more self-assured than I felt.

But strangely, as others seem to flock to online forums to check their baby's progress, or their parenting against others, I have an underlying confidence as a mum. I know, for sure, that my instinct, common sense and awareness make me the best parent I can be for my children.

This has carried through to other areas of my life where I'm quicker to make decisions, less hung up on detail and less cautious than I once was. In short, the me I am now is who I was always meant to be, and becoming a mum is what has taken me there."

Jenny, Mother to Matthew, 3 and Lucy, 14 months

Certainly, there are opportunities for such growth in all aspects of life, yet mothering, in all her biological, hormonal, spiritual, loving, challenging, mundane intensity, holds us within these flames of transformation fiercely, and for decades. We use, in unison, our hearts, homes, hormones, energy, bodies, intellect, relationships, blueprints and memories of childhood alongside conscious learning to love, care, nurture and discipline, day by day and year by year. Mothering, and the unconditional love for our children that it ignites, creates the perfect environment to explore, heal and nurture manifold aspects of ourselves, allowing us to deepen into our strength;

"Being a mother has made me realise I am stronger than I ever knew. I never thought I was strong. Being a mother has kicked me into living a life full of purpose. Most of all I want to show my children how to live true to yourself by modelling that to them."

Harriet, Mother to Riley, 4 and Leon, 1

The milestones
Our milestones of motherhood refer to our learning, growth, understanding, surrender and deepening as we adventure, strive and struggle along our mothering path. And whilst our experiences are unique, we walk upon a shared landscape where the terrain is made up of manifold manifestations of love, trust, understanding and surrender. Initially, we learn to give, placing the needs of another before our own. Yet to even begin to do this, we must learn an extensive new language as we try to fathom what our baby is communicating.

Soon we realise that this is not only a journey of loving and giving, but also of trust, in our babies and ourselves. We have to believe that we can understand, respond and continue to be there for our babies, and when we fear we cannot do these things, to keep on trying come what may. Similarly, we realise that this faith in ourselves extends to learning to trust our intuition; to dare to hear, then act upon our inner knowing, filtering out unhelpful advice we receive from others.

And permeating all of this are the journeys of love; the awakening surges of overpowering, protective, heart melting love; the rise of anxiety and vulnerability provoked by this immense love; the silent searching for feelings we know, and hope, will be there; the attempts to love ourselves, our babies, partners or, perhaps, the memories of the babies we've loved and lost. And as we feel such intense love for our children, we realise how truly precious they are and how we dearly want to do our best for them. We feel the crushing urges to be perfect for them, and the fearful realisations that we are not. Hence, we meet milestones of acceptance, surrender and authenticity. We are who we are and all we can do is the very best we can with the physical, emotional and financial resources we hold at any given time.

The transformative waves of growth, change and realisation begin to work their way around the spiral as our years of mothering accrue. We realise that perfection exists in our minds only, and that it is better to strive to be authentic and genuine; to create a mothering style which aligns with our values, passions and truths. We can give what we have to give, and what we come to realise our children need. As we do this, we deepen into ourselves, meeting milestones of recognition and validation. For whilst we may not be paid for loving, feeding and tending our children, we begin to see the very real, intrinsic and lifelong worth inherent in committed, responsive mothering. We come to value what we do and know its true worth.

And certainly, through the decades we may experience a resurgence of doubts, fears and anxieties, especially as our children leave behind the now-familiar terrain of early and middle childhood to traverse their way through adolescence. Once again, we find ourselves feeling, and sometimes losing, our way through the new challenges. Yet all we can do is continue onwards; to keep on communicating, empathizing and understanding. And this is truly demanding work.

We realise, time and again, the need for the full circle of unconditional love. For if we are to continue giving, to continue loving, guiding and sustaining our babies, children and teens through their years of development, we must allow some of this unconditional love to flow towards ourselves also. Loving and giving is not one way, and cannot be sustained if we never allow our own needs to be recognised and met. For our heart to pump blood constantly, it must also receive that blood back with every beat. So we meet milestones of inner awareness, vulnerability and gentle healing as we allow the powerful, alchemic balm of unconditional love to flow towards ourselves also.

We can allow this love to soothe the parts of us which are aching, worn out, worn down and overlooked. Decades of responsive, caring mothering are so worthwhile; we know this and see the results as our babies grow into more of the beautiful, capable people they are becoming. Yet this kind of life work takes its toll. So as our children step further into their own independence, we can allow the small spaces this opens up to become opportunities to turn our nurturing attentive gaze upon ourselves. Let our milestones continue as our children grow, and let us simultaneously love, nurture and listen to ourselves as we do for our growing children.

Love is the path
Meeting our mothering milestones is not always a smooth or rosy process, yet unconditional love teaches us that love *is* the path and to continue as best we can.

Once again, we are seeing how the path of mothering brings us back, full circle, to the message, experience and embodiment of *unconditional love*. Our children are not destined to become mini versions of ourselves, or the embodiment of our ideas, ideals or unfulfilled hopes, although we may want this for them in the beginning. Rather, they are unique in their own right, complete with their own identities, strengths and vulnerabilities. They have their own lives to create in accordance with their own wishes and inclinations. Let our milestones be of nurturing their unfolding, clearing away our controlling tendencies, holding a space for them, and us, to grow and unfold into more of who we are.

And when we are far from our best, worn out, anxious and frustrated, fearing we cannot go on, fearing we are not enough, that we are broken by the enormity of it all, let us see their tenderness amidst our own struggles, and hold on to the knowledge that loving them will be enough. And it is, for as we progress ever onwards on our mothering path, as we face the twists and turns of the terrain – the celebrations, the struggles, the simple, quiet days and the difficult, fraught days and hours where all of our tempers are frayed – we gain the perspective that we are upon a *journey*; a journey of change, a journey of love. And all we are required to do is continue onwards, with love, as best we can.

Awakening Femininity
Mothering milestones invite us to explore a new kind of Femininity; to think about feminism from new perspectives and to embody more

of our innate power, wisdom and gentleness. This is not a feminism where we compete to be equals within the dominant patriarchal model of success, striving for strength, power, status, control and accumulation of wealth, nor attempting to conform to externally defined modes of appearance, attractiveness or acceptability. Rather, we walk in a different direction, *deepening into our own selves*. We embark upon freeing journeys of exploration and discovery, these journeys bringing forth our *own* versions of strength, life, creativity and success through expressing, valuing and celebrating the truths of our own inner landscapes.

Our biological, emotional and spiritual experiences of motherhood see raw Feminine energy, power, love, instinct, nurture and wisdom awakened and embodied, perhaps for the first time in our lives. We have the potential to be awakened to another way; not *their* way or *the* way, but rather our own way, illuminated from within;

"My journey to motherhood enabled me to become a more conscious human being. We need to deeply trust our instincts and override the cultural conditioning that teaches us to mistrust them. This is a time to be fully in the Feminine and cast aside the necessity to control, be goal orientated or prove one's equality to the Masculine."

Alex, Mother to Jude, 9 months

Motherhood teaches us of our strength *and* vulnerability, with neither being less valuable than the other. This brings us opportunities to re-envision and experience all aspects of our Femininity. Our job *is* to be sensitive, open and vulnerable, for it is into this soft openness which we welcome, receive and begin to love our babies. Our breasts are places of warmth, love and softness, yet the milk they produce is a fierce and mighty living substance, imbued with nutrients, stem cells and immunity boosting properties to build brains, cells and bones. Breastfeeding so very effectively lays down the physical and emotional foundations of lifelong health.

Our sensitivity becomes the foundation of our empathy and compassion, qualities *essential* to mothering, and sorely needed in the wider world. Our strength enables us to persevere, to birth babies, to overcome the loss of miscarriage and birth trauma. It empowers us to defend our children's interests where necessary.

We are the embodiment of the fierce, protective mother archetype, the wolf, the lioness, the Hindu goddesses, Kali and

Shakti. We are the most powerful force of the universe in our bringing forth and sustaining of life. *Within* our wisdom, gentleness and capacity for love and connection, we hold immense power. With reflection it is easy to see how the *combination* of such qualities is essential for balanced, wise, loving families, societies, governments and nations. These qualities also help to bring a much-needed focus on the needs of the natural environment. Let us re-envision a world where the *Qualities of the Mother*, these *Qualities of the Feminine* hold influence at the structural and global level.

I am currently experiencing the application of these *Qualities of the Feminine* in a very tender, personal way as my children's grandfather, a dear and kind man, nears the end of life. Whilst receiving extensive medical care, control and intervention, I find myself sitting with him, holding his hand and stroking his head in the quiet. Asking if there is anything he would like to say, then listening intently as I try to decipher his speech. When he says he can't talk any longer, I tell him I'll stay with him in the quiet, and I do, holding his hand and stroking his head until he falls asleep again. And here, I recognise these *Qualities of the Mother*, *Qualities of the Feminine*, expressing themselves through me as they did in my initiation into motherhood when nurturing my babies.

I love him and mother him. He simply needs love, presence and tenderness, someone to be still, quiet, aware and connected; someone to hold the space for him as he journeys inwards and onwards. And it is here that I truly deepen into these milestones; understanding that we need the qualities of both the Feminine and the Masculine, but for these qualities to be equally recognised, expressed and valued. For there to be balance, there needs to be respect and reverence of both. And in a world which currently fails to recognise and fully value the Feminine, mothering and fathering are powerful catalysts in awakening and honing such qualities. These *Qualities of the Feminine*, which of course dwell within both women and men, allow us to hold and nurture one another, and ourselves, through birth, life and death, bringing to the fore the value of *being* and *connection*.

Mother to the world

Mothering sharpens our awareness and brings into focus what is most important to us. We realise that social, political and environmental issues are no longer the concerns of others, but that they shape the world within which our children will be attempting to create their lives. As mothers and fathers, let us not underestimate our power as agents for change; we have developed immense skills, capabilities and a capacity for empathy and connection through loving our children, and we are sensitised to the importance of creating meaningful and lasting change right *now*, in our and our children's lifetimes;

"Being a mother has changed me immeasurably, and in most respects for the better, and being an adoptive mother has been the best thing I could ever have done. I don't think I've changed deep down, but being a parent has given me a depth that I don't think I had before. I was always an empathetic person, but raising boys has made me much more so.

I have always cared about what happens in the world, but now I have this added responsibility as a parent, I am super-conscious of what happens out there and am much more willing to help initiate change where needed. For example, since having the boys I've set up a local group for the national campaigning organisation Compassion in World Farming, which seeks to improve the lives of farmed animals, and I'm currently standing in our local elections for the Green Party. I'm not sure I would have done either of these without the boys being here.

In a way, I think being a mother to the boys has helped me realise that I also have a duty to be a mother to the world, in the sense of safeguarding other people, other beings and the environment. Being a parent seems to have opened up a super-capable, ultra-nourishing and very confident part of myself that I didn't really know I had. I'm basically a much improved (or, rather, 'improving') version of the person I was before!"

Tess, Mother to Adam and Aidan, 8 and Shaun, 6

Do not be afraid to share your awakening through motherhood and the inspiration for change this ignites. May your milestones propel you more fully into your own power as you create a life which nurtures your children and resonates beautifully with the truth and wisdom of your heart and inner landscapes. Become a flame of inspiration, inspiring others to awaken to their own truths, empowering them to create lives according to the whisperings of their own hearts.

At times the path is tough and the terrain inhospitable; be gentle with yourself as you would be with your child. You are doing such vital life work; hold yourself with tenderness through your vulnerabilities, cherish yourself and see the true worth and value you bring to your children each day. Bestow upon yourself the same, fierce, unconditional love and all-encompassing acceptance you shower upon your children, and gift yourself the space and compassion to blossom, heal and grow from your own self-nurturing.

Give yourself full permission to enjoy the good times, for these are the sunshine of your world. Allow the love and laughter to soak into your bones, let the warmth of cuddles and a small hand held in your own become part of your cellular memory. Know what it means to be a mother – to love another so fiercely that without hesitation you would give your all to protect that person – and deepen into an understanding of the purpose and mystery of life. Let this love and the good times, as well as the knowledge of your power, be your beacon of light and hope when your path feels dark and uncertain. Strive to carry on so that you can experience the light once again.

Recognise and remind yourself that you are performing valuable *life work* by loving your children with compassion and empathy. You are making a lifelong contribution to humanity; your work is never time wasted, but always love invested. Shine these *Qualities of the Mother*, these *Qualities of the Feminine*, upon your children, yourself, and the world beyond with pride. *You* are part of this wave of awakening understanding which recognises, validates and celebrates the immense worth and value conscious mothering brings to ourselves, our children and the world beyond.

Embrace your mothering as a path of change, an opportunity to learn, grow and transform. Let go of what you no longer need, of what holds you back in fear, limiting and preventing your growth. And as you let go into the void, remember you are surrendering into deepening *trust*; a relinquishing of control, and a realisation that you really *are* able to trust in yourself, your wisdom, your heart, your children and the ever-unfolding process of life. Recognise mothering not as a task, but a process, a journey, a way of life; the *Journey of the Feminine*, and celebrate your milestones with love.

Clare, Mother to Surya, 12, Shanti, 9 and Sol, 7

Resources

Pregnancy and Birth

Balaskas, Janet, 1990, *New Active Birth: A Concise Guide to Natural Childbirth*

Gaskin, Ina May, 2008, *Ina May's Guide to Childbirth*

Hill, Milli, 2017, *The Positive Birth Book: A New Approach to Pregnancy, Birth and the Early Weeks*

Odent, Michel, 1994, *Birth Reborn: What Childbirth Should Be*

Tommy's. Research, information and support for all aspects of pregnancy loss: www.tommys.org

Association for Improvements in the Maternity Services (AIMS). Birth information, resources, campaigns: www.aims.org.uk

Home Birth Reference Site. Information and resources for all aspects of homebirth: www.homebirth.org.uk

Gestational Diabetes UK. Resources, diets and information for all aspects of gestational diabetes: www.gestationaldiabetes.co.uk

Maternity Voices Partnerships (MVP) is an NHS working group: a team of women and their families, commissioners and providers (midwives and doctors) working together to review and contribute to the development of local maternity care. Find your local group: www.nationalmaternityvoices.org.uk

First Times

Sears, William M.D. 2007, *Nighttime Parenting: How to Get Your Baby and Child to Sleep*

The Lullaby Trust. Safer sleep for babies, support for families: www.lullabytrust.org.uk

Unicef and the Baby Friendly Initiative. Resources and information about safe sleeping, breastfeeding and other infant health matters. www.unicef.org.uk/babyfriendly

Breastfeeding Journeys

Palmer, Gabrielle, 2009, *The Politics of Breastfeeding: When breasts are bad for business*

La Leche League International, Weissinger, Diane; West, Diana, and Pitman, Teresa, 2010, *The Womanly Art of Breastfeeding*

Kate Evans, 2008, *The Food of Love: Your formula for successful breastfeeding*

Flower, Hilary, 2003, *Adventures in Tandem Nursing: Breastfeeding During Pregnancy and Beyond*

Bumgarner, Norma Jane, 2000, *Mothering Your Nursing Toddler*

La Leche League GB (LLLGB). Friendly breastfeeding support from pregnancy onwards, telephone, online and local support and training: www.laleche.org.uk and Breastfeeding Helpline 0345 120 2918

Association of Breastfeeding Mothers (ABM). Breastfeeding support, training and information, online, telephone support and local groups: www.abm.me.uk and Breastfeeding Helpline 0300 330 5453

The Breastfeeding Network. Breastfeeding support, information and national helpline: www.breastfeedingnetwork.org.uk and Breastfeeding Helpline 0300 100 0212

Sadness When Breastfeeding, D-MER Network. Support and information for Dysphoric Milk Ejection Reflex, https://d-mer.org

National Childbirth Trust (NCT). Information, support and courses for parents from pregnancy, birth and beyond: www.nct.org.uk

The Mothering Journey

Aldort, Naomi, 2006, *Raising Our Children, Raising Ourselves: Transforming parent-child relationships from reaction and struggle to freedom, power and joy*

Bellamy, Teika, 2012, *Musings on Mothering: About pregnancy, birth and breastfeeding, an anthology of art, poetry and prose*

Mountney, Ross, 2013, *Mumhood: How to handle it, why it matters*

Pearce, Lucy, 2013, *The Rainbow Way: Cultivating Creativity in the Midst of Motherhood*

Pearce, Lucy, 2016, *Moods of Motherhood: The inner journey of mothering*

Stadlen, Naomi, 2005, *What Mothers Do: Especially when it looks like nothing*

Stadlen, Naomi, 2015, *How Mothers Love: And how relationships are born*

Challenging Times and Changing the Legacy

Alcoholics Anonymous. Support with recovery from alcoholism, directory of local groups: www.alcoholics-anonymous.org.uk

McBride, Karyl, Ph.D. 2009, *Will I Ever Be Good Enough? Healing the daughters of narcissistic mothers*
More information can be found here: www.willieverbegoodenough.com

Streep, Peg, 2009, *Mean Mothers: Overcoming the legacy of hurt*

The Qualities of the Mother

Dinsmore-Tuli, Uma, 2014, *Yoni Shakti: A Woman's Guide to Power and Freedom through Yoga and Tantra*

Pearce, Lucy, 2016, *Burning Woman*

Pearce, Lucy, 2018, *Medicine Woman: Reclaiming the soul of healing*

Pope, Alexander and Hugo Wurlitzer, Sjanie, 2017, *Wild Power: Discover the power of your menstrual cycle and awaken the feminine path to power*

Dr Weaver, Libby, 2017, *Rushing Woman's Syndrome: The impact of a never-ending to-do list and how to stay healthy in today's busy world*

Supporting Fathers

Houser, Patrick, 2007, *Fathers to Be Handbook: A Road Map for the Transition to Fatherhood*

Also, Steve Biddulph and William Sears write a lot about supporting fathers:
www.stevebiddulph.co.uk
www.askdrsears.com

Reflections on Your Own Journey

How have *you* changed through learning to love and nurture your children? Have you even had the time to ask yourself this question? You can use this section of the book to explore your own journey of change, learning and transformation through motherhood. Reflect in a quiet moment, or use a journal to explore your own journey in more depth.

Conception, pregnancy and birth

Reflect upon your hopes, fears, memories and milestones surrounding the conception of your first child. Cast your mind back to how your life was before you became a mother. Reflect upon your pregnancy journey, your physical and emotional experiences as your pregnancy unfolded week by week. What were the milestones of change for you? Reflect upon your connection with your growing baby, explore your joyful, exciting and challenging memories of that first pregnancy.

Can you recall the labour and birth of your first child? Explore what stands out for you, how do you feel about this birth now? How do you feel you have changed from these experiences, what did you learn, about the birth process, and about yourself, your voice and your power? Reflect on the memories of meeting your baby for the first time, your emotions in the very beginning.

Perhaps you experienced miscarriage at some point along your journey to motherhood. Hold yourself in tenderness as you explore these memories and emotions; how does this loss fit within your wider mothering landscapes now?

Early days and feeding

Reflect on the steep learning curve of the early days and weeks; what do you see as some of your small milestones. Explore your journeys of love, trust, of both yourself and your baby, your confidence, understanding and getting to know and love your baby. What was unfolding upon your emotional landscapes?

What were your experiences of feeding? How did you hope to feed your baby, what do you recall from those early weeks and months of nurturing your baby? Explore your own learning around understanding your baby, your feelings of insecurity, trust, love and emerging confidence.

Explore the challenges of these early times and your growth

through them. Which memories stand out as joyful, positive and happy from this period? How do you feel your identity changed and grew through the early times? Reflect upon your learning, challenges and journeys of change.

Becoming a family
How has your mothering changed as your children have grown? How have family relationships evolved? What stands out as significant milestones in your development as a mother as your babies and children have grown? How have you experienced love, trust and connection both within yourself and with your children as the years have passed?

Have you become pregnant again? Explore your experiences of pregnancy with your next babies. Were these pregnancies different to your first? Reflect upon the different experiences of later pregnancy, labour, birth and caring for your next babies. How did these experiences illustrate how you have changed and grown through mothering your first child? What was different? What did you find challenging and what did you enjoy? Reflect upon the unfolding relationships between your children, their different personalities, dynamics, joys and tensions.

Challenging times and past reflections
What stands out as times of difficulty or challenge for you? Do you still feel challenged by these times now? Can you draw out your own learning from these times, how do you feel you have grown in strength, compassion and understanding? Have these times brought a deepening into love, trust or connection? What would you say to support others going through similar times?

Reflect upon how you yourself were parented. Explore the memories and emotions which arise. How do you feel your own childhood influences how you mother your own children? Do you strive to do anything differently with your children to what you experienced? Explore these memories and draw out the elements of mothering which seem most important to you now.

Identity and independence
How do you feel you have changed from the child and young woman you once were, to the mother you are now? Explore how you have grown in trust, love, confidence, identity, self-knowledge and awareness, spirituality, empathy, empowerment and compassion.

How has your identity shifted over the years? Which stages of mothering did/do you feel most comfortable in, and where do you feel most challenged? To what extent do you feel valued in your mothering work? Do you value this yourself? Explore your own journey of self-worth as a mum; have you put yourself under pressure to be perfect? Have you experienced milestones of acceptance, surrender and letting go? What have you let go and what have you embraced?

What can you most celebrate about your mothering journey? Explore what you feel proud of, what makes you feel happy, joyful and glad. Are there any areas you are struggling with? To what extent do you feel your identity is linked to being a mum? How much do you value yourself as a mother and the mothering work you do? To what extent do you feel valued by others, and by wider society as a mother? How does it feel to hold yourself in the same fierce, unconditional love with which you hold your children? How do you think the work and worth of mothering can be more widely recognised?

What are your experiences of your children growing into their independence? Explore the feelings that come up as your children grow more into their independence. How do you feel about them growing up, have you felt the contradiction of holding them close, yet letting them go?

Where do you feel empowered, strong and confident, and where does fear, anxiety and vulnerability show up? How are you experiencing love, trust and connection in your current stage of mothering and where are you challenged? How do you anticipate your milestones and transformation to unfold in the future?

Reflect on the enormity of your journey so far and all you have accomplished. Remember that no work on the mothering path is ever time wasted, but always love invested. Reflect upon your changing relationships, the journey from conception, pregnancy, infancy, to where your children are now. Look at the enormity of the energy you have invested, celebrate this and be proud of it. And remember to hold yourself in the same, fierce, unconditional love in which you hold your children.

Acknowledgements

I would like to thank the Milestones Contributors, the busy mothers who resonated with the book in its infancy and found the time to share their own experiences of transformation through learning to love and mother their children. Without you, this book would be merely academic musings; you bring it to life and make it real through sharing your wisdom, your tears, your experiences and your journeys through the joys and challenges of loving your children. I am forever grateful to you. Thank you, also, for your continued interest in the progress of the book, and your words of positivity and encouragement. Writing alongside children is tough and your words of encouragement meant so much.

Special thanks to Teika Bellamy, editor and founder of Mother's Milk Books. Thank you for seeing the potential for the book, for nurturing its development and my progression as a writer and for holding unwavering belief in its value and purpose. Thank you for your patience, your editorial support and beautiful cover design. Thank you to Katrina Rourke and Angela Topping for the beautiful poems, and also to Dr Karyl McBride.

Writing a book around family life is a long process, and I have been supported and encouraged by many people. Thank you Hatti, Natalie, Alison, Jenny, Kat, Angela, Margaret, Debs, Sarah, Tim, Tammy and all of the other kind and inspirational people who continually enquired as to how the book was going and offered words of encouragement and support both in person and online. Your words really meant so much. Thank you for believing in me, and for the inspiration you provide as you love and nurture your children and grow through what motherhood has to bring with such grace and consciousness.

Thank you Neil, for your continued support through the long process of writing, and to my children Surya, Shanti and Sol. It is through loving you that I learned of the depth and transformative potential of the mothering path.

And most of all thank you, dear reader, for connecting with the book. I hope the milestones resonate with you and inspire you to continue walking your path and welcoming the love, trust, understanding and surrender which unfolds.

Clare xx

About the Author

Photo courtesy Clare Cooper

Clare is a mother of three, a writer, yoga teacher and doula living in Cumbria. She specialises in Pregnancy and Women's Wellness Yoga, offering writing and practices which nurture, inspire and empower our journeys through Femininity. Clare is passionate about the value of time spent nurturing children and hopes her work will support others as they walk this valuable, and at times challenging, path. Clare also runs a small Family Forest School where children and parents get to explore, climb and play in the mud.

You can connect with Clare through: www.beautifulbeginnings.org.uk and through Facebook:
MilestonesofMotherhoodBook and BeautifulBeginningsYoga

Mother's Milk Books
is an independent press, founded and managed by
at-home mother Dr Teika Bellamy.

The aim of the press is to celebrate femininity
and empathy through images and words,
with a view to normalizing breastfeeding.
The annual Mother's Milk Books Writing Prize,
which welcomes poetry and prose
from both adults and children,
runs from September to the end of January.
Mother's Milk Books also produces and sells art
and poetry prints, as well as greetings cards.
For more information about the press,
and to make purchases from the online store,
please visit: www.mothersmilkbooks.com